LESSON PLANS & TEACHER'S MANUAL
BUILDING THINKING SKILLS®
Book 2

SERIES TITLES
BUILDING THINKING SKILLS®—PRIMARY
BUILDING THINKING SKILLS®—BOOK 1
BUILDING THINKING SKILLS®—BOOK 2
BUILDING THINKING SKILLS®—BOOK 3 FIGURAL
BUILDING THINKING SKILLS®—BOOK 3 VERBAL

SANDRA PARKS AND HOWARD BLACK

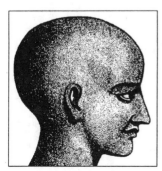

© 1987, 1998
CRITICAL THINKING BOOKS & SOFTWARE
www.criticalthinking.com
P.O. Box 448 • Pacific Grove • CA 93950-0448
Phone 800-458-4849 • FAX 831-393-3277
ISBN 0-89455-321-6
Printed in the United States of America

Table of Contents

INTRODUCTION

Program Design v

Types of Instructional Methods vii

Rationale and Description of Skills x

Evaluating Building Thinking Skills Instruction xiii

Evaluation Recommendations xv

Instructional Recommendations xvi

Vocabulary and Synonyms xvii

Guide to Using the Lesson Plans xx

LESSON PLANS

CHAPTER ONE—DESCRIBING SHAPES

Describing Shapes—Select 1

Describing Shapes—Explain 3

Describing Position—Select 5

Describing Position—Explain 6

Characteristics of a Shape 9

CHAPTER TWO—FIGURAL SIMILARITIES AND DIFFERENCES

Matching Figures/Shapes 13

Which Shape/Figure Does Not Match? 15

Finding Shapes 17

Finding and Tracing Patterns 19

Combining Shapes 21

Dividing Shapes into Equal Parts—A 23

Dividing Shapes into Equal Parts—B 25

Paper Folding—Select 28

Paper Folding—Supply 30

Symmetrical Patterns—Supply 33

Axis of Symmetry—Supply 36

Covering a Surface 38

Which Shape Completes the Square? 41

Which Shapes Completes the Square? 43

Copying or Enlarging Figures 46

Reducing Figures 49

Comparing Shapes—Explain 52

CHAPTER THREE—FIGURAL SEQUENCES

Sequence of Figures—Select 55

Sequence of Figures—Supply 62

Tumbling—Shading/Turning (Rotating) Figures 64
Pattern Folding—Select/Supply 68
Stacking Shapes—Select 71
Stacking Shapes—Supply 73
Stacking Shapes—Explain 76

CHAPTER FOUR—FIGURAL CLASSIFICATIONS

Describing Classes 79
Matching Classes by Shape/Pattern 81
Classifying More than One Way—Matching 82
Changing Characteristics—Select 85
Changing Characteristics—Supply 86
Draw Another 88
Classifying by Shape/Pattern—Sorting 90
Classifying More Than One Way—Sorting 90
Overlapping Classes—Intersection 92
Overlapping Classes—Matrix 94
Deduce the Class 98

CHAPTER FIVE—FIGURAL ANALOGIES

Figural Analogies—Select 101
Complete the Pair/Figural Analogies—Complete 104
Figural Analogies—Supply 107
Figural Analogies—Follow the Rule 110

CHAPTER SIX—DESCRIBING THINGS

Describing Things—Select 113
Identifying Characteristics 115
Describing Things—Explain 116
Naming Things—Supply 119
Writing Descriptions: Describing an Object 120
Writing Descriptions: Describing an Event 123

CHAPTER SEVEN—VERBAL SIMILARITIES AND DIFFERENCES

Opposites—Select 127
Opposites—Supply 131
Similarities—Select 134
Similarities—Supply 139
How Alike?—Select 141
How Alike and How Different? 143
Word Web—Select and Supply 145
Compare and Contrast—Graphic Organizers 148

CHAPTER EIGHT—VERBAL SEQUENCES

Following Directions—Select 153
Following Directions—Supply 155
Writing Directions 157
Recognizing Direction—A 159
Recognizing Direction—B 161
Describing Locations 163
Describing Directions 165
Time Sequence—Select, Rank, Supply 167
Degree of Meaning—Select, Rank, Supply 170
Transitivity—Comparison/Common Sequences 173
Transitivity—Family Tree 176
Deductive Reasoning 179
Following Yes–No Rules—A 184
Following Yes–No Rules—B 187
Writing Yes–No Rules 187
Completing True–False Tables 189
Following If–Then Rules—A 191
Graphic Organizers—Cycles 197
Graphic Organizers—Time Lines 200

CHAPTER NINE—VERBAL CLASSIFICATIONS

Parts of a Whole—Select 203
Class and Members—Select 205
Sentences Containing Classes and Subclasses 208
How Are These Words Alike?—Select 211
How Are These Words Alike?—Explain 212
Explain the Exception 214
Sorting into Classes 217
Branching Diagrams 219
Diagramming Classes—Select 221
Diagramming Classes—Select and Explain 224
Overlapping Classes—Matrix 229
Relationships—Explain 232
Classifying Shapes—Graphic Organizers 234

CHAPTER TEN—VERBAL ANALOGIES

Analogies—Select 237
Analogies—Select a Pair/Two 239
Analogies—Explain 243
Analogies—Supply 245
Analogies—Explain and Supply a Pair/Analogies—Produce 247

TRANSPARENCY MASTERS

Transparency Masters 251

INTRODUCTION

PROGRAM DESIGN

Skills in *Building Thinking Skills*

- **Figural Skills**: describing shapes, figural similarities and differences, figural sequences, figural classifications, figural analogies

- **Verbal Skills**: describing things, verbal similarities and differences, verbal sequences, verbal classifications, verbal analogies

The five cognitive skills developed in this series (describing, finding similarities and differences, sequencing, classifying, and forming analogies) were selected because of their prevalence and relevance in academic disciplines. These analysis skills are required in all content areas, including the arts. Since improved school performance is an important goal of thinking skills instruction, many variations of each of these thinking skills are demonstrated in *Building Thinking Skills* exercises.

These five analysis skills are sequenced in the same order that a child develops intellectually. A child first learns to observe and describe objects, recognizing the characteristics of an object and then distinguishing similarities and differences between the objects. These skills are integral to a learner's ability to put things in order, to group items by class, and to think analogically. Each analysis skill is presented first in the concrete figural form and then in the abstract verbal reasoning form.

Teaching Options

The teacher may select one of three alternatives for teaching the activities: (1) teaching skills in the order in which they are presented in the student book, i.e., completing the figural exercises first and then the verbal exercises; (2) alternating between figural and verbal forms of each skill; or (3) scheduling the thinking skills exercises as they occur in content objectives. Using any of these alternatives, the exercises dealing with *description* and *similarities and differences* in figural and verbal forms should be offered before more complex ones.

The following flowchart illustrates the first two teaching options:

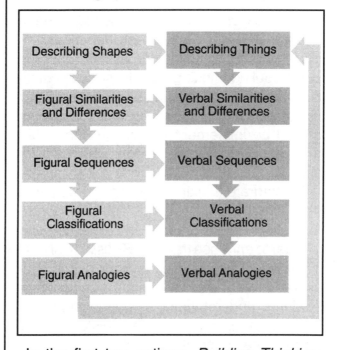

In the first two options, *Building Thinking Skills* is used as a structured program. Students are offered considerable explanation of and practice in skillful thinking and are able to recognize their growing competence in carrying out the thinking tasks required in school. The careful sequencing of the complexity of the exercises and the repeated practice of consecutive lessons produces greater cognitive development gains than spreading the skill exercises over the academic year to correlate with similar content lessons. For special education instruction, compensatory education classes, or bilingual programs, teaching thinking skills sequentially produces better results on tests of cognitive ability, vocabulary, and achievement than correlating *Building Thinking Skills* activities to content objectives does.

The third teaching option involves linking thinking skills instruction to content objectives. By identifying thinking skills in the curriculum, one can offer a structured thinking skills program tailored for teaching content objectives to district needs rather than offering a "packaged program." This articulated program allows supervisors to identify and evaluate instruction, but is accepted by teachers because thinking skills instruction makes content learning more effective.

The Curriculum Applications section of each *Building Thinking Skills* lesson identifies common content objectives and assists teachers in scheduling thinking skills lessons to correlate with appropriate curriculum material. For effective transfer, thinking skills activities should be implemented in conjunction with, and just prior to, content lessons which feature similar processes.

To integrate thinking skills into content lessons, teachers must provide sufficient opportunities for explicit practice and metacognition in order to enhance transfer. By using *Building Thinking Skills* activities in conjunction with similar content lessons, teachers can confirm students' understanding of a variety of thinking processes and can plan systematically through the school year to develop students' competence and confidence in their thinking and learning.

The decision whether to use thinking skills instruction as a lesson supplement or as a sequential series to improve learning skills depends on several factors:

(1) how thinking skills instruction can be effectively scheduled within the school program

(2) how thinking skills instruction can be most easily managed and evaluated

(3) whether teachers are more receptive to using a structured program with a carefully developed sequence of lessons or to correlating thinking skills lessons to existing instructional objectives

(4) the extent to which student achievement on objective tests and in classroom performance is expected to improve

Item Design

In both the figural and verbal strands, exercises have been designed in the manner that the developing child learns: *cognition, evaluation,* and *convergent production.* The simplest form of a task is recognizing the correct answer among several choices. These cognition exercises have the direction *select.*

Next in difficulty is the ability to explain or rank items. This evaluation step helps the learner clarify relationships between objects or concepts. The evaluation exercises contain the direction *rank* or *explain.*

When the learner must supply a single correct answer from his own background and memory, the task becomes more difficult. This convergent production step is designated by the heading *supply.* Teachers may find it helpful to explain concepts in any discipline by remembering the simple "select, explain, then supply" process. The increasing difficulty of cognition, evaluation, and convergent production processes follows J. P. Guilford's *Structure of Intellect* model.

Vocabulary Level

The vocabulary level of *Building Thinking Skills Book 1* utilizes the first thousand words that a child learns to read. Vocabulary designation is based on the *New Horizon Ladder Dictionary of the English Language* by John and Janet Shaw (New American Library, Inc., 1970). Lesson directions and a few items contain words from the second thousand words. *Building Thinking Skills Book 1* contains pictures to allow learners with limited reading abilities to develop more complex thinking skills.

Building Thinking Skills Book 2 includes the second thousand words, with occasional word choices in the third thousand words. This level of difficulty corresponds to the reading vocabulary typically used in grades 4–6. Because the vocabulary level is compounded by the thinking skills component, the resulting exercises in both books may be more difficult than the vocabulary level suggests.

TYPES OF INSTRUCTIONAL METHODS

Piagetian learning theory indicates that the learner proceeds from the concrete manipulative form of a task to the semiconcrete paper-and-pencil form of the task and, finally, to the abstract verbal form. The *Building Thinking Skills* program is based on that progression. Ideally, students should practice each cognitive task in concrete form. Manipulatives, such as attribute blocks, pattern blocks, and interlocking cubes, are commonly available or easily made from inexpensive materials.

The student book provides the paper-and-pencil form of the thinking task. Doing paper-and-pencil tasks alone does not offer the same cognitive benefit as combining thinking skills tasks in all three forms—manipulative, paper-and-pencil, and discussion.

The third step in this process—abstract, verbal expression of the task—involves class discussion of the exercises. Discussion reinforces and confirms the thinking processes which the learner used to carry out the task. The discussion process clarifies the information the learner considered in formulating an answer and differentiates that thinking process from similar ones.

Discussion demonstrates differences in learning styles, allowing students to recognize and understand other ways of arriving at an answer and to value other people's processes for solving problems. For gifted students, discussion provides insight regarding how other equally bright learners can produce correct answers by different analyses.

Discussion reinforces the learner's memory of the thinking process, increasing transfer to similar tasks in content applications. Carrying out a thinking task in a nonthreatening learning situation enhances the learner's confidence in his or her ability to solve similar problems in a different context.

Figural and Verbal Development

Class discussion also provides verbal stimulation for figural learners and is particularly helpful for the student whose language skills are underdeveloped. Since the intellectual development of the learner continues in spite of the lack of language stimulation, figural tasks are likely to be cognitive strengths of students with a limited language background or auditory impairment. Implementation of *Building Thinking Skills* with limited English, learning disabled, or hearing impaired students has indicated that developing one's thinking through figural tasks is also an effective strategy for language acquisition.

Figural observation skills are integral to scientific observation. Undeveloped figural skills may explain why a student who can make good grades on textbook tests may sometimes perform less satisfactorily in a laboratory exercise.

Figural exercises offer figural stimulation for verbal learners. The verbal proficiency of academically achieving learners may mask limited conceptualization. For example, students may memorize the patterns of words for solving various types of mathematical problems, rather than conceptualizing the mathematical principles and visualizing the process. When the learner forgets the formula or algorithm, he or she no longer has a basis for knowing how to do the problem. As verbal learners practice the figural exercises, such students may need to use verbal skills to reinforce and clarify figural perceptions until they become skillful enough to perceive relationships without verbalizing the task.

Discussion Principles

Discussion allows learners to clarify subtle aspects of their mental processing of the exercises. This clarification distinguishes a thinking task from other kinds of instructional tasks and provides alternative and creative ways of getting an answer. Through discussion, the learner ties a thinking skill to other tasks in his or her experience and anticipates situations when using that thinking skill will be helpful.

For effective explanation and transfer of the skill, the lesson proceeds from previous experience to new experience. When introducing a skill, the teacher should identify a real world or academic experience in which the learner has used that skill, cueing the learner that he or she has already had some experience and competence doing that thinking task.

Tying the activity into previous experience signals the learner that the activity is useful and reduces his or her anxiety about being able to accomplish it skillfully. While improved thinking skills often enhance school performance, low-functioning students seldom expect such improvement. For learners who have not been successful in school, the relevance and usefulness of thinking skills may influence how thoroughly the learner will attend to the lesson.

After explanation and guided practice of the thinking skill, the learner should identify other contexts in which he or she has used this skill. This association with past personal experience increases the learner's confidence in reasoning and encourages transfer of the skill.

Because an important goal of thinking skills instruction is improved school performance, both teachers and students should identify thinking skills as they experience them in the content curriculum. Skillful thinking enhances newly mastered skills, improves student confidence, and facilitates new content learning.

Those benefits are best realized by frequent identification of the five thinking skills (describing, finding similarities and differences, sequencing, classifying, and forming analogies) whenever teachers and students encounter similar examples or applications.

The Thinking About Thinking section of each lesson reminds students of the thinking process practiced in the lesson and prompts students to express their thinking clearly. Research on thinking process instruction indicates that unless students can express the thinking they practice in such instruction, subsequent transfer and demonstrated competence in improved thinking are greatly re-duced. Metacognition is fostered by peer discussion, by class discussion as outlined in the lesson plan, by creating posters to describe the thinking process, or by student journaling.

Types of Graphic Organizers

The following graphic organizers are used in *Building Thinking Skills* activities. Each diagram cues a different thinking process.

Central idea graphs are used to aid in writing descriptions; to depict a main idea and supporting details; to depict parts of a given object, system, or concept; to depict general classes and subclasses of a system; to depict factors leading to or resulting from a given action; to narrow or broaden proposed topics for a paper or speech; to organize thoughts in writing essay questions or in preparing a speech; to depict alternatives or creative connections in decision making and creative thinking.

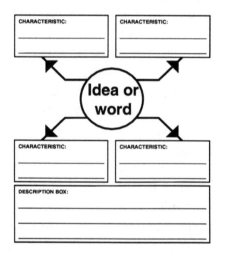

Transitive Order graphs are used to record the inferred order or sequence of information from written materials.

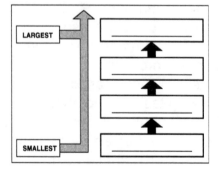

Compare and contrast diagrams are used to compare and contrast two terms or ideas, to organize thinking to respond to essay questions, to clarify the meaning of terms in reviewing for a test.

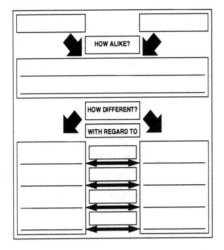

Flowcharts are used to sequence steps in an arithmetic problem; to write instructions; to depict the consequences of decisions; to plan a course of action; to sequence events in plots, historical eras, or laboratory instructions; to picture stages in the development of organisms, social trends, or legislative bills.

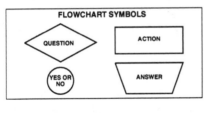

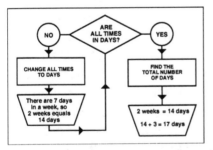

Class relationship diagrams are used to depict class membership and to depict part/whole relationship.

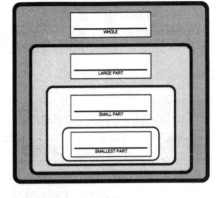

Supplemental Materials

The following books and software published by CTB&S may be used to extend the lessons in *Building Thinking Skills Book 2*

- *Building Thinking Skills Book 3 (Verbal and Figural)*—can be used to further extend or advance students' skills in all areas
- *Think Ahead Figural* software—can be used in conjunction with the Figural Sequences section
- *What's My Logic* software—offers an excellent supplement to the Figural Classification section
- *Language Smarts Book A-1* and *B-1*—offer supplemental activities in Verbal Similarities and Differences, Verbal Sequences, and Verbal Classification
- *Mind Benders® A-1* and *A-2*—provide further practice in the deductive reasoning exercises presented in Verbal Sequences
- *A Case of Red Herrings*—practice discerning multiple word meanings (Verbal Classification)
- *ThinkAnalogy* software—can be used in conjunction with Verbal Analogies
- *Organizing Thinking Book 1*—is an excellent resource in using the graphic organizers presented in Verbal Sequences

RATIONALE AND DESCRIPTION OF SKILLS

Describing Shapes

The exercises in chapter 1 help students express the properties of figures that they observe. The characteristics of geometric figures (sides, angles, area), as well as definitions of basic polygons, are featured in these exercises. Students systematically observe basic features of figures, discuss the features, and write about the properties of the figures.

Types of exercises include the following:

1. Selecting a description of a shape
2. Writing the description of a shape
3. Following directions
4. Writing directions
5. Describing position
6. Describing characteristics of a shape

Figural reasoning instruction allows primary gifted students or mature students with low reading ability to carry out complex analysis and evaluation tasks. Since these activities do not require an extensive English vocabulary or well-developed reading skills, these exercises can be used successfully by non-English speaking students.

Figural Similarities and Differences

Chapter 2 features activities to develop visual discrimination skills and to improve students' perception of congruence and similarity. The ability to discern similarities and differences is necessary before the learner can place objects in order, classify them, or make analogous comparisons.

Visual discrimination in its simplest forms involves recognizing geometric shapes and the appearance of letters. In elementary school mathematics programs, the concepts of congruence and similarity are involved in establishing geometric definitions and developing perceptions of area and volume.

Visual discrimination activities may be helpful in promoting word decoding for upper elementary students having reading difficulty. Reading development requires the learner to recognize subtle differences in the shapes and sequences of letters or the appearance of a whole word.

Visual discrimination skills are fundamental to elementary science and mathematics instruction. Relational observations of rotation, reflection, size change, and shape change are basic observations in geometry, botany, zoology, and geology.

In the Figural Similarities and Differences strand, students exercise cognition in selecting the correct shape among subtly different ones. The learner evaluates whether or not a shape matches others or appears in a more complex design.

Types of exercises in this strand include the following:

1. Analyzing and matching shapes
2. Finding and combining shapes
3. Evaluating and producing equal shapes
4. Recognizing shapes necessary to complete a whole figure

Figural Sequences

Chapter 3 provides exercises to develop visual discrimination and to promote sequential reasoning. Identifying sequences in figural form sharpens observational skills and promotes students' reasoning abilities regardless of language development.

In the Figural Sequences strand, students demonstrate a variety of skills in sequencing: adding or subtracting detail in figures; changing size, shape, or color of figures in a sequence; rotation and reflection of shapes; and rearrangement of figures in a sequence.

Types of exercises in this strand include the following:

1. Recognizing the next figure in a sequence
2. Producing the next figure in a sequence
3. Recognizing rotation and reflection
4. Folding paper

Figural Classification

Figural Classification exercises in chapter 4 develop the ability to group or organize objects by similar characteristics. Classification is a significant concept-building process, associated with science concepts. However, classification is a helpful study skill, promoting visual discrimination, memory, observation, and organizing skills.

The student uses classification as an observational tool. By identifying similar or different characteristics, the learner systematically examines and understands new material. Classification is involved in assimilating new information and accommodating old categories to include new information or experiences.

Classification assists the student in visualizing relationships and provides a practical problem-solving technique. Venn diagrams and matrices are useful for showing class relationships by showing that items have some or all variables in common. Classification techniques are integral to computer logic and set theory.

The Figural Classification exercises increase in complexity and difficulty throughout the chapter. The exercises proceed through the following learning sequence:

1. Classifying by shape
2. Classifying by pattern
3. Classifying by shape and pattern
4. Describing characteristics of a class
5. Matching classes
6. Completing or forming a class
7. Producing another member of a class
8. Using diagrams to depict overlapping classes

Figural Analogies

Chapter 5 provides exercises to develop visual discrimination skills and to promote analogical reasoning. Teaching students to identify analogous relationships in figural form sharpens observational skills and promotes students' reasoning abilities.

Analogous relationships are basic to all fields of study. Analogies are expressed as imagery in literature, ratios in mathematics, and analysis techniques in geometry, natural science, and social sciences. While teachers use analogies in explaining concepts, students seldom practice this useful relational technique before they encounter analogies on objective tests.

In the Figural Analogies strand, students are introduced to analogous relationships ("A" is to "B" as "C" is to "D"). Students analyze the components, recognize the relationships, and complete the analogies by selecting or drawing the missing figure.

The exercises in this strand are nongraded and require little reading skill.

Types of Figural Analogies include the following:

1. Color or size change
2. Rotations and reflections
3. Change in detail

Describing Things

In chapter 6, students discuss and define the characteristics of key concepts in the elementary school curriculum such as occupations, food, animals, vehicles, buildings, common objects, etc. Students practice using precise language to describe or define things they study.

Types of exercises include the following:

1. Matching a description to a drawing
2. Writing descriptions of objects
3. Matching a description to a word
4. Supplying a word that fits a description

Verbal Similarities and Differences

Chapter 7 introduces synonyms and antonyms. The ability to discern similarity and difference in meaning is integral to reading comprehension, vocabulary development, and writing skills.

Synonym and antonym exercises are presented in picture form, using line drawings suitable for primary children or nonreading adults.

Types of exercises in this chapter include the following:

1. Selecting similar and opposite words
2. Selecting how words are alike and how they are different
3. Explaining how words are alike and how they are different
4. Supplying similar and opposite words

Verbal Sequences

Chapter 8 introduces verbal sequences. Students must recognize word relationships in order to understand subtle differences in meaning, to recognize chronological order, and to organize and retrieve information. Language arts research indicates that students learn vocabulary effectively through context. Context may be paragraphs or clusters of words that give meaning to the word or words being learned.

In some of the Verbal Sequence exercises, two of the three words suggest a progression in size, rank, or order that the next word should continue. If the student knows the meaning of some of the words in the sequence, he or she can infer the meaning of the missing word.

Verbal sequence exercises include distinguishing transitive order. From a written passage, students rank objects or people being compared according to some characteristic (weight, age, height, score, etc.). Transitive order is applied in solving deductive reasoning puzzles.

Some verbal sequences involve degree. Recognizing degree of meaning fosters correct inference in reading and listening and promotes clarity in writing and speech. This clarification alerts students to differences in meaning and reinforces the meaning of new words. Vocabulary and reading comprehension test items frequently involve slight differences in meaning.

Achievement tests contain items which require the student to number sentences in chronological order. The student recognizes and organizes a commonly known sequence or relies on the context of the passage to determine order.

Verbal sequence is also involved in following simple directions and distinguishing Yes-No rules and True-False values. More complex directions include describing direction and location, as commonly found in map reading.

Verbal Classifications

Chapter 9 features activities to improve students' conceptualization of class relationships and formation of clear definitions. Classification promotes the understanding and recall of the meaning of words. *Classes* are the categories in any definition of nouns. In the definition of *bicycle* as a "vehicle having two wheels," "vehicle" is the class and "two wheels" are the descriptors.

Classification provides a basis for storing and retrieving information. Just as a computer stores, organizes, and recalls bits of information, our human memory uses categories or classes to organize and retain otherwise unconnected items and ideas. The learner remembers categories or associations as an aid to recalling details.

Classification of collections allows learners to find items or information easily. Commonly, students are introduced to conventional classification systems (library classification systems, biological phyla, the periodic chart, etc.). Less often, however, do students learn how to classify. Classification brings order to everyday tasks, such as arranging items on storage shelves, managing a family budget, keeping records, sorting collections, or scheduling family activities.

Verbal classification exercises are presented in picture form, using pictures sufficiently sophisticated to allow use with either primary students or nonreading adults.

Types of exercises include the following:
1. Distinguishing parts of a whole
2. Distinguishing between class and members of that class
3. Selecting and explaining common characteristics of a class
4. Explaining the exception to a class
5. Sorting words into classes

Verbal Analogies

The Verbal Analogies strand in Chapter 10 features activities to sharpen students' perceptions of analogical relationships and to sharpen vocabulary. Analogies are basic to all fields of study: expressed as imagery in literature, ratios in mathematics, and analysis techniques in geometry and the natural and social sciences. Practicing verbal analogies prepares students for similar exercises on achievement tests.

The types of analogies include synonyms, antonyms, part of, kind of (classification), something used to, and association.

Analogy exercises include the following:

1. Selecting the word to complete an analogy

2. Naming the kind of analogy

3. Supplying the word to complete an analogy

4. Selecting analogous pairs of words to complete an analogy

EVALUATING BUILDING THINKING SKILLS INSTRUCTION

School district implementation of the *Building Thinking Skills* program has been evaluated using many assessment procedures:

- Student performance on cognitive abilities tests

- Student performance on normed-referenced achievement tests

- Student performance on teacher-designed, criterion-referenced tests

- Student performance on language proficiency tests

- Student performance on writing assessments

- Number of students placed in heterogeneous grouped classes, or advanced academic programs, as well as students' subsequent successful performance in gifted or academic excellence classes

Cognitive Abilities Tests

Cognitive abilities tests indicate students' capabilities to perform thinking tasks that are related to school performance but do not require content knowledge. Such tasks include figural and verbal forms of tasks that require certain analysis skills. Because *Building Thinking Skills* is a cognitive development program that emphasizes language development, the figural and verbal subtests of cognitive abilities tests are closely correlated to *Building Thinking Skills* goals and activities.

Pretesting with cognitive abilities tests offers baseline data on student performance on various thinking skills and guides teachers' planning regarding suitability of the level of vocabulary and difficulty of the exercises. Pretest information also can identify cognitive strengths that are not easily uncovered in daily classwork.

Post-testing gives information to teachers, students, parents, administrators, and the community about the effectiveness of thinking instruction in improving students' thinking and learning. Correlated with achievement information (tests, products, performance), post-instruction performance on cognitive abilities tests offers an indicator of how well a student is performing relative to his or her ability.

A list of cognitive abilities tests that have been used in program effectiveness evaluation of thinking instruction using the *Building Thinking Skills* series is provided on page xi.

Norm-referenced Achievement Tests

Composite scores on norm-referenced achievement tests are generally poor indicators of improved thinking skills. Total language scores include grammar, spelling, and literacy items that do not reflect analysis meaningfully. Total mathematics scores include a significant number of items to measure computation, rather than improved analysis in mathematics.

However, some subtests do reflect the analysis skills addressed in *Building Thinking Skills* instruction. Program evaluation using this series has indicated substantial gains in subtests which measure reading comprehension, mathematics concepts, and mathematics problem solving. If achievement test information is needed to report the effectiveness of *Building Thinking Skills* instruction, only those subtests should be monitored.

Teacher-designed, Criterion-referenced Tests

To address improved content learning as a result of thinking skills instruction, criterion-referenced tests (tests that measure students' understanding of what was taught) should also show improvement in students' comprehension of content. Teacher-designed tests, given at the end of an instructional unit, should show gain in several kinds of items:

- Open-response writing involving definition, description, chronological order or prioritizing, or analogy
- Multiple choice, short response, or matching items involving definition, analogy, transitive order, rank, chronological order, or prioritizing
- Interpreting graphs or diagrams or completing graphic organizers to show learning

Language Proficiency Tests

Because one of the goals of the *Building Thinking Skills* program is language development, increased vocabulary can be shown on a variety of language tests. Tests commonly used to evaluate the effect of thinking instruction on language development include the following:

- *Peabody Picture Vocabulary Test*
- ESOL proficiency tests

Writing Assessments

Writing assessment can involve many forms of evaluation:

- Students' evaluation of their own writing portfolios, showing vocabulary and writing skills early in the school year and after participation in thinking instruction
- Pre- and post-instruction on the types of writing used on state writing assessment tests: descriptive, expository, and narrative writing are the types of prompts most related to the *Building Thinking Skills* program
- End-of-unit essay questions requiring description, compare/contrast, definition, sequential order, or analogy

Inclusion and Performance in Mainstream or Advanced Academic Programs

Building Thinking Skills is commonly used to promote access to academic excellence programs or to prepare students to be successful in mainstream classes from special services programs (Chapter 1 classes, bilingual programs, ESOL classes, special education classes, or remedial programs). The key statistics for evaluating this goal are the number of students who gain access to programs, the speed with which the transition is accomplished, and the students' level of achievement when included in general classes.

EVALUATION RECOMMENDATIONS

1. Any standardized content test currently utilized byyour district will reflect increases in students' academic performance that result from better thinking skills can be used to measure the effectiveness of the Building Thinking Skills® series.

2. Tests are also available to specifically measure growth in cognitive skills. These tests include the following:

- *Cognitive Abilities Test*
  (*Woodcock-Johnson*)
  Riverside Publishing Company
  425 Spring Lake Dr.
  Itasa, IL 60143
  800-323-9540 • 312-693-0325 (fax)

- *Developing Cognitive Abilities Test*
  American College Testronics
  (formerly   American Testronics)
  P.O. Box 2270
  Iowa City, IA 52244
  800-533-0030 • 319-337-1578 (fax)

- *Differential Aptitude Tests*
  Psychological Corporation
  Order Service Center
  P.O. Box 839954
  San Antonio, TX 78283-3954
  800-228-0752 • 800-232-1223 (fax)

- *Otis-Lennon School Ability Test*
  (OLSAT-7)
  Harcourt Brace Educational
  Measurement
  555 Academic Court
  San Antonio, TX 78204
  800-228-0752, 210 299-1061
  (fax) 800-232-1222

- *Structure of Intellect Learning Abilities Test*
  S.O.I. Institute
  P.O. Box D
  Vida, OR 97488
  503-896-3936 • 503-896-3983 (fax)

- *Test of Cognitive Skills*
  CTB-McGraw Hill
  P.O. Box 150
  Monterey, CA 93942-0150
  800-538-9547 • 800-282-0266 (fax)

- *WISC-III*
  Psychological Corporation
  Order Service Center
  P.O. Box 839954
  San Antonio, TX 78283-3954
  800-228-0752 • 800-232-1223 (fax)

INSTRUCTIONAL RECOMMENDATIONS

- **Use real objects or detailed pictures whenever possible.** Observation and vocabulary acquisition are enhanced by carefully examining pictures. Supplement the pictures, whenever possible, with real objects.

- **Do description exercises first.** Description requires that students observe significant characteristics of food, plants, animals, people, buildings, and vehicles.

- **Do similarities and differences exercises next.** Sequencing, classification, and analogy require that students observe significant characteristics and distinguish important similarities and differences.

- **Encourage peer discussion.** Program evaluation suggests that the quality of student responses, students' willingness to participate, and the attentiveness of easily distracted students significantly improve when peers discuss their answers prior to full class discussion.

- **Conduct short exercises.** Do only a few activities in each session—lasting not more than twenty minutes. Thoroughly discuss a few items with ample time for students to explain their thinking, rather than attempting to conduct additional exercises.

- **Identify and use students' background knowledge.** Teachers who have used *Building Thinking Skills* comment that the richness of the group's background exceeds the limited experience of individual marginal students in the class. Use these sessions as diagnostic indicators of students' prior knowledge. Remember the language that students use in their descriptions. Use the same words to remind students of the thinking processes in subsequent content lessons.

- **Use *Building Thinking Skills* lessons to introduce an activity in content areas.** The curriculum applications supplied in the lesson plans offer a wide variety of ways to integrate thinking skills into content areas.

- **Examine concepts in other content areas using the same processes.** Use correct terms to cue students to use a thinking process in other lessons. Use the same methods (peer and class discussion, observation of pictures or objects) in other contexts.

- *Building Thinking Skills* lessons are not to be given as strictly independent activities, such as homework assignments. The lessons in *Building Thinking Skills* are designed to enhance cognitive development through discussion and observation. Independent practice exercises may be used to reinforce mastery or build confidence but should never be used as a substitute for class discussions.

- **Use the "language of thinking" in thinking skills activities and in other lessons.** Encourage students to express their thinking with the terms listed in the Vocabulary section (p. xix). Your use of the vocabulary of thinking helps students transfer the thinking skills they practice in this program and other contexts. Encourage students to use these analysis terms when they discuss their thinking in *Building Thinking Skills* exercises, in content lessons, and in personal applications. Frequent, natural use of the language of thinking promotes precision in using these terms and confidence in expressing one's thoughts.

- **Use graphic organizers to cue various thinking processes.** *Building Thinking Skills* features the following graphic organizers: central idea graph, compare and contrast diagram, transitive order graph, flowchart, and class relationship diagram. Each diagram cues a different thinking process.

VOCABULARY AND SYNONYMS

Reinforce the language of thinking in thinking skills activities and in other lessons. The following list includes terms that teachers and students can use in *Building Thinking Skills* lessons, content lessons, and personal applications. Students may create a "thinking thesaurus" of the words and idioms they use to describe their thinking. Encourage them to express their thinking using the terms below.

WORD	SYNONYMS
Adjust	modify, adapt, fit
Alternate	replace, substitute, vary, use instead of
Analogies	comparisons, metaphors, similarities
Antonyms	opposites, least like
Appropriate	fitting, correct, proper, suitable
Arrange	place, order, rank, organize
Assemble	put together, gather, build, organize
Associate	correlate, link, connect, is similar to
Attribute	feature, property, characteristic
Category	classification, class, kind, type, form
Characteristic	attribute, quality, style, traits
Chart	map, outline, graph, diagram, matrix
Chronological	time-order, consecutive, sequential
Clarity	being clear, direct, well-defined, understanding
Class	group, set, category, kind, type, sort
Classification	arrangement, assortment, grouping
Clockwise	rotating to the right like the hands of a clock
Combine	connect, link, join, assemble, put together
Common	familiar, ordinary, similar, have the same characteristic, frequently occurring

WORD	SYNONYMS
Compare	relate, match, find similarities
Conclude	decide, complete, end, determine, finish, realize, comprehend
Conclusion	understanding, result, finish, outcome, completion, decision, determination, realization
Confirm	prove, explain, agree, make sure, show, determine, check
Consecutive	next, sequential, following, continuing
Construct	build, create, compose, invent, put together, assemble
Contrasts	differs, is unlike
Corresponds to	is the same as, compares with, parallels, is like, is similar, has the same qualities as
Counterclockwise	turning in a left direction, opposite movement from the hands of a clock
Decreasing	lessening, diminishing, shrinking, becoming smaller
Definition	meaning, explanation, description
Demonstrate	show, illustrate, enact, make clear
Describe	explain, clarify, give details of
Detail	part, piece, feature, component
Determine	decide, find out, learn, arrange, conclude, figure out, show

Diagram .... graph, layout, outline, design

Differences .... dissimilarity, unlike qualities, contrasts

Disassemble ..... separate, divide, take apart, dismantle, disconnect

Discuss .... talk about, describe, explain, explore, express, exchange ideas

Distinguish .... clarify, differentiate, analyze, show how it is different

Elaborate .... expand, explain, add details, tell more

Elements .... parts, features, portions, details, components, particles

Eliminate .... remove, take out, erase, end

Enable .... allow, approve, permit, make possible

Equal .... same, matching, evenly divided, same size, congruent

Examine .... find the details, analyze, inspect, explore, investigate, look at, observe closely

Express .... declare, say, tell, signify, verbalize

False .... not true, not real, untrue, unreal, not valid

Figural .... pictured, drawn, illustrated, geometric

Figure .... picture, shape, structure, illustration, diagram, outline, drawing

Frequency .... occuring often, recurrence, regularity

Geometric .... Figural, having shape, many-sided

Graph .... diagram, chart, outline

Hidden .... unclear, not distinct, camouflaged

Identify .... find, recognize, pick out, know, indicate, show, specify

Illustrate .... draw, depict, show, represent, picture, portray, model

Indicate .... show, identify, point out, specify

Inequality .... difference, unequal, not matching, dissimilar

Interpret .... convey, explain, make clear,

define, show, mode, paraphrase, tell another way

Intersect .... cross, divide, meet, converge, pass through

Justify .... explain, offer reasons for, defend, show how, evaluate

Locate .... identify, place, find

Location .... place, position, point

Matching .... equal, making an equal pair, congruent

Matrix .... chart, graph with rows and columns, grid

Member .... belongs to a group or class

Observe .... pay attention to, examine, look at carefully, perceive

Order .... rank, sequence, organization

Overlap .... intersection, comes together, overlay, belongs to both

Part .... piece, fragment, segment, section, detail

Pattern .... arrangement, design, repetition

Point/position .... location, spot

Precise .... clear, accurate, definite, correct

Prepare .... produce, create, arrange, ready, plan

Produce .... generate, make, create, assemble

Quality .... characteristic, attribute, trait, standard

Rank .... order, class, grade, type

Recognize .... identify, be familiar with, verify, indicate

Reinforce .... strengthen, make sure

Relationship ..... tie, connection, how related or similar

Represent .... show, depict, model, typify

Select .... pick out, identify, locate, decide

Sequence .... steps, order, rank, consecutive arrangement, change or shift

Series .... group, succession, sequence, order

Set .... group, category, collection, class, type

Shape .... figure, form, pattern, outline, drawing

Significant......... important, key, basic, meaningful

Similarity .... likeness, sameness, resemblance

Solution .... answer, result, resolution, clarification, outcome

Solve .... figure out, think, interpret, resolve, find answer, find out why

Sort.................. group, classify, file, organize

Specify .... identify, show, point out, detail, stipulate, clarify

Sufficient .... acceptable, adequate, enough, satisfactory

Supply .... provide, furnish, produce

Support............ assist, defend, reason, detail, give evidence for, explain

Transparent ...... revealing, clear, see-through

True .... real, accurate, precise

Unique .... rare, one of a kind, distinctive

Verbal .... spoken, expressed in words, oral

Visualize .... imagine, picture mentally, envision

Whole .... entire, complete, total

Chapter No.

GUIDE TO USING THE LESSON PLANS

EXERCISES ## LESSON TITLE

> **ANSWERS**
> Lists exercises and pages covered in student book.
> **Guided Practice:** Provides answers to guided practice exercises.
> **Independent Practice:** Lists independent practice answers.

LESSON PREPARATION

OBJECTIVE AND MATERIALS
OBJECTIVE: Explains for the teacher the thinking objective of the lesson.
MATERIALS: Lists materials or supplies for modeling the lesson

CURRICULUM APPLICATIONS
Lists content objectives which feature the skill or require it as a prerequisite.

TEACHING SUGGESTIONS
Alerts the teacher to special vocabulary or concepts in the lesson. Guided practice should be followed by class discussion of the exercises, with the teacher clarifying significant terms and concepts. Discussion should also include student explanations, reasons for rejecting incorrect answers, and confirmation of correct responses.

MODEL LESSON

LESSON

Introduction
- Indicates to the learner when he or she has seen or used a similar kind of learning.

Explaining the Objective to the Students
Q: Explains to the student what he or she will learn in the lesson.

Class Activity
- Offers a concrete form of the thinking task (and/or illustrates the task by modeling). Students may also prepare models or materials similar to those suggested. When conducting the lesson, teachers should verbalize their own thinking process. This modeling provides cues to students for executing the thinking task skillfully.

GUIDED PRACTICE
Controlled practice allows the teacher to identify errors or omissions in students' processing. Guided practice should be followed by class discussion.

INDEPENDENT PRACTICE
- Provides practice exercises for promoting skill mastery.

THINKING ABOUT THINKING
Helps the student clarify and verbalize the thinking process: metacognition.

PERSONAL APPLICATION
Relates the skill to the learner's experience and cues the learner regarding possible future uses of the skill.

Chapter 1

DESCRIBING SHAPES
(Student book pages 2–16)

DESCRIBING SHAPES—SELECT

ANSWERS A-1 through A-22 — Student book pages 2–6
Guided Practice: A-1 tall and wide; **A-2** tall and narrow; **A-3** short and wide; **A-4** tall and wide
Independent Practice: A-5 four, four; **A-6** three, three; **A-7** five, five; **A-8** six, six; **A-9** four, four, All (or four); **A-10** four, four, All (or four); **A-11** five, five, Two; **A-12** six, six, None; **A-13** triangle, three, all (or three) (an equilateral triangle) **A-14** square, four, all (or four); **A-15** triangle, three, two (an isosceles triangle); **A-16** trapezoid, four, two; **A-17** rectangle, four, two (actually two pairs); **A-18** triangle, three, none (a scalene triangle); **A-19** pentagon, five, two (two pairs); **A-20** quadrilateral, four, none; **A-21** parallelogram, four, two (two pairs); **A-22** hexagon, six, all (or six)

**LESSON
PREPARATION**

OBJECTIVE AND MATERIALS
OBJECTIVE: Students will describe shapes by name and by characteristics.
MATERIALS: Transparencies of Transparency Masters (TMs) 1 and 2

CURRICULUM APPLICATIONS
LANGUAGE ARTS: Using visual discrimination in word recognition
MATHEMATICS: Completing similarity and congruence exercises, distinguishing between arithmetic problems by operational signs ($+$, $-$, $\times$, $\div$)
SCIENCE: Comparing shapes of leaves, insects, shells, etc.; finding or putting away laboratory equipment
SOCIAL STUDIES: Describing artifacts, ornaments, tools, costumes, or implements of various cultures; describing buildings or architectural features
ENRICHMENT AREAS: Recognizing shapes of road signs; discerning different patterns in art, written music, or dance steps

TEACHING SUGGESTIONS
Reinforce the following vocabulary emphasized in this lesson: *right angle, acute angle, obtuse angle, hexagon, scalene triangle, isosceles triangle, equilateral triangle, polygon.* Students may describe a square corner as a right angle; angles smaller than a right angle are acute and angles larger than a right angle are obtuse. Students may remember that a hexagon has six sides by recalling that both *six* and *hexagon* contain an x.

A triangle with no equal sides is called scalene. If two sides are equal, a triangle is called isosceles. If all three sides are equal, it is an equilateral triangle. All many-sided, closed shapes are called polygons.

MODEL LESSON

LESSON

Introduction
Q: With a partner, review the names of some of the basic shapes.

Explaining the Objective to Students

Q: In these exercises you will describe shapes by their names and by their characteristics.

Class Activity

* Project TM 1 and review the names of the polygons shown on the transparency: (1) *triangle*, (2) *parallelogram*, (3) *rectangle*, (4) *trapezoid*, (5) *pentagon*, (6) *hexagon*.

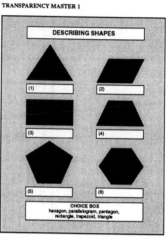

TRANSPARENCY MASTER 1

Q: What is the name of any three-sided, closed shape?

A: Triangle

Q: Four-sided shapes are called quadrilaterals. Can you name some special quadrilaterals?

A: Square, rectangle, parallelogram

Q: What is special about a square?

A: All the sides are equal and all the angles have square corners.

Q: What is special about a rectangle?

A: All the corners are "square" (right angles), but the sides are not all equal—the opposite sides are equal.

* Project a transparency of TM 2, uncover questions 1 and 2.

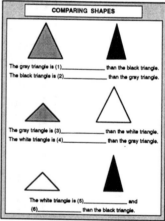

TRANSPARENCY MASTER 2

Q: Compare these two triangles.

A: The gray triangle is (1) wider than the black triangle. The black triangle is (2) thinner or narrower than the gray triangle.

* Expose questions 3 and 4.

Q: Compare these two triangles.

A: The gray triangle is (3) shorter than the white triangle. The white triangle is (4) taller than the gray triangle.

* Expose questions 5 and 6.

Q: Compare these two triangles.

A: The white triangle is (5) wider and (6) shorter than the black triangle.

GUIDED PRACTICE

EXERCISES: **A-1** through **A-4**

* Give students sufficient time to complete these exercises. Then ask students to discuss and explain their choices.

INDEPENDENT PRACTICE

* Assign exercises **A-5** through **A-22**.

THINKING ABOUT THINKING

Q: What did you pay attention to when you picked a word that described a shape?

1. I read the words (characteristics) in the choice box.

2. I looked for those characteristics in each shape.

3. I picked the word that best described the shape.

4. I checked to see why the other words didn't describe the shape.

PERSONAL APPLICATION

Q: When do you need to describe the shape of something?

A: Examples include describing objects or organisms in order to clarify your meaning, or to identify or locate an object.

EXERCISES A-23 to A-25

DESCRIBING SHAPES—EXPLAIN

ANSWERS A-23 through A-25 — Student book pages 7–8

Guided Practice: A-23 This triangle has one square corner. The triangle is three inches high and two inches wide. (The terms *right triangle* and *two-inch base* may also be used.)

Independent Practice: A-24 This trapezoid has two equal sides. The trapezoid is two inches high, has a four-inch lower base and a two-inch top. **A-25** This pentagon has two pairs of equal sides. The vertical sides are each two inches long. The slanted sides are equal in length. The base of the pentagon is two inches and the height is three inches.

LESSON PREPARATION

OBJECTIVE AND MATERIALS

OBJECTIVE: Students will practice describing shapes by the length of the sides, measured in inches.

MATERIALS: Transparency of page 7 • washable transparency marker

CURRICULUM APPLICATIONS

LANGUAGE ARTS: Using visual discrimination, discriminating between punctuation marks

MATHEMATICS: Distinguishing between geometric shapes

SCIENCE: Comparing shapes of leaves, insects, shells, etc.; choosing proper laboratory utensils by size or shape

SOCIAL STUDIES: Using legends to locate map features, e.g., parks, airports, rest areas, historical monuments; recognizing graphic variations in charts or graphs

ENRICHMENT AREAS: Using shape to distinguish purposes of traffic or road signs, separating architectural periods by comparing typical styles, distinguishing different note values in music

TEACHING SUGGESTIONS

Remind students of the terms they used in the previous lesson to describe geometric shapes. Explain the meaning of *dimensions* and *units of measure*. Encourage students to use these terms in their descriptions. When discussing the exercises, describe the sentence patterns and key words that most students use in their descriptions.

MODEL LESSON | **LESSON**

Introduction

Q: In the previous lesson you described shapes by names and characteristics.

Explaining the Objective to the Students

Q: In these exercises you will practice describing shapes by the length of their sides, measured in inches.

Class Activity

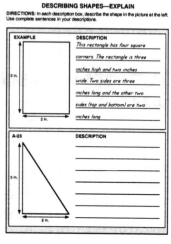

- Project transparency of page 7—cover the description.

  Q: Name this shape.
    A: It is a rectangle.

  Q: What is special about this shape?
    A: It has four square corners.

  Q: Remember that *in.* is the abbreviation for inches. How tall is the rectangle?
    A: 3 inches

  Q: How wide is the rectangle?
    A: 2 inches

  Q: Use these features to write a description of this shape.

- Allow time for writing. Ask for student descriptions then uncover the description on the transparency and compare them.

GUIDED PRACTICE

EXERCISES: **A-23**

- Give students sufficient time to complete this exercise.

INDEPENDENT PRACTICE

- Assign exercises **A-24** and **A-25**.

THINKING ABOUT THINKING

Q: What did you pay attention to when you picked a word that described a shape?

  1. I recalled the name of the shape.

  2. I looked at special features of the shape (square corners, equal sides, length of sides).

  3. I named the shape and described its special features.

PERSONAL APPLICATION

Q: When might you need to describe shapes?
  A: Examples include describing organisms in order to identify them; identifying objects (tools, toys, clothing, vehicles, games); describing symbols, including icons on computer displays; describing landforms or buildings.

EXERCISES A-26 to A-31

DESCRIBING POSITION—SELECT

ANSWERS A-26 through A-31 — Student book pages 9–11
Guided Practice: A-26 above, below; **A-27** above, left
Independent Practice: A-28 below, right, below; **A-29** left, center, left;
A-30 larger, smaller, left; **A-31** smaller, right, above

LESSON PREPARATION

OBJECTIVE AND MATERIALS
OBJECTIVE: Students will complete sentences describing the locations of shapes and then draw additional shapes according to the given directions.
MATERIALS: Transparency of student workbook page 9 • washable transparency marker

CURRICULUM APPLICATIONS
LANGUAGE ARTS: Diagramming sentences; placing words in sentences according to function or slot, e.g., subject, direct object; following directions for formatting written materials, e.g., business or personal letters, outlines, essays; writing descriptive or instructive paragraphs; proofreading and editing
MATHEMATICS: Plotting graph coordinates, constructing geometric shapes by following directions, constructing bar graphs
SCIENCE: Plotting or reading a plot of an archaeological dig or ecological study area, seeing and describing strata in natural formations
SOCIAL STUDIES: Interpreting and constructing maps, graphs, time lines, or diagrams; locating details in pictures or diagrams
ENRICHMENT AREAS: Taking tests; art, physical education, or dance activities involving position or location; following drill, marching band, or sports instructions involving location, direction, or movement

TEACHING SUGGESTIONS
Encourage students to discuss their answers. Class discussion is a valuable technique for allowing children to share their acquired knowledge. Often a child's words will express characteristics meaningfully and with originality.

MODEL LESSON

LESSON

Introduction
Q: In previous exercises you identified a figure or shape by its dimensions.

Explaining the Objective to Students
Q: In these exercises you will complete sentences describing the locations of shapes and draw additional shapes according to the given directions.

Class Activity
• Project exercise **A-26** from the transparency of page 9.
Q: You will choose words from the choice box to complete each description. The first sentence says, "The square is _____ the circle."

DESCRIBING POSITION—SELECT
DIRECTIONS: Write the words from the choice box that correctly complete the sentences. Draw a figure as directed.

CHOICE BOX
above, below, center, circle, left, right, square, triangle

A-26
The square is _____ the circle. The circle is _____ the square.
Draw a triangle below the circle.

A-27
The triangle is _____ the square. The circle is on the _____ side of the square.
Draw a black triangle to the right of the square.

- Point to the figures.
  Q: Select words from the choice box to describe their positions.
    A: Above or below

  Q: Which word correctly completes the first sentence?
    A: Above

- Write "above" in the blank.
  Q: The second sentence says, "The circle is _____ the square." Which word from the choice box correctly completes this sentence?
    A: Below

- Write "below" in the blank.
  Q: The last sentence tells you, "Draw a triangle below the circle." NOTE: The word *below* refers to the bottom third of the large square. Add the word *directly*, as in directly below, to indicate a specific location.

- Draw a triangle below the circle anywhere on the transparency.
  Q: If I put a triangle here, have I followed the directions?
    A: Yes

GUIDED PRACTICE
EXERCISE: **A-26**, **A-27**
- Give students sufficient time to complete this exercise. Ask students to discuss and explain their choices.

INDEPENDENT PRACTICE
- Assign exercises **A-28** through **A-31**.

THINKING ABOUT THINKING
Q: What did you pay attention to when you described the location of something?
1. I read the clue.

2. I looked for the shape mentioned in the clue.

3. I decided what word from the "choice box" completes the sentence.

4. I wrote the answer on the blank.

PERSONAL APPLICATION
Q: When might you need to describe, find, or place something in a given location?
A: Examples include assembling games or models; using computer-tabulated questionnaires or answer sheets; playing games involving location or direction; giving directions to someone; reading directions regarding placement or location of answers; following square dance, drill, or sports instructions.

**EXERCISES
A-32 to A-36**

DESCRIBING POSITION—EXPLAIN

ANSWERS A-32 through A-36 — Student book pages 12–4
Guided Practice: A-32 The white square is to the right of the gray circle.

© 1998 CRITICAL THINKING BOOKS & SOFTWARE • WWW.CRITICALTHINKING.COM • 800-458-4849

OR The gray circle is to the left of the white square.

Independent Practice: A-33 (Relative to the center) The center shape is a black triangle. Above the triangle is a gray square and below the triangle is a white circle. OR (Relative to the bottom) The shape at the bottom is a white circle. Above the circle is a black triangle and above the triangle is a gray square. OR (Relative to the top) The shape at the top is a gray square. Below the square is a black triangle and below the triangle is a white circle. **A-34** (Relative to the center) The center shape is a white square. To the left of the square is a black triangle and to the right of the square is a gray circle. OR (Relative to the left side) The shape at the left is a black triangle. To the right of the triangle is a white square and to the right of the square is a gray circle. OR (Relative to the right side) The shape at the right is a gray circle. To the left of the circle is a white square and to the left of the square is a black triangle. **A-35** (Relative to the middle right) The middle right shape is a black circle. To the left of the circle is a white triangle and above the circle is a gray square. OR (Relative to the middle left) The middle left shape is a white triangle. To the right of the triangle is a black circle and above the circle is a gray square. OR (Relative to the top right) The top right shape is a gray square. Below the square is a black circle. To the left of the circle is a white triangle. **A-36** (Relative to the lower middle) The lower middle shape is a gray triangle. To the right of the triangle is a white circle and above the triangle is a black square. OR (Relative to the lower right) The lower right shape is a white circle. To the left of the circle is a gray triangle and above the triangle is a black square. OR (Relative to the upper middle) The upper middle shape is a black square. Below the square is a gray triangle. To the right of the triangle is a white circle.

LESSON PREPARATION

OBJECTIVE AND MATERIALS

OBJECTIVE: Students will describe the color, shape, and position of two or three shapes.

MATERIALS: Transparency of student workbook page 12 • washable transparency marker

CURRICULUM APPLICATIONS

LANGUAGE ARTS: Diagramming sentences; placing words in sentences according to function or slot, e.g., subject, direct object; following directions for formatting written materials, e.g., business or personal letters, outlines, essays; writing descriptive or instructive paragraphs; proofreading and editing

MATHEMATICS: Plotting graph coordinates; constructing geometric shapes by following directions; creating diagrams, flowcharts, or graphs by following directions or using manuals.

SCIENCE: Plotting or reading a plot of an archaeological dig or ecological study area; seeing and describing strata in natural formations

SOCIAL STUDIES: Interpreting and constructing maps, graphs, time lines, or diagrams

ENRICHMENT AREAS: Taking tests; art, physical education, or dance activities involving position or location; following drill, marching band, or sports instructions involving location, direction, or movement

TEACHING SUGGESTIONS

There will be several ways to describe the relative positions of the shapes. During class discussion, compare alternative descriptions and note the sentence patterns used to express the same relative positions, shapes, and colors. Remind students of the words they used in the previous lesson to describe shape and location.

MODEL LESSON

LESSON

Introduction

Q: In previous exercises you completed sentences describing locations of shapes.

Explaining the Objective to Students

Q: In these exercises you will describe the color, shape, and position of two or three shapes.

Class Activity

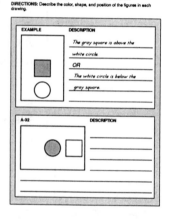

- Project the example from the transparency of page 12. (Keep the description covered.)

    Q: Name these shapes.
      A: Square and circle

    Q: Describe the colors of the shapes.
      A: White or gray

    Q: Describe the positions of the shapes.
      A: Above or below

    Q: Put these ideas together into a description.

- Allow time for writing. Ask for students' descriptions. Compare their answers to the text by uncovering the description.

GUIDED PRACTICE
EXERCISE: **A-32**

INDEPENDENT PRACTICE

- Assign exercises **A-33** through **A-36**.

THINKING ABOUT THINKING

Q: What did you pay attention to when you described two or three shapes?

1. I looked to see if the shapes were black, white, or gray.

2. I named each shape (square, circle, or triangle).

3. I combined the color and shape name (black circle, etc.).

4. I described the position of the shapes (above or below, left or right, middle or corner, etc.)

5. I combined all of the above ideas in a description.

PERSONAL APPLICATION

Q: When would you describe the position of an object?

A: Examples include describing the positions of players in a game, filling out an automobile accident report, requesting the installation of an appliance or telephone, describing the movement of the cursor on a computer display, etc.

EXERCISES A-37 to A-38

CHARACTERISTICS OF A SHAPE

ANSWERS A-37 through A-38 — Student book pages 15–6

Guided Practice: TM 3 Characteristic: gray in color; Characteristic: three sides (triangle); Characteristic: three-inch base; Characteristic: one inch high; Characteristic: All the angles are smaller than a square corner (acute angles). Characteristic: Two sides are equal (isosceles). NOTE: Students will not necessarily list all these characteristics. Description: This gray triangle has a three-inch base and is one inch high. All the angles are smaller than a square corner.

Independent Practice: A-37 Characteristic: gray in color; Characteristic: five sides (pentagon); Characteristic: two one-inch sides, making a square corner; Characteristic: The other four angles are larger than a square corner (obtuse angles). Description: This gray pentagon has one square corner formed by sides that are each one inch long. The three remaining sides form four angles that are each larger than a square corner (obtuse angles). **A-38** Characteristic: gray in color; Characteristic: six sides (hexagon); Characteristic: two vertical one-inch sides opposite one another (parallel); Characteristic: All the angles are larger than a square corner (obtuse angles). Description: This gray hexagon has two vertical sides that are one inch long. All the angles are larger than a square corner.

LESSON PREPARATION

OBJECTIVE AND MATERIALS

OBJECTIVE: Students will combine the characteristics of a shape to describe it accurately.

MATERIALS: Transparency of TM 3 (optional), transparency and photocopies of TM 4, transparency of TM 5 (optional) • washable transparency marker

CURRICULUM APPLICATIONS

LANGUAGE ARTS: Writing descriptions

MATHEMATICS: Describing area and perimeter

SCIENCE: Describing crystals or gems, describing locomotion

SOCIAL STUDIES: Describing map features, landforms, lots, parks, or features of buildings.

ENRICHMENT AREAS: Describing designs or patterns

TEACHING SUGGESTIONS

Relate the description process to forming a definition. Discuss how a description of a specific polygon is similar to and different from a definition of the term for that class of polygons (see graphic organizer on next page).

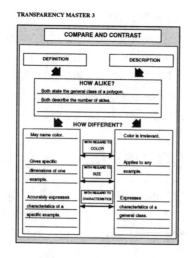

MODEL LESSON

LESSON

Introduction

Q: In the previous exercises you described the color, shape, and position of two or three shapes.

Explaining the Objective to Students

Q: You will combine characteristics of a shape to describe it accurately.

Class Activity

- Project TM 4 and distribute photocopies to students.

  Q: List a characteristic of this shape in each of the four characteristic boxes.

  A: Characteristic: gray in color; Characteristic: three sides (triangle); Characteristic: three-inch base; Characteristic: one inch high; Characteristic: all the angles are smaller than a square corner (acute angles); Characteristic: two sides are equal (isosceles) NOTE: Students will not necessarily list all these characteristics.

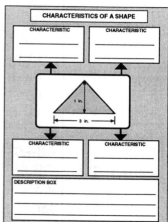

- Allow time for writing. Discuss students' answers.

  Q: Put these characteristics together into a description.

  A: This gray triangle has a three-inch base and is one inch high. All the angles are smaller than a square corner.

GUIDED PRACTICE

EXERCISE: TM 4

INDEPENDENT PRACTICE

- Assign exercises **A-37** and **A-38**.

EXTENSION ACTIVITY (optional)

- Write the following definitions on the board and review them with students:
  1. Quadrilateral—any closed, four-sided shape

2. Parallelogram—a closed, four-sided shape with two sets of parallel sides

3. Rectangle—a parallelogram with four right angles

4. Square—a rectangle with four equal sides

5. Trapezoid—a quadrilateral with only one pair of parallel sides

- Project TM 5.
   Q: Look at the first shape on the left. Which of the characteristics does this shape have?
      A: It has four sides so it is a quadrilateral.

- Make a check mark under quadrilateral.
   Q: Does this shape have the characteristics of any of the other shapes listed (i.e., are the sides parallel, does it have square corners, etc.)?
      A: No

- Continue the same process with the rest of the figures, marking each appropriate box.

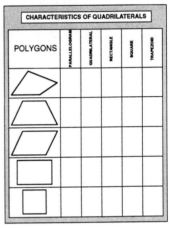

TRANSPARENCY MASTER 5

THINKING ABOUT THINKING

Q: What did you pay attention to when you described the shape?

1. I looked for special characteristics such as equal sides, equal angles, lines going in the same direction (parallel lines).

2. I described each characteristic.

3. I combined the characteristics to make a complete description.

PERSONAL APPLICATION

Q: When would you describe the characteristics of an object?

   A: Examples include when describing tools, areas of materials (plots of ground, clothing material, building materials, etc.), lot size.

Chapter 2 | FIGURAL SIMILARITIES AND DIFFERENCES
(Student book pages 18–73)

EXERCISES B-1 to B-32

MATCHING FIGURES/SHAPES

> **ANSWERS B-1 through B-32 — Student book pages 18–24**
> **Guided Practice: B-1** d; **B-2** b; **B-3** a; **B-4** d
> **Independent Practice: B-5** c; **B-6** b; **B-7** d; **B-8** a; **B-9** c; **B-10** b;
> **B-11** d; **B-12** c; **B-13** a; **B-14** d; **B-15** a, c, and e; **B-16** b and c; **B-17** b and
> d; **B-18** b and e; **B-19** b and d; **B-20** b and e; **B-21** c and e; **B-22** b, c, and
> e; **B-23** c and e **B-24** a and d; **B-25** a and c; **B-26** b and c; **B-27** a and c;
> **B-28** b and d; **B-29** c and d; **B-30** a and d; **B-31** b and d; **B-32** a and c

LESSON PREPARATION

OBJECTIVE AND MATERIALS
OBJECTIVE: Students will match a shape or figure with one that is exactly like it.
MATERIALS: Transparency of TM 6 (top section cut apart as indicated)

CURRICULUM APPLICATIONS
LANGUAGE ARTS: Using visual discrimination in word recognition
MATHEMATICS: Completing similarity and congruence exercises, distinguishing between arithmetic problems by operational signs (+, −, ×, ÷)
SCIENCE: Comparing shapes of leaves, insects, shells, etc.; finding or putting away laboratory equipment
SOCIAL STUDIES: Matching puzzle sections to geographic features on map puzzles; using legends to locate map features, e.g., parks, airports, rest areas, historical monuments
ENRICHMENT AREAS: Recognizing shapes of road signs; discerning different patterns in art, written music, or dance steps

TEACHING SUGGESTIONS
Explain the difference between the terms *shape* and *figure*. A shape is the general configuration or outline of an object, such as a circle or square. A figure is a more complex geometric form consisting of any combination of points, lines, or planes. Reinforce the following words and phrases emphasized in these exercises: *square, circle, rectangle, right triangle, parallelogram, triangle,* and *trapezoid.* For spelling or vocabulary review, you may list terms that describe location (*center, corner*), position (*above, below, left, right*), or size (*large, small*). Encourage students to be as specific as possible in describing shapes or figures and their similarities and differences; e.g., taller, pointed, shorter, wider. Emphasize direction in exercises **B-10** through **B-14**, for three of the choices are rotations of the given figure. The matching figures must face in the same direction.

MODEL LESSON

LESSON

Introduction
Q: When you were very young, you learned to pick out things that were similar to each other. You could find a ball, regardless of the color or size,

because you knew what a ball looked like. Think about a situation when someone asked "Please bring me one just like this." Describe to a partner what you had to think about to be sure that what you brought was exactly like what you were shown.

Explaining the Objective to Students

Q: In these exercises you are going to match a shape or figure with one that is exactly like it. There should be no difference in the lines or the direction a figure faces.

Class Activity

TRANSPARENCY MASTER 6

- Project the example figure from TM 6. Reposition the figure to show its mobility.

  Q: You are going to look for a figure that is exactly like this one. In these exercises, direction makes a difference.

- Project the remaining figures.

  Q: Which of these figures matches the first one? Remember that you cannot turn the example figure to make it fit.

- Place the example figure over the figure *a*.

  Q: Are these figures the same? Explain your answer.

  A: No, there is an extra line in the lower part of the shape.

- Place the example figure over figure *b*.

  Q: Are these figure the same? Explain your answer.

  A: No, figure *b* is too narrow.

- Place the example figure over figure *c*.

  Q: Are these figures the same? Explain your answer.

  A: Yes, all the lines match.

- Place the example figure over figure *d*.

  Q: Are these figures the same? Explain your answer.

  A: No, shape *d* is too short.

  Q: Since all the lines match in the example figure and figure *c*, these figures are the same. Circle figure *c* .

GUIDED PRACTICE

EXERCISES: **B-1** through **B-4**

- Give students sufficient time to complete these exercises. Ask students to discuss and explain their choices.

INDEPENDENT PRACTICE

- Assign exercises **B-5** through **B-32**. NOTE: These exercises may be divided after **B-14** and after **B-23** if needed.

THINKING ABOUT THINKING

Q: What did you pay attention to when you matched these figures?

1. I looked carefully at the details (size of the figure, length of the sides, size of the angle, pattern or color, similarity to some common object, etc.).

2. I matched equal parts (side, angle, etc.).

3. I checked that all the sides and angles were the same.

4. I checked how those figures that didn't match are really different.

PERSONAL APPLICATION

Q: When might you need to match shapes or figures?

A: Examples include putting away blocks, toys, dishes, silverware, hardware, or tools; matching model parts; recognizing differences in makes of cars.

EXERCISES B-33 to B-45

WHICH SHAPE/FIGURE DOES NOT MATCH?

ANSWERS B-33 through B-45— Student book pages 25–7
Guided Practice: B-33 a, c, and d; B-34 b, c, and e; B-35 a and c; B-36 b and c
Independent Practice: B-37 b; B-38 b; B-39 c; B-40 c; B-41 c; B-42 b; B-43 a; B-44 c; B-45 c

LESSON PREPARATION

OBJECTIVE AND MATERIALS

OBJECTIVE: Students will practice finding the shape or figure that is different from the others in the group.

MATERIALS: Transparency of TM 7 (top section cut apart as indicated) • washable transparency marker • attribute blocks, pattern blocks, or hand-made facsimiles (optional)

CURRICULUM APPLICATIONS

LANGUAGE ARTS: Using visual discrimination in reading, discriminating between punctuation marks

MATHEMATICS: Distinguishing between geometric shapes

Science: Comparing shapes of leaves, insects, shells, etc.; choosing proper laboratory apparatus by size or shape

SOCIAL STUDIES: Using legends to locate map features, e.g., parks, airports, rest areas, historical monuments; recognizing graphic variations in charts or graphs

ENRICHMENT AREAS: Using shape to distinguish purpose of traffic or road signs, separating architectural periods by comparing typical styles, distinguishing different note values in music

TEACHING SUGGESTIONS

Remind students of the words they used in the previous lesson to describe shapes and figures. The difference between this exercise and the previous one is the emphasis on the word *not*. Terms emphasized in this lesson should include: *square, circle, right triangle, rectangle, parallelogram, triangle,* and *pentagon.*

MODEL LESSON

LESSON

Introduction

Q: You have been finding shapes or figures that are exactly the same.

Explaining the Objective to Students

Q: In these exercises you are going to practice finding the shape or figure that is different from the others in the group.

Class Activity—Option 1

• Optional demonstration using blocks: Using attribute or design blocks, arrange a set of three triangles and one square on the overhead projector. NOTE: On the projector, these blocks will be seen as silhouettes, so color is not a factor.

Q: Which block is not like the others? Which block doesn't belong?

• After students respond, ask them to explain their answers.

Class Activity—Option 2

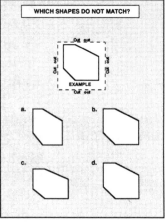

TRANSPARENCY MASTER 7

• Demonstration using transparency: Project TM 7. Reposition the figure to show its mobility then project the remaining shapes.

Q: You will compare these shapes to determine which are exactly like the movable figure and which are different.

• Place the example shape over shape *a*.

Q: These two shapes are not the same. The example is wider than shape *a*. Since this shape does not match the example, mark it with an X.

• Move the example shape to shape *b*.

Q: All sides match exactly, so you won't mark this one.

• Place the example shape over shape *c*.

Q: Shape *c* is too short. How should you mark this shape?
  A: Mark an X through it. Move the example shape to shape *d*.

Q: All sides match exactly. What should be done to this shape?
  A: Nothing; it should not be marked.

GUIDED PRACTICE

EXERCISES: **B-33** through **B-36**

• Give students sufficient time to complete these exercises. Ask students to discuss and explain their choices.

INDEPENDENT PRACTICE

• Assign exercises **B-37** through **B-45**.

THINKING ABOUT THINKING

Q: What did you pay attention to when you matched these figures?
  1. I looked carefully at the details (size of the figure, length of the sides, size of the angle, pattern or color, similarity to a common object, etc.).

2. I matched equal parts (side, angle, etc.).

3. I checked that all the sides and angles were the same.

4. I checked how those figures that didn't match are really different.

PERSONAL APPLICATION

Q: When might you be asked to find something shaped or patterned differently from others in a group?

A: Examples include sorting utensils, tools, or hardware that are improperly stored; finding errors or exceptions in needlework patterns; distinguishing between motor or engine parts.

EXERCISES B-46 to B-50

FINDING SHAPES

> **ANSWERS B-46 through B-50 — Student book pages 28–30**
> **Guided Practice: B-46** c, and d; **B-47** b and c
> **Independent Practice: B-48** a, b, c, d, e, and f; **B-49** b, c, and d; **B-50** a, b, and c

LESSON PREPARATION

OBJECTIVE AND MATERIALS

OBJECTIVE: Students will decide which shapes from a group are included in a given figure.
MATERIALS: Transparency of TM 8 • piece of clothing with obvious seams • attribute blocks or handmade tangrams (optional)

CURRICULUM APPLICATIONS

LANGUAGE ARTS: Recognizing phonemes and/or syllables, recognizing component parts of compound words
MATHEMATICS: Describing geometric shapes within larger designs or constructions
SCIENCE: Recognizing parts of trees, plants, insects, and animals; recognizing components of compound materials
SOCIAL STUDIES: Recognizing components of continents, countries, states, and cities; comparing aerial photos or topographic maps with maps showing governmental divisions and subdivisions, e.g., cities, counties, states, and countries
ENRICHMENT AREAS: Locating or duplicating sections of a larger work of art; recognizing parts of a stanza of music, e.g., clef sign, bar, time signature, notes, rests; recognizing individual steps in a dance routine; recognizing moves or patterns in sports plays

TEACHING SUGGESTIONS

Students should know the terms used in the first two lessons to describe the shapes and sizes in these exercises. Emphasize the following comparative terms: *taller, shorter, wider, more narrow,* or *less pointed.* Encourage students to use these words with qualifiers, e.g., slightly smaller, much larger.

Students may have difficulty verbalizing these figural perceptions. These exercises contribute valuable language training only if the words are used, reinforced, and become functional in the vocabulary of the learner. For spelling or vocabulary review, you may list the following synonyms for "put together:" *assemble, connect, join, combine, build,* etc.

MODEL LESSON

LESSON

Introduction

• Show the seamed piece of clothing, indicating the parts of the whole.
Q: Have you ever watched someone making a shirt? He or she seems to see just how the pieces fit to become a single garment. If you look closely, you can see where the pieces have been put together.

Explaining the Objective to Students

Q: In these exercises you are going to decide which shapes from a group are included in a given figure.

Class Activity—Option 1

• Optional demonstration using blocks: Join any two blocks together and project them on the overhead. Select four additional blocks, two the same size and shape as the pattern pieces, and place them separately below the figure. Ask students to identify the two blocks which were combined to make the figure. Encourage them to state why they did not choose the other shapes. NOTE: Color is not a factor in this demonstration.

Class Activity—Option 2

• Demonstration using transparency: Project TM 8. Point to shapes *a, b, c,* and *d.*
Q: You need to identify which of these shapes are included in the top figure.

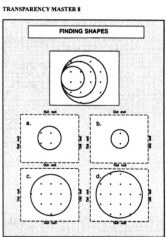

TRANSPARENCY MASTER 8

FINDING SHAPES

• Place shape *a* on the figure.
Q: This shape matches the inside circle exactly.

• Replace with shape *b.*
Q: This shape is smaller than any circle of the figure.

• Replace with shape *c.*
Q: This shape is larger than the middle circle.

• Replace with shape *d.*
Q: This shape is the same as the outer circle of the figure. To show that these two shapes…

• Indicate shapes *a* and *d.*
Q: …are included in the given figure, circle each of them.

• Mark shapes *a* and *d*

GUIDED PRACTICE

EXERCISES: **B-46, B-47**

• Give students sufficient time to complete these exercises. Ask students to discuss and explain their choices.

INDEPENDENT PRACTICE
- Assign exercises **B-48** through **B-50**.

THINKING ABOUT THINKING
Q: What did you pay attention to when you found parts of these figures?
1. I looked carefully at the details of the shapes in the choice box (size of the figure, length of the sides, size of the angle, similarity to some common object, etc.).
2. I looked at the figure box to see which shapes I might find there.
3. I matched equal parts (side, angle, etc.).
4. I checked that all the sides and angles were the same.
5. I checked how those shapes that didn't match were really different.

PERSONAL APPLICATION
Q: When might you need to recognize the parts of something after it has been put together?
A: Examples include art activities; furniture or clothing items; parts of tools, motors, or gears; picture puzzles.

**EXERCISES
B-51 to B-55**

FINDING AND TRACING PATTERNS

> **ANSWERS B-51 through B-55 — Student book pages 31–3**
> **Guided Practice: B-51** c and d
> **Independent Practice: B-52** a and d; **B-53** a and d; **B-54** d; **B-55** b and c

**LESSON
PREPARATION**

OBJECTIVE AND MATERIALS
OBJECTIVE: Students will find and trace a pattern hidden in a larger design.
MATERIALS: Transparency of TM 9 • colored washable transparency marker • crayons or markers for each student (optional)

CURRICULUM APPLICATIONS
LANGUAGE ARTS: Identifying position of topics and subtopics in outlines, identifying rhyme patterns in poetry, finding hidden words in larger words, finding repeated letter patterns in words
MATHEMATICS: Finding patterns or shapes within geometric figures
SCIENCE: Tracing the path of blood or any system through the body, recognizing patterns in soil stratification or cloud formations
SOCIAL STUDIES: Following or indicating a historical trip on a map, e.g., Oregon Trail, Pony Express route, travels of Lewis and Clark; locating boundaries of national parks or forests, counties, states, countries, etc., on a map
ENRICHMENT AREAS: Finding repeated interval patterns in music, reproducing sections of art projects, identifying steps in a dance sequence, recognizing or drawing pattern plays in team sports

TEACHING SUGGESTIONS
Encourage students to describe patterns accurately. Use the technique of identifying key patterns in a figure to eliminate rather than to confirm

responses. Darkening the patterns will emphasize the design. Markers or crayons may be used for greater contrast. This figure-ground exercise is more difficult than it appears.

MODEL LESSON

LESSON

Introduction

Q: In the previous exercise you recognized parts that make up a whole. Sometimes these parts were hard to see because other lines or shapes got in the way.

Explaining the Objective to Students

Q: In these exercises you will find and trace a pattern hidden in a larger design. The pattern must face the same direction in the complex design as it does in the given figure.

Class Activity

TRANSPARENCY MASTER 9

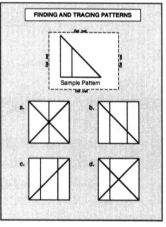

- Project TM 9. Move the sample pattern piece around as you explain the activity.
  Q: Any time you move the sample pattern you must keep it facing in the same direction. Do not turn the sample pattern as you move it, just slide it. You are going to use this pattern to determine if it is hidden in each figure.

- Place the sample pattern over figure *a*.
  Q: The outside lines of the sample pattern are in this figure, but the vertical line is missing, so the sample pattern is not found in figure *a*.

- Move the sample pattern over figure *b*.
  Q: All lines in the sample pattern fit the figure exactly, so this pattern is hidden in figure *b*.

- Trace the sample pattern in the figure using a colored transparency marker.

- Move the sample pattern over figure *c*.
  Q: The outside edges match and the vertical line is the same, but the diagonal line isn't in the right position. This pattern is not hidden in figure *c*.

- Move the sample pattern over figure *d*.
  Q: Is the sample pattern hidden in this figure? If so, how can you tell?
    A: Yes; all the lines in the sample pattern fit the figure exactly, so this pattern is hidden in figure *d*.

- Trace the pattern in the figure using a colored transparency marker.

GUIDED PRACTICE
EXERCISE: **B-51**

- Give students sufficient time to complete this exercise. Ask students to state their reasons for selecting or eliminating each choice.

INDEPENDENT PRACTICE

- Assign exercises **B-52** through **B-55**.

THINKING ABOUT THINKING

Q: What did you pay attention to when you matched these figures?

1. I looked carefully at the details in the shape on the left (size of the figure, length of the sides, size of the angle, similarity to a common object, etc.).

2. I looked for matching equal parts (side, angle, etc.) in each of the four figures in the exercise.

3. I checked that all the sides and angles were the same.

4. I checked how those figures that didn't match were really different.

PERSONAL APPLICATION

Q: When might you need to find or follow a line or pattern within a larger design?

A: Examples include reading a map; doing weaving or needlework, tracing electrical circuits, reproducing furniture or clothing, solving maze puzzles

EXERCISES B-56 to B-60

COMBINING SHAPES

> **ANSWERS B-56 through B-60 — Student book pages 34–6**
> **Guided Practice: B-56** b and c
> **Independent Practice: B-57** c and d; **B-58** b and d; **B-59** b and d; **B-60** a, b, and c

LESSON PREPARATION

OBJECTIVE AND MATERIALS

OBJECTIVE: Students will practice recognizing what the whole figure looks like when the individual parts are put together.

MATERIALS: Transparency of TM 10 (cut apart as indicated) • washable transparency marker • dress or shirt pattern • attribute blocks or handmade tangrams (optional)

CURRICULUM APPLICATIONS

LANGUAGE ARTS: Preparing layouts for newspapers, yearbooks, posters, or magazines
MATHEMATICS: Recognizing fractional parts of geometric shapes; rearranging irregular polygons into recognizable, regular shapes
SCIENCE: Recognizing connections in skeletal structure and body parts of animals; recognizing parts of plants, animals, or compounds; assembling science apparatus
SOCIAL STUDIES: Recognizing subdivisions of areas on a map, e.g., wards, cities, townships, counties, states, regions, countries, and continents
ENRICHMENT AREAS: Recognizing sections of orchestras or bands; making collages in art

TEACHING SUGGESTIONS

Review synonyms for the following terms: *joining, size, shape,* and *location*. Ask students to identify common objects which combine geometric shapes, noting how the part appears within the whole; e.g., ceiling tiles, floor tiles, concrete block or brick walls, window panes.

MODEL LESSON | **LESSON**

Introduction

Q: Sometimes parts don't look quite the same as you expect they should after they have been put together. When you are making a garment, for example, the pattern piece that looks like this…

- Hold up a sleeve pattern piece.
  Q: …becomes the part of the garment that is here.

- Indicate a sleeve.
  Q: Each piece looks slightly different after it has become part of a whole garment.

Explaining the Objective to Students

Q: In these exercises you are going to practice recognizing what the whole figure looks like when the individual parts are put together.

Class Activity—Option 1

- Optional demonstration using blocks: Show attribute block or handmade tangram shapes separately first, then joined to make a figure. Ask students to describe the shape of the total figure, then point to and name the separate shapes that make up the figure.

Class Activity—Option 2

- Demonstration using transparency: Project TM 10, transparency of the example on student workbook page 34. Show that the cutout shapes can be moved around.
  Q: You need to determine which figures…

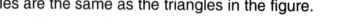

TRANSPARENCY MASTER 10

COMBINING SHAPES

- Indicate the answer choices.
  Q: …can be made by combining these three shapes.

- Indicate the movable shapes.
  Q: To form these figures, you can turn the shapes in any direction or flip them over.

- Place the movable shapes on figure *a* with edges matching.
  Q: All the edges match, so this figure can be made by joining these shapes.

- Put a check mark on figure *a* to show these three shapes make this figure.

- Place the shapes over figure *b*.
  Q: The shapes do not fit this figure. The triangles match, but the base rectangle is too long. You cannot make this figure by joining these shapes.

- Place the shapes over figure *c*.
  Q: Can you form this figure with these shapes?
    A: No.

  Q: Are any of these shapes found in the figure?
    A: Yes; both triangles are the same as the triangles in the figure.

Q: How is the rectangle different?
  A: It is longer than the rectangle in the figure.

Q: Since one shape is different, this figure cannot be made by joining these shapes.

• Place the shapes over figure *d.*
Q: Can this figure be made by combining these shapes?
  A: Yes.

Q: Since all the edges match, these shapes can make figure *d.*

• Put a check mark on figure *d.*

GUIDED PRACTICE
EXERCISE: **B-56**
• Give students sufficient time to complete this exercise. Ask students to discuss and explain their choices and give reasons for eliminating the other answers.

INDEPENDENT PRACTICE
• Assign exercises **B-57** through **B-60**.

THINKING ABOUT THINKING
Q: What did you pay attention to when you matched these figures?
1. I looked at the shapes to be joined.
2. I mentally moved the shapes to see if I could form the combination.
3. I checked that the combination I mentally formed matched the combination to be formed.
4. If I could not form a combination, I checked on the reason I could not.

PERSONAL APPLICATION
Q: When might you need to recognize how parts have been rearranged or combined to form a whole?
  A: Examples include making a sandwich, identifying gears or motor parts, matching parts of picture puzzles or tangrams, copying objects made from construction toys, following needlework or sewing patterns.

**EXERCISES
B-61 to B-71**

DIVIDING SHAPES INTO EQUAL PARTS—A

ANSWERS B-61 through B-71 — Student book pages 37–9
Guided Practice: B-61 Yes, the parts are the same size and shape and all lines match. **B-62** Yes, the parts are the same size and shape and all lines match. **B-63** No, part G (top section) is larger than part H (bottom section)
Independent Practice: B-64 Yes; the parts are the same size and shape and all lines match. **B-65** No; part K (top section) is larger than part L (bottom section); the shortest side of the top section is longer than the shortest side of the bottom section. **B-66** Yes; the parts are the same size and shape and all lines match. **B-67** No; part O (top section) is smaller

than part P (bottom section); the shortest side of the top section is shorter than the shortest side of the bottom section. **B-68** Yes; the parts are the same size and shape and all lines match. **B-69** No; part S (top section) is smaller than part T (bottom section); the common line divides the sections unequally so they do not match. **B-70** Yes; the parts are the same size and shape and all lines match. **B-71** No; the parts have the same base and height measurements, but the common line divides the sections unequally so they do not match.

LESSON PREPARATION

OBJECTIVE AND MATERIALS

OBJECTIVE: Students will determine whether or not a shape has been divided in half.

MATERIALS: Transparency of TM 11

CURRICULUM APPLICATIONS

LANGUAGE ARTS: Dividing a long poem into parts

MATHEMATICS: Comparing similarity and congruence of geometric shapes

SCIENCE: Recognizing symmetry in natural objects, e.g., leaves, shells, etc.

SOCIAL STUDIES: Applying legends to perceive distances on a map

ENRICHMENT AREAS: Doing artistic paper folding (origami); making models of symmetrical objects; dividing copy into equal columns in journalism; doing geometric art designs

TEACHING SUGGESTIONS

Use the following terms if students are familiar with them: *perimeter, area, radius, base,* and *height.* If the shape has been divided unequally, students should explain how the sections are unequal. They should identify positions of parts (upper, lower, left, right), compare sizes (larger, smaller), and compare lengths (longer, shorter, same). Also ask students to identify shapes within the classroom that can and cannot be divided into equal parts and explain how each can be divided.

MODEL LESSON

LESSON

Introduction

- Using a symmetrical object, show that it can be divided into two equal parts. Then divide an asymmetrical object to show that some objects cannot be divided into equal portions. Point out the unequal parts.
  Q: Sometimes it's easy to see that something is divided exactly in half.

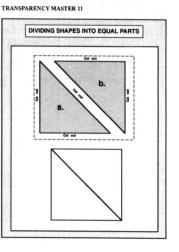

TRANSPARENCY MASTER 11

Explaining the Objective to Students

Q: In these exercises you will determine whether or not a shape has been divided in half.

Class Activity

- Project the undivided square from TM 11 on the top section of the overhead, then lay triangles

A and B on the lower section of the overhead so students see they can be moved around.

Q: You are going to determine whether this square has been divided into equal parts.

- Lay triangles A and B on top of the square.

  Q: These two triangles fit the square exactly. If the square has been divided in half, these two triangles will match each other.

- Move the two triangles to another part of the projector and stack one on the other to form a single triangle.

  Q: Since all the edges match exactly, the triangles are equal. The square must have been divided into equal parts.

GUIDED PRACTICE

EXERCISES: **B-61** through **B-63**

INDEPENDENT PRACTICE

- Assign exercises **B-64** through **B-71**.

THINKING ABOUT THINKING

Q: What did you pay attention to when you divided the shapes into equal parts?

1. I looked carefully to see if a similar paper shape could be folded into equal parts.

2. I built the two parts.

3. I checked to see that the parts were equal by pulling the halves apart and stacking them on top of one another.

PERSONAL APPLICATION

Q: When might you need to decide whether something is divided into two equal parts?

 A: Examples include sharing food, cutting or folding paper, constructing symmetrical models.

EXERCISES B-72 to B-77

DIVIDING SHAPES INTO EQUAL PARTS—B

> **ANSWERS B-72 through B-77—** Student book pages 40–2
> **Guided Practice: B-72** and **B-73** See next page.
> **Independent Practice: B-74** through **B-77** See next page.

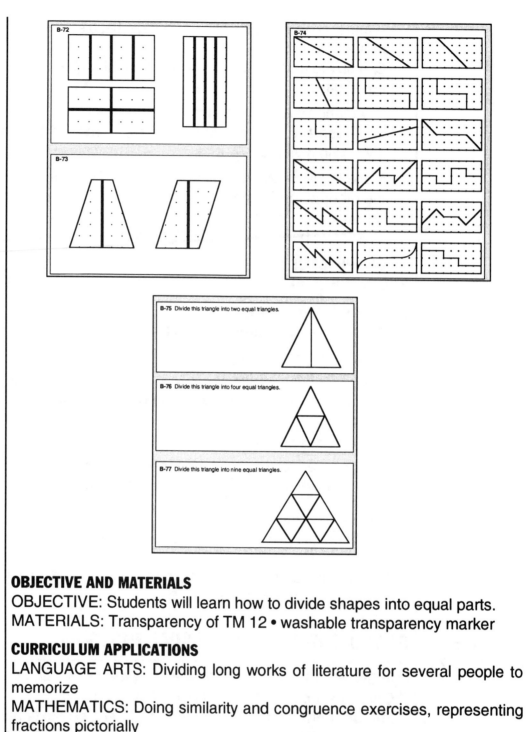

LESSON PREPARATION

OBJECTIVE AND MATERIALS
OBJECTIVE: Students will learn how to divide shapes into equal parts.
MATERIALS: Transparency of TM 12 • washable transparency marker

CURRICULUM APPLICATIONS
LANGUAGE ARTS: Dividing long works of literature for several people to memorize
MATHEMATICS: Doing similarity and congruence exercises, representing fractions pictorially
SCIENCE: Dividing materials equally for experiments; identifying symmetry in body parts or natural phenomena, e.g., leaves, plants, shells
SOCIAL STUDIES: Making or interpreting charts and graphs, dividing historical time lines into intervals
ENRICHMENT AREAS: Dividing materials in home economics, art, or industrial arts; creating geometric or symmetrical designs in art

TEACHING SUGGESTIONS
Keys to this lesson are the concept of equality and the process of confirming visually that two parts are or are not equal. The following synonyms for equal

should be used to help reinforce this concept: *congruent, symmetrical, same, as wide as,* and *as long as.* NOTE: The rectangle in exercise **B-74** can be divided into congruent parts in many ways. Encourage students who draw any different or unusual divisions to draw them on the dot grid on the transparency.

MODEL LESSON

LESSON

Introduction

Q: In the previous exercise you learned to recognize whether or not a shape had been divided into equal parts, as you do when you judge whether a candy bar has been equally divided.

Explaining the Objective to Students

Q: In these exercises you will learn how to divide shapes into equal parts.

Class Activity

• Project TM 12 onto the chalkboard. Write on the chalkboard or use a washable transparency marker to divide the rectangular grid by drawing a vertical line one dot off from the center.

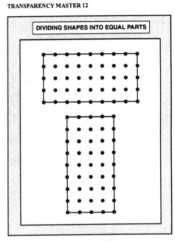

TRANSPARENCY MASTER 12

DIVIDING SHAPES INTO EQUAL PARTS

Q: If this shape is divided along this line, will it be divided exactly into equal parts?

    A: Students should respond that one part looks larger than the other.

Q: How can you tell if one part is larger than the other?

    A: Students should explain that counting spaces between dots will determine the width of each part. NOTE: It is helpful to count spaces instead of dots. The dots are spaced one-fourth inch apart. If one counts dots, the first dot should be counted as the zero dot (dots that fall on the outer edges of the figure may not be visible, but should always be counted.)

Q: If you want to divide this grid into four rectangles of equal size, you can do it several ways. For example, you can use one horizontal line and one vertical line.

• Divide the rectangle horizontally and vertically into four equal rectangles.
Q: Are there four equal parts?

• Check accuracy by counting spaces down and across for each smaller rectangle, then have students open their workbooks to page 40, exercise **B-72**.
Q: Use your pencil to divide the rectangle into four equal rectangles as demonstrated.

• After students have completed the division, erase the lines from the transparency.
Q: This rectangle can be divided several different ways to make it into four equal rectangular parts. Use the second grid to show a different way of

dividing this rectangle into four equal rectangles. Count the spaces to confirm that the sections are equal.

GUIDED PRACTICE
EXERCISES: **B-72, B-73**
• Check to see that students have divided the shapes correctly. Discuss how to count the spaces between the dots to confirm whether the shapes are equal.

INDEPENDENT PRACTICE
• Assign exercises **B-74** through **B-77**.

THINKING ABOUT THINKING
Q: What did you pay attention to in deciding if the shapes were divided into equal parts?
1. I looked to see if the pieces were the same shape.
2. I looked to see if the pieces were the same size.

PERSONAL APPLICATION
Q: When might you need to decide whether something is divided into equal parts?
A: Examples include sharing food, cutting paper, constructing models or projects, paper folding.

Q: Why is it sometimes important to divide things equally?
A: Examples include to show fairness to others, to give artistic value, to simplify constructions or instructions.

EXERCISES B-78 to B-84

PAPER FOLDING—SELECT

ANSWERS B-78 through B-84 — Student book pages 43–4
Guided Practice: **B-78** b
Independent Practice: **B-79** b; **B-80** d; **B-81** c; **B-82** c; **B-83** b; **B-84** b

LESSON PREPARATION

OBJECTIVE AND MATERIALS
OBJECTIVE: Students will identify the pattern which produced a particular design.
MATERIALS: 5" × 8" models of TM 13, the example patterns from student workbook page 43 • using a hole punch and brightly colored paper, make one model each of items *a, b,* and *c* (marked *a, b,* or *c* on the folded front) and two models of item *d*—one marked *d* and one unmarked • paper and scissors for teacher and each student

CURRICULUM APPLICATIONS
LANGUAGE ARTS: Doing word search puzzles, recognizing sound or letter patterns
MATHEMATICS: Doing symmetry exercises, using visual perception skills, drawing geometric shapes to form patterns
SCIENCE: Determining symmetry in natural forms, reproducing crystal or snowflake patterns, predicting appearance or position of stars or planets

SOCIAL STUDIES: Seeing patterns in charts, graphs, or schedules
ENRICHMENT AREAS: Creating computer-generated designs, identifying basic steps in a dance routine or art project, memorizing printed music patterns

TEACHING SUGGESTIONS

Students must distinguish the folded edge from the outer edges. Identify these distinctions and encourage students to use the terms *right, left,* and *center.* These directional words will be practiced in more complex forms in the section on following directions. *Inner, outer,* and *near* are relative terms requiring some point for comparison. You may want to introduce the concepts of curve and symmetry.

MODEL LESSON

LESSON

Introduction

NOTE: In paper-folding lessons, the word *pattern* refers to the folded item; the word *design* refers to the unfolded item.

> Q: Have you ever noticed that when you cut a design in a folded paper pattern, it looks different after it has been unfolded than it did when you cut the pattern?

- As the class watches, cut a fancy, sharply curved pattern from an edge of a piece of folded scrap paper. Project the pattern and unfold the paper.
  Q: When you unfold the pattern, you have a lovely design. Now two sides have the same curves as the one edge that was cut.

- Fold the paper again. Select a noticeable curve and point as you explain.
  Q: This curve…

- Point to identify the curve as you slowly open the pattern.
  Q: …becomes two curves.

- Point to both curves.
  Q: Practice by cutting the fanciest pattern you can.

- Allow time for students to cut patterns and discuss their designs.
  Q: Because the patterns have such large curves, the unfolded design is lovely. You can easily see the two edges that result…

- Point to both edges of a sample student pattern.
  Q: …from the one you cut.

- Refold the pattern and point to the corresponding curve.
  Q: It may not be so easy, however, to see which curve makes a particular edge on a pattern that is not as fancy as this one.

Explaining the Objective to Students

> Q: In these exercises you will identify the pattern which produced a particular design.

Class Activity

- Place the folded patterns marked *a, b, c,* and *d* on the chalkboard tray or tabletop. Unfold and hold up the unmarked pattern *d,* then place it to the left of the folded patterns.

Q: You need to determine which pattern—*a*, *b*, *c*, or *d*—will make this design when it is unfolded. Pattern *a* cannot make this design because both holes of the pattern are near the fold and will not match up when the pattern is unfolded and put in front of the design.

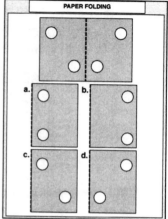

PAPER FOLDING

- Confirm answers by unfolding each pattern.
  Q: Can pattern *b* be the answer?
  A: No, because both holes are near the edge, away from the fold.

  Q: Can pattern *c* be the answer?
  A: No, because the upper hole is near the center and the lower hole is near the edge.

  Q: Can pattern *d* be the answer?
  A: Yes, the holes will be matching.

GUIDED PRACTICE
EXERCISE: **B-78**
- Give students sufficient time to complete this exercise. Then, using the demonstration methodology above, have them discuss and explain their choice.

INDEPENDENT PRACTICE
- Assign exercises **B-79** through **B-84**. NOTE: In exercises **B-79** and **B-80**, students will select the pattern which makes a given design after it has been folded. In exercises **B-81** through **B-84**, students will reverse the process, selecting the design which results when a given pattern has been unfolded. Have students make models of any patterns they find difficult.

THINKING ABOUT THINKING
Q: What did you pay attention to when you decided which figure came next?
1. I looked carefully at the location of the holes.
2. In my mind, I lined up the fold lines.
3. I matched the pattern and design.

PERSONAL APPLICATION
Q: When must you be able to figure out which pattern created a design?
A: Examples include refolding a map, cutting a pattern to make a particular snowflake design, finding the correct pattern piece

EXERCISES B-85 to B-89

PAPER FOLDING—SUPPLY

ANSWERS B-85 through B-92 — Student book pages 45–6
Guided Practice: B-85 to B-86, and B-89 to B-90 See next page.
Independent Practice: B-87 to B-88, B-91 to B-92 See next page.

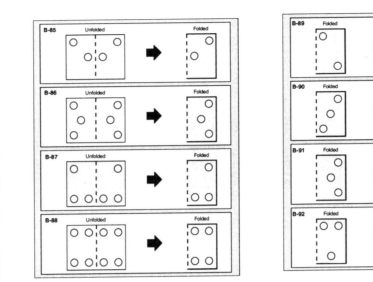

LESSON PREPARATION

OBJECTIVE AND MATERIALS
OBJECTIVE: Students will draw either the design that results from a given pattern or the pattern that produces a given design.
MATERIALS: Paper model of exercise **B-85**, student workbook page 45 • paper model of exercise **B-89**, student workbook page 46

CURRICULUM APPLICATIONS
LANGUAGE ARTS: Doing word search puzzles, recognizing sound or letter patterns
MATHEMATICS: Doing symmetry exercises, using visual perception skills, forming geometric patterns
SCIENCE: Determining symmetry in natural forms, reproducing crystal or snowflake patterns, predicting appearance or position of stars or planets
SOCIAL STUDIES: Seeing patterns in charts, graphs, or schedules
ENRICHMENT AREAS: Creating computer-generated designs, breaking down dance routines or art projects into groups of steps, memorizing printed music patterns

TEACHING SUGGESTIONS
Students must perceive the folded edges and distinguish them from outer edges. Encourage students to use the terms *right, left,* and *center.* These directional words will be practiced in a more complex form in the section on following directions. *Inner, outer,* and *near* are relative terms requiring some point for comparison. Emphasize and repeat these contrasting terms: *right/ left/center, inner/outer, edge/fold, pattern/design (folded/unfolded).* You may want to introduce the concepts of curve and symmetry.

MODEL LESSON

LESSON

Introduction
NOTE: *Pattern* refers to the folded item; *design* refers to the unfolded item.
> Q: In the previous exercise, you practiced recognizing which pattern, when unfolded, creates a particular design and which design is made from a given pattern.

Explaining the Objective to Students

Q: In these exercises you will draw either the design that results from a given pattern or the pattern that produces a given design.

Class Activity

- Hold up the **B-85** design.

  Q: You need to determine what this design will look like when it has been folded. To reproduce the pattern made by this design, you must decide which side of the design represents the folded pattern. Where is the fold in the pattern?

  A: On the left.

  Q: On the design the dotted line represents the vertical fold line. If the pattern has the fold on the left, which part of the design has a dotted line on the left?

  A: The right side

  Q: Draw the pattern that results when the design is folded.

  A: It will be a reproduction of the right half of the **B-85** design, i.e., it will have two holes, one near the top right corner and one centered vertically near the fold line.

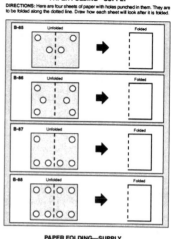

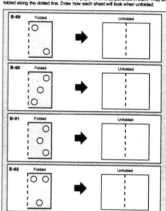

- Hold up the model of **B-85**, fold it and verify the answer. After class discussion, continue the lesson.

- Draw a horizontal rectangle on the chalkboard with a vertical dotted line in the center. Hold up a model of **B-89**.

  Q: You need to determine what this pattern will look like when it has been unfolded. In this pattern, the fold line is on the left side, like the spine of a book. If the pattern opens like a book, what will the left side look like after it is opened?

  A: One hole will be at the top center near the fold line and one hole will be in the lower left corner.

- Draw in the design, then unfold the pattern so students can confirm the design.

GUIDED PRACTICE

EXERCISES: **B-86** and **B-90**

- Give students sufficient time to complete these exercises. Then, using the demonstration methodology above, have them discuss and explain their choices.

INDEPENDENT PRACTICE

- Assign exercises **B-87** to **B-88**, **B-91** to **B-92**.

THINKING ABOUT THINKING

Q: What did you pay attention to when you drew the folded pattern?

1. I identified the fold line of the design.

2. I decided where the hole would go when the design was folded.

3. I drew the pattern the design would make when it was folded.

4. I followed the same process to draw the design of the unfolded pattern.

PERSONAL APPLICATION

Q: When must you be able to recognize what something looks like when it has been folded or unfolded?

  A: Examples include getting towels from a shelf or clothes from a drawer; paper cutting; symmetry in cut patterns; finding correct pattern pieces in sewing, particularly facings.

EXERCISES B-93 to B-114

SYMMETRICAL PATTERNS—SUPPLY

ANSWERS B-93 through B-114 — Student book pages 47–51
Guided Practice: B-93 to B-94, B-101 to B-102 See below.
Independent Practice: B-95 through B-100, B-103 through B-114 See below and next page.

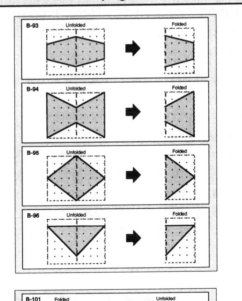

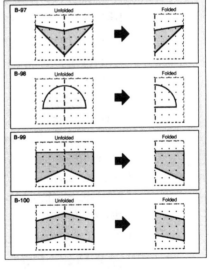

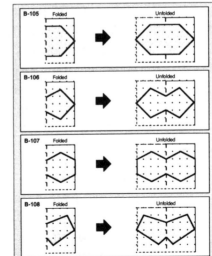

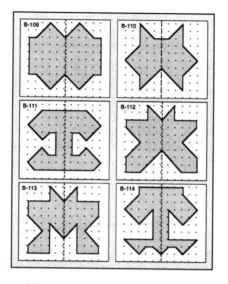

LESSON
PREPARATION

OBJECTIVE AND MATERIALS
OBJECTIVE: Students will draw either the design that results from a given pattern that is non-rectangular or the non-rectangular pattern that produces a given design.
MATERIALS: Paper model of exercise **B-93**, student workbook page 47 • paper model of exercise **B-101**, student workbook page 49

CURRICULUM APPLICATIONS
LANGUAGE ARTS: Doing word search puzzles, recognizing sound or letter patterns
MATHEMATICS: Doing symmetry exercises, using visual perception skills, forming geometric patterns
SCIENCE: Determining symmetry in natural forms, reproducing crystal or snowflake patterns, predicting appearance or position of stars or planets
SOCIAL STUDIES: Seeing patterns in charts, graphs, or schedules
ENRICHMENT AREAS: Creating computer-generated designs, breaking down dance routines or art projects into groups of steps, memorizing printed music patterns

TEACHING SUGGESTIONS
Students must perceive the folded edges and distinguish them from outer edges. Encourage students to use the terms *right, left,* and *center.* These directional words will be practiced in a more complex form in the section on following directions. *Inner, outer,* and *near* are relative terms requiring some point for comparison. Emphasize and repeat these contrasts: *right/left/ center, inner/outer, edge/fold, pattern/design (folded/unfolded).* You may want to introduce the concepts of curve and symmetry.

MODEL LESSON

LESSON
Introduction
NOTE: *Pattern* refers to the folded item; *design* refers to the unfolded item.
    Q: In the previous exercise, you practiced drawing either the design that resulted from a given rectangular pattern with holes or the pattern that produces a given design.

Explaining the Objective to Students

Q: In these exercises you will draw either the design that results from a given pattern that is not a rectangle or the non-rectangular pattern that produces a given design.

Class Activity

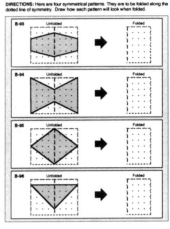

SYMMETRICAL PATTERNS—SUPPLY

DIRECTIONS: Here are four symmetrical patterns. They are to be folded along the dotted line of symmetry. Draw how each pattern will look when folded.

- Hold up the **B-93** design.

  Q: You need to determine what this design will look like when it has been folded. To reproduce the pattern made by this design, you must decide which side of the design represents the folded pattern. Where is the fold in the pattern?

  A: On the left

  Q: On the design, the dotted line represents the vertical fold line. If the pattern has the fold on the left, which part of the design has a dotted line on the left?

  A: The right side

  Q: Draw the pattern that results when the design is folded.

  A: It will be a reproduction of the right half of the **B-93** design.

- Hold up the model of **B-93**, fold it and verify the answer. After class discussion, continue the lesson.

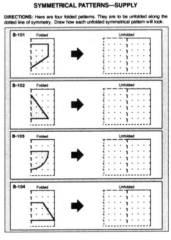

SYMMETRICAL PATTERNS—SUPPLY

DIRECTIONS: Here are four folded patterns. They are to be unfolded along the dotted line of symmetry. Draw how each unfolded symmetrical pattern will look.

- Draw a horizontal rectangle on the chalkboard with a vertical dotted line in the center. Hold up a model of **B-101**.

  Q: You need to determine what this pattern will look like when it has been unfolded. In this pattern, the fold line is on the left side, like the spine of a book. If the pattern opens like a book, what will the left side look like after it is opened?

  A: The design on the left is a mirror image of the design on the right. The first line is a horizontal line to the left connecting the top three dots. The second line goes down two dots vertically, making a square corner. The design continues in a slant line down and back to the center fold line.

- Draw in the design, then unfold the pattern of **B-101** so students can confirm the design.

GUIDED PRACTICE

EXERCISES: **B-93** to **B-94** and **B-101** to **B-102**

- Give students sufficient time to complete these exercises. Ask students to discuss and explain their choices.

INDEPENDENT PRACTICE

• Assign exercises **B-95** through **B-100** and **B-103** through **B-114**.

THINKING ABOUT THINKING

Q: What did you pay attention to when you drew your pattern for exercises **B-93** through **B-100**?

1. I observed that the fold was on the left. This meant that I needed to copy the right half of the pattern.

Q: What did you pay attention to when you drew your pattern for exercises **B-101** through **B-114**?

1. I observed that the fold was on the left.

2. I copied the pattern on the right side of the fold line.

3. I counted the spaces on the right side of the pattern and moved my pencil the same number of spaces on the left side of the pattern to find the locations of important points.

4. I located a number of important points in the left half of the unfolded design and then connected them to form the finished design.

PERSONAL APPLICATION

Q: When must you be able to recognize what something looks like when it has been folded or unfolded?

A: Examples include getting towels from a shelf or clothes from a drawer; paper cutting; finding symmetry in cut patterns; finding correct pattern pieces in sewing, particularly facings.

EXERCISES B-115 to B-125

AXIS OF SYMMETRY—SUPPLY

> **ANSWERS B-115 through B-125 — Student book pages 52–3**
> **Guided Practice: B-115** See below.
> **Independent Practice: B-116** through **B-125** See below.

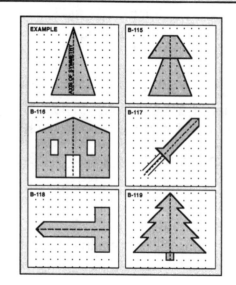

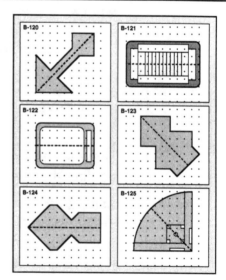

LESSON PREPARATION

OBJECTIVE AND MATERIALS

OBJECTIVE: Students will draw the line that divides a design into two equal parts. Such a line is called an "axis of symmetry."
MATERIALS: Photocopies of Transparency Master 14

CURRICULUM APPLICATIONS

MATHEMATICS Doing symmetry exercises, using visual perception skills, forming geometric patterns
SCIENCE: Determining symmetry in natural forms, reproducing crystal or snowflake patterns, predicting appearance or position of stars or planets
SOCIAL STUDIES: Seeing patterns in charts, graphs, or schedules
ENRICHMENT AREAS: Creating computer-generated designs, breaking down dance routines or art projects into groups of steps, memorizing printed music patterns

TEACHING SUGGESTIONS

If students have difficulty, encourage them to cut out the designs and fold them.

MODEL LESSON

LESSON

Introduction

Q: In the previous exercise you practiced drawing either the design that resulted from a given non-rectangular pattern or the non-rectangular pattern that produced a given design.

Explaining the Objective to Students

Q: In these exercises you will draw the line that divides a design into two equal parts. Such a line is called an "axis of symmetry."

Class Activity

- Distribute photocopies of TM 14.
  Q: Cut out and fold the triangle so that the two parts fit on top of one another exactly.

- Allow time for cutting and folding the triangle.
  Q: Where did you fold the design?
    A: Along a line that makes a square corner (right angle) with the short side (base) and goes through the point at the top (opposite vertex)

  Q: Open the triangle and draw a line along your fold line.

- Allow time for drawing.
  Q: What is this line called?
    A: The axis of symmetry

- Hold up the rectangle.
  Q: Cut out and fold the rectangle so that the two halves fit on top of one another exactly.

- Allow time for cutting and folding the rectangle.

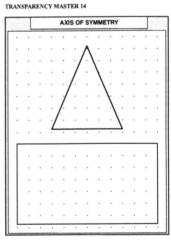

TRANSPARENCY MASTER 14

AXIS OF SYMMETRY

Q: Where did you fold the design?
   A: Up and down or across

Q: Open the rectangle and draw a line along your fold lines.

• Allow time for drawing.
   Q: What are these lines called?
      A: The axes of symmetry

GUIDED PRACTICE
EXERCISE: **B-115**

• Give students sufficient time to complete this exercise. Using the demonstration methodology above, have them discuss and explain their choices.

INDEPENDENT PRACTICE
• Assign exercises **B-116** through **B-125**.

THINKING ABOUT THINKING
Q: What did you think about to find an axis of symmetry?
1. I counted the number of spaces from the left side of the object to the right side.

2. I divided the number of spaces in half and counted in that many spaces from the side.

3. I marked the dot at that point and drew a line through it from top to bottom.

PERSONAL APPLICATION
Q: When must you be able to find an axis of symmetry?
   A: Examples include getting towels from a shelf or clothes from a drawer; paper cutting; symmetry in cut patterns; finding correct pattern pieces in sewing, particularly facings

**EXERCISES
B-126 to
B-129**

COVERING A SURFACE

ANSWERS B-126 through B-129 — Student book pages 54–7
Guided Practice: B-126 to B-127 See below.
Independent Practice: B-128 to B-129 See next page.

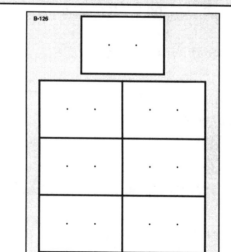

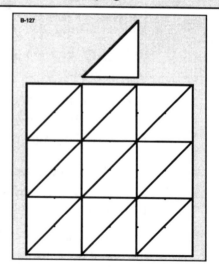

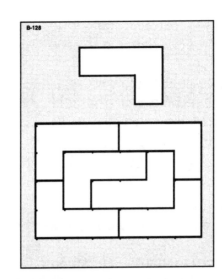 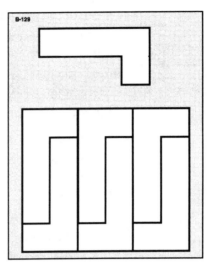

LESSON PREPARATION

OBJECTIVE AND MATERIALS
OBJECTIVE: Students will cover a given surface with a number of equal parts.
MATERIALS: Transparency of student workbook page 54 (cut out top rectangle) • washable transparency marker

CURRICULUM APPLICATIONS
LANGUAGE ARTS: Estimating how many words are on or will fit on a given page, e.g., in a composition or newspaper layout
MATHEMATICS: Doing exercises in tessellation, estimating area problems
SCIENCE: Recognizing tessellation in natural forms, e.g., crystals, honeycombs; dividing bacteria cultures into segments to count the number of organisms per segment
SOCIAL STUDIES: Estimating comparative sizes of mapped areas
ENRICHMENT AREAS: Determining how many typed lines will fit on a page, fitting copy to a layout design in newspaper or other journalism exercises

TEACHING SUGGESTIONS
If students have trouble visualizing this process, encourage them to trace the pattern, cut it out, and move it about as in the demonstration. The process of covering a surface completely is known as tessellation. NOTE: It is helpful to count spaces instead of dots. The dots are spaced one inch apart. If one counts dots, the first dot should be counted as the zero dot.

MODEL LESSON

LESSON

Introduction
    Q: In the previous exercise you divided shapes into equal parts.

Explaining the Objective to Students
    Q: In these exercises you will cover a given surface with a number of equal parts.

Class Activity
• Project the larger grid from the transparency of page 54 then place the cutout rectangle in the top left corner of the grid with the wide part on top.
    Q: Using this smaller rectangle as a pattern, see if shapes this size…

- Move the smaller rectangle around the grid to demonstrate its mobility, returning it to the top left corner.

  Q: …will fit next to one another so the whole grid can be covered. This is similar to what a carpenter does when installing rectangular ceiling tiles.

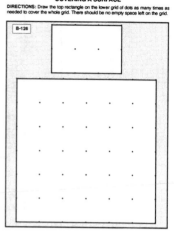

- Mark the outline of the rectangle each time you move it so students can see the parts. Slide the pattern to the top right corner.

  Q: As you can see, two of these rectangles just fit across the top of the grid. How wide is the pattern rectangle?

    A: Three spaces (Students should understand that they can count the number of spaces between dots to find the width of the rectangle.)

  Q: How tall is the pattern rectangle?
    A: Two spaces

  Q: How tall is the grid that is being covered?
    A: Six spaces

  Q: How many pattern rectangles will fit the height of the large square grid?
    A: Three

  Q: How do you know that?
    A: The larger grid is six spaces high and the pattern rectangle is two spaces high. Three smaller rectangles will exactly fill the height of the larger grid. (Six divided by two equals three.) Trace the edges of the smaller rectangle as indicated to cover the left portion of the grid on the transparency.

  Q: How many pattern rectangles are needed to cover the entire grid?
    A: Six

  Q: How do you know that?
    A: The larger grid is two pattern pieces wide and three pattern pieces high. (Two times three equals six.) Move the pattern rectangle, tracing its edges each time until the grid is completely covered.

  Q: Is it possible to completely cover this same surface by turning the rectangles another way?
    A: Yes. Have students open their workbooks to page 54, exercise **B-126**.

  Q: Use your pencil to show a different way of covering the surface by sketching in the small rectangles.

GUIDED PRACTICE
EXERCISE: **B-127**
- Check to see that students covered the surface completely. Since many alternatives are possible, have students sketch any unique solutions on the transparency grid.

INDEPENDENT PRACTICE
- Assign exercises **B-128** and **B-129**.

THINKING ABOUT THINKING
Q: What did you pay attention to when you worked out your answer?

1. If I could not visualize the small shapes covering the large shape, I counted the number of spaces in the small shape and then counted the same number of spaces on the large shape to draw in each small shape.

2. I cut out a single small shape and traced around it several times until I had covered the large shape.

3. I cut out a number of the small shapes and moved them around until they covered the large shape.

PERSONAL APPLICATION
Q: When might you need to cover a surface completely with a given shape?

A: Examples include installing floor tiles, ceiling tiles, wall paneling, siding, or roofing; doing needlework.

EXERCISES B-130 to B-137

WHICH SHAPE COMPLETES THE SQUARE?

ANSWERS B-130 through B-137 — Student book pages 58–60
Guided Practice: B-130 d
Independent Practice: B-131 d; **B-132** d; **B-133** b; **B-134** b; **B-135** a; **B-136** c; **B-137** d

LESSON PREPARATION

OBJECTIVE AND MATERIALS
OBJECTIVE: Students will visualize the part that will complete the square shape.
MATERIALS: Transparency of TM 15 (cut apart as indicated) • colored markers or crayons for each student (optional)

CURRICULUM APPLICATIONS
LANGUAGE ARTS: Completing "shape poems"
MATHEMATICS: Estimating complementary angles; confirming that the sum of the angles in a triangle is 180° by drawing a triangle, cutting the three angles at the vertices, and laying the angles next to one another to show they form a straight line
SCIENCE: Completing drawings of symmetrical natural objects
SOCIAL STUDIES: Completing a map, graph, or chart
ENRICHMENT AREAS: Doing art, home economics, or industrial arts projects involving patterns

TEACHING SUGGESTIONS
Reinforce the following key concepts in this lesson: *completes* and *equals*. Make a list on the chalkboard of words students use to explain why the shape did not complete the square. NOTE: Students may sketch in the completed square if they are unable to do the exercises otherwise. An optional strategy for teaching this lesson involves giving students colored markers or crayons.

Ask them to color the missing area of the square and the area of the four shapes using the same color. The similarity of the colored area is a helpful visual cue for young children.

MODEL LESSON

LESSON

Introduction

Q: In previous exercises you divided shapes and saw how it can be important to estimate visually whether something has been divided into equal parts.

Explaining the Objective to Students

Q: In these exercises it is also important to correctly visualize a part of a whole. This time you need to visualize the part that will complete the square shape.

Class Activity

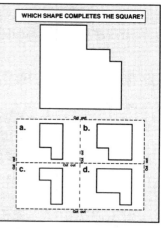

TRANSPARENCY MASTER 15

* Project TM 15. Arrange the four shapes next to the incomplete square in the original order.
  Q: You need to determine which of these shapes…

* Indicate the choices.
  Q: …will complete the square.

* Place shape *a* over the space on the square.
  Q: Does this shape complete the square?
  A: No

  Q: Why not?
  A: The height and the base are the same, but the top line is not long enough and the step does not have the same shape.

* Replace shape *a* with shape *b*.
  Q: Does shape *b* complete the square?
  A: No

  Q: Why not?
  A: The height and the top line are the right size, but the base is too long and the step is not the same shape. Replace shape *b* with shape *c*.

  Q: Does shape *c* complete the square?
  A: No

  Q: Why not?
  A: The height and the base match, but the steps are not the same shape and the top line is too short. Replace shape *c* with shape *d*.

  Q: Does shape *d* complete the square?
  A: Yes.

  Q: How can you tell?
  A: All of the steps fit exactly and the outside lines complete the square shape.

GUIDED PRACTICE
EXERCISE: **B-130**
- Give students sufficient time to complete this exercise. Then, using the demonstration methodology above, have them discuss and explain their choice.

INDEPENDENT PRACTICE
- Assign exercises **B-131** through **B-137**.

THINKING ABOUT THINKING
Q: What did you pay attention to when deciding what shape completes the square?
1. I looked at the shape of the missing part.
2. I looked at the four shapes for similar shapes.
3. When I found a similar shape, I checked to see if it was the same size as the missing shape.
4. If I was uncertain, I checked the size of the piece with a ruler.

PERSONAL APPLICATION
Q: When might you want to determine what shape is needed to complete a given object?
A: Examples include deciding how many pieces of something are missing, deciding which puzzle piece you need, determining missing parts of a model or pattern.

EXERCISES B-138 to B-145

WHICH SHAPES COMPLETE THE SQUARE?

ANSWERS B-138 through B-145 — Student book pages 61–3
Guided Practice: B-138 a and d; **B-139** a and c
Independent Practice: B-140 a and c; **B-141** a and d; **B-142** b and c;
B-143 b and c; **B-144** b and d; **B-145** a and c or b and d

---

LESSON PREPARATION

OBJECTIVE AND MATERIALS
OBJECTIVE: Students will choose two shapes which, when combined, will complete a square.
MATERIALS: Transparency of TM 16 • colored markers or crayons for each student (optional)

CURRICULUM APPLICATIONS
LANGUAGE ARTS: Deciding which letter or ending completes a word
MATHEMATICS: Estimating complementary angles; confirming that the sum of the angles in a triangle is 180° by drawing a triangle, cutting the three angles at the vertices, and laying the angles next to one another to show they form a straight line
SCIENCE: Deciding which bones complete a skeleton
SOCIAL STUDIES: Deciding which fragments complete an archaeological artifact

ENRICHMENT AREAS: Doing art, home economics, or industrial arts projects involving patterns; doing jigsaw puzzles

TEACHING SUGGESTIONS

Reinforce the following key concepts in this lesson: *completes, combines,* and *equals*. Make a list on the chalkboard of words students use to explain why the shape did not complete the square. NOTE: Students may draw lines to sketch in the completed square if they are unable to do the exercises otherwise. An optional strategy for teaching this lesson involves giving students colored markers or crayons. Ask them to color the missing area of the square and the areas of the four shapes using the same color. The similarity of the colored area is a helpful visual cue for young children.

MODEL LESSON

LESSON

Introduction

Q: In the previous exercise you completed a square with a single shape and saw how important it was to be able to estimate visually which part was needed to complete a square shape.

Explaining the Objective to Students

Q: In these exercises you will choose two shapes which, when combined, will complete a square.

Class Activity

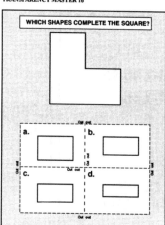

TRANSPARENCY MASTER 16

WHICH SHAPES COMPLETE THE SQUARE?

- Project TM 16, transparency of example on student workbook page 61. Arrange the four shapes next to the big square in the original order.

   Q: You are going to determine which combination of shapes…

- Indicate the choices.

   Q: …will complete the square.

- Place shape *a* in the space on the square.

   Q: Could shape *a* be one of the shapes needed to complete the square?

     A: Possibly

   Q: Why?

     A: It is the right width and fits within the open space in the big square.

- Leave shape *a* in place and move in shape *b*.

   Q: Can shape *b* combine with shape *a* to complete the square?

     A: Yes

   Q: Why?

     A: It just fills the remaining space. Shapes *a* and *b* are each half as large as the open space.

- Replace shapes *a* and *b* with shape *c*.

Q: Could shape *c* be one of the shapes needed to complete the square?
  A: Possibly

Q: Why?
  A: It is the right width and fits within the open space in the big square.

- Leave shape *c* in place and move in shape *d*.
Q: Can shape *d* combine with shape *c* to complete the square?
  A: No

Q: Why not?
  A: It is the right height, but it is not wide enough.

- Remove *c* and *d*, replacing them with shape *a*.
Q: Can either shape *c* or shape *d* combine with shape *a* to complete the square?
  A: No, shape *c* is the right width, but it is too tall when combined with either *a* or *b*; shape *d* is the right height but the wrong width.

Q: Can *c* or *d* combine with *b* to complete the square?
  A: No; since shape *a* and shape *b* are the same, the same reasons apply.

- Move shapes *a* and *b* back into the space.
Q: These two shapes are the only possible combination for completing the square.

- Circle shapes *a* and *b* on the transparency.

GUIDED PRACTICE
EXERCISES: **B-138, B-139**
- Give students sufficient time to complete these exercises. Ask students to discuss and explain their choices.

INDEPENDENT PRACTICE
- Assign exercises **B-140** through **B-145**.

THINKING ABOUT THINKING
Q: What did you pay attention to when you selected the shapes that make squares?
  A: I imagined rotating each piece inside the big square to see which shapes would fit together to complete the square.

PERSONAL APPLICATION
Q: When might you need to decide which combination of shapes completes an object?
  A: Examples include deciding how many pieces of something are missing, deciding which puzzle pieces you need, determining missing parts of a model or pattern.

**EXERCISES
B-146 to
B-154**

COPYING OR ENLARGING FIGURES

ANSWERS B-146 through B-154 — Student book pages 64–7
Guided Practice: B-146 through **B-150** (The drawings for **B-146** through **B-148** should be the same size as the given drawings.) See below.
Independent Practice: B-151 through **B-154** See below.

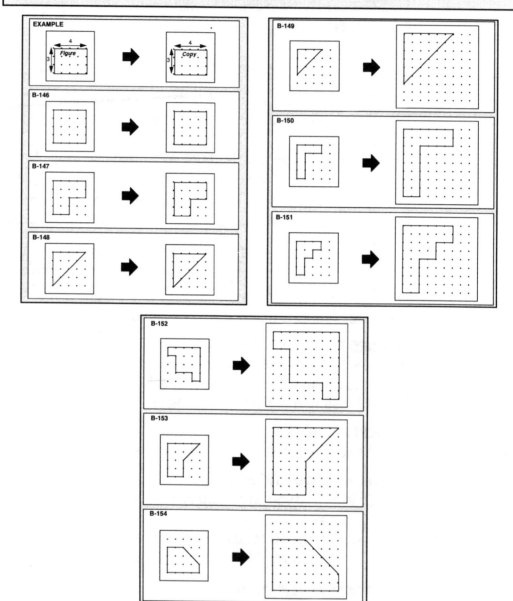

**LESSON
PREPARATION**

OBJECTIVE AND MATERIALS

OBJECTIVE: Students will draw a shape with sides twice the size of a given shape.
MATERIALS: Transparency of page 64 • transparency of TM 17 or photocopies for each student • washable transparency marker

CURRICULUM APPLICATIONS

LANGUAGE ARTS: Preparing visual aids for oral presentations
MATHEMATICS: Copying geometric shapes using correct proportions
SCIENCE: Drawing images for laboratory reports or science fair projects

SOCIAL STUDIES: Enlarging charts, graphs, or maps
ENRICHMENT AREAS: Doing art projects, enlarging scale drawings in industrial arts or drafting

TEACHING SUGGESTIONS

Students should accurately describe the shapes they have drawn. You may wish to have various students give you oral directions for reproducing each shape on the overhead. Be sure to draw exactly what they tell you! If students have not used the quarter-inch dot grid before, you may need to emphasize the importance of counting spaces instead of dots. NOTE: If one counts dots, call the first dot zero. From the zero dot to the first dot is one space.

MODEL LESSON

LESSON

Introduction

Q: Sometimes it is necessary to enlarge a drawing or sketch so people can see it in greater detail.

Explaining the Objective to Students

Q: In these exercises you will draw a shape with sides twice the size of a given shape.

Class Activity

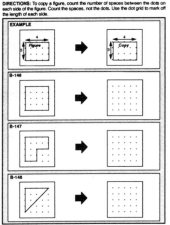

COPYING A FIGURE

DIRECTIONS: To copy a figure, count the number of spaces between the dots on each side of the figure. Count the spaces, not the dots. Use the dot grid to mark off the length of each side.

- Project transparency of page 64.
  Q: Before we learn to enlarge figures let's practice copying a figure. Open your book to page 64 and do exercise **B-146**.

- Check that students are counting spaces between the dots and not the dots themselves.

- Project TM 17.
  Q: You will draw a quadrilateral with sides twice as long as this one. First, find the starting point on the dot grid for the enlarged quadrilateral. Start in the lower left corner (marked starting point S).

- Mark the starting point with a small circle.
  Q: How many spaces wide is the given quadrilateral along the bottom?
    A: Two spaces

TRANSPARENCY MASTER 17

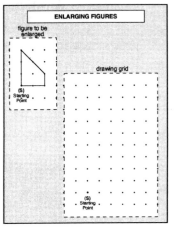

Q: If each side of the enlarged quadrilateral is to be twice as long as the same side on the given quadrilateral, how wide should you draw the bottom of the enlarged quadrilateral?
    A: Four spaces

Q: Why?
    A: The sides are supposed to be twice as long, and two times two spaces is four

spaces. Beginning at the marked starting point, draw the bottom of the enlarged quadrilateral.

Q: How tall is the given quadrilateral on the right side?
  A: One space

Q: How tall should the enlarged quadrilateral be on the right side?
  A: Two spaces

Q: Where should this line begin on the drawing?
  A: It should begin at the point where the line four spaces long ends.

Q: How tall is the given quadrilateral on the left side?
  A: Three spaces

Q: How tall should the enlarged quadrilateral be on the left side?
  A: Six spaces

Q: Where should this line begin on the drawing?
  A: It should begin at the point S and go upward. Draw a vertical line six spaces long from the original starting point.

Q: You have three lines, one four spaces long, one two spaces long, and another six spaces in length. How do you finish the drawing?
  A: Use a straightedge (ruler) to connect the two end points.

GUIDED PRACTICE
EXERCISES: **B-146** through **B-150**
• When students have had sufficient time to complete these exercises, check their drawings.

INDEPENDENT PRACTICE
• Assign exercises **B-151** through **B-154**.

THINKING ABOUT THINKING
Q: What did you pay attention to when you drew the shape twice as large?
1. I counted the spaces in the small figure.

2. I doubled that number.

3. I drew a line with twice as many spaces.

4. I repeated the first three steps until I completed the enlarged figure.

PERSONAL APPLICATION
Q: When might you have to enlarge something proportionally?
  A: Examples include drawing a mural, writing a sign or poster to be read from a distance, writing on a chalkboard, increasing the size of a pattern, reproducing a map or section of a map from a smaller picture or drawing.

EXERCISES B-155 to B-163

REDUCING FIGURES

ANSWERS B-155 through B-163 — Student book pages 68–70
Guided Practice: B-155 through **B-157** NOTE: On **B-157**, the reduced shape should be two spaces wide and three spaces high. Notice that the diagonal line does not go through dots except at the end points. See below.
Independent Practice: B-158 through **B-163** See below.

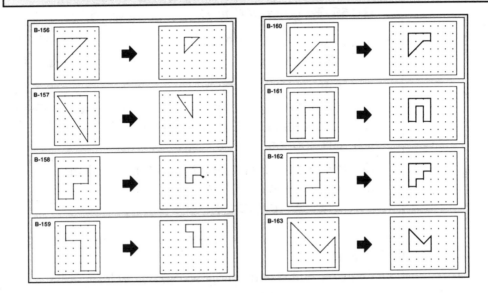

LESSON PREPARATION

OBJECTIVE AND MATERIALS
OBJECTIVE: Students will draw a shape with sides half the size of a given shape.
MATERIALS: Transparency of page 68 in the student book • transparency of TM 18 • washable transparency marker

CURRICULUM APPLICATIONS
MATHEMATICS: Reducing geometric shapes using correct proportions
SCIENCE: Drawing body parts or larger objects from nature
SOCIAL STUDIES: Reducing charts, graphs, or maps
ENRICHMENT AREAS: Charting pattern plays in sports, making scale drawings in industrial arts or drafting, drawing dance-step patterns, doing art projects

TEACHING SUGGESTIONS
If students have not used the quarter-inch dot grid before, you may need to emphasize the importance of counting spaces instead of dots. If one counts dots, call the first dot zero. From the zero dot to the first dot is one space.

MODEL LESSON

LESSON

Introduction
Q: In the previous exercise you learned that it is sometimes necessary to enlarge a drawing or figure.

Explaining the Objective to Students
Q: Sometimes it is necessary to reduce a larger drawing so it is a more

convenient size. In these exercises you will draw shapes with sides half the size of given shapes.

Class Activity

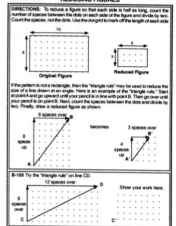

- Project the transparency of student workbook page 68 exercise **B-155**.
  Q: Before you try to reduce shapes, practice reducing a diagonal line like the one in exercise **B-155**. To go from *C* to *D*, first go upward.

- Illustrate on transparency.
  Q: Then go across.

- Illustrate on transparency.
  Q: Count the spaces between the dots. How many spaces tall is the upward line?
    A: Six spaces

  Q: How do you draw a line that is half as tall as a six-space line?
    A: Draw a line three spaces tall.

- Draw a vertical three-space line, starting at the lower left corner of the blank grid.
  Q: Look at the line going across. How long is it?
    A: Twelve spaces

  Q: How do you draw a line that is half as long as a twelve-space line?
    A: Draw a line six spaces long.

- Draw a corresponding line six spaces long on the reduced figure grid
  Q: If you now draw a diagonal line connecting the end points of the two reduced lines, this line will be half as long as the original line.

- Students may wish to measure to confirm their answer. Project transparency of TM 18.
  Q: You need to draw a pentagon with sides half as long as this one. Use the starting point printed on the dot grid for the reduced pentagon. How many spaces wide is the top of the given pentagon?
    A: Four spaces

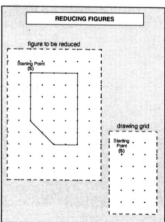

  Q: If the reduced pentagon is to have sides half as long, how wide should you draw the top horizontal line?
    A: Two spaces

  Q: Why?
    A: The sides are supposed to be half as long as the given pentagon, and one-half of four spaces is two spaces.

- Draw the top of the reduced pentagon.

Q: How tall is the right side of the large pentagon?
  A: Six spaces

Q: How tall should you make the reduced pentagon?
  A: Three spaces

Q: Where should the vertical line begin on the drawing?
  A: It should start at the right end of the top line.

- Draw the line.
  Q: How tall is the left side of the large pentagon?
    A: Four spaces

  Q: How tall should you make the reduced pentagon?
    A: Two spaces

  Q: Where should the vertical line begin on the drawing?
    A: It should start at the left end of the top line.

- Draw the line.
  Q: You now have three lines; the horizontal one is two spaces long and the vertical ones are two or three spaces long. How can you finish the reduced drawing?
    A: Use a straightedge (ruler) to connect the two end points.

  Q: Notice that this line goes through three dots. Diagonal lines do not always fall on the dots of a grid.

GUIDED PRACTICE
EXERCISES: **B-155** through **B-157**
- When students have had sufficient time to complete this exercise, check their drawings.

INDEPENDENT PRACTICE
- Assign exercises **B-158** through **B-163**.

THINKING ABOUT THINKING
Q: What did you pay attention to when you drew the shape half as large?
1. I counted the spaces in the large figure.

2. I divided that number by two.

3. I drew a line with half as many spaces.

4. I repeated the first three steps until I completed the enlarged figure.

PERSONAL APPLICATION
Q: When might you need or want to reduce a shape or figure proportionally?
  A: Examples include copying a large map or chart to paper; copying notes from a chalkboard or projection screen; scale drawings of full-sized houses, machines, parts, etc.

EXERCISES B-164 to B-166

COMPARING SHAPES—EXPLAIN

ANSWERS B-164 through B-166 — Student book pages 71–3
Guided Practice: B-164 ALIKE: Both are closed, white figures, both are made with straight lines, both have a base length of two inches and are two inches high. DIFFERENT: The triangle has three sides, the trapezoid has four. The triangle has three angles, the trapezoid has four. The triangle has no parallel sides and the trapezoid has two (top and bottom).
B-165 ALIKE: Both are white, both have four sides, both are two inches high. Both have two pairs of parallel sides. DIFFERENT: The square has four equal sides located all around the square. Only the opposite sides are equal in the parallelogram. The square has a two-inch base. The parallelogram has a one-inch base.
Independent Practice: B-166 ALIKE: Both are white, four-sided shapes, both have a one-inch base and are two inches high, both have opposite sides parallel and the same length. DIFFERENT: The rectangle has four equal (right) angles. The parallelogram has two pairs of equal angles. The equal angles of the rectangle are located on all corners. The equal angles of the parallelogram are located on opposite corners. (Corners are called vertices—the plural of vertex.) All the angles of the rectangle are the same size (right angle or 90°). Two angles of the parallelogram are smaller than a right angle and two are larger than a right angle. (One pair is acute, i.e., less than 90°; the other is obtuse, i.e., more than 90°.)

LESSON PREPARATION

OBJECTIVE AND MATERIALS
OBJECTIVE: Students will use a graphic organizer to compare and contrast two shapes.
MATERIALS: Transparencies of exercise **B-164** on student workbook page 71, TM 19 • washable transparency marker

CURRICULUM APPLICATIONS
LANGUAGE ARTS: Diagramming sentences according to functions of words, eliminating certain reference books when researching reports, recognizing sentences that do not support a topic, making an outline as a prewriting exercise by choosing only those subheads or points which support the main idea
MATHEMATICS: Distinguishing between types of arithmetic problems, recognizing numerical or geometrical properties
SCIENCE: Naming and recognizing plants or animals that do not belong in a particular phyla, naming and recognizing differing properties of elements or compounds, classifying foods into basic food groups or determining nutritional values
SOCIAL STUDIES: Eliminating architectural structures, governmental divisions, or community institutions that do not fit a given class of functions or other attributes
ENRICHMENT AREAS: Recognizing types of dance, art, or music that do not fit stated criteria; naming functions and attributes of different tools in art, shop, or home economics

TEACHING SUGGESTIONS

Use TM 19 to compare two shapes such as parallelogram and trapezoid, parallelogram and rectangle, parallelogram and rhombus, or pentagon and hexagon, etc. Note: The bottom of a trapezoid is sometimes called the large base or *B*. The top is sometimes referred to as the small base or *b*.

MODEL LESSON

LESSON

Introduction

Q: We make comparisons every day. Can you name some comparisons you make?

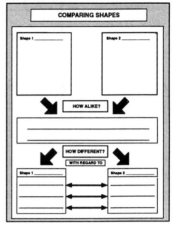

Explaining the Objective to Students

Q: In these exercises you will use a graphic organizer to compare and contrast two shapes.

Class Activity

• Project the transparency of exercise **B-164** onto the chalkboard.

Q: How are the triangle and trapezoid alike?

A: Both are closed, gray figures; both are made with straight lines; both have a base length of two inches and are two inches high.

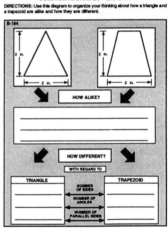

• Write in answers as the discussion proceeds.

Q: How are the shapes different with regard to number of sides?

A: The triangle has three sides and the trapezoid has four.

Q: How are the shapes different with regard to number of angles?

A: The triangle has three angles and the trapezoid has four.

Q: How are the shapes different with regard to number of parallel sides?

A: The triangle has no parallel sides and the trapezoid has two parallel sides (top and bottom).

GUIDED PRACTICE

EXERCISES: **B-164** to **B-165**

INDEPENDENT PRACTICE

• Assign exercise **B-166**.

THINKING ABOUT THINKING

Q: What did you pay attention to when you compared shapes?

1. I paid attention to the important characteristics in the two shapes.

2. I gave names to those characteristics.

3. I combined the names and characteristics into a description.

4. I checked to see that my description was complete.

PERSONAL APPLICATION

Q: When might you be asked to compare two things?

A: Examples include putting away items at home or in school; replacing items in a supermarket, warehouse, workshop, or library; finding items in a supermarket, hardware store, mall directory, telephone book yellow pages, or classified ads.

Chapter 3

FIGURAL SEQUENCES
(Student book pages 76–100)

SEQUENCE OF FIGURES—SELECT

ANSWERS C-1 through C-9 — Student book pages 76–9
Guided Practice: C-1 d (rotation to the right, or clockwise rotation)
Independent Practice: C-2 b (reflection or flip about the horizontal); **C-3** d (adding detail, or increasing the number of parts); **C-4** a (rotation to the left, or counterclockwise rotation); **C-5** d (reflection about the diagonal); **C-6** d (reflection or flip about the vertical); **C-7** d (rotation to the left, or counterclockwise rotation); **C-8** d (rotation to the right, or clockwise rotation); **C-9** c (adding detail)

**LESSON
PREPARATION**

OBJECTIVE AND MATERIALS
OBJECTIVE: Students will determine the sequence of changes in a series of figures.
MATERIALS: Transparencies of TMs 20, 21, 21, and 23 (cut apart as indicated) • attribute or design blocks (optional)

CURRICULUM APPLICATIONS
LANGUAGE ARTS: Repeating patterns can be seen in decoding unfamiliar words and in recognizing alliteration, flipping is connected to letter discrimination (b/d, d/p) or to inverting letter order in words, rotation is an important skill in developing letter discrimination abilities, adding and subtracting detail is used in forming new words by adding or subtracting prefixes and suffixes
MATHEMATICS: Repeating patterns can be used as a memorization technique for mathematical tables; flips can be shown in methods of checking basic mathematics problems, e.g., inverting fractions and using addition to check subtraction accuracy; rotation is used in arranging basic problems differently, e.g., horizontal or vertical addition, and in recognizing geometrical position or pattern changes; adding and subtracting detail is used in making charts and graphs
SCIENCE: Repeating patterns are seen in leaves, shells, and life cycles; flips can be used to show symmetry in plants or animals and in mirror-image exercises; rotation is an important concept in understanding the operation of gears, wheels, motors, or kaleidoscopes and for recognizing the rotation of planets; adding and subtracting detail can be seen in changes of plants or animals
SOCIAL STUDIES: Repeating patterns are used to show geographic changes or types of topography on maps, flips can be seen when using or making graphs that show negative and positive changes, rotations are used when orienting maps, adding and subtracting detail can be illustrated by comparing different types of maps that show the same geographic area or when comparing photographs to maps

ENRICHMENT AREAS: Doing art exercises involving rotation, reflection, or positive and negative space; repeating interval patterns in music; playing games that call for taking turns or doing rotations, e.g., musical chairs, relay races, positions on a volleyball court

TEACHING SUGGESTIONS

Remember the importance of discussing each individual exercise. Students should know and correctly use the following words in describing exercises and solutions: *repeating, flip, sequence, horizontal, vertical, diagonal, rotation,* and *axis.* The proper term for flip is *reflection.* The terms *clockwise* and *counterclockwise* may be used to name directions of rotations.

MODEL LESSON

LESSON

Introduction

Q: A sequence is defined as an arrangement of things having regular patterns or regular changes. Where in this room can you see examples of patterns?

A: Examples include fabric in clothing, cement block or brick walls, floor or ceiling tiles, Venetian blinds, leaf arrangements on plants.

Explaining the Objective to Students

Q: These exercises deal with sequences. You will determine what the sequence is by looking for the pattern of changes in a series of figures.

Class Activity—Option 1

• Optional demonstration using blocks: Use attribute or design blocks to set up the following sequence on the chalkboard tray or tabletop. (NOTE: This set will be used at the beginning of the demonstration.)

LARGE	LARGE	LARGE	LARGE	LARGE
BLUE	BLUE	BLUE	BLUE	BLUE
SQUARE	CIRCLE	TRIANGLE	SQUARE	CIRCLE

• Set up this second sequence of blocks to the right, a considerable distance from the first. (NOTE: This set will be used by the students in the middle of the demonstration.)

LARGE	LARGE	LARGE	LARGE	LARGE	LARGE
RED	BLUE	RED	BLUE	RED	BLUE
CIRCLE	CIRCLE	TRIANGLE	TRIANGLE	SQUARE	SQUARE

Q: Here you see a row of shapes.

• Point to the first set on the left.
Q: Look for a pattern so you can determine the next shape in the series. If you compare the first and second shapes, you will notice they are the same size and color, but they have different shapes. This one…

• Point to the large blue square.
Q: …is a large blue square, and this one…

• Point to the large blue circle.
Q: …is large and blue, but it is a circle. Compare the second and third shapes in this series and determine what was changed.

A: The shape changed from circle to triangle, but the color and size stayed the same.

Q: The first three shapes in this pattern are large blue square, large blue circle, large blue triangle. The color and size do not change, but the shape does. Look at the rest of the row. The pattern of shape change seems to be starting over again with a blue square. Can anyone see a pattern in the row?

A: The shape is changing from square to circle to triangle.

Q: Which figure should come next?
A: The large blue triangle

- Place a large blue triangle at the end of the sequence.
  Q: How did you know that a large blue triangle came next?
  A: The large blue square signals that the pattern (square-circle-triangle) is beginning again.

- Reinforce the pattern by pointing to the shapes and saying…
  Q: Square—circle—triangle; square—circle—triangle.

- Point to the set of red and blue shapes to the right.
  Q: What sequences can you make with these shapes?

- Allow time for students to create several patterns.

Class Activity—Option 2
- Demonstration using transparencies
  Q: You can see several kinds of sequences using shapes. The first type of sequence is a repeating pattern of shapes.

- Write "repeating pattern of shapes" on the chalkboard.
  Q: That is the pattern you just identified with the blocks.

- Point to the set of blue shapes on the left.
  Q: You found and continued a repeating pattern of shapes, square—circle—triangle.

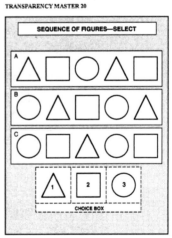

TRANSPARENCY MASTER 20

- Project a transparency of TM 20 showing sequence A. Point as you explain.
  Q: The pattern given here is triangle—square—circle, triangle—square—____. The sound of that tells us this pattern is repeating the words triangle—square—circle, so the next shape should be a circle.

- Move shape 3 (the circle) into position at the end of the sequence. Point to sequence B.
  Q: The pattern given here is circle—triangle—square, circle—triangle—____. To continue this pattern, circle—triangle—square, the next shape should be a square.

- Move shape 2 (the square) into position at the end of the sequence. Point to sequence C.

Q: The pattern given here is circle—square—triangle, circle—square—
____. To continue the pattern, the next shape should be a triangle.

• Move shape 1 (the triangle) into position at the end of the sequence.

• Project a transparency of TM 21 showing sequence A. Cover sequences B, C, & D, leaving the vertical choice box column exposed.
Q: Look at this sequence. How does the second figure differ from the first figure?
  A: It has been flipped from top to bottom.

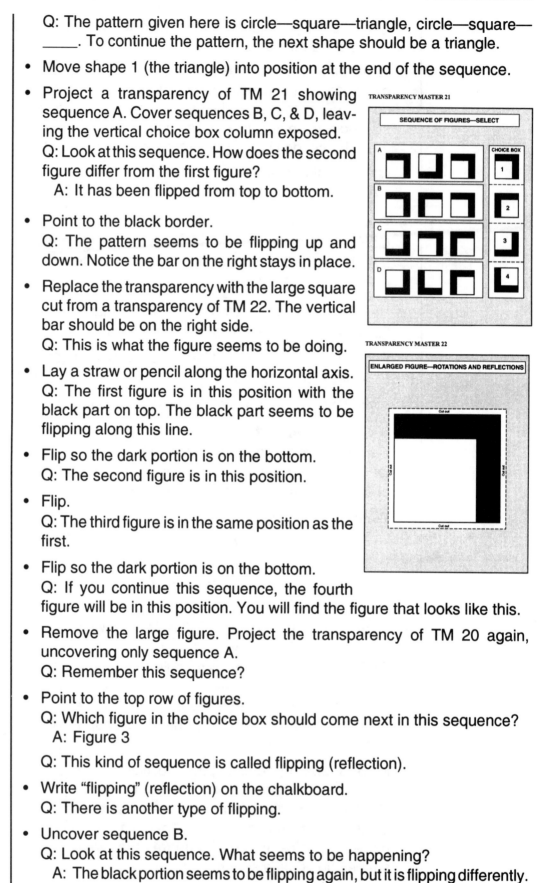

• Point to the black border.
Q: The pattern seems to be flipping up and down. Notice the bar on the right stays in place.

• Replace the transparency with the large square cut from a transparency of TM 22. The vertical bar should be on the right side.
Q: This is what the figure seems to be doing.

• Lay a straw or pencil along the horizontal axis.
Q: The first figure is in this position with the black part on top. The black part seems to be flipping along this line.

• Flip so the dark portion is on the bottom.
Q: The second figure is in this position.

• Flip.
Q: The third figure is in the same position as the first.

• Flip so the dark portion is on the bottom.
Q: If you continue this sequence, the fourth figure will be in this position. You will find the figure that looks like this.

• Remove the large figure. Project the transparency of TM 20 again, uncovering only sequence A.
Q: Remember this sequence?

• Point to the top row of figures.
Q: Which figure in the choice box should come next in this sequence?
  A: Figure 3

Q: This kind of sequence is called flipping (reflection).

• Write "flipping" (reflection) on the chalkboard.
Q: There is another type of flipping.

• Uncover sequence B.
Q: Look at this sequence. What seems to be happening?
  A: The black portion seems to be flipping again, but it is flipping differently.

• Replace the transparency with the large square. The square should have the

same orientation as the square in the exercise, with the black portion along the right side and bottom. Place a pencil or straw along the vertical axis.
Q: This time the figure seems to be flipping back and forth. In the first position, the black bar is on the right.

- Flip the figure.
Q: In the next position, the black bar is on the left but the top bar stays in place.

- Flip the figure.
Q: In the third position, the black bar is on the right again. What will the fourth figure look like?
   A: The black bar should be back on the left.

- Flip. Replace the large square with TM 20, uncovering sequence B.
Q: Find the figure that matches this one. Look for the one with the black bar on the left. Which figure in the choice box continues this sequence?
   A: Figure 2

- Uncover sequence C and the choice box.
Q: What seems to be happening in this sequence?
   A: The square seems to be turning one position to the left each time.

- Replace the transparency with the large square. Check to see that the dark portion is to the right and on top.
Q: This is the first figure.

- Rotate one position to the left.
Q: The figure has been turned one position to the left. One position means that it has been turned to the next flat surface.

- Turn the large square one more position to the left.
Q: The third figure in the sequence has been turned one more position to the left. To find the next figure in this sequence, what should be done?
   A: Turn the figure one position to the left.

- Demonstrate the movement.
Q: Now the dark sections are on the bottom and the left side.

- Point. Replace the large square with TM 20, exposing sequence C.
Q: Find the figure in the choice box that continues this sequence.
   A: Figure 4

Q: This kind of sequence is called rotation or turning.

- Write "rotation" on the chalkboard. Remove the transparency.
Q: You have looked at three kinds of sequences: repeating patterns of shapes, flips, and rotations.

- Refer to the chalkboard.
Q: There is a difference between flips and rotations.

- Project the large square again.
Q: To flip the square, one side stays in place and the other sides move up. You must pick up the square and turn it over.

- Demonstrate vertical flip twice.
  Q: You can flip it left and right about the vertical axis…

- Demonstrate horizontal flip twice.
  Q: …or you can flip it up and down about the horizontal axis…

- Demonstrate each diagonal flip twice.
  Q: …or you can flip it diagonally about a diagonal axis. But each time you must move the square through space by picking it up and putting it down. In rotations you don't pick up the figure.

- Turn the square to the right through four positions.
  Q: You can rotate it to the right (clockwise)…

- Turn the square to the left through four positions.
  Q: …or you can rotate it to the left (counterclockwise). Whichever way it is rotated, it is not picked up. All edges stay on the surface.

- Project TM 20 and uncover sequence D and the choice box.
  Q: Look at the last sequence of figures. Is each square being flipped or rotated?
     A: Rotated to the right

  Q: Find the figure in the choice box that continues this sequence.
     A: Figure 1

- Project figure 1 from TM 23.
  Q: Other sequential patterns may be formed by adding or subtracting detail. In this figure, only a bar across the bottom is black.

- Place figure 2 directly over the first figure.
  Q: Now the black section has increased to about one-third of the figure.

- Place figure 3 directly over the first two figures.
  Q: In this figure, the black part covers about half of the square.

- Place figure 4 directly over the first three figures.
  Q: Now most of the square is black. This sequence is known as adding detail.

- Write "adding detail" on the chalkboard.
  Q: The reverse process is called subtracting detail, and is done almost the same way as you subtract numbers.

- Write "subtracting detail" on the chalkboard.
  Q: This kind of sequence starts with a lot of shading or lines and each time has less. Use this figure as an example. To begin, the whole square is black.

- Remove figure 4.
  Q: Now, some of the black space has been subtracted.

- Remove figure 3.
  Q: More of the color has been removed, leaving only half the square black.

TRANSPARENCY MASTER 23

ADDING OR SUBTRACTING DETAIL

- Remove figure 2.
  Q: Now only the bar at the bottom remains. Some of the black space has been subtracted each time. Detail has been removed. In this example, the detail being subtracted is the amount of black space. (NOTE: You may have a student who recognizes the difference in positive and negative space and perceives that in the first demonstration you were subtracting white and in the second you were adding white. That perception is correct and should be encouraged.)

- Have students examine the examples on page 76 in their workbooks.

GUIDED PRACTICE
EXERCISE: **C-1**
- Give students sufficient time to complete this exercise. Using the demonstration methodology above, have them discuss and explain their choices.

INDEPENDENT PRACTICE
- Assign exercises **C-2** through **C-9**.

THINKING ABOUT THINKING
Q: What did you pay attention to when you decided which figure should come next?

1. I looked carefully at the shapes.

2. I looked for a pattern of changes.

3. I figured out what the next shape would be if the pattern continued.

4. I checked that the other shapes didn't fit the pattern.

PERSONAL APPLICATION
Q: When do you remember seeing repeating patterns or shapes?
A: Examples include fabric, concrete block or brick walls, floor or ceiling tiles, Venetian blinds, leaf arrangements on plants, beads, sequences of letters or numbers, model building.

Q: When do you remember having to determine whether something has been flipped?
A: Examples include recognizing reversed letters or numerals, seeing a sign in a mirror (especially AMBULANCE in a rearview mirror), using patterns which have to be reflected to cut a second piece, printmaking, photography, working on an automobile engine from underneath.

Q: When do you have to recognize that something has been turned?
A: Examples include art activities, fitting puzzle pieces, reading a map.

Q: When might you need to predict what something will look like when details have been added?
A: Examples include art projects, model building, computer graphics, sewing, woodworking.

Q: When might you have to predict what something will look like when details have been removed?
A: Examples include looking for basic shapes in pictures, scenes, or designs.

EXERCISES C-10 to C-19

SEQUENCE OF FIGURES—SUPPLY

ANSWERS C-10 through C-19 — Student book pages 80–1
Guided Practice: C-10 Tumbling to the left (rotation counterclockwise); **C-11** Adding detail
Independent Practice: C-12 Subtracting detail; **C-13** Tumbling to the right (rotation clockwise); **C-14** Subtracting detail (removing two black squares at a time around the edges; **C-15** Flipping about a diagonal (the NE—SW diagonal); **C-16** Flipping like the pages in a book (reflection about a vertical line); **C-17** Flipping like a calendar (reflection about a horizontal line); **C-18** Flipping about a diagonal (the NW–SE diagonal); **C-19** Flipping about a diagonal (the NE–SW diagonal)

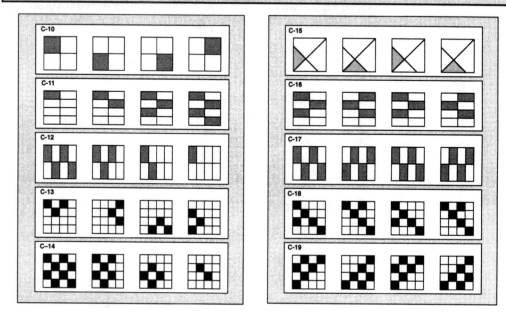

LESSON PREPARATION

OBJECTIVE AND MATERIALS

OBJECTIVE: Students will correctly shade a figure to continue a sequence.
MATERIALS: Transparency of TM 24 • washable black transparency marker

CURRICULUM APPLICATIONS

LANGUAGE ARTS: Choosing the right picture to fill in or complete a story sequence
Mathematics: Supplying missing shapes in a sequence, completing a mathematical table
SCIENCE: Recording biological stages in the development of animals or plants, duplicating order of steps in experiments
SOCIAL STUDIES: Reading and interpreting maps, developing a time-line pattern
ENRICHMENT AREAS: Doing art projects requiring construction of repeated patterns, memorizing music or dance patterns

TEACHING SUGGESTIONS

Students should always identify the type of sequence and explain how they changed the final figure to complete the sequence. Students should know and use the terms *increasing size, decreasing size,* and *hexagon* in addition to the terms used in the previous lesson.

MODEL LESSON | **LESSON**

Introduction
- Write a list of sequence types on the chalkboard.
  Q: In previous exercises you chose a figure to continue a sequence and learned to recognize several types of sequences: repeating patterns of shapes, flips, rotations, adding detail, and subtracting detail.

Explaining the Objective to Students
Q: In these exercises you will shade a figure to make it correctly continue a sequence.

Class Activity
- Project row 1 (the diamonds) from a transparency of TM 24, covering the bottom section with a piece of heavy paper.
  Q: What pattern do you see?
    A: White diamond, gray diamond, white diamond
  Q: What kind of sequence is this?

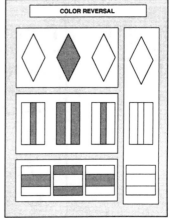

TRANSPARENCY MASTER 24

COLOR REVERSAL

- Refer to list on the chalkboard.
    A: Repeating pattern of shapes.

  Q: What must be done to the next shape to continue this sequence?
    A: Shade it gray. Use a black washable transparency marker to lightly shade in the final diamond.

- Move the cover down to project the row of rectangles.
  Q: This example shows another type of sequence. What pattern can you see in these rectangles?
    A: The part that is white in the first rectangle is gray in the next rectangle and the part that is gray in the first rectangle is white in the next rectangle. This type of sequence is called color opposite or color reversal.

- Write "color reversal" on the chalkboard.
  Q: What must be done to the next figure to continue this sequence?
    A: Shade the two outside sections and leave the center section white. Shade in the sections on the transparency as indicated.

GUIDED PRACTICE
EXERCISES: **C-10, C-11**
- Give students sufficient time to complete these exercises. Using the demonstration methodology above, have them discuss and explain their choices.

INDEPENDENT PRACTICE
• Assign exercises **C-12** through **C-19**.

THINKING ABOUT THINKING
Q: What did you pay attention to when you decided which figure came next?

1. I looked carefully at the details (position of the figure, added or subtracted detail, pattern or color) to decide what characteristic was changed.

2. I looked for a pattern of changes like rotating, reflecting, more detail, less detail, etc.

3. I figured out what the next figure would look like if the pattern continued.

4. I drew the next figure in the pattern.

PERSONAL APPLICATION
Q: When might you need to predict and/or make the next item in a pattern?
A: Examples include knitting, weaving, art activities, construction projects.

EXERCISES C-20 to C-31

TUMBLING—SHADING/TURNING (ROTATING) FIGURES

ANSWERS C-20 through C-31 — Student book pages 82–6
Guided Practice: C-20 See below.
Independent Practice: C-21 to **C-27** See below. **C-28** 2 turns right; **C-29** 1 turn right; **C-30** 2 turns left; **C-31** 3 turns right

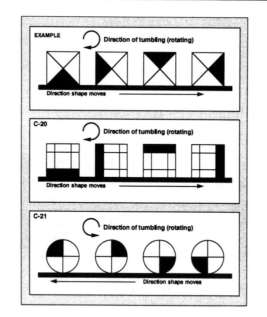

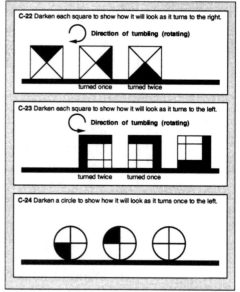

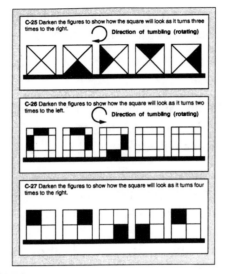

LESSON PREPARATION

OBJECTIVE AND MATERIALS

OBJECTIVE: Students will estimate how a figure will look after it has been turned.

MATERIALS: Transparencies of TM 25 and TM 26 • large cardboard square marked like the example on student workbook page 82 • wooden puzzle (optional)

CURRICULUM APPLICATIONS

LANGUAGE ARTS: Recognizing mirror-imaged words, e.g., mom, wow, mow, dad, pop, etc.

MATHEMATICS: Rotating geometric shapes, reversing processes to check accuracy

SCIENCE: Explaining rotation of the earth and the solar system, lunar and solar eclipses

SOCIAL STUDIES: Reading a map for longitude and latitude, orienting with a map, redrawing charts or graphs

ENRICHMENT AREAS: Following folk or square dancing patterns; doing quilting, sewing, and needlework; taking courses in such fields as architecture, engineering, construction, drafting, design, etc.

TEACHING SUGGESTIONS

Key words used in this lesson are: *clockwise, counterclockwise, and rotation*. A helpful association is that the surface of a stereo turntable or a CD rotates. Ask students to identify objects in school or movements in sports using these terms.

Students should explain their choices, accurately state the location of each interior shape, and identify the direction in which the figure was turned (right or clockwise and left or counterclockwise). Remind students that in exercises **C-28** through **C-31**, they are to write the number of terms and the direction of turning.

LESSON

Introduction

• Project the cut pieces from TM 25 (not arranged).

Q: When you put a puzzle together, sometimes you must turn the pieces to make them fit.

- Turn the pieces until they fit together to form a square.

Explaining the Objective to the Students

Q: In these exercises you will estimate how a figure will look after it has been turned.

Class Activity—Option 1

Optional demonstration using the large cardboard square of the example on student workbook page 81.

- Use the chalk tray or other flat surface as a track.

Q: You are to predict how a figure will look when it has been turned one position so that it comes to rest again.

- Turn the square slowly as you explain so students can see what "coming to rest in the next position" means.

Q: The square starts at rest, turns one position, and comes to rest again. If you turn the square to the right, its points move like the hands of a clock. Turning something to the right is called clockwise.

- On the chalkboard, draw a curved arrow to the right and label it clockwise.

Q: Turning something to the left makes it move in the other direction, the direction opposite to the way the hands of a clock move. "Counter" means against, so if you turn something to the left...

- Turn the triangular block to the left.

Q: ...the direction is called counterclockwise.

- On the chalkboard, draw a curved arrow to the left and label it counter-clockwise.

Class Activity—Option 2

- Project TM 26, cut apart as indicated. Using the gray bar as a track, demonstrate the following rotations as you explain.

Q: If you turn this square one position to the right, where will the black triangle be?

　A: On the left

Q: If you turn this square one additional position to the right, where will the black triangle be?

　A: On top

Q: If you turn this square one additional position to the right, where will the black triangle be?

　A: On the right

TRANSPARENCY MASTER 25

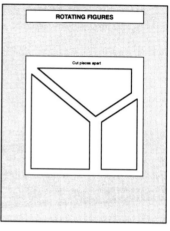

TRANSPARENCY MASTER 26

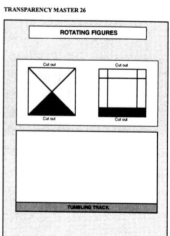

Q: What word describes the direction that the square has been turned?
   A: Clockwise

- Return the movable square to its original position with the black triangle on the bottom.
  Q: If you turn this square one position to the left, where will the black triangle be?

- Demonstrate this movement.
    A: On the right

  Q: If you turn this square one additional position to the left, where will the black triangle be?
    A: On top

  Q: If you turn this square one additional position to the left, where will the black triangle be?
    A: On the left

  Q: What word describes the direction that the square has been turned?
    A: Counterclockwise

  Q: The word that describes turning something on the same surface is rotation.

- Write "rotation" on the chalkboard.

GUIDED PRACTICE
EXERCISE: **C-20**
- Give students sufficient time to complete this exercise.

INDEPENDENT PRACTICE
- Assign exercises **C-21** through **C-31**.

THINKING ABOUT THINKING
   Q: What did you pay attention to when you decided how a figure would look when it was turned?
   1. I looked carefully at the details (color of cubes, pattern) to decide what to look for as the object tumbled.
   2. I looked for a pattern of tumbling to the right (clockwise) or to the left (counterclockwise).
   3. I determined what the next figure would look like if the pattern continued.

PERSONAL APPLICATION
   Q: When might you need to predict what a shape or pattern will look like after it has been turned?
     A: Examples include assembling puzzle pieces, reading a map, assembling models or dress patterns, rotating position in certain team sports or games.

**EXERCISES
C-32 to C-44**

PATTERN FOLDING—SELECT/SUPPLY

**ANSWERS C-32 through C-44 — Student book pages 87–90
Guided Practice: C-32 b; C-34 See below.
Independent Practice: C-33 b; C-35 to C-44 See below.**

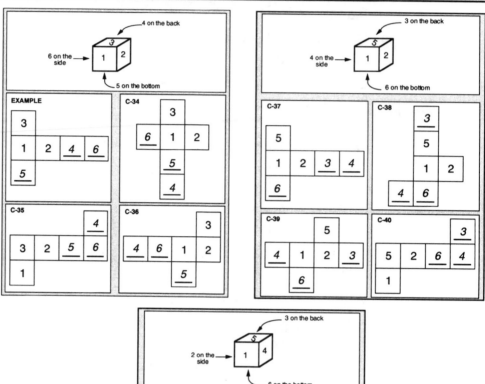

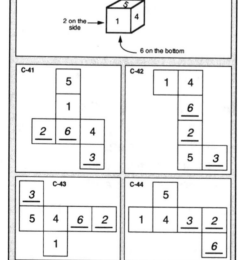

**LESSON
PREPARATION**

OBJECTIVE AND MATERIALS

OBJECTIVE: Students will first identify which solid can be covered by a given pattern, and then complete a pattern using the relative position of the faces of a given solid.

MATERIALS: Shoe box with rectangular ends • newsprint wrapper pattern for the shoe box, similar to the example on student page 87 • a building block or other cube-shaped object • masking tape • black marker • scrap paper • model of the cube shown on student workbook page 88 • transparencies of student workbook pages 87 and 88

CURRICULUM APPLICATIONS

LANGUAGE ARTS: Visualizing a complex sequence of directions

MATHEMATICS: Doing visual perceptual exercises, completing surface area problems

SCIENCE: Building or drawing models of crystals

SOCIAL STUDIES: Modeling globes or other three-dimensional maps

ENRICHMENT AREAS: Doing art and industrial arts projects involving covering surfaces

TEACHING SUGGESTIONS

If students have difficulty visualizing what a pattern will look like after it has been folded, they may disassemble cardboard boxes or create paper patterns to fold. If students have difficulty visualizing positions of the faces, they can trace the pattern and fold it or fit it over a cube. Ask students to discuss how they determined the relative position of the number and describe the manner in which the pattern wraps the cube.

MODEL LESSON

LESSON

Introduction

Q: In previous exercises you folded and unfolded patterns to make and recognize specific designs.

Explaining the Objective to Students

Q: In the exercises on workbook page 87, you will identify which solid can be covered by a given pattern. In the exercises on pages 88 through 90, you will use the relative position of the faces on a given solid to complete a pattern.

Class Activity

• Hold up the shoe box and the shoe box wrapper pattern.
  Q: Here is a box and a piece of paper. See how this paper can be wrapped around the box to cover the whole surface.

• Demonstrate, then unfold the wrapper and identify pairs of parts.
  Q: Notice there are two pieces like this...

• Point.
  Q: ...covering the top and bottom. There are two like this...

• Point.
  Q: ...covering the ends. There are two like this...

• Point.
  Q: ...covering the sides.

• Project the transparency of student page 87.
  Q: Look at the example on page 87 in your workbook. This pattern...

• Indicate the pattern.
  Q: ...is somewhat like the one for the shoe box. What is different about this pattern?
    A: The parts that cover the ends are square.

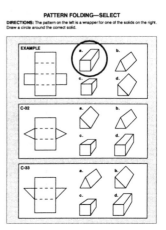

PATTERN FOLDING—SELECT

DIRECTIONS: The pattern on the left is a wrapper for one of the solids on the right. Draw a circle around the correct solid.

Q: Which of these solids has square ends?

- Indicate the choices.
    A: *a* and *c*

    Q: Which solid has the right-sized sides?
    A: *a* Circle choice *a* on the transparency.

- Make a model of the cube shown on student workbook page 88 by covering a block with masking tape and marking the faces as shown. Project the top section from the transparency of page 88.
    Q: Look at the cube on page 88 in your workbook. This cube…

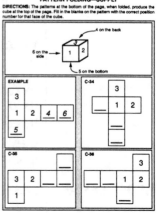

- Hold up the cube with number 1 facing the class.
    Q: …has been marked like the one on the screen. According to the diagram on the screen, if the number 1 is on the front, what number is on the back?
    A: *4* Turn the block around so students can see that 4 is opposite 1. Turn the block so 2 is facing the class.

    Q: What number is opposite side 2?
    A: *6* Repeat this line of questioning until all pairs of opposite sides have been identified.

- Point to the example.
    Q: Look at the example. You said that 1 and 4 are on the front and back of the cube. Look at the positions of numbers 1 and 4 on the pattern.

- Point to numbers 1 and 4.
    Q: The numbers 2 and 6 are also on opposite sides of the cube. Look at the positions of these numbers.

- Point to numbers 2 and 6.
    Q: Now find the numbers that are on the top and bottom of the cube. Where are the 3 and 5 located on the pattern?
    A: The 3 is above the 1 and the 5 is below the 1.

    Q: If you could fold this pattern into a cube, it would look like the cube at the top of the screen.

GUIDED PRACTICE
EXERCISES: **C-32** and **C-34**

- Give students sufficient time to complete this exercise. Then, using the demonstration methodology above, have them discuss and explain their choices.

INDEPENDENT PRACTICE

- Assign exercises **C-33** and **C-35** through **C-44**.

THINKING ABOUT THINKING

Q: What did you pay attention to when you did the pattern-folding exercises?

1. If I could not visualize the positions of the numbers, I made a cube and wrote numbers on it.

2. I cut out the patterns and folded them on the cube.

3. I copied the numbers from the cube onto the pattern.

PERSONAL APPLICATION

Q: When must you be able to recognize which solid can be wrapped by a given pattern?
   A: Examples include model building, wrapping gifts or packages, upholstering furniture.

Q: When might you need to recognize the relative position of the faces on a solid?
   A: Examples include model building, assembling boxes or display racks.

EXERCISES C-45 to C-52

STACKING SHAPES—SELECT

ANSWERS C-45 through C-52 — Student book pages 91–2
Guided Practice: C-45 d; **C-46** e; **C-47** f
Independent Practice: C-48 c; **C-49** f; **C-50** h; **C-51** g; **C-52** a

OBJECTIVE AND MATERIALS

OBJECTIVE: Students will select a diagram which correctly represents a given arrangement of stacked shapes.
MATERIALS: Transparency of student workbook page 91 • Shapes cut from colored paper (optional): four red squares, two blue hexagons, two yellow triangles

CURRICULUM APPLICATIONS

LANGUAGE ARTS: Following directions in formatting outlines, letters, memos, or layouts
MATHEMATICS: Solving a multistep problem, recognizing order or position of numbers or shapes in a sequence, following geometric constructions and proofs
SCIENCE: Following multistep directions for experiments and recognizing that they have been followed correctly; recognizing, following, or explaining the sequence of systems, e.g., circulatory system or electrical system
SOCIAL STUDIES: Reading or constructing charts, graphs, or maps
ENRICHMENT AREAS: Learning a sequence of dance steps or musical movements; recognizing and following correct procedures in art, industrial arts, or vocational education projects; learning marching band or drill team pattern sequences

TEACHING SUGGESTIONS

Encourage students to discuss their answers. Class discussion is a valuable technique for having children share their acquired knowledge. Often a child's words will communicate in a more meaningful way than words a teacher may use.

MODEL LESSON

LESSON

Introduction

Q: In the previous exercise you practiced writing directions.

Explaining the Objective to Students

Q: In these exercises you will select the diagram which correctly represents a given arrangement of stacked shapes.

Class Activity—Option 1

- Demonstration using paper shapes: Use the cutout paper shapes to build each of the following stacks: (1) square on triangle, (2) triangle on square, (3) hexagon on square, (4) square on hexagon.
- Hold up stack 1 (square on triangle) for students to see.
  Q: Describe this stack of shapes.
    A: The square is on the triangle (or the triangle is under the square).

- Hold up stack 2 (triangle on square).
  Q: Describe this stack.
    A: The triangle is on the square (or the square is under the triangle).

- Hold up stack 3 (hexagon on square).
  Q: Describe this stack.
    A: The hexagon is on the square (or the square is under the hexagon).

- Hold up stack 4 (square on hexagon).
  Q: Describe this stack.
    A: The square is on the hexagon (or the hexagon is under the square).

  Q: Which stack fits this description: "The square is under the hexagon"?
    A: Stack 3

  Q: Which stack fits this description: "The square is on the triangle"?
    A: Stack 1

  Q: Which stack fits this description: "The hexagon is under the square"?
    A: Stack 4

  Q: Which stack fits this description: "The triangle is on the square"?
    A: Stack 2

  Q: When you stack shapes, you can always see all of the shape that is on top of the stack. For example, in this stack…
    A: Hold up stack 2

  Q:…you can see all of the triangle, but only part of the square. This tells you that the triangle is on the square.

Class Activity—Option 2

- Demonstration using transparency: Project the lettered figure stacks from the bottom of the transparency of student workbook page 91.

Q: Which stack matches the statement "The hexagon is on the square"?

  A: *c*

Q: How do you know that the square isn't on top?

  A: If the square were on top, it would be completely visible.

Q: Which stack matches the statement: "The triangle is on the circle"?

  A: *a*

Q: How can you be sure that the triangle is on top of the stack?

  A: You can see all of the top shape and only part of the bottom shape. In this stack, you can see all of the triangle and only part of the circle, so the triangle is on top.

STACKING SHAPES—SELECT

DIRECTIONS: Look at the four shapes in the top box. At the bottom of the page are six combinations formed by placing one shape on another. Select the stack that fits each description.

EXAMPLE: The hexagon is on the square.   Answer: *c*

C-45   The circle is on the triangle.   Answer: _____

C-46   The triangle is on the square.   Answer: _____

C-47   The square is on the hexagon.   Answer: _____

GUIDED PRACTICE

EXERCISES: **C-45** through **C-47**

- Give students sufficient time to complete these exercises. Then, using the demonstration methodology above, have them discuss and explain their choices.

INDEPENDENT PRACTICE

- Assign exercises **C-48** through **C-52**.

THINKING ABOUT THINKING

Q: What did you pay attention to when you selected the stack that matched the description?

1. If I could not visualize the positions of the shapes, I cut out the shapes and stacked them according to the description.

2. I looked through the answers until I found the picture that matched my model.

PERSONAL APPLICATION

Q: When might you need to recognize the order in which something has been arranged?

  A: Examples include model building; assembling toys or bikes; crafts, sewing, cooking, cleaning, or household repairs; learning or recognizing pattern plays in sports; using a filing system in an office or at home.

EXERCISES C-55 to C-67

STACKING SHAPES—SUPPLY

ANSWERS C-53 through C-67 — Student book pages 93–6
Guided Practice: C-53 to C-55 See next page.
Independent Practice: C-56 through C-67 See next page.

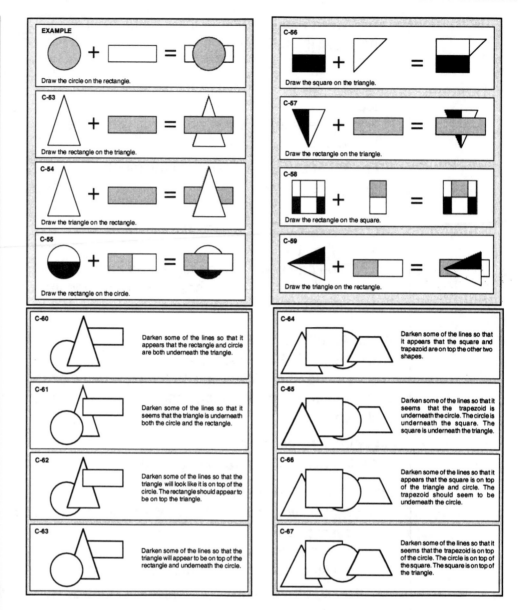

LESSON PREPARATION

OBJECTIVE AND MATERIALS

OBJECTIVE: Students will draw a stack of shapes to represent a given description.

MATERIALS: Transparency of page 93 of the student book • washable transparency marker

CURRICULUM APPLICATIONS

LANGUAGE ARTS: Following directions in formatting outlines, letters, memos, or layouts

MATHEMATICS: Doing geometry constructions and proofs

SCIENCE: Following sequential directions in science demonstrations or experiments

SOCIAL STUDIES: Reading or constructing charts, graphs, or maps

ENRICHMENT AREAS: Following art, industrial arts, or vocational education procedures; visualizing and learning positions and movements in marching band or drill team formations

TEACHING SUGGESTIONS

Encourage students to describe stacks in terms of "on top of" rather than "under." This gives a recognizable sequence from the bottom to the top of a stack. Encourage students to discuss and explain their answers.

MODEL LESSON | **LESSON**

Introduction

Q: In the previous exercises you matched a stack of shapes with a statement describing it.

Explaining the Objective to Students

Q: In these exercises you will draw a stack of shapes to represent a given description.

Class Activity

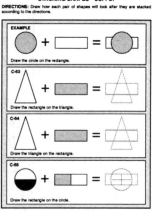

- Project the example on page 93. Notice the instructions are to draw the circle on the rectangle. Which shape is completely visible?

    A: The circle

Q: Look at **C-53**. The instructions are to draw the rectangle on the triangle. Which shape will be completely visible?

    A: The rectangle

Q: Which shape will be only partly visible?

    A: The triangle

Q: How can you shade the outline in your book to show that the rectangle is on the triangle?

- Pause for student response.

    A: The whole rectangle is shaded. The peak and the base of the triangle are unshaded.

GUIDED PRACTICE

EXERCISES: **C-53** through **C-55**

- Give students sufficient time to complete these exercises. Then, using the demonstration methodology above, have them discuss and explain their choices.

INDEPENDENT PRACTICE

- Assign exercises **C-56** through **C-67**.

THINKING ABOUT THINKING

Q: What did you pay attention to when you selected the stack that matched the description?

1. If I could not visualize the positions of the shapes, I cut out the shapes and stacked them according to the description.

2. I drew a picture that matched my model.

PERSONAL APPLICATION

Q: When might you need to follow directions in stacking or arranging something?

A: Examples include putting away or reshelving items, e.g., dishes, records, tools, or books; following directions for errands or chores; assembling models or toys; following directions for crafts, sewing, cooking, cleaning, or household repairs; arranging notebooks or projects according to specifications.

EXERCISES C-68 to C-77

STACKING SHAPES—EXPLAIN

ANSWERS C-68 through C-77 Student book pages 97–100
Guided Practice: C-68 The triangle is on top of the square. **C-69** The circle is on top of the square.
Independent Practice: C-70 The hexagon is on top of the square. **C-71** The hexagon is on top of the circle. **C-72** The triangle is on top of the hexagon. **C-73** The dark gray triangle is on top of the gray square which is on top of the white circle. **C-74** The gray square is on top of the dark gray circle which is on top of the white triangle. **C-75** The checked square is on top of the striped circle, which is on top of the gray triangle. **C-76** The gray square is on top of the checked circle which is top of the striped triangle. **C-77** The gray circle is on top of the striped square, which is on top of the checked triangle.

LESSON PREPARATION

OBJECTIVE AND MATERIALS

OBJECTIVE: Students will write directions for stacking two or three shapes into a given arrangement.
MATERIALS: Transparency of student workbook page 97 • washable transparency marker

CURRICULUM APPLICATIONS

LANGUAGE ARTS: Organizing demonstration speeches; writing or presenting instructions for doing, constructing, or operating something
MATHEMATICS: Doing geometry constructions and proofs
SCIENCE: Recognizing and stating correct instructions for scientific demonstrations or experiments, writing laboratory reports
SOCIAL STUDIES: Explaining the organization of charts, graphs, schedules, or map legends
ENRICHMENT AREAS: Recognizing and explaining art, industrial arts, or vocational education procedures; explaining written music; writing directions for a dance or drill formation

TEACHING SUGGESTIONS

Encourage students to discuss their answers. Class discussion is valuable for sharing acquired knowledge. Often a child's words will communicate in a more meaningful way than words a teacher may use.

NOTE: Answers may be reversed by using the word *under*, although *on top of* is preferred.

MODEL LESSON | LESSON

Introduction

Q: In the previous exercise you shaded diagrams to illustrate different descriptions of a stack of shapes.

Explaining the Objective to Students

Q: In these exercises you will write directions for stacking two or three shapes into a given arrangement.

Class Activity

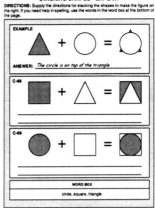

- Project the example from the transparency of page 97, covering the answer.

  Q: The example shows a gray triangle and a white circle. Which shape is completely visible in the stack?

  A: The circle

Q: Describe the position of the circle.

A: The circle is on top of the triangle.

Q: Which shape is only partly visible?

A: The triangle

Q: Describe the position of the triangle.

A: The triangle is under the circle.

Q: What statement would explain the positions of the shapes in this stack?

A: The circle is on top of the triangle (or the triangle is under the circle).

GUIDED PRACTICE

EXERCISES: **C-68**, **C-69**

- Give students sufficient time to complete these exercises. Using the demonstration methodology above, have them discuss and explain their choices.

INDEPENDENT PRACTICE

- Assign exercises **C-70** through **C-77**.

THINKING ABOUT THINKING

Q: What did you pay attention to when you wrote a description of a stack of shapes?

1. I recognized that the only whole shape was on top.

2. If I could not visualize the positions of the remaining shapes, I cut out the shapes and stacked them like the picture.

3. I described how I built my stack.

PERSONAL APPLICATION

Q: When might you need to explain how something has been arranged or organized?

A: Examples include explaining how models or toys have been constructed; giving directions for crafts, sewing, cooking, or household repair projects; explaining how to find something in a library or store.

Chapter 4 | FIGURAL CLASSIFICATIONS
(Student book pages 102–31)

EXERCISES D-1 to D-8

DESCRIBING CLASSES

> **ANSWERS D-1 through D-8 — Student book pages 102–3**
> **Guided Practice: D-1** a and d; **D-2** a, b, c, and d; **D-3** a and c
> **Independent Practice: D-4** a and c; **D-5** d; **D-6** a, b, and d; **D-7** c; **D-8** b and d

LESSON PREPARATION

OBJECTIVE AND MATERIALS
OBJECTIVE: Students will select statements to describe the characteristics of a class.
MATERIALS: Transparency of TM 27 • Washable transparency marker

CURRICULUM APPLICATIONS
LANGUAGE ARTS: Describing the way things or people look, writing or giving directions for constructing something or going somewhere
MATHEMATICS: Describing and/or reproducing geometric shapes
SCIENCE: Matching items to classification statements based on appearance, describing the results of an experiment or demonstration
SOCIAL STUDIES: Interpreting charts and graphs, drawing inferences from pictures or artifacts
ENRICHMENT AREAS: Answering questions about a work of art or a dance

TEACHING SUGGESTIONS
The important word is *all*. All members of a class must be distinguished by common characteristics or attributes. Since most classes possess more than a single common attribute, students must read each descriptive phrase, examine each member of the class, and decide if the statement is true of each one. They should also accurately state why unchosen answers do not describe the class and give a single-sentence description of each class. During class discussion, ask individual students why he or she believes a particular statement to be true or false. This exercise promotes thoroughness in description and examination.

MODEL LESSON

LESSON

Introduction
Q: You call yourselves a class of students. All students in this class have things in common. In this class, everyone is about the same age, meets in the same room, studies the same things, and has me as a teacher. You all have these things in common. *Class* can mean a group having one or more characteristics in common. When you describe the group using those characteristics, you are classifying.

Explaining the Objective to Students

Q: In these exercises you will choose statements which describe the characteristics of a class.

Class Activity

- Project a transparency of TM 27.

  Q: You need to determine which of these statements describe the shapes on the page. The first statement says all the shapes are rectangular. Is this true of each shape?

  A: No

  Q: The second statement says all the shapes are gray. Is this true of each shape on the page?

  A: Yes. Circle this statement to indicate that it is one correct description of this class.

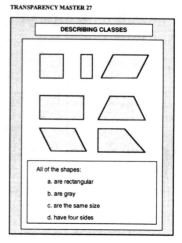

TRANSPARENCY MASTER 27

DESCRIBING CLASSES

All of the shapes:
a. are rectangular
b. are gray
c. are the same size
d. have four sides

- Circle choice *b.*

  Q: Are all of these shapes the same size?

  A: No

  Q: Do all of these shapes have four sides?

  A: Yes

- Circle *d* on the transparency.

  Q: You have determined that all of these shapes are gray and they have four sides. Can you describe this class in a single sentence?

  A: The class is a group of gray quadrilaterals (four-sided shapes).

GUIDED PRACTICE

EXERCISES: **D-1** through **D-3**

- Give students sufficient time to complete these exercises. Encourage students to discuss and explain their choices.

INDEPENDENT PRACTICE

- Assign exercises **D-4** through **D-8**.

THINKING ABOUT THINKING

Q: What did you think about when you classified each group of shapes?

1. I looked carefully at the group of shapes.

2. I read each statement.

3. I decided if the statement was true for all the figures in the group.

PERSONAL APPLICATION

Q: When might you be asked to identify statements which accurately describe the characteristics of what you see?

A: Examples include field trip observations; reporting an accident, injury, or fire to officials; describing the appearance of something to someone who cannot see it.

**EXERCISES
D-9 to D-21**

MATCHING CLASSES BY SHAPE/PATTERN

ANSWERS D-9 through D-21 — Student book pages 104–6
Guided Practice: D-9 d (triangles) **D-10** a (rectangles); **D-11** b (squares);
D-12 c (circles)
Independent Practice: D-13 c; **D-14** e; **D-15** a; **D-16** b; **D-17** d; **D-18** e;
D-19 a; **D-20** b; **D-21** c

**LESSON
PREPARATION**

OBJECTIVE AND MATERIALS

OBJECTIVE: Students will match groups of figures which have the same characteristics.
MATERIALS: Transparency of student workbook page 104 • washable transparency marker

CURRICULUM APPLICATIONS

LANGUAGE ARTS: Matching letter styles by placement and punctuation, e.g., business letters, friendly letters, memos
MATHEMATICS: Comparing numbers using place values, using arithmetic symbols to group like problems, grouping geometric shapes
SCIENCE: Classifying by shape or pattern, e.g., leaves, insects, flowers, shells, birds; identifying symmetry and geometric forms found in the environment
SOCIAL STUDIES: Examining pictures or artifacts for drawing inferences; finding the same location on different types or sizes of maps; using legends to read graphs, maps, charts
ENRICHMENT AREAS: Locating types of books or items in a library; matching type faces, fonts, or page designs in journalism; classifying musical instruments by tone, design, or shape, e.g., winds, reeds, percussion; classifying works of art by medium

TEACHING SUGGESTIONS

Encourage students to use precise vocabulary in describing shape and pattern. Encourage geometric terms (*right triangle, trapezoid,* etc.) if the words are familiar to students. Imaginative similes (arrowhead, home plate, etc.) are encouraged when unconventional shapes are used. After completing the exercises, have students explain their choices and state class descriptions and reasoning processes as precisely as possible.

MODEL LESSON

LESSON

Introduction

Q: In the previous exercise you chose statements which described a group of shapes.

Explaining the Objective to Students

Q: In these exercises you will match groups which have the same characteristics.

Class Activity

• Project the transparency of page 104. Using the washable marker, follow this procedure.

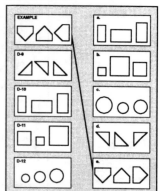

MATCHING CLASSES BY SHAPE
DIRECTIONS: Draw a line from each group of shapes on the left to a group on the right that belongs to the same class.

Q: Describe the shapes in the example group.
  A: They are all white five-sided shapes (pentagons).

Q: Which group in the right column has the most characteristics in common with those in the example group?
  A: Group *e*

Q: Why does group *e* match?
  A: Group *e* also contains only white five-sided shapes of the same size. Notice that a line has been drawn connecting the example to *e*.

Q: Describe the shapes in group **D-9**.
  A: They are all gray triangles with a square corner (right triangles).

Q: Which group in the right column has the most characteristics in common with those in **D-9**?
  A: Group *d*

Q: Why does group *d* match?
  A: Group *d* also contains only white triangles.

• Connect **D-9** to *d*.

GUIDED PRACTICE
EXERCISES: **D-9** through **D-12**
• Give students sufficient time to complete these exercises.

INDEPENDENT PRACTICE
• Assign exercises **D-13** through **D-21**.

THINKING ABOUT THINKING
Q: What did you pay attention to when you classified the figures?
  1. I looked carefully at the shape and/or the pattern of the figure on the left.
  2. I looked for a group of figures that had the same characteristic(s) as the first shape.
  3. I drew a line connecting the shape to the group.

PERSONAL APPLICATION
Q: When might you want to match objects by their common characteristics?
  A: Examples include sorting construction toys, eating utensils, clothing, or tools; reshelving or locating items in a store, warehouse, library, or workshop.

**EXERCISES
D-23 to D-34**

CLASSIFYING MORE THAN ONE WAY—MATCHING

ANSWERS D-22 through D-34—Student book pages 107–8
Guided Practice: D-22 e (divided shapes); **D-23** c (parallelograms) and
f (black); **D-24 b** (horizontal congruent parts; top part shaded); possibly

c (quadrilaterals), d (congruent parts, one-half shaded), or e (two congruent parts)
Independent Practice: D-25 a (checkered shape) and c (parallelogram); **D-26** d (shape with left half-gray and right half-black); **D-27** c (gray shape); **D-28** b (one-fourth black) and e (rectangle); **D-29** c (triangle) and f (black); **D-30** a (circle) and e (gray); **D-31** d (parallelogram) and f (black); **D-32** e (gray) and f (trapezoid); **D-33** a (half-black), b (square), c (half-black), and d (half-black); **D-34** a (half-black), c (half-black), d (half-black), and e (rectangle)
NOTE: The most common answers are given here. Additional matches may be justified if students state legitimate classifying criteria.

LESSON PREPARATION

OBJECTIVE AND MATERIALS

OBJECTIVE: Students will match a given figure with all classes to which it can belong.
MATERIALS: Transparency of student workbook page 107 • washable transparency marker

CURRICULUM APPLICATIONS

LANGUAGE ARTS: Arranging groups of words using various categories, e.g., initial letters, alphabetical order, words that end in —ing
MATHEMATICS: Using the same numbers to create different problems, sorting geometric shapes and patterns
SCIENCE: Using matrices to classify items by shape, pattern, or color
SOCIAL STUDIES: Making different types of charts or graphs illustrating results of a poll or other statistical information; grouping artifacts using various categories, e.g., material, use, design
ENRICHMENT AREAS: Selecting proper materials for an art project from available supplies; classifying music using different categories, e.g., type, instrument, purpose

TEACHING SUGGESTIONS

Encourage students to be specific when explaining why each shape or figure belongs to some classes and not to others.

MODEL LESSON

LESSON

Introduction

Q: In previous exercises you described classes by determining common characteristics and matched classes by shape and pattern.

Explaining the Objective to Students

Q: In these exercises you will match a given figure with all classes to which it can belong.

Class Activity

• Project the transparency of page 107.
Q: The gray triangle given as an example belongs in class f because all the shapes in that class are

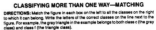

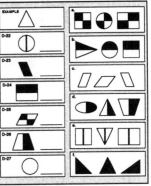

CLASSIFYING MORE THAN ONE WAY—MATCHING
DIRECTIONS: Match the figure in each box on the left to all the classes on the right to which it can belong. Write the letters of the correct classes on the line next to the figure. For example, the gray triangle in the example belongs to both class c (the gray class) and class f (the triangle class).

triangles. It also belongs in class *c* because it is gray and all the shapes in that class are gray. The triangle doesn't fit in any of the other classes because they all have characteristics other than triangular shape or gray color. The figures in class *a* are all checkered with opposite congruent parts shaded black. What are the characteristics of class *b?*

A: Symmetrical figures divided horizontally into two congruent parts with top part shaded black

Q: What are the characteristics of class *c?*

A: Gray parallelograms NOTE: Students may see these as quadrilaterals, which will add matches not included in the answer section.

Q: What are the characteristics of class *d?*

A: Symmetrical figures divided vertically into two congruent parts; left part shaded gray and the right part shaded black

Q: What are the characteristics of class *e?*

A: Figures divided vertically into two congruent parts

Q: What are the characteristics of class *f?*

A: Triangles; shaded black

Q: Describe figure **D-22**.

A: It is a circle divided into two congruent parts by a vertical line.

Q: Name one of the classes on the right to which it can be matched.

A: Answers may vary, but **D-22** most obviously belongs in class *e*. Students might also justify matching it to class *c* as a gray figure, or to classes *b* and *d* as figures with two congruent parts. Write all accepted answers on the transparency.

GUIDED PRACTICE
EXERCISES: **D-22** through **D-24**
• Give students sufficient time to complete these exercises. Then, using the demonstration methodology above, have them discuss and explain their choices.

INDEPENDENT PRACTICE
• Assign exercises **D-25** through **D-34**.

THINKING ABOUT THINKING
Q: What did you think about when you classified each figure?
1. I looked at the characteristics of the figure.
2. I looked for a class of figures with the same characteristic as the given figure.

PERSONAL APPLICATION
Q: When do you sort objects in more than one way?
A: Examples include sorting tools or materials for different projects; arranging books or toys on shelves; arranging collections of objects, e.g., using country of origin, denomination, or date of issuance to sort stamps or money.

**EXERCISES
D-35 to D-42**

CHANGING CHARACTERISTICS—SELECT

ANSWERS D-35 through D-42 — Student book pages: 109–10
Guided Practice: **D-35** Size: D, Shape: D, Color: S; **D-36** Size: D, Shape: D, Pattern: D
Independent Practice: D-37 Size: D, Shape: D, Color: S, Position: S; **D-38** Size: S, Shape: S, Pattern: D, Position D; **D-39** Size: D, Shape: S, Pattern: D; **D-40** Size: S, Shape: S, Pattern: D, Position: D (congruent triangles); **D-41** Size: D, Shape: S, Pattern D, Position: D; **D-42** Size: S, Shape: S, Pattern: D, Position: D (congruent arrows)

**LESSON
PREPARATION**

OBJECTIVE AND MATERIALS
OBJECTIVE: Students will compare the characteristics of two given shapes.
MATERIALS: Transparency of student workbook page 109

CURRICULUM APPLICATIONS
LANGUAGE ARTS: Differentiating between proper and common nouns or adjectives; identifying singular, plural, and possessive forms of words
MATHEMATICS: Reading graphs; doing rotation, reflection, similarity, and congruence exercises; differentiating between specialized geometric shapes, e.g., quadrilaterals: squares, rectangles, rhombuses, trapezoids
SCIENCE: Observing life cycles of living organisms; describing changes in cloud formations; observing effects of different elements on the earth, e.g., soil erosion or caking; observing physical changes caused by forest fires; describing changes in science experiments
SOCIAL STUDIES: Observing changes in artifacts, architectural styles, dress, and social, political, or judicial systems over a period of time
ENRICHMENT AREAS: Observing changes over a period of years in such areas as dance, music, art, or furniture styles; observing changes in an artist's style

TEACHING SUGGESTIONS
Students should always explain the similarity or difference they see. They should also be able to make a statement that describes the common classification for each set of figures.

MODEL LESSON

LESSON

Introduction
Q: In previous exercises you described classes, classified by shape or pattern, and learned that a single object can be classified in more than one way.

Explaining the Objective to Students
Q: In these exercises you will decide whether certain characteristics of two given shapes are the same or different.

Class Activity
• Project the example from the transparency of student page 109.
  Q: Are these shapes the same size?
    A: Yes

Q: These two shapes are the same size, so S, meaning same, is circled in the size row. Are these shapes the same shape?
  A: Yes, they are both triangles.

Q: Since they are the same shape, S has been circled in the shape row. Are these shapes the same color?
  A: No, one is gray and the other black.

Q: Circle the D, meaning different, in the color row. Are the shapes in the same position?
  A: No, the triangles face in opposite directions.

Q: The D has been circled in the direction row. Describe this class of shapes.
  A: Equal (congruent) triangles

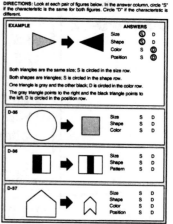

GUIDED PRACTICE
EXERCISES: **D-35, D-36**
- Give students sufficient time to complete these exercises. Then, using the demonstration methodology above, have them discuss and explain their choices.

INDEPENDENT PRACTICE
- Assign exercises **D-37** through **D-42**.

THINKING ABOUT THINKING
Q: What did you think about when you compared the two shapes?
1. I looked at the size and shape of each figure to see if they were the same or different.
2. I looked at the color and pattern of each figure to see if they were the same or different.
3. I looked at each figure to see if it was in the same position as the other figure.
4. I circled S or D for each characteristic that I compared.

PERSONAL APPLICATION
Q: When might you need to identify changed characteristics?
  A: Examples include choosing correct tools, utensils, or materials for a project; differentiating between similar, but not identical, objects.

EXERCISES D-43 to D-51

CHANGING CHARACTERISTICS—SUPPLY

ANSWERS D-43 through D-51 — Student book pages 111–2
Guided Practice: D-43 any large black square CLASS: black squares; **D-44** any non-gray triangle facing another direction CLASS: congruent isosceles triangles

Independent Practice: D-45 any larger circle with the same pattern CLASS: half-black circles; **D-46** any arrow of the same size and shape, with a different pattern, pointing in a different direction; **D-47** any large black non-triangle CLASS: large black non-triangles; **D-48** any small gray non-hexagon CLASS: small gray non-hexagons; **D-49** any small gray and black non-square with the same pattern; **D-50** any large non-gray right triangle in a different position; **D-51** any large non-hexagon with the top half black and the bottom gray
NOTE: There are many possible answers to the above exercises.

LESSON PREPARATION

OBJECTIVE AND MATERIALS
OBJECTIVE: Students will make specific changes to a given figure and draw the new figure.
MATERIALS: Transparency of student workbook page 111 • washable transparency marker

CURRICULUM APPLICATIONS
LANGUAGE ARTS: Reproducing letters or essays with changes in form
MATHEMATICS: Doing rotation, reflection, congruence, or similarity exercises
SCIENCE: Drawing different stages in life cycles of living objects
SOCIAL STUDIES: Depicting statistical information using a different format, e.g., changing from pictograph to bar graph or pie chart
ENRICHMENT AREAS: Reproducing art, industrial art, or craft projects with changes; changing parts in music or dance compositions; modifying dramatic performances or sports plays

TEACHING SUGGESTIONS
Students should always explain the similarity or difference they see. They should also be able to make a statement describing the common classification for each set of figures.

MODEL LESSON

LESSON

Introduction
Q: In previous exercises you have chosen words that are useful for classifying and describing characteristics of shapes or figures.

Explaining the Objective to Students
Q: In these exercises you are given a drawing and specific directions for changing it. You are then asked to draw (produce) the figure that results from making those changes.

Class Activity
• Project the example and its directions from the transparency of page 111.
Q: In this example, you are to keep the shape and color the same. Describe the shape that results from these instructions.

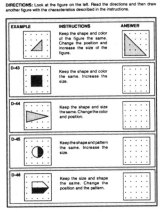

A: It will be a gray triangle

Q: You are to change the position. In what position will the new drawing face?

A: It can be turned any direction, but it must be turned.

Q: You are also to increase the size. Can you now describe the resulting figure?

A: A larger gray triangle that has been turned a different way.

- Project the answer.

Q: Does this shape meet the given directions?

A: Yes; it meets all the criteria.

Q: Is this the only figure that can be drawn given these changes?

A: Students should recognize that many different figures will fit the criteria and not all correctly produced shapes or figures will look the same.

Q: What statement would describe the class for these two shapes?

A: Gray right triangles

GUIDED PRACTICE
EXERCISES: **D-43, D-44**

- Give students sufficient time to complete these exercises. Check their drawings, then have them discuss and explain their choices.

INDEPENDENT PRACTICE

- Assign exercises **D-45** through **D-51**.

THINKING ABOUT THINKING

Q: What did you think about to produce a new figure?

1. I looked at the given figure.

2. I read the directions to determine what characteristcs would stay the same and what charactersitics would change.

3. I drew a new figure with the correct changes.

PERSONAL APPLICATION

Q: When are you asked to produce something with certain characteristics changed?

A: Examples include drawing graphs, altering patterns or recipes.

**EXERCISES
D-52 to D-61**

DRAW ANOTHER

ANSWERS D-52 through D-61 — Student book pages 113–4
Guided Practice: D-52 any gray parallelogram; **D-53** any square with a wide black band through the center
Independent Practice: D-54 any half-black symmetrical shape divided vertically; **D-55** any shape divided into two congruent parts; **D-56** any trapezoid having two right angles; **D-57** any rectangle divided diagonally and shaded half gray and half black; **D-58** any oval with a line along the long axis; **D-59** any half-black symmetrical shape divided horizontally;

D-60 any triangle or trapezoid that is divided horizontally and shaded gray and black; **D-61** any gray shape that has a similar small black shape inside it

LESSON PREPARATION

OBJECTIVE AND MATERIALS

OBJECTIVE: Students will draw a shape or figure that belongs to a given class.
MATERIALS: Transparency of student workbook page 113 • washable transparency marker

CURRICULUM APPLICATIONS

LANGUAGE ARTS: Categorizing words based on word configuration rather than meaning, e.g., -ing words, -ance words, doubled consonant words; identifying punctuation and proofreading marks
MATHEMATICS: Adding numbers or shapes to given sets, constructing geometric shapes
SCIENCE: Naming items that could belong to a class, identifying cloud formations
SOCIAL STUDIES: Naming states by geographic region or other given category, using an atlas to find regions sharing particular attributes, adding information to an existing chart or graph
ENRICHMENT AREAS: Creating different art projects using the same type of material; adding to lists of instrument types, e.g., percussion, woodwinds, brass, strings

TEACHING SUGGESTIONS

Students should describe the shape and pattern and name the class in each exercise. Give students sufficient time to complete this exercise, encouraging them to draw a large shape.

MODEL LESSON

LESSON

Introduction

Q: In previous exercises you described and formed classes of shapes and figures.

Explaining the Objective to Students

Q: In these exercises you will draw a shape or figure that belongs to a given class.

Class Activity

• Project exercise **D-52** from the transparency of page 113.

   Q: What are the characteristics of this class?
     A: Shape: parallelogram; color: gray

   Q: If you wanted to add another shape to this class, what would it have to look like?
     A: It would have to be a gray parallelogram.

• Draw the figure on the grid provided.

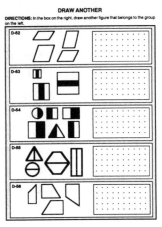

DRAW ANOTHER
DIRECTIONS: In the box on the right, draw another figure that belongs to the group on the left.

GUIDED PRACTICE
EXERCISE: **D-52, D-53**
- Using the demonstration methodology above, have students discuss and explain their choice.

INDEPENDENT PRACTICE
- Assign exercises **D-54** through **D-61**.

THINKING ABOUT THINKING
Q: How did you decide what figure to draw in the box?
1. I determined the characteristics of the class.
2. I drew a figure that fit those specific characteristics.

PERSONAL APPLICATION
Q: When are you asked to determine a class, then provide another member?
A: Examples include reshelving books in a library; locating substitute parts for models, motors, or gears; locating objects that illustrate specific geometric shapes.

EXERCISES D-62 to D-65

CLASSIFYING BY SHAPE/PATTERN—SORTING
CLASSIFYING MORE THAN ONE WAY—SORTING

ANSWERS D-62 through D-65 Student book pages 115–8
Guided Practice: D-62 Shapes with Three Sides: 2,4,6,8, Shapes with Four Sides: 1,3,5,7,9
Independent Practice: D-63 Shapes with Four Sides: 1, 2, 4, 7, 8; Shapes with Five Sides: 3, 5, 10, 12; Shapes with Six Sides: 6, 9, 11; **D-64** Shapes with One Vertical Line: 4, 5, 11; Shapes with a Horizontal Line and Vertical Line: 2, 7, 9; Shapes Shaded Vertically: 3, 8, 10; Shapes Shaded Diagonally: 1, 6, 12; **D-65** White Shapes: 1, 2, 4, 8; Half-white Shapes: 3, 5, 6, 7; Squares: 1, 3, 4; Rectangles 1, 2, 3, 4, 5 (squares are also rectangles); Shapes with Four Sides: 1, 2, 3, 4, 5; Circles: 6, 7, 8; Small Shapes: 1, 2, 7, 8; Large Shapes: 3, 4, 5, 6

LESSON PREPARATION

OBJECTIVE AND MATERIALS
OBJECTIVE: Students will sort all given shapes or figures into classes.
MATERIALS: Transparency of TM 28 (cut apart as indicated)

CURRICULUM APPLICATIONS
LANGUAGE ARTS: Grouping lists of words according to configuration rather than meaning, e.g., —ing words, —ance words
MATHEMATICS: Placing numerical information onto charts or graphs
SCIENCE: Classifying groups of objects or items into given categories; indexing days of the week or month according to given weather parameters, e.g., temperature, fog, rain, snow
SOCIAL STUDIES: Placing events or dates on a given time line; deciding which information to include and how to arrange it on a chart, map, or graph

ENRICHMENT AREAS: Classifying crayons, paints, or markers according to color family or other category; classifying music or art media according to categories

TEACHING SUGGESTIONS

Encourage students to use precise vocabulary to describe shape and pattern. Geometric terms (*right triangle, trapezoid,* etc.) are encouraged if the words are familiar to the students. Imaginative similes (arrowhead, home plate, etc.) should be encouraged when unconventional shapes are used.

MODEL LESSON

LESSON

Introduction

Q: In previous exercises you sorted some given shapes or figures into classes.

Explaining the Objective to Students

Q: In these exercises you will sort all given shapes or figures into classes.

Class Activity

* Project TM 28.
  Q: In these exercises, each shape belongs in one of the classes shown.

TRANSPARENCY MASTER 28

CLASSIFYING BY SHAPE—SORTING

SHAPES WITH 3 SIDES SHAPES WITH 4 SIDES

Cut along dotted lines.

* Point to the columns titled Shapes with 3 Sides and Shapes with 4 Sides. Pick up one of the shapes.
  Q: How many sides does this shape have?
    A: Three or four (depending on the shape selected)

* Pause for students' response.
  Q: In which class does it belong?
    A: In the box for 3- (or 4-) sided figures.

* Repeat the above questions until all shapes have been sorted.

GUIDED PRACTICE

EXERCISE: **D-62**

* Give students sufficient time to complete this exercise. Then, using the demonstration methodology above, have them discuss and explain their choices.

INDEPENDENT PRACTICE

* Assign exercises **D-63** through **D-65**.

THINKING ABOUT THINKING

Q: What did you pay attention to when you classified the figures?
  1. I read the heading on the sorting box.

  2. I found all the figures in the shape box that had the given characteristic.

  3. I drew the shapes in the correct sorting box.

PERSONAL APPLICATION

Q: When might you need to sort a group of objects into given classes?

A: Examples include sorting toys, utensils, tools, books, or supplies; sorting items into boxes for moving or packing

EXERCISES D-66 to D-111

OVERLAPPING CLASSES—INTERSECTION

ANSWERS D-66 through D-111 Student book pages 119–25
Guided Practice: D-66 Darken left section; **D-67** Darken center section; **D-68** Darken the right section; **D-69** B; **D-70** A
Independent Practice: D-71 B; **D-72** A; **D-73** B; **D-74** I; **D-75** B; **D-76** I; **D-77** I; **D-78** B; **D-79** O; **D-80** A (striped—five sides); **D-81** B; **D-82** I; **D-83** O (black with five sides); **D-84** O (black with three sides) **D-85** squares **D-86** black shapes; **D-87** black squares; **D-88** B; **D-89** A; **D-90** B; **D-91** I; **D-92** O; **D-93** A; **D-94** circles; **D-95** striped shapes; **D-96** striped circles; **D-97** B; **D-98** A; **D-99** B; **D-100** A; **D-101** O (The black triangle is not a circle and is not striped); **D-102** I; **D-103** black shapes; **D-104** triangles; **D-105** black triangles; **D-106** A; **D-107** B; **D-108** A; **D-109** O; **D-110** I **D-111** O

LESSON PREPARATION

OBJECTIVE AND MATERIALS

OBJECTIVE: Students will sort shapes by one or two characteristics.
MATERIALS: Transparencies of student workbook pages 119 (optional) and 120 • washable transparency marker • attribute blocks (optional)

CURRICULUM APPLICATIONS

LANGUAGE ARTS: Classifying words by configuration rather than meaning, e.g., double consonant words, —ie words,—ance words; choosing appropriate illustrations for an original story or book
MATHEMATICS: Doing set theory exercises and attribute block exercises; sorting geometric shapes
SCIENCE: Sorting natural objects into overlapping classes; indexing days according to different weather parameters, e.g., morning rain, afternoon rain, all-day rain, night rain
SOCIAL STUDIES: Interpreting graphic information, using a legend to read a map, understanding the concept of classes and subclasses
ENRICHMENT AREAS: Classifying types of musical instruments, e.g., woodwind, string, etc.; classifying categories of art, e.g., era, gender of artist, medium used

TEACHING SUGGESTIONS

Using the demonstration methodology below, encourage students to discuss and explain their choices. You may want to review student page 119 first. On pages 123–5, students must observe and determine the characteristics of the set.

MODEL LESSON

LESSON

Introduction

Q: In the previous exercise you sorted by one or more characteristics.

Explaining the Objective to Students

Q: In these exercises you will sort some shapes by one characteristic and other shapes by two characteristics.

Class Activity—Option 1

• Demonstration using attribute blocks: On a table, place two rings about one foot apart. Select the following blocks from the attribute block set: Small blue triangle, large blue triangle, small red square, large red hexagon, large red triangle, small red rectangle, large yellow triangle.

• Point to the ring representing red shapes.
Q: This ring contains the class "red shapes."

• Point to the ring representing triangles.
Q: This ring contains the class "triangles." You are to chose the class that best describes each block.

• Pick up the small blue triangle. (Save the large red triangle until last.)
Q: Where does this block go?
  A: In the triangle ring.

• Place the shape inside the triangle ring. Continue until all the blocks except the large red triangle have been placed, then hold up the red triangle.
Q: Where does this block belong?
  A: In the red ring (or in the triangle ring).

Q: Yes, it is red (or a triangle), but that doesn't describe its shape (color).
  A: No, put it in the other ring.

Q: Yes, it is a triangle (red), but that doesn't describe its color (shape), does it? Does anybody know a way to show that this shape is both red and a triangle?

• Students will probably try to move the block back and forth between the rings or place it in the space between the two rings. Encourage students to move the rings. If they do not move the rings, you should move them so they overlap as shown on page 120.

Class Activity—Option 2

• Project the transparency of student page 120 and point to the circle on the right.
Q: The right circle represents a class of white shapes.

• Point to the circle on the left.
Q: The left circle is a class of squares. Name the shape in the example box.
  A: White rectangle

Q: Does the shape belong in the right circle or the left circle?
  A: The right circle because it is white

Q: Notice that the right section of the small diagram in the box has been darkened.

OVERLAPPING CLASSES—INTERSECTIONS
DIRECTIONS: Using the information in the top diagram, darken part of the small overlapping circles diagram next to each figure to show where that figure would belong.

EXAMPLE: In the large overlapping diagram above, the white square is in the intersection of the diagram because it is both white and square. In the example below, the right part of the diagram has been darkened to show that the white rectangle belongs only in the part of the diagram labeled white shapes.

Q: In which class does the shape in **D-66** belong?
  A: The left circle because it is a square

- Darken the left section of the **D-66** diagram.
  Q: Now look at the shape in exercise **D-67**. In which class does it belong?
    A: It can go into the right circle because it is white and into the left circle because it is a square.

- Indicate the overlapping section (intersection) on the large diagram.
  Q: This center section shows an area of overlapping classes. This is where you would put shapes that fit in both classes.

- Darken the center section of the **D-67** diagram.

- Do guided practice exercise **D-68** next.
  Q: Notice that in the large diagram on page 120, the sections of the diagram are labeled. In exercises **D-69** and **D-70**, you will be writing an "A" for the left side of the diagram, a "B" for the right side, or an "I" for the overlapping part or intersection.

GUIDED PRACTICE
EXERCISES: **D-66** through **D-70**
- Give students sufficient time to complete these exercise

INDEPENDENT PRACTICE
- Assign exercises **D-71** through **D-111**. You may wish to divide this exercise into two assignments.

THINKING ABOUT THINKING
Q: What did you pay attention to when you classified the figures?
  1. I looked carefully at the details to decide how the figures in a sorting circle were alike (size of the figure, shape, pattern, or color).
  2. I checked to be sure that any figure added to the circle had the same characteristic(s).
  3. If a figure had the characteristics of both sorting circles, I placed it in the overlapping part of the diagram (intersection).

PERSONAL APPLICATION
Q: When would you sort objects into classes, some of which might overlap?
  A: Examples include finding books or materials in a library; locating products in a grocery store; using tools or materials in different ways, e.g., using one side of a claw hammer to drive in nails and the other side to pull them out.

EXERCISES D-112 to D-117

OVERLAPPING CLASSES—MATRIX

> **ANSWERS D-112 through D-117 — Student book pages 126–8**
> **Guided Practice: D-112 to D-113** See next page.
> **Independent Practice: D-114 to D-117** See next page.

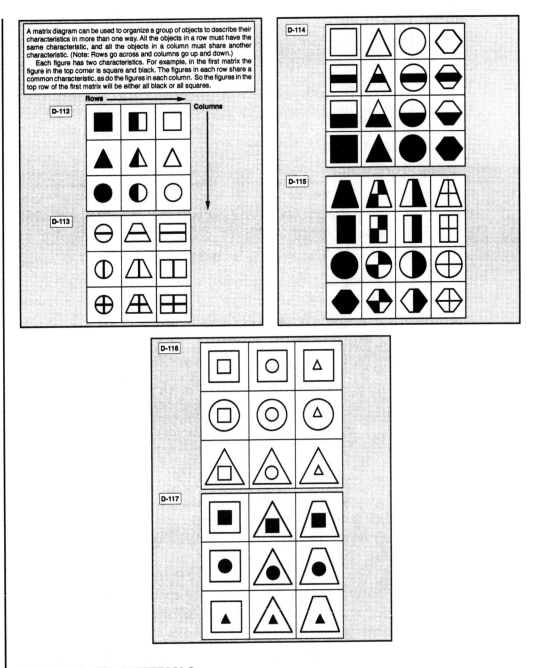

A matrix diagram can be used to organize a group of objects to describe their characteristics in more than one way. All the objects in a row must have the same characteristic, and all the objects in a column must share another characteristic. (Note: Rows go across and columns go up and down.)

Each figure has two characteristics. For example, in the first matrix the figure in the top corner is square and black. The figures in each row share a common characteristic, as do the figures in each column. So the figures in the top row of the first matrix will be either all black or all squares.

LESSON PREPARATION

OBJECTIVE AND MATERIALS
OBJECTIVE: Students will use a matrix to classify figures by more than one characteristic.
MATERIALS: Transparency of TM 29 • Washable transparency marker • attribute blocks (optional)

CURRICULUM APPLICATIONS
LANGUAGE ARTS: Locating information from graphs, tables, or schedules
MATHEMATICS: Reading addition, subtraction, or multiplication tables
SCIENCE: Classifying information using more than one characteristic; using tables or charts, e.g., periodic chart, probability chart
SOCIAL STUDIES: Making a graph or chart of survey results, using matrices to depict data

ENRICHMENT AREAS: Using mileage matrices on road maps, comparing or contrasting works of art or pieces of music using multiple categories, comparing or contrasting works of two artists or composers

TEACHING SUGGESTIONS

Encourage students to use precise vocabulary when describing shape and pattern. Using the demonstration methodology below, have them discuss and explain their choices.

MODEL LESSON

LESSON

Introduction

Q: In the previous exercise some shapes could be classified by more than one characteristic. The overlapping-circles diagram you used to show that relationship is called a Venn diagram.

Explaining the Objective to Students

Q: In these exercises all the given figures can be classified by more than one characteristic. For this kind of classification, you will use a diagram called a matrix.

Class Activity—Option 1

- Demonstration using attribute blocks: Draw a nine-cell matrix on the floor or sidewalk with chalk or on a piece of cardboard with either chalk or a marker. Label the rows and columns as indicated, placing the correct attribute blocks in their corresponding cells. As you draw the matrix, explain which are rows and which are columns.
  Q: What shape belongs in the top middle (Row 1, Column 2) cell?
    A: A red circle.

	Column 1 squares	Column 2 circles	Column 3 triangles
Row 1 red	red square	red circle	red triangle
Row 2 yellow	yelllow square		
Row 3 blue	blue square		

- By asking similar questions, lead students to complete the matrix.

  NOTE: An alternate method might be to assign "cell values" to various students, then ask the class to place them on a floor matrix. For example: Q: [Student's name], you are a blue square.

- Hand student a blue square to hold.
  Q: Where should we place [student's name] on this matrix?

- Students should be specific as to the location of the correct cell, naming it by row and column. After students respond, have the student holding the blue square stand in or place the object in the indicated cell. Continue in this manner until all students with "cell values" have been placed and the matrix is complete.

Class Activity—Option 2

- Demonstration using transparency: Project transparency TM 29.
  Q: This example shows a different way of demonstrating overlapping

classes. This type, called a matrix, is used when all given objects can be classified in more than one way. Look for a row that has two cells filled in.

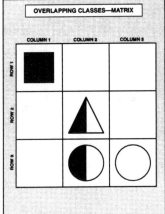

TRANSPARENCY MASTER 29

- Point to Row 3.
  Q: What do the two figures in Row 3 have in common?
    A: They are circles.
- Write "circles" to the left of Row 3.
  Q: Now look for a column that has two cells filled in.

- Point to Column 2.
  Q: What do the figures in Column 2 have in common?
    A: They have a half-black pattern. Write "half-black" at the top of Column 2.

  Q: It seems that in this matrix all the figures in a row have the same shape, and all the figures in a column have the same color or pattern. That's row for shape and column for pattern.

- Write in the names for the other rows and columns: Column 1—Black, Column 3— White; Row 1—Squares, Row 2—Triangles.
  Q: What figure should be drawn in Row 3, Column 1?
    A: A black circle

- Draw it in.
  Q: What figure should be drawn in Row 2, Column 1?
    A: A black triangle

- Draw it in. Turn to page 125 and finish the matrix for exercise **D-112**.

GUIDED PRACTICE
EXERCISES: **D-112, D-113**
- Give students sufficient time to complete these exercises.

INDEPENDENT PRACTICE
- Assign exercises **D-114** through **D-117**.

THINKING ABOUT THINKING
  Q: What did you pay attention to when you classified the figures?
  1. I looked carefully at the row and column headings.

  2. I checked to be sure that any figure added to the matrix had the characteristics of both the row and the column.

PERSONAL APPLICATION
  Q: When might you need to read, construct, or complete a matrix?
    A: Examples include using charts and class schedules, solving puzzles by filling in clues

DEDUCE THE CLASS

ANSWERS D-118 through D-127 — Student book pages 129–31
Guided Practice: D-118 Yes, it has four sides; **D-119** No, it does not have four sides (some say it has an infinite number of sides); **D-120** No, because it has three sides not four; **D-121** Yes, because it is closed and has four sides; **D-122** No, because it has five sides
Independent Practice: D-123 No, the triangle has three sides, a pentagram has five. **D-124** Yes, it is a closed, five-sided shape. **D-125** No, the oval does not have five sides. **D-126** No, it has four sides. **D-127** Yes, it is a closed, five-sided shape.

**LESSON
PREPARATION**

OBJECTIVE AND MATERIALS

OBJECTIVE: Students will determine the characteristics of a given class and then decide which given shapes belong to that class.
MATERIALS: Transparencies of student workbook pages 129 and 130

CURRICULUM APPLICATIONS

LANGUAGE ARTS: Classifying spelling words according to general rules
MATHEMATICS: Classifying geometric shapes and irregular polygons
SCIENCE: Describing given classes of plants or animals
SOCIAL STUDIES: Making deductions about geographical features using given information, identifying the culture to which artifacts belong based on knowledge about similar artifacts
ENRICHMENT AREAS: Using prior knowledge to classify or modify newly gained information

TEACHING SUGGESTIONS

Encourage students to discuss their answers using precise vocabulary to describe shapes and classes.

MODEL LESSON

LESSON

Introduction

Q: In previous exercises you classified figures and shapes by many different characteristics and drew and named classes.

Explaining the Objective to Students

Q: In these exercises you are given a class of shapes and several additional shapes, some of which belong to the class and some of which do not. You are to determine the characteristics of the given class and decide whether or not each additional shape belongs to the given class.

Class Activity

• Project the transparency of student page 129 and go over the steps for determining the characteristics of a class.

DEDUCE THE CLASS

DIRECTIONS: In the next group of exercises, you will continue to classify figures, but now you must determine the characteristics of the class. Look at the figures that belong to the class. Then look at the figures that do not belong to that class.
By looking at the clue figures, decide what is true of the members of the group or class. You may wish to look at the number of straight lines and the number of curved lines in each figure.
After you have decided (deduced) the characteristics of the class, you will decide which of the given figures belong to that class.

HERE ARE THE STEPS:

1. Carefully study the "clue" figures.

2. Decide (deduce) the characteristics of the "clue figures" by asking yourself:

   a. How are the clue figures alike?

   b. How are the clue figures different?

3. Look at the figures in the questions and decide if they belong in the class.

- Project Clue 1 from the transparency of student page 130, covering the other shapes.
  Q: This is a quad. Describe this shape.
    A: It is a shape with four sides (isosceles trapezoid; quadrilateral).

- Project the Clue 2 shape.
  Q: This is a quad. Describe this shape.
    A: A shape with four sides (quadrilateral).

- Project the Clue 3 shape.
  Q: This is not a quad. Describe this shape.
    A: A shape with three sides (triangle).

- Project the Clue 4 shape.
  Q: This is a quad. Describe this shape.
    A: A shape with four sides (square).

- Project the Clue 5 shape.
  Q: This is not a quad. Describe this shape.
    A: A shape made with a curved line or no straight lines (oval or ellipse).

  Q: What do all the shapes, both quads and non-quads, have in common?
    A: They are all closed shapes.

  Q: What is the difference between a quad and a non-quad?
    A: The number of sides; quads have four sides.

- Project exercise **D-118**.
  Q: Describe this shape.
    A: A shape with four sides with opposite sides parallel (a parallelogram).

  Q: Is it a quad?
    A: Yes, it has four sides.

- Write "yes" on the line.

GUIDED PRACTICE
EXERCISES: **D-118** through **D-122**
- Give students sufficient time to complete these exercises. Then, using the demonstration methodology above, have them discuss and explain their choices.

INDEPENDENT PRACTICE
- Assign exercises **D-123** through **D-127**.

THINKING ABOUT THINKING
  Q: What did you pay attention to when you classified the figures?
  1. I looked carefully at the figures in the class to see what characteristics they had in common.
  2. I looked carefully at the figures that were not in the class to see how they were different.

3. I looked at the details of each given shape to determine if it fit the characteristics of the class.

PERSONAL APPLICATION

Q: When might you need to determine the characteristics of a class from given examples?

A: Examples include examining evidence of any kind, utilizing inquiry methods in learning science or social studies.

Chapter 5

FIGURAL ANALOGIES
(Student book pages 133–53)

FIGURAL ANALOGIES—SELECT

ANSWERS E-1 through E-14 — PAGES: 134–8
Guided Practice: TM 27 prob. 1 A (rotation to the right) TM 27 prob. 2 C (reflection about a vertical line); **E-1** c (adding detail diagonally); **E-2** d (rotation to the left)
Independent Practice: E-3 c (rotation to the right and darken color); **E-4** d (reflection about the vertical and color opposite); **E-5** c (color opposite); **E-6** d (reflection about the diagonal and decrease size); **E-7** d (reflection about the diagonal and decrease size); **E-8** b (increase size and color opposite); **E-9** b (rotate one position, increase size, and color opposite); **E-10** c (reflection about the vertical); **E-11** a (rotate left and decrease size); **E-12** b (rotate right one-quarter turn and increase size); **E-13** c (rotate right and decrease size); **E-14** d (reflection about the diagonal) **E-15** d (small is to large); **E-16** e (reflection about the diagonal); **E-17** a (subtracting detail—halving—or two parts are to one part as four parts are to two); **E-18** b (rotate left one-quarter turn); **E-19** c (reflection about the diagonal); **E-20** d (adding detail—doubling—or two parts are to four parts as four parts are to eight); **E-21** e (rotate one-quarter turn); **E-22** a (color opposite or rotate one-half turn); **E-23** b (reduce size)

LESSON PREPARATION

OBJECTIVE AND MATERIALS
OBJECTIVE: Students will recognize the relationship in a figural analogy.
MATERIALS: Transparencies of TMs 30 and 31 • washable transparency marker • attribute blocks (optional)

CURRICULUM APPLICATIONS
LANGUAGE ARTS: Comparing or contrasting pictorial or graphic information
MATHEMATICS: Creating charts or graphs from numeric information, comparing or contrasting angles or polygons
SCIENCE: Recognizing the relationship of cloud formations and weather, recognizing analogous body parts or structural elements in different organisms
SOCIAL STUDIES: Recognizing parallel structures of governments, e.g., local to state to federal, monarchy to federalist; recognizing similar patterns in artifacts or in styles of architecture; comparing and/or contrasting information from maps, charts, or graphs
ENRICHMENT AREAS: Developing test-taking skills; comparing and/or contrasting two types of music, art, or dance

TEACHING SUGGESTIONS
Encourage students to use precise vocabulary when describing shape and pattern. You may need to remind them of the vocabulary they used to describe sequential changes in the section on Figural Sequences.

MODEL LESSON | **LESSON**

Introduction

Q: In previous exercises you identified relationships by examining how shapes or figures were alike and how they were different, putting them into order, and separating them into classes.

Explaining the Objective to Students

Q: In these exercises you will recognize how two pairs of figures are related. This relationship is called an analogy.

Class Activity—Option 1

Demonstration using blocks: Set up the following attribute blocks on the chalk rail. Leave a space about a foot wide between the triangles and the circle.

Small red triangle, large red triangle   Small red circle

• Point to the pair of red triangles.

Q: Compare these two shapes. How are they alike?
   A: They are both red triangles (same shape and color).

Q: How are they different?
   A: The second triangle is larger than the first (different size).

Q: Now look at the small red circle.

• Point to the circle.

Q: Which block would complete this second pair of blocks to make it like the first pair? Both pairs must have the same relationship, so you need a block with the same shape and the same color, but a different size.
   A: A large red circle.

Q: The large red circle has the same shape and color as the small red circle, but has a different (larger) size. This relationship, called an analogy, means that each pair is related in the same way: shape to shape, color to color, and size to size. You read analogies like this: a is to b as c is to d.

• Mark an "a" on the chalkboard over the small red triangle. Make a pair of the small dots (:) over the words "is to." Mark a "b" over the large red triangle. Make four dots(::) over the word "as." Mark a "c" over the small red circle and a "d" over the large red circle. Put a pair small dots over the words "is to."

Class Activity—Option 2

• Demonstration using transparencies: Project the top box on TM 30, covering the bottom section.

Q: Compare the first two shapes. How are they alike?
   A: They are both gray triangles (same shape and same color/pattern).

Q: How are these triangles different?
   A: The second triangle is larger (different size).

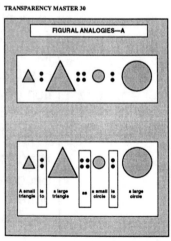

Q: What has been done to the first shape to make the second shape?
　A: It has been enlarged.

Q: Now look at the last two shapes. How are they alike?
　A: They are both gray circles (same shape and same color/pattern).

Q: How are these circles different?
　A: The second circle is larger (different size).

Q: To make the first circle into the second circle, you would have to enlarge it. The circles have been changed in the same way as the triangles. These four shapes, or two pairs of shapes...

• Point to the pair of triangles, then to the pair of circles.
Q: ...are called a figural analogy. The groups of dots (: and ::) represent words.

• Uncover the bottom half of the transparency.
Q: In place of the two dots (:) you read "is to," and in place of the four dots (::) you read "as." So now the figural analogy reads, "A small gray triangle is to a large gray triangle as a small gray circle is to a large gray circle."

• Project exercise 1 from TM 31.

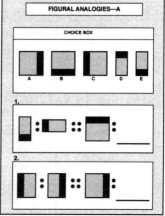

TRANSPARENCY MASTER 31

Q: Compare the first two figures. How are they alike?
　A: Both figures are gray rectangles with a black bar on one end.

Q: How are these two rectangles different?
　A: The second rectangle has been rotated clockwise to the right.

Q: Now look at the next figure. It is a gray square with a black bar on one side. Which figures in the choice box are similar to this square?
　A: Figures A, B, and C

Q: To show the same relationship as the first two figures, the second square must be rotated to the right. Which square should you choose?
　A: A

• Complete the second exercise using the same method.

GUIDED PRACTICE
EXERCISES: TM 30, **E-1**, **E-2**
• Give students sufficient time to complete these exercises. Then, using the demonstration methodology above, have them discuss and explain their choices.

INDEPENDENT PRACTICE
• Assign exercises **E-3** through **E-23**.

THINKING ABOUT THINKING
Q: What did you pay attention to when you found analogies between pairs of figures?

1. I looked carefully at the details (size, shape, pattern or color).

2. I looked at the first pair to see how the two figures were different (change of size, shape, pattern, or color).

3. I looked at the second pair to see if the two figures were different in the same way as the first pair.

4. I explained the relationship as an analogy: *a* is to *b* as *c* is to *d*.

PERSONAL APPLICATION

Q: When might you need to recognize how two pairs of shapes, figures, or patterns are related?

A. Examples include assembling needlework projects; choosing replacement parts for models, gears, or motors; matching containers with the correct lids; choosing articles of clothing and accessories to mix or match.

EXERCISES E-24 to E-47

COMPLETE THE PAIR/FIGURAL ANALOGIES—COMPLETE

ANSWERS E-24 through E-47 — Student book pages 141–7
Guided Practice: E-24 (see below) **E-33** reflect about the vertical; **E-34** rotate to the left (see below)
Independent Practice: E-25 through **E-32** (see below); **E-35** rotate to the right; **E-36** rotate to the left; **E-37** reflect about a diagonal; **E-38** reflect about a vertical; **E-39** reflect about a diagonal; **E-40** opposite color; **E-41** rotate to the right; **E-42** reflect about a horizontal; **E-43** reflect about a vertical; **E-44** reflect about a horizontal; **E-45** rotate to the right; **E-46** reflect about a diagonal; **E-47** rotate to the right

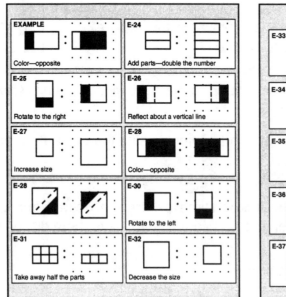

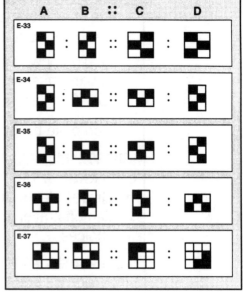

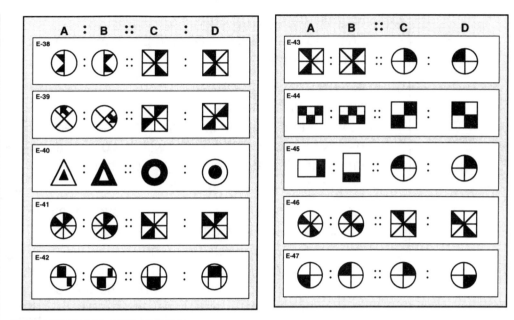

LESSON PREPARATION

OBJECTIVE AND MATERIALS
OBJECTIVE: Students will complete an analogy by shading or drawing the correct figure.
MATERIALS: Transparencies of student workbook pages 142 and 143 • optional transparency of student page 141 • washable transparency marker

CURRICULUM APPLICATIONS
LANGUAGE ARTS: Recognizing correct pronunciation of words by comparing letter patterns
MATHEMATICS: Doing geometry exercises involving similarity, congruence, rotation, or reflection; recognizing equivalent fractional parts; working with ratios; writing and recognizing arithmetic problems in pictorial form
SCIENCE: Seeing and stating relationships between different natural phenomena, animal or plant classes, or minerals and rocks; naming analogous body parts of different organisms; comparing and/or contrasting organisms or tissue types
SOCIAL STUDIES: Recognizing and stating the relationships between people and events, recognizing and stating causal relationships
ENRICHMENT AREAS: Learning new vocabulary in a foreign language; recognizing types of music by listening to the rhythm, e.g., march, rumba, waltz; drawing things to scale

TEACHING SUGGESTIONS
Encourage students to describe the markings and the relationships using the following terms learned in the section on Figural Sequences: *opposite, reflection* or *flip, rotation* or *turn, clockwise,* and *counterclockwise.* Student page 141 gives examples of types of figural analogies.

MODEL LESSON

LESSON

Introduction
Q: In previous exercises you selected the figure that completed the analogy.

Explaining the Objective to Students

Q: In these exercises you will complete analogies by shading or drawing the correct figure.

Class Activity

- Project the transparency of page 142.

    Q: Look at the example on page 142. The directions say to draw a similar figure with the opposite color. Notice the rectangle on the right has been drawn following these directions.

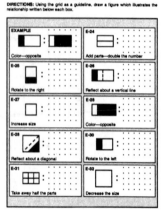

COMPLETE THE PAIR

DIRECTIONS: Using the grid as a guideline, draw a figure which illustrates the relationship written below each box.

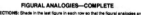

- Project the transparency of page 143 covering all but exercise **E-33**. Indicate figures A and B.

    Q: How are these figures the same?

    A: Possible answers are same shape, size, and direction; equal number of parts; shading of alternate parts.

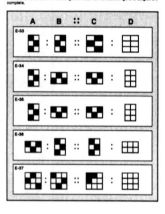

FIGURAL ANALOGIES—COMPLETE

DIRECTIONS: Shade in the last figure in each row so that the figural analogies are complete.

Q: How are they different?

A: The sections that are white on the first rectangle are black on the second. The sections that are black on the first rectangle are white on the second (color opposite).

Q: Are there other ways to explain how rectangles A and B are different?

A: Rectangle A has been flipped (reflected) about a vertical axis, or it has been rotated two positions.

Q: How should the fourth figure be shaded to show that the same relationship exists between figures C and D as between figures A and B?

A: The shaded sections should be opposite.

GUIDED PRACTICE

EXERCISES: **E-24**, **E-33** to **E-34**

- Give students sufficient time to complete these exercises. Then, using the demonstration methodology above, have them discuss and explain their choices.

INDEPENDENT PRACTICE

- Assign exercises **E-25** through **E-32**, and **E-35** through **E-47**

THINKING ABOUT THINKING

Q: What did you pay attention to when you completed the pair of figures?

1. I looked carefully at the details (size of the figure, position of the figure, pattern or color).

2. I looked at the first pair to see how the two figures were different (change of the size, pattern, or color).

3. I looked at the second pair to see if the two figures were different in the same way as the first pair.

4. I explained the relationship as an analogy: *a* is to *b* as *c* is to *d.*

PERSONAL APPLICATION

Q: When might you need to draw or supply something that has the same relationship as another pair or set?

A: Examples include repeating weaving or needlework patterns in different colors; matching clothing or linens; selecting proper hardware for construction projects; wood, metal, or leather working projects.

EXERCISES E-48 to E-70

FIGURAL ANALOGIES—SUPPLY

ANSWERS E-48 through E-70 — Student book pages 146–50
Guided Practice: E-48 to E-49 See below. **E-63** any reduction in size
Independent Practice: E-50 through E-62 See below and next page.
E-64 any clockwise rotation; **E-65** any reflection about the vertical; **E-66** any color reversal; **E-67** any reflection about a diagonal; **E-68** any increase in the number of parts in a 1 to 3 ratio; **E-69** any reflection about the horizontal; **E-70** any increase in size with color reversal

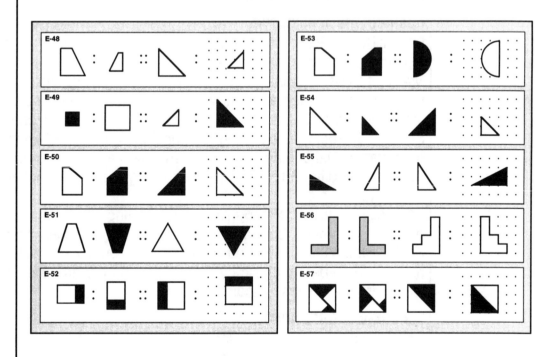

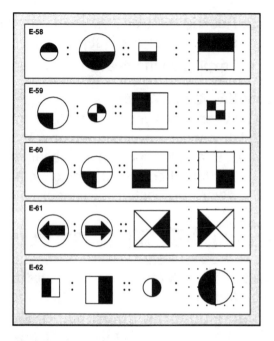

LESSON PREPARATION

OBJECTIVES AND MATERIALS

OBJECTIVE: Students will complete an analogy by drawing the correct figure or pair of figures.

MATERIALS: Transparencies of student workbook pages 146 and 149 • washable transparency marker

CURRICULUM APPLICATIONS

LANGUAGE ARTS: Recognizing correct pronunciation of words by comparing letter patterns

MATHEMATICS: Doing geometry exercises involving similarity, congruence, rotation, or reflection; recognizing equivalent fractional parts; working with ratios; writing and recognizing arithmetic problems in pictorial form

SCIENCE: Seeing and stating relationships between different natural phenomena, animal or plant classes, or minerals and rocks; naming analogous body parts of different organisms; comparing and/or contrasting organisms or tissue types

SOCIAL STUDIES: Recognizing and stating the relationships between people and events, recognizing and stating causal relationships

ENRICHMENT AREAS: Learning new vocabulary in a foreign language; recognizing types of music by listening to the rhythm, e.g., march, rumba, waltz; drawing things to scale

TEACHING SUGGESTIONS

Encourage students to describe the markings and the relationships using the following terms learned in the section on Figural Sequences: *opposite*, *reflection* or *flip*, *rotation* or *turn*, *clockwise*, and *counterclockwise*.

For exercises **E-63** through **E-70**, students will draw a pair of figures. Since many alternative are possible, this offers an opportunity for interesting discussions.

MODEL LESSON | **LESSON**

Introduction

Q: In previous exercises you completed an analogy by shading a figure.

Explaining the Objective to Students

Q: In these exercises you will draw a figure or pair of figures to complete an analogy.

Class Activity

- Project the transparency of student page 146. Q: Look at exercise **E-48** on page 146. The directions say to draw a figure that will complete the analogy. How are the first two figures the same

  A: Both figures are the same shape.

  Q: How are the two figures different?
  A: The second figure is reduced in size and reflects the first figure along the vertical axis.

  Q: Look at the third figure in the analogy. What figure should you draw next to show the same kind of relationship?
  A: A smaller right triangle that reflects the larger triangle about the vertical.

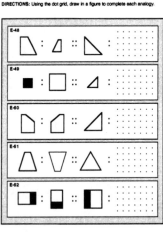

FIGURAL ANALOGIES—SUPPLY
DIRECTIONS: Using the dot grid, draw in a figure to complete each analogy.

- Project the transparency of student page 149. Q: Look at exercise **E-63** on page 149. In this activity, you will draw the last two figures to complete the analogy. How is the first pair of figures the same?
  A: They are both triangles.

  Q: How is the first pair of figures different?
  A: The second figure is smaller than the first figure.

  Q: What could you draw for the second pair of figures?
  A: Two figures of the same shape, such as two squares, two circles, etc.

  Q: How will the two figures be related?
  A: The second figure will be smaller than the first.

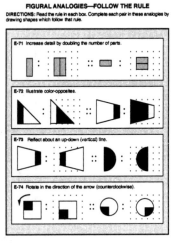

FIGURAL ANALOGIES—FOLLOW THE RULE
DIRECTIONS: Read the rule in each box. Complete each pair in these analogies by drawing shapes which follow that rule.

E-71 Increase detail by doubling the number of parts.

E-72 Illustrate color-opposites.

E-73 Reflect about an up-down (vertical) line.

E-74 Rotate in the direction of the arrow (counterclockwise).

- Draw two figures on the transparency to complete the analogy.

GUIDED PRACTICE
EXERCISES: **E-48, E-63**

INDEPENDENT PRACTICE

- Assign exercises **E-49** through **E-62**, and **E-64** through **E-70**.

THINKING ABOUT THINKING

Q: What did you pay attention to when you completed the pair of figures?

1. I looked carefully at the details (size of the figure, position of the figure, pattern or color).

2. I looked at the first pair to see how the two figures were different (change of the size, pattern, or color).

3. I drew a second pair of figures that were different in the same way as the first pair.

4. I explained the relationship as an analogy: *a* is to *b* as *c* is to *d*.

PERSONAL APPLICATION

Q: When might you need to draw or supply something that has the same relationship as another pair or set?

A: Examples include repeating weaving or needlework patterns in different colors; matching clothing or linens; selecting proper hardware for construction projects; wood, metal, or leather working projects.

EXERCISES E-71 to E-82

FIGURAL ANALOGIES—FOLLOW THE RULE

ANSWERS E-71 through E-82 — Student book pages 151–3
Guided Practice: E-71 to E-72 See below.
Independent Practice: E-73 through E-82 See below and next page.

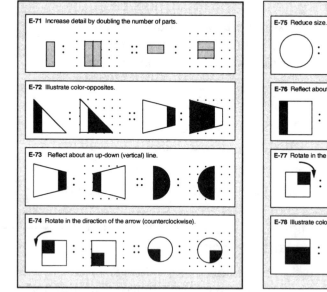

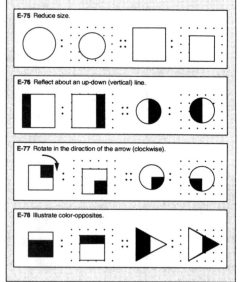

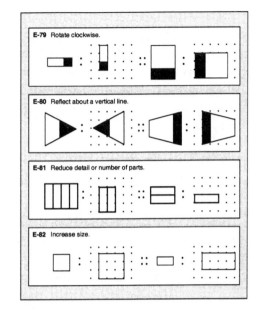

LESSON PREPARATION

OBJECTIVE AND MATERIALS
OBJECTIVE: Students will follow the written instructions for drawing a pair of figures to complete an analogy.
MATERIALS: Transparency of student workbook page 151 • Washable transparency marker

CURRICULUM APPLICATIONS
LANGUAGE ARTS: Changing formats of letters, outlines, or compositions
MATHEMATICS: Comparing angles or polygons, recognizing and illustrating changes in formats of mathematical problems
SCIENCE: Observing and describing analogous structures in plants and animals; observing and describing changes in weather patterns, cloud formations, etc.
SOCIAL STUDIES: Changing charts or graphs to reflect changed information
ENRICHMENT AREAS: Changing parts of art, home economics, or industrial art projects according to instructions; making or recognizing changes in pattern plays in sports.

TEACHING SUGGESTIONS
Encourage students to draw their analogies on the chalkboard or a transparency for class viewing and discussion.

MODEL LESSON

LESSON

Introduction
Q: In previous exercises you completed analogies by drawing one or two figures.

Explaining the Objective to Students
Q: In these exercises you will follow the written instructions for drawing two figures to complete each analogy.

Class Activity
• Project exercise **E-71** from the transparency of page 151.

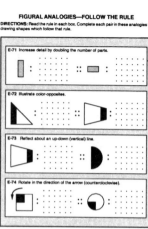

Q: The instructions say to double the number of parts to complete this analogy. Notice that only the first figure of each pair is given. What figure would complete the first part of the analogy?

    A: Students will probably reply that another section should be added beside the given figure.

• Draw the figure as directed by the students, then have them confirm that you followed the given rule.

Q: Now what figure should be drawn in the last grid to correctly complete the analogy?

    A: Students should guide your drawing and confirm by discussion that the analogy is correct and complete.

Q: Are there any other figures that would correctly complete this analogy?

    A: Students should recognize that the number of parts can be doubled by dividing the rectangles along any line of symmetry, i.e., vertically, horizontally, or diagonally.

NOTE: However the first figure is drawn, draw the second figure using the same method.

GUIDED PRACTICE
EXERCISES: **E-71**, **E-72**

• Give students sufficient time to complete these exercises. Then have them discuss and explain their choices and check their drawings.

INDEPENDENT PRACTICE
• Assign exercises **E-73** through **E-82**.

THINKING ABOUT THINKING
Q: What did you pay attention to when you drew the second figures?

1. I read the written instructions carefully.

2. I looked at the given figure for each pair.

3. I decided what figure would complete the first part of the analogy and drew it.

4. I then decided what figure to draw to complete the analogy.

5. I checked both figures to make sure they followed the instructions.

PERSONAL APPLICATION
Q: When might you need to provide drawings or items to reflect specific changes in an original?

    A: Examples include drawing or changing geometric shapes according to instructions; making directed changes in blueprints, drafting projects, or patterns.

Chapter 6

DESCRIBING THINGS
(Student book pages 156–83)

DESCRIBING THINGS—SELECT

ANSWERS F-1 through F-17 — Student book pages 156–61
Guided Practice: F-1A cucumber; **F-1B** zucchini; **F-2A** water; **F-2B** milk
Independent Practice: F-3A moose; **F-3B** elk; **F-4A** moth; **F-4B** wasp;
F-5A sea lion; **F-5B** walrus; **F-6A** moped; **F-6B** motorcycle; **F-7A** crane;
F-7B backhoe; **F-8A** all terrain vehicle; **F-8B** motocross bicycle; **F-9A** channel; **F-9B** canal; **F-10A** mesa; **F-10B** basin; **F-11A** isthmus; **F-11B** peninsula; **F-12A** dental hygienist; **F-12B** dental assistant; **F-13A** inhalation therapist; **F-13B** physical therapist; **F-14A** data clerk; **F-14B** computer engineer; **F-15A** computer memory; **F-15B** computer processing unit; **F-16A** modem; **F-16B** internet; **F-17A** Random Access Memory (RAM); **F-17B** Read Only Memory (ROM)

OBJECTIVE AND MATERIALS
OBJECTIVE: Students will match the description of an item with its name.
MATERIALS: Transparency of student book page 156 • washable transparency marker • large pictures of the food, animals, vehicles, buildings, and occupations featured in the lesson (optional)

CURRICULUM APPLICATIONS
LANGUAGE ARTS: Doing dictionary activities and vocabulary development, using precise words, doing reading comprehension activities using illustrations and context
MATHEMATICS: Matching terms with operations, recognizing sets
SCIENCE: Matching scientific terms with their descriptions; identifying types of plants, animals, etc.
SOCIAL STUDIES: Recognizing and matching topographic or geographic areas with their correct terms, identifying pictures of historical artifacts
ENRICHMENT AREAS: Identifying art styles, techniques, and artists' works; recognizing different types and periods in art and music

TEACHING SUGGESTIONS
Encourage students to discuss reasons for their choices and why the other items don't fit. The following cues model the discussion procedure demonstrated in the explanation and help students determine the correct answer.

1. Read the word choices.

2. Read the description.

3. If the description has more than one part, select the word that best matches all parts of the description.

4. Verify that no other word fits the description.

Note: This method simulates how to determine correct answers and eliminate incorrect answers on multiple choice tests.

MODEL LESSON | **LESSON**

Introduction

Q: In the figural exercises you sometimes selected or drew figures that were opposite in color or position to another figure.

Explaining the Objective to Students

Q: In this lesson you will match the description of something to its name.

Class Activity

- Project the directions and the example from the transparency of student book page 156.

  Q: This is a picture of page 156 in your book. The word choices are *corn, rice, and wheat.*

  Q: What do these words name?

  A: These words name seeds used to make breakfast cereals.

DESCRIBING FOODS—SELECT

DIRECTIONS: Each exercise contains the names of three foods, followed by descriptions of two of the words. Choose the word that fits each description and write it in the blank.

EXAMPLE

WORD CHOICES: corn, rice, wheat

A. We eat the seeds of this yellow vegetable. The seeds are protected by husks that grow on a tall stalk.   corn

B. We eat the seeds of this grain, which grows as a tall grass. The seeds are often ground into flour to make bread.   wheat

F-1 WORD CHOICES: cucumber, yellow squash, zucchini

A. This long, round, green, salad vegetable is often made into pickles.

B. This squash looks like a cucumber and is eaten boiled or fried.

F-2 WORD CHOICES: cucumber, yellow squash, zucchini

A. This liquid has no nutritional value, but we need to drink 6 to 8 glasses of it each day. It makes up most of our body.

B. This liquid is an important source of calcium to build strong teeth and bones. You can drink it or pour it on your cereal.

- Read Example A. The first part of the sentence says "We eat the seeds of this yellow vegetable."

  Q: Which of the choices names a yellow vegetable?

  A: Corn

  Q: Read the rest of the sentence, "The seeds are protected by husks that grow on stalks." Does this describe either rice or wheat?

  A: No, rice and wheat look like tall grass.

- Read Example B. The second part of the sentence gives the clue "The seeds are often ground into flour to make bread."

  Q: What food does this describe?

  A: Wheat

  Q: Why is rice not the answer?

  A: Wheat flour is used more in bread making than rice flour.

GUIDED PRACTICE

EXERCISE: **F-1** through **F-2B**

- When students have had sufficient time to complete these exercises, check answers by discussion to determine whether they have answered correctly. Discuss why the incorrect answers were eliminated.

INDEPENDENT PRACTICE

- Assign exercises **F-3** through **F-17**. Note: You may wish to make these exercises into more than one lesson.

THINKING ABOUT THINKING

Q: How did you match the word to the description?

1. I defined each of the words given.

2. I compared the differences in meaning between the words given.

3. I matched my definition of the word with the description in the activity.

PERSONAL APPLICATION
Q: When do you need to match a word to a description?
A: Examples include solving word puzzles, reading directions, and understanding someone's description of an experience.

**EXERCISES
F-18 to F-25**

IDENTIFYING CHARACTERISTICS

ANSWERS F-18 through F-25 — Student book pages 162–5
Guided Practice: F-18 Students may list the four following characteristics of a pizza: flat, round bread base; covered with tomato sauce; covered with cheese; covered with a variety of other ingredients. **F-19** Students may list any four of the following characteristics of butter: yellow in color, a dairy product, made by stirring milk, is the butterfat found in milk, is made into sticks, is sold by grocers.
Independent Practice: F-20 Students may list any four of the following characteristics of an owl: large bird, large head, flat face, forward-directed eyes, hooked beak, sharp claws, soft feathers. **F-21** Students may list any four of the following characteristics of a lizard: reptile, rough skin, four legs, tail, lives in dry regions, hatches from an egg. **F-22** Students may list the four following characteristics of an ambulance: emergency vehicle, takes an injured or sick person to the hospital, has a bed inside, has other emergency medical equipment. **F-23** Students may list the four following characteristics of a tug boat: small boat, maneuverable, has strong engines, assists larger ships in and out of harbors. **F-24** Students may list the four following characteristics of a volcano: a mountain, central core that leads to the molten part of the earth, can erupt, lava spills out. **F-25** Students may list the four following characteristics of a glacier: large mass of compressed ice and snow, weight causes it to move slowly, carries along rocks and sediments, varies in size from a half mile to more than the size of the United States.

**LESSON
PREPARATION**

OBJECTIVE AND MATERIALS
OBJECTIVE: Students read descriptions and list the characteristics of the thing being described.
MATERIALS: • Transparency of page 162 • washable marker • (optional) large pictures of the items featured in the lesson • transparency of TM 32 (optional)

CURRICULUM APPLICATIONS
LANGUAGE ARTS: Writing descriptive sentences and paragraphs, doing vocabulary enrichment activities, using precise words
MATHEMATICS: Writing and solving word problems
SCIENCE: Defining scientific terms and processes; explaining the results of an experiment; describing and classifying animals, plants, etc.
SOCIAL STUDIES: Describing historical figures and events, identifying topographic and geographic areas
ENRICHMENT AREAS: Describing works of art and music

TEACHING SUGGESTIONS

Read a description and ask students to list the characteristics they heard. Whenever possible, we recommend using actual objects; however, pictures usually offer sufficient detail, even for students with limited backgrounds. A blank web transparency (TM 32) is included with the Transparency Masters and can be used for further practice.

MODEL LESSON

LESSON

Introduction

Q: You have matched words with their descriptions.

Explaining the Objective to Students

Q: In this lesson you will read descriptions and then list the important characteristics of the thing being described.

Class Activity

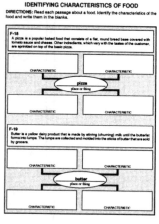

* Project **F-18** from the transparency of page 162.

* Ask a student to read the description of a pizza. Ask students to tell the characteristics of a pizza.

* Write the student responses on the transparency.

GUIDED PRACTICE

EXERCISES: **F-18** and **F-19**

INDEPENDENT PRACTICE

* Assign exercises **F-20** through **F-25**.

THINKING ABOUT THINKING

Q: What did you pay attention to as you read the description?

1. I looked for the main characteristics (size, shape, color, etc.) of the item.

2. I wrote each characteristic in the boxes provided.

PERSONAL APPLICATION

Q: When do you need to mention the important characteristics of something you have read?

A: Examples include giving directions for going somewhere or making something; following directions that are given in pictures or diagrams; describing a gift, person, book, movie, or experience.

**EXERCISES
F-26 to F-40**

DESCRIBING THINGS—EXPLAIN

ANSWERS F-26 through F-40 — Student book pages 166–70
Guided Practice: F-26 rice: This grassy plant requires a steady supply of water. It is often planted in swampy soil. People eat the seeds of this plant. Rice that has been milled to remove its outer hull is white. Brown rice retains the outer bran layer and has more nutrient value and flavor, but takes longer to cook. The world rice crop feeds more people than the wheat crop. Rice is eaten boiled. or as a component of breakfast cereals or rice

cakes. **F-27 lettuce:** This green-leaved plant is the most popular of all salad crops. It grows close to the ground. The most popular lettuce is the iceberg head lettuce. Other varieties include Boston lettuce and romaine. **Independent Practice: F-28 strawberry:** This low-growing perennial plant has red fruit that is eaten fresh or used to make jelly, pies, cakes, or ice cream flavoring. **F-29 turtle:** This hard-shelled reptile lives in tropical or temperate zones in land, freshwater, and marine habitats. Turtles range in size from 4 inches to 8 feet. Turtles can retract their heads and four legs into their shells for protection. Since turtle eggs and meat provide food for people and other animals, some freshwater turtles are near extinction. **F-30 clam:** Clams are a large group of often edible, mostly marine, bivalve mollusks. They are closely related to the oyster, scallop, and mussel. The body of the clam consists of two symmetrical shells held closed by two large muscles. They have large gills that serve as food collectors. **F-31 hamster:** This rodent ranges in size from 2.5 to 11 inches long. They have long, soft, dark or yellowish fur, and short tails. Cheek pouches are used for storing food. Golden hamsters are frequently kept as pets. **F-32 pickup truck:** This small, motorized, four-wheeled vehicle has a flat surface in the rear that is used to carry cargo. They are often used by craftsmen to carry their tools, paint, and building materials. They are used for recreation as well as work. **F-33 ferry boat:** A large boat that carries passengers, automobiles, trucks, and buses across stretches of water that are difficult to bridge. **F-34 helicopter:** This versatile aircraft has blades which rotate above it and permit it to take off or land almost straight up or down. It is capable of hovering motionless. This versatile vehicle can be used to quickly airlift injured people to hospitals. They are also used for traffic patrol, crop dusting, sight-seeing, and military purposes. **F-35 tributary:** A stream that flows into a larger river. **F-36 plateau:** An uplifted area of fairly level land. With continued erosion by rivers, a plateau may leave large uneroded tracts (mesas) or smaller isolated hills (buttes). **F-37 equator:** An imaginary line around the center of the earth that divides the northern hemisphere from the southern hemisphere. **F-38 pilot:** Pilots fly airplanes or helicopters. Their aircraft carry passengers or cargo. Their flight may be to a nearby city or to a distance place. Pilots work hard to earn their pilot's license. There are many kinds of pilots – instructors, test pilots, commercial airline pilots, pilots who own private planes, agricultural pilots, and pilots who fly planes owned by a company to take their employes where they are needed. **F-39 physician:** A physician, or doctor, is a well-trained professional who finds out the cause of an illness and treats it with diet, medicine, and rest. Physicians also fix broken bones, and repair or remove diseased or damaged organs. The first person to see for health care is a family practice physician who can diagnose most illnesses. If the illness or injury is complex, the doctor will refer the patient to a specialist who deals with specific parts of the body. **F-40 architect:** This trained professional combines art and engineering to design buildings. An architect works with engineers and builders to see that the designed buildings are constructed properly. An architect goes to college for many years before she/he is licensed.

LESSON PREPARATION

OBJECTIVE AND MATERIALS
OBJECTIVE: Students write a descriptions of things.
MATERIALS: Transparency of student workbook page 166 • washable marker • (optional) large pictures of the items featured in the lesson

CURRICULUM APPLICATIONS
LANGUAGE ARTS: Writing descriptive sentences and paragraphs, doing vocabulary enrichment activities, using precise words
MATHEMATICS: Writing and solving word problems.
SCIENCE: Defining scientific terms and processes; explaining the results of an experiment; describing and classifying animals, plants, etc.
SOCIAL STUDIES: Describing historical figures and events, identifying topographic and geographic areas
ENRICHMENT AREAS: Describing works of art and music

TEACHING SUGGESTIONS
Ask students to describe a family member and list the types of characteristics that students mention (age, gender, relationships to other members of the family, roles, feelings about them, interests or experiences that make them special). Students may use these characteristics to develop a story.

Ask students to describe a job and list the types of characteristics that students mention (specific tools or skills required, goods or services provided and what consumer seeks these goods or services, work location, training, and how the person spends his/her time). Emphasize the tasks that a person having this job carries out.

Whenever possible, we recommend using actual objects; however, pictures usually offer sufficient detail even for students with limited backgrounds. Encourage students to discuss their descriptions and why a description is or is not accurate. The suggested answers should be modified to fit the vocabulary level and needs of students. Remember the language that students use to describe food, animals, etc. Use the same words to remind students of the key characteristics of objects or people in this lesson and subsequent ones.

MODEL LESSON

LESSON

Introduction
  Q: You have matched words with their descriptions.

Explaining the Objective to Students
  Q: In this lesson you will write descriptions.

Class Activity
• Point to exercise **F-26** on the transparency.
  Q: How can we describe rice?
    A: Class discussion will result in a number of responses: color, size,

shape, uses, how it is grown, etc. Students may recognize that we eat the long seeds of the grasslike plant.

- After class discussion write the consensus description on the transparency.

GUIDED PRACTICE
EXERCISE: **F-26** and **F-27**

INDEPENDENT PRACTICE
- Assign exercises **F-28** through **F-40**.

THINKING ABOUT THINKING
Q: What did you pay attention to when you wrote the description?

1. I thought of common characteristics to identify the item.

2. I thought of specific characteristics that were unique to the item.

3. I wrote as accurate a description as possible.

PERSONAL APPLICATION
Q: When do you need to describe something?

A: Examples include giving directions for going somewhere or making something, following directions that are given in pictures or diagrams; describing a gift, person, book, movie, or experience.

EXERCISES F-41 to F-58

NAMING THINGS—SUPPLY

ANSWERS F-41 through F-58 — Student book pages 171–3
Guided Practice: F-41 mule; **F-42** toad; **F-43** gorilla
Independent Practice: F-44 snake; **F-45** crocodile; **F-46** ostrich; **F-47** cantaloupe or muskmelon; **F-48** tangerine; **F-49** cactus; **F-50** cabbage; **F-51** palm; **F-52** pine; **F-53** monorail; **F-54** helicopter; **F-55** bus; **F-56** marsh; **F-57** island, lake; **F-58** delta

LESSON PREPARATION

OBJECTIVE AND MATERIALS
OBJECTIVE: Students will supply the word that is described.
MATERIALS: • transparency of student workbook page 171

CURRICULUM APPLICATIONS
LANGUAGE ARTS: Doing vocabulary enrichment activities, using precise words, writing comparison paragraphs
MATHEMATICS: Analyzing and solving word problems, recognizing sets
SCIENCE: Identifying processes, types of animals, plants, etc.
SOCIAL STUDIES: Comparing topographic or geographic areas.
ENRICHMENT AREAS: Writing or giving directions for creating dance movements or art projects; comparing two pieces of music, two works of art, two dances, or two athletic activities

TEACHING SUGGESTIONS
For exercise **F-51** students may not know that palm oil is used to make soap. Palmolive, a brand of soap, was named for its ingredients.

Remember the language that students use in their descriptions. Use the same words to remind students of the key characteristics of objects in this lesson and subsequent ones. When students have had sufficient time to complete the guided exercises, check descriptions by discussion to help improve their description skills.

MODEL LESSON

LESSON

Introduction

Q: In the last exercises you wrote descriptions.

Explaining the Objective to Students

Q: In this lesson you will read a description and supply the answer from your own knowledge of animals.

Class Activity

• Project the transparency of student book page 171.

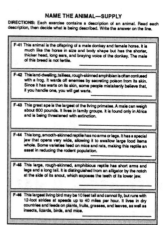

Q: Read **F-41**. What animal is like both a donkey and a horse?
  A: A mule

Q: Read **F-42**. What animal has warts and is similar to a frog?
  A: A toad

Q: Read **F-43**. What is the largest ape?
  A: A gorilla

GUIDED PRACTICE
EXERCISES: **F-41** through **F-43**

INDEPENDENT PRACTICE

• Assign exercises **F-44** through **F-58**. Note: You may wish to divide this into two or three lessons.

THINKING ABOUT THINKING

Q: How did you remember the word that fits the description?
1. I looked for clues in the description.
2. I searched my memory for a word that fit <u>all</u> the clues.
3. If I didn't know the answer, I looked up the clue words in references.

PERSONAL APPLICATION

Q: When do you need to find a word that matches a description?
  A: Examples include solving word puzzles, reading directions, and understanding someone's description of an experience.

EXERCISES F-59 to F-61

WRITING DESCRIPTIONS: Describing an Object

ANSWERS F-59 through F-61 — Student book pages 174–7
Guided Practice: F-59 See next page for sample answers.
Independent Practice: F-60 and **F-61** See diagrams on next page.

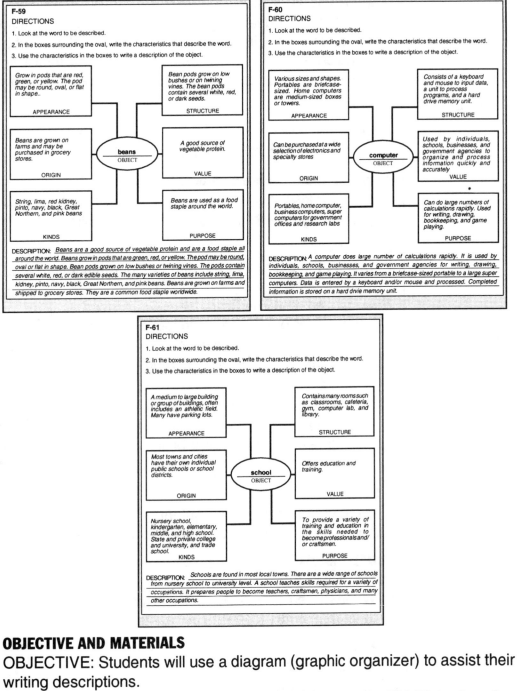

F-59
DIRECTIONS

1. Look at the word to be described.

2. In the boxes surrounding the oval, write the characteristics that describe the word.

3. Use the characteristics in the boxes to write a description of the object.

Grow in pods that are red, green, or yellow. The pod may be round, oval, or flat in shape.. — APPEARANCE

Bean pods grow on low bushes or on twining vines. The bean pods contain several white, red, or dark seeds. — STRUCTURE

Beans are grown on farms and may be purchased in grocery stores. — ORIGIN

beans OBJECT

A good source of vegetable protein. — VALUE

String, lima, red kidney, pinto, navy, black, Great Northern, and pink beans — KINDS

Beans are used as a food staple around the world. — PURPOSE

DESCRIPTION: Beans are a good source of vegetable protein and are a food staple all around the world. Beans grow in pods that are green, red, or yellow. The pod may be round, oval or flat in shape. Bean pods grow on low bushes or twining vines. The pods contain several white, red, or dark edible seeds. The many varieties of beans include string, lima, kidney, pinto, navy, black, Great Northern, and pink beans. Beans are grown on farms and shipped to grocery stores. They are a common food staple worldwide.

F-60
DIRECTIONS

1. Look at the word to be described.

2. In the boxes surrounding the oval, write the characteristics that describe the word.

3. Use the characteristics in the boxes to write a description of the object.

Various sizes and shapes. Portables are briefcase-sized. Home computers are medium-sized boxes or towers. — APPEARANCE

Consists of a keyboard and mouse to input data, a unit to process programs, and a hard drive memory unit. — STRUCTURE

Can be purchased at a wide selection of electronics and specialty stores — ORIGIN

computer OBJECT

Used by individuals, schools, businesses, and government agencies to organize and process information quickly and accurately — VALUE

Portables, home computer, business computers, super computers for government offices and research labs — KINDS

Can do large numbers of calculations rapidly. Used for writing, drawing, bookkeeping, and game playing. — PURPOSE

DESCRIPTION: A computer does large number of calculations rapidly. It is used by individuals, schools, businesses, and government agencies for writing, drawing, bookkeeping, and game playing. It varies from a briefcase-sized portable to a large super computers. Data is entered by a keyboard and/or mouse and processed. Completed information is stored on a hard drive memory unit.

F-61
DIRECTIONS

1. Look at the word to be described.

2. In the boxes surrounding the oval, write the characteristics that describe the word.

3. Use the characteristics in the boxes to write a description of the object.

A medium to large building or group of buildings, often includes an athletic field. Many have parking lots. — APPEARANCE

Contains many rooms such as classrooms, cafeteria, gym, computer lab, and library. — STRUCTURE

Most towns and cities have their own individual public schools or school districts. — ORIGIN

school OBJECT

Offers education and training. — VALUE

Nursery school, kindergarten, elementary, middle, and high school. State and private college and university, and trade school. — KINDS

To provide a variety of training and education in the skills needed to become professionals and/or craftsmen. — PURPOSE

DESCRIPTION: Schools are found in most local towns. There are a wide range of schools from nursery school to university level. A school teaches skills required for a variety of occupations. It prepares people to become teachers, craftsmen, physicians, and many other occupations.

LESSON PREPARATION

OBJECTIVE AND MATERIALS

OBJECTIVE: Students will use a diagram (graphic organizer) to assist their writing descriptions.

MATERIALS: Transparency of student book page 174 • TM 32 (optional)

CURRICULUM APPLICATIONS

LANGUAGE ARTS: Doing reading comprehension exercises and vocabulary enrichment activities

MATHEMATICS: Matching terms and operations, analyzing and solving word problems, recognizing sets and set complements

SCIENCE: Recognizing scientific processes; identifying categories of plants, animals, etc.

SOCIAL STUDIES: Identifying topographic or geographic areas, and historical events and periods

ENRICHMENT AREAS: Identifying types of art or music, periods in art , etc.

TEACHING SUGGESTIONS

Remember the language that students use in their descriptions. Use the same words to remind students of the key characteristics of objects in this lesson and subsequent ones. If students need additional instruction or practice, use a transparency or photocopies of TM 32 to create your own lessons.

MODEL LESSON

LESSON

Introduction

Q: You have practiced writing descriptions.

Explaining the Objective to Students

Q: In this lesson you will use a diagram (a *graphic organizer*) to help guide your thoughts about the description you will write.

Class Activity

*   Project the example from the transparency of student page 174.

    Q: Notice that the word being described is written in the oval. Look at the four boxes on the arms. How are they labeled?

    A: Appearance, Structure, Kinds, and Purpose.

    Q: Give a definition for each of the words.

    A Appearance—how something looks; structure—how something is built, what its parts are; kinds—different types; purpose—how or why is it used

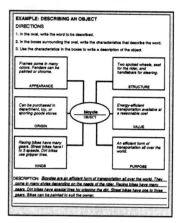

*   Have students read the contents of each box and then ask students to notice how the parts fit into the whole description.

GUIDED PRACTICE

EXERCISES: **F-59**

*   When students have had sufficient time to complete this exercise, ask them to share their descriptions of *beans*.

INDEPENDENT PRACTICE

*   Assign exercises **F-60** and **F-61**.

THINKING ABOUT THINKING

Q: What did you pay attention to as you completed the diagram?

A: I gave my attention to one feature at a time instead of thinking about the total description.

PERSONAL APPLICATION

Q: When do you need to give complete descriptions?

A: Giving directions for going somewhere or making something, following directions that are given in pictures or diagrams; describing a gift, person, book, movie, or experience.

**EXERCISES
F-62 to F-64**

WRITING DESCRIPTIONS: Describing an Event

ANSWERS F-62 through F-64 — Student book pages 178–81
Guided Practice: F-62 See examples below.
Independent Practice: F-63 and **F-64** See examples below.

F-62
DIRECTIONS
1. In the oval, write the event to be described.
2. In each box, write the information requested.
3. Use the information to write a description of the event.

102 Pilgrims aboard the ship Mayflower. Myles Standish and John Alden were among the passengers.
WHO

To bring the Pilgrims to America. They had separated from the Church of England and wished to establish a new church.
WHY

65 days from September 16, 1620 to December 21, 1620.
WHEN

Voyage of the Mayflower
EVENT

A group of English merchants, the Plymouth Company, sponsored the Pilgrims.
HOW

From Southampton, England to Plymouth, Massachusetts.
WHERE

Wrote the Mayflower Compact, the first laws establishing a government of and by the people in America.
SIGNIFICANCE

DESCRIPTION: *On September 16, 1620 the Mayflower left Southampton, England with 102 Pilgrams. The Pilgrims had separated from the Church of England and wished to establish a new church. Sixty-five days later, on December 21, 1610, they landed at Plymouth, Massachusetts. The Pilgrims drafted the Mayflower Compact, the first American laws based on government of and by the people.*

F-63
DIRECTIONS
1. In the oval, write the event to be described.
2. In each box, write the information requested.
3. Use the information to write a description of the event.

The Continental Congress approved the Declaration. Written mainly by Thomas Jefferson. All 56 members of Congress signed it.
WHO

To declare the independence of the 13 colonies from Great Britain.
WHY

Declaration approved by Continental Congress on July 4, 1776. Formal signing began August 2, 1776.
WHEN

The Signing of the Declaration of Independence
EVENT

TheCongress charged Thomas Jefferson to write the Declaration.
HOW

Independence Hall in Philadelphia, Pennsylvania.
WHERE

Led to the Revolutionary War against Britain and united the colonies into one nation.
SIGNIFICANCE

DESCRIPTION: *The Continental Congress approved the Declaration of Independence on July 4, 1776 in Philadelphia, Pennsylvania. It declared that the 13 colonies were independent from Great Britain, which led to the Revolutionary War.*

F-64
DIRECTIONS
1. In the oval, write the event to be described.
2. In each box, write the information requested.
3. Use the information to write a description of the event.

Northern states and Southern states
WHO

Southerners wanted less government control over their lives, especially in regards to slavery.
WHY

1861–1865
WHEN

The United States is divided by Civil War
EVENT

Most battles were fought on land.
HOW

Most battles were fought in the Southern states, in Virginia and west. One famous exception was the battle at Gettysburg, Pennsylvania.
WHERE

The Northern victory ended slavery.
SIGNIFICANCE

DESCRIPTION: *From 1861 to 1865, the United States was divided by civil war. The Northern and Southern states fought one another. Southerners wanted less control by the government, particularly in regards to slavery. Slavery was ended when the Northerners won the war.*

LESSON PREPARATION

OBJECTIVE AND MATERIALS
OBJECTIVE: Students will use a diagram (graphic organizer) to assist their writing descriptions of events.
MATERIALS: Transparency of student book page 178.

CURRICULUM APPLICATIONS
LANGUAGE ARTS: Doing reading comprehension and vocabulary enrichment activities

MATHEMATICS: Matching terms and operations, analyzing and solving word problems, recognizing sets and set complements
SCIENCE: Recognizing scientific processes; identifying categories of plants, animals, etc.
SOCIAL STUDIES: Identifying topographic or geographic areas and historical events and periods
ENRICHMENT AREAS: Identifying types of art or music, periods in art history, etc.

TEACHING SUGGESTIONS
Remember the language that students use in their descriptions. Use the same words to remind students of the key characteristics of objects in this lesson and subsequent ones.

MODEL LESSON

LESSON

Introduction
Q: You have used diagrams to help organize your thoughts when writing descriptions.

Explaining the Objective to Students
Q: In this lesson you will use a diagram (a *graphic organizer*) to help guide your thoughts about an event you will describe.

Class Activity
- Project the example from the transparency of student page 178.
Q: Notice that the event being described is written in the oval. Look at the four boxes. How are they labeled?
   A: Who, where, when, and why

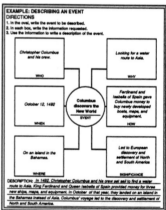

- Have students read the contents of each of the boxes and then ask students to notice how the parts fit into the whole description.

GUIDED PRACTICE
EXERCISES: **F-62**
- When students have had sufficient time to complete these exercises, ask them to share their descriptions of the voyage of the *Mayflower*.

INDEPENDENT PRACTICE
- Assign exercises **F-63** and **F-64**.

THINKING ABOUT THINKING
Q: What did you pay attention to as you completed the diagram?
   1. I gave my attention to one feature at a time instead of thinking about the total description.
   2. I combined the information in the features to write a description.

PERSONAL APPLICATION

Q: When do you need to give complete descriptions of an event?
A: Reporting on an accident you witnessed, describing a gift, person, book, movie, or experience.

EXTENSION ACTIVITY (Optional)

• Use student book pages 182–3.

The blank graphic organizers shown below are for students to use to prepare special projects or reports. These extended diagrams allow for greater detail. Students fill in all three diagrams before writing a description.

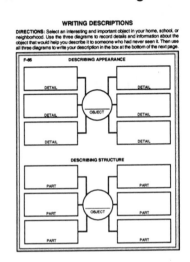

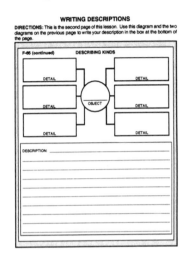

Chapter 7

VERBAL SIMILARITIES AND DIFFERENCES
(Student book pages 186–215)

OPPOSITES—SELECT

> **ANSWERS G-1 through G-36 — Student book pages 186–8**
> **Guided Practice:** G-1 c; G-2 a; G-3 a; G-4 c
> **Independent Practice:** G-5 c; G-6 a; G-7 c; G-8 c; G-9 b; G-10 c; G-11 a; G-12 c; G-13 b; G-14 c; G-15 b; G-16 b; G-17 c; G-18 a; G-19 c; G-20 c; G-21 a; G-22 b; G-23 c; G-24 c; G-25 c; G-26 a; G-27 a; G-28 c; G-29 b; G-30 c; G-31 c; G-32 a; G-33 c; G-34 b; G-35 c; G-36 b

DETAILED SOLUTIONS

NOTE: The key definition and its opposite are underlined throughout this section. The four words in each exercise are italicized.

G-1 c; *Play* means to do something for fun. Look for a word that means to do something that is not primarily for fun. *Work* means to labor and is not always fun. *Amuse* and *entertain* both mean to enjoy oneself. **G-2** a; *Allow* means to let an action occur. Look for a word that means to prevent an action. *Deny* means to refuse something. *Let* and *permit* both mean to allow. **G-3** a; *Mend* means to fix or repair. Look for a word that means to damage or destroy. *Break* means to crack or shatter into pieces. *Correct* and *patch* refer to fixing or repairing. **G-4** c; *Save* means to keep or put aside for later use. Look for a word that means to use or not put aside. *Spend* means to use something. *Collect* means to accumulate, as for a hobby. *Store* means to keep for future use. **G-5** c; *Harm* means to injure. Look for a word that means to heal or help. *Benefit* means to help or aid. *Damage* means to break or impair. *Hurt* means to injure. **G-6** a; *Doubt* means to question the truth of something. Look for a word that means to accept as true. *Believe* means to accept the truth of something. *Challenge* means to demand an explanation. *Question* means to inquire. **G-7** c; *Reduce* means to make smaller in size. Look for a word that means to make larger in size. *Increase* means to make larger. *Cut* and *diminish* mean to make smaller. **G-8** c; *Conclude* means to end. Look for a word that means to begin. *Open* means to begin, e.g., the play opened. *Close* and *finish* mean to end. **G-9** b; *Approach* means to come toward. Look for a word that means to go away. *Leave* means to go away. *Arrive* and *reach* mean to attain a goal or objective. **G-10** c; *Escape* means to run away. Look for a word that means to come back. *Return* means to come back. *Depart* and *flee* mean to leave or run away. **G-11** a; *Reject* means to refuse or disagree. Look for a word that means to take or agree. *Accept* means to approve or to take without protest. *Dismiss* means to reject from consideration. *Overlook* means to miss or neglect. **G-12** c; *Overlook* means to pass over or neglect. Look for a word that means to select or notice. *Choose* means to select or accept. *Miss* and *ignore* mean to pass over. **G-13** b; *Neat* means tidy or in order. Look for a word that means untidy or out of order. *Messy* means disorderly or untidy.

Clean and *orderly* both mean tidy or in order. **G-14** c; *Tight* means <u>securely fixed or held together</u>. Look for a word that means <u>not securely fixed, or unattached</u>. *Loose* means not securely fixed. *Close* means having little or no space between, as close fitting. *Firm* means securely fixed or held together. **G-15** b; *Rude* means <u>having bad manners</u>. Look for a word that means <u>having good manners</u>. *Polite* means having good manners. *Discourteous* means rude. *Vulgar* means lacking taste or manners. **G-16** b; *Timid* means <u>fearful or shy</u>. Look for a word that means <u>fearless</u>. *Bold* means fearless. *Bashful* and *shy* mean the same as timid. **G-17** c; *Familiar* means <u>well-known</u>. Look for a word that means <u>unknown</u>. *Strange* means unknown or different. *Common* means ordinary or plentiful. *Known* means familiar. **G-18** a; *Plain* means <u>undecorated or without ornamentation</u>. Look for a word that means <u>decorated or adorned</u>. *Fancy* means decorated. *Ordinary* and *simple* mean common or plain. **G-19** c; *Public* means <u>open to all people</u>. Look for a word that means <u>closed to some people</u>. *Private* means open to members only. *Free* means costing nothing or publicly supported. *Open* means accessible to all. **G-20** c; *Sharp* means <u>keen or intelligent</u>. Look for a word that means <u>not intelligent</u>. *Slow* can mean unintelligent. *Alert* means observant. *Bright* can mean intelligent. **G-21** a; *Honest* means <u>truthful</u>. Look for a word that means <u>dishonest</u>. *Unethical* means dishonest. *Lawful* and *truthful* both mean honest. **G-22** b; *Diverse* means <u>varied</u>. Look for a word that means <u>same</u>. *Identical* means same. *Different* and *varied* are synonyms for diverse. **G-23** c; *Lively* means <u>full of energy and spirit</u>. Look for a word that means <u>lacking energy</u>. *Sluggish* means lacking energy. *Alert* and *bright* are synonyms for lively. **G-24** c; *Worthless* means <u>without value</u>. Look for a word that means <u>having value or importance</u>. *Valuable* means having value. *Useless* means having little use or worth. *Trivial* means unimportant. **G-25** c; *Accidentally* means <u>unplanned</u>. Look for a word that means <u>planned</u>. *Purposefully* means with purpose. *Randomly* means without plan. *Incidentally* means occurring unpredictably. **G-26** a; *Afterward* means <u>happening at a later time</u>. Look for a word that means <u>happening at an earlier time</u>. *Before* means happening prior to. *Later* and *next* mean to happen at a subsequent time. **G-27** a; *Barely* means <u>not quite enough</u>. Look for a word that means <u>more than enough</u>. *Amply* means more than enough. *Hardly* and *scarcely* mean not quite enough. **G-28** c; *Maybe* means <u>perhaps</u>. Look for a word that means <u>definitely</u>. *Surely* means for sure. *Perhaps* and *possibly* are synonyms of maybe. **G-29** b; *Deeply* means <u>to a great depth</u>. Look for a word that means <u>shallowly or barely</u>. *Hardly* means to a shallow depth or barely. *Intensely* means deeply felt. *Greatly* means to a large extent. **G-30** c; *Concisely* means <u>briefly and to the point</u>. Look for a word that means <u>lengthily</u>. *Wordily* means spoken or written with more words than necessary. *Accurately* and *briefly* mean to the point. **G-31** c; *Gradually* means <u>to happen over a period of time</u>. Look for a word that means <u>to happen now or at once</u>. *Suddenly* means to happen unexpectedly. *Slowly* and *eventually* mean to happen over a long period of time. **G-32** a; *Capably* means <u>ably or well-done</u>. Look for a word that means <u>poorly done</u>. *Incompetently* means <u>badly done</u>. *Exceptionally* and *superbly* mean well-done. **G-33** c; *Eternally* means <u>never-ending</u>. Look for a word that means <u>rarely happening</u>. *Seldom* means not often, rarely. *Always* and *forever* are synonyms of eternally. **G-34** b; *Onward* means <u>toward the front</u>. Look for a word that means <u>toward the rear</u>. *Backward* is the opposite of onward. *Ahead* and *forward* are similar to onward. **G-35** c; *Mightily* means <u>powerfully</u>. Look for a word that means <u>with little power</u>. *Weakly* means with little power. *Forcefully* and *strongly* mean with strength and power. **G-36** b; *Rarely* means <u>not happening frequently</u>. Look for a word that means <u>happening frequently</u>. *Often* means happening frequently. *Infrequently* and *seldom* mean happening occasionally or infrequently.

LESSON PREPARATION

OBJECTIVE AND MATERIALS

OBJECTIVE: Students will select a word that means the opposite of a given word.

MATERIALS: Transparencies of student workbook pages 151 and 186 • washable transparency marker

CURRICULUM APPLICATIONS

LANGUAGE ARTS: Doing vocabulary enrichment activities and antonym exercises, using precise words, writing contrastive paragraphs, describing contrasting characteristics in a work of literature, debating or expressing an opposite opinion

MATHEMATICS: Recognizing and using inverse operations; using fractions and reciprocals; recognizing set and set complements; checking basic arithmetic problems by reversing the process, e.g., checking subtraction by addition

SCIENCE: Recognizing reversed processes in simple experiments, describing differences between two objects or concepts, disassembling and reassembling motors or models

SOCIAL STUDIES: Contrasting topographic or geographic areas, locating and expressing contrasting details between two or more topics

ENRICHMENT AREAS: Writing or giving directions for creating dance movements or art projects; expressing the differences between two pieces of music, two works of art, two dances, or two athletic activities

TEACHING SUGGESTIONS

Encourage students to discuss reasons for their choices and why the other words are incorrect. Remember the words that students use to describe their choices and use those same words to remind students of the key characteristics of objects or people in this lesson and subsequent ones. The definitions should be tailored to the vocabulary level and needs of the students. Use the cues provided below to encourage the discussion procedure demonstrated in the lesson.

1. Recognize/pronounce word.

2. Define word.

3. Define opposite word.

4. Select opposite (answer).

5. Eliminate detractors (confirmation).

MODEL LESSON | LESSON

Introduction

- Project the transparency of page 151.
  Q: In the figural analogy exercises you selected or drew figures that had the opposite position or the opposite color. In exercise **E-72**, you illustrated opposite color. In exercise **E-73**, you illustrated opposite position.

Explaining the Objective to Students

Q: In these exercises you will select a word that means the opposite of a given word.

Class Activity

- Project exercise **G-1** from the transparency of student page 186.
  Q: You will look for the word that is most unlike the given word. After you have selected a word, check the other words to confirm that they are not opposites. In exercise **G-1,** you are given the word *play* and three words that might be opposite to *play*. *Play* means to do something for fun. Look for a word that means to do something which is not primarily for fun.

- Point to item *c*.
  Q: *Work* means to labor and is not always fun.

- Point to items *a* and *b*.
  Q: *Amuse* is not an opposite because it means to keep busy with something enjoyable. *Entertain* is not an opposite because it also means to amuse. *Work* is the word most unlike *play* and should be underlined.

- Underline the word "work."

GUIDED PRACTICE

EXERCISES: **G-1** through **G-4**

- Give students sufficient time to complete these exercises. Then, using the method demonstrated above, have them discuss and explain their choices.

INDEPENDENT PRACTICE

- Assign exercises **G-5** through **G-36**.

THINKING ABOUT THINKING

Q: What did you pay attention to in order to find a word with the opposite meaning?

1. I thought about what the first word meant.

2. I looked for another word that had an opposite meaning.

3. I substituted this word for the given word to check whether the words had opposite meanings.

4. I read the other words to see why they did not have opposite meanings.

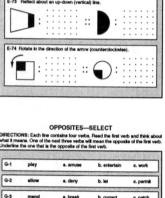

FIGURAL ANALOGIES—FOLLOW THE RULE
DIRECTIONS: Read the rule in each box. Complete each pair in these analogies by drawing shapes which follow that rule.

E-71 Increase detail by doubling the number of parts.

E-72 Illustrate color-opposites.

E-73 Reflect about an up-down (vertical) line.

E-74 Rotate in the direction of the arrow (counterclockwise).

OPPOSITES—SELECT
DIRECTIONS: Each line contains four verbs. Read the first verb and think about what it means. One of the next three verbs will mean the opposite of the first verb. Underline the one that is the opposite of the first verb.

G-1	play	a. amuse	b. entertain	c. work
G-2	allow	a. deny	b. let	c. permit
G-3	mend	a. break	b. correct	c. patch
G-4	save	a. collect	b. store	c. spend
G-5	harm	a. damage	b. hurt	c. benefit
G-6	doubt	a. believe	b. challenge	c. question
G-7	reduce	a. cut	b. diminish	c. increase
G-8	conclude	a. close	b. finish	c. open
G-9	approach	a. arrive	b. leave	c. reach
G-10	escape	a. depart	b. flee	c. return
G-11	reject	a. accept	b. dismiss	c. overlook
G-12	overlook	a. miss	b. ignore	c. choose

PERSONAL APPLICATION

Q: When might you find it helpful to know or be able to define a word that means the opposite of another word?

A: Examples include solving crossword puzzles; giving directions; following reverse directions, e.g., turning left when you go to your friend's house and turning right when you go back home; reassembling models or appliances.

EXERCISES G-37 to G-72

OPPOSITES—SUPPLY

ANSWERS G-37 through G-72 — Student book pages 189–91
Guided Practice: G-37 subtract; **G-38** accept; **G-39** quiet; **G-40** increase
Independent Practice: G-41 divide; **G-42** disapprove; **G-43** release; **G-44** freeze; **G-45** grant; **G-46** de-emphasize; **G-47** arrive; **G-48** join; **G-49** dusk or end; **G-50** happiness; **G-51** payment; **G-52** answer; **G-53** adult; **G-54** little; **G-55** failure; **G-56** foreigner; **G-57** exterior; **G-58** attic; **G-59** conclusion; **G-60** surplus; **G-61** active; **G-62** new; **G-63** negative; **G-64** extraordinary; **G-65** sad; **G-66** terrible; **G-67** complete; **G-68** future; **G-69** easy; **G-70** unpopular; **G-71** patient; **G-72** worthless

DETAILED SOLUTIONS

NOTE: Possible definitions for words and their opposites are underlined throughout this section; the given word and possible answers are italicized. Additional answers may result through discussion.

G-37 *Add* means to combine or increase. Think of a word that means to take apart or take away. Possible answers: *subtract, reduce, remove.* **G-38** *Reject* means to refuse or ignore. Think of a word that means to receive willingly or pay attention to. Possible answers: *accept, choose, select.* **G-39** *Excite* means to make active or cause strong feelings. Think of a word that means to calm. Possible answers: *quiet, bore, soothe, silence.* **G-40** *Decrease* means to make smaller in size or amount. Think of a word that means to make larger in size or amount. Possible answers: *increase, multiply, add, expand.* **G-41** *Multiply* means to increase in number. Think of a word that means to decrease in number. Possible answers: *divide, reduce, lessen, diminish.* **G-42** *Approve* means to find acceptable. Think of a word that means to find unacceptable. Possible answers: *disapprove, decline, dismiss, refuse, reject, disfavor, frown, object.* **G-43** *Capture* means to catch. Think of a word that means to let go. Possible answers: *release, free, discharge, loose, liberate, unbind.* **G-44** *Melt* means to change from solid to liquid. Think of a word that means to change from liquid to solid. Possible answers: *freeze, become solid, harden, solidify, gel.* **G-45** *Deny* means to not allow. Think of a word that means to allow. Possible answers: *grant, allow, acknowledge.* **G-46** *Emphasize* means to bring out what is important. Think of a word that means to omit or play down what is important. Possible answers: *de-emphasize, depreciate, minimize, underrate, understate.* **G-47** *Depart* means to go. Think of a word that means to return. Possible answers: *arrive, remain, abide.* **G-48** *Separate* means to disconnect or take apart. Think of a word that means to put together.

Possible answers: *join, connect, combine.* **G-49** *Dawn* means <u>daybreak or beginning</u>. Think of a word that means <u>nightfall or ending</u>. Possible answers: *dusk, twilight, evening, sunset, conclusion, finale.* **G-50** *Sorrow* means <u>a sad or troubled feeling</u>. Think of a word that means <u>not sad, or untroubled</u>. Possible answers: *happiness, joy, gladness, contentment.* **G-51** *Debt* means <u>something owed</u>. Think of a word that means <u>something paid</u>. Possible answers: *payment, credit, compensation, income.* **G-52** *Question* means <u>something asked about, an inquiry</u>. Think of a word that means <u>something told in response</u>. Possible answers: *answer, reply, response.* **G-53** *Youth* means <u>one who is in an early stage of life or development</u>. Think of a word that means <u>one who is in a late stage or well-developed</u>. Possible answers: *adult, elder, senior.* **G-54** *Plenty* means <u>a large supply</u>. Think of a word that means <u>a small supply</u>. Possible answers: *little, scarcity, lack, shortage, deficit.* **G-55** *Success* means <u>having a desired or favorable outcome</u>. Think of a word that means <u>not having a desirable outcome</u>. Possible answers: *failure, ruin, disappointment, defeat, disaster.* **G-56** *Native* refers to <u>someone born in a particular place</u>. Think of a word that refers to <u>someone born outside a particular place</u>. Possible answers: *foreigner, alien, nonnative.* **G-57** *Interior* refers to <u>the inner part of something</u>. Think of a word that refers to <u>the outer part of something</u>. Possible answers: *exterior, outside.* **G-58** *Basement* is <u>the lowest level of a building</u>. Think of a word that <u>means the highest level of a building</u>. Possible answers: *attic, penthouse, top floor.* **G-59** *Introduction* means <u>something that serves as a preliminary</u>. Think of a word that means <u>something that serves as an ending</u>. Possible answers: *conclusion, withdrawal, epilogue, afterword, ending.* **G-60** *Shortage* means <u>less than the necessary amount</u>. Think of a word that means <u>more than the necessary amount</u>. Possible answers: *surplus, excess, overage, overabundance, overflow.* **G-61** *Still* means <u>without movement or noise</u>. Think of a word that means <u>moving or not quiet</u>. Possible answers: *active, mobile, restless, noisy.* **G-62** *Ancient* means <u>old or out-of-date</u>. Think of a word that means <u>young or up-to-date</u>. Possible answers: *new, modern, recent, fresh.* **G-63** *Positive* means <u>accepting or very sure</u>. Think of a word that means <u>opposed to or unsure</u>. Possible answers: *negative, uncertain, doubtful, pessimistic.* **G-64** *Ordinary* means <u>routine and usual</u>. Think of a word that means <u>different and unusual</u>. Possible answers: *extraordinary, exceptional, uncommon, rare, unique, exciting.* **G-65** *Glad* means <u>happy or joyful</u>. Think of a word that means <u>unhappy</u>. Possible answers: *sad, depressed, miserable, sorry.* **G-66** *Excellent* means <u>superior</u>. Think of a word that means <u>inferior</u>. Possible answers: *terrible, poor, unsatisfactory, imperfect, awful.* **G-67** *Partial* means <u>incomplete or biased</u>. Think of a word that means <u>whole or fair</u>. Possible answers: *complete, finished, total, impartial, objective.* **G-68** *Past* means <u>no longer current</u>. Think of a word that means <u>to come</u>. Possible answers: *future, coming, present, now.* **G-69** *Difficult* means <u>hard to do</u>. Think of a word that means <u>not hard to do</u>. Possible answers: *easy, effortless, uncomplicated, simple.* **G-70** *Popular* means <u>liked or favored</u>. Think of a word that means <u>not well-liked</u>. Possible answers: *unpopular, rejected, disliked, hated.* **G-71** *Impatient* means <u>intolerant or restless</u>. Think of a word that means <u>tolerant</u>. Possible answers: *patient, easygoing, calm, quiet, understanding.* **G-72**

Valuable means <u>having worth</u>. Think of a word that means <u>having no worth</u>. Possible answers: *worthless, inferior, mediocre, poor, valueless.*

LESSON PREPARATION

OBJECTIVE AND MATERIALS

OBJECTIVE: Students will supply a word that means the opposite of a given word.

MATERIALS: Transparency of student workbook page 189 • washable transparency marker

CURRICULUM APPLICATIONS

LANGUAGE ARTS: Using precise words, doing vocabulary enrichment activities and antonym exercises, writing contrastive paragraphs, describing contrasting elements in a work of literature, debating or expressing an opposite opinion

MATHEMATICS: Recognizing and using inverse operations; using fractions and reciprocals; recognizing set and set complements; checking basic arithmetic problems by reversing processes, e.g., checking subtraction by addition

SCIENCE: Recognizing reversed processes in simple experiments; accurately describing differences between two objects or concepts; disassembling and reassembling motors, gears, or models

SOCIAL STUDIES: Contrasting topographic or geographic areas, locating and expressing contrasting details when comparing topics from grade-level texts

ENRICHMENT AREAS: Writing or giving directions for creating dance movements or art projects; accurately expressing the differences between two pieces of music, two works of art, two dances, or two athletic activities

TEACHING SUGGESTIONS

Encourage students to list as many acceptable antonyms as possible, then discuss and define their words. Class discussion is a valuable technique for having students share their acquired knowledge. Definitions and antonyms should be tailored to the vocabulary level and needs of the students. These activities are excellent exercises for dictionary and thesaurus use. Use the following cues to encourage the discussion procedure demonstrated:

1. Recognize/pronounce word.
2. Define word.
3. Define opposite word.
4. Supply opposite word (answer).
5. Recognize/use other antonyms.

MODEL LESSON

LESSON

Introduction

Q: In the previous exercise you selected a word that meant the opposite of a given word.

Explaining the Objective to Students

Q: In these exercises you will supply a word that means the opposite of a given word.

Class Activity

- Project exercise **G-37** from the transparency of student page 189.

  Q: You will think of a word (or words) that means the opposite of the given word. The first word you are given is *add*. Before you give an answer, think of the definition of *add*.

  > A: Possible answers: to combine parts or increase in number

  Q: The opposite meaning of the word *add* is to take apart or take away. What are some words that mean the opposite of *add*?

  > A: Possible answers: subtract, remove, reduce, deduct, withdraw

OPPOSITES—SUPPLY

DIRECTIONS: Each line contains a verb. Read the verb and think about what it means. Think of another verb (or verbs) that means the opposite of the given verb. Write the verb(s) in the box.

G-37	add
G-38	reject
G-39	excite
G-40	decrease
G-41	multiply
G-42	approve
G-43	capture
G-44	melt
G-45	deny
G-46	emphasize
G-47	depart
G-48	separate

- Write all answers on the transparency. Students may confirm answers by giving examples of each antonym or by using them in a sentence.

GUIDED PRACTICE

EXERCISES: **G-37** through **G-40**

- Give students sufficient time to complete these exercises. Then, using the demonstration methodology above, have them discuss and explain their choices.

INDEPENDENT PRACTICE

- Assign exercises **G-41** through **G-72**.

THINKING ABOUT THINKING

Q: What did you pay attention to in order to supply a word with the opposite meaning?

1. I defined the given word.

2. I thought about what the opposite meaning was.

3. I thought of words that had the opposite meaning.

4. I substituted the other word for the given one to check whether the words had opposite meanings.

PERSONAL APPLICATION

Q: When might you need to think of a word that means the opposite of a given word?

> A: Examples include solving crossword puzzles; giving directions; following reverse directions, e.g., turning left when you go to your friend's house and turning right when you go back home; reassembling models or appliances; taking tests.

EXERCISES G-73 to G-120 | SIMILARITIES—SELECT

ANSWERS G-73 through G-120 — Student book pages 192-5
Guided Practice: G-73 a; **G-74** b; **G-75** a

Independent Practice: G-76 b; G-77 c; G-78 a; G-79 c; G-80 c; G-81 b; G-82 c; G-83 b; G-84 c; G-85 a; G-86 c; G-87 b; G-88 b; G-89 a; G-90 b; G-91 a; G-92 a; G-93 b; G-94 b; G-95 c; G-96 b; G-97 a; G-98 a; G-99 a; G-100 b; G-101 c; G-102 a; G-103 b; G-104 a; G-105 b; G-106 c; G-107 b; G-108 a; G-109 b; G-110 a; G-111 b; G-112 b; G-113 c; G-114 c; G-115 b; G-116 b; G-117 a; G-118 a; G-119 a; G-120 a

DETAILED SOLUTIONS

NOTE: The key definitions are underlined throughout this section. The four verbs in each exercise are italicized.

G-73 a; *Break* means to separate into parts. *Crack* means to break or split. *Mend* and *repair* both mean to put something back into good or working condition. **G-74** b; *Lead* means to show the way. *Direct* means to tell or show the way. *Attempt* means to try. *Follow* means to come after. **G-75** a; *Seem* means to give an impression of being. *Appear* means to come into sight or being. *Have* means to possess or own. *Need* means to lack something. **G-76** b; *Begin* means to take the first step. *Start* means to make the first move. *Make* means to cause or build. *Try* means to attempt. **G-77** c; *Jog* means to move at a rate faster than walking. *Run* means to move rapidly. *Hike* means to take an extended walk. *Pace* means to walk back and forth. **G-78** a; *Manage* means to direct or run affairs. *Control* means to exercise authority. *Start* and *stop* mean to begin and to end, respectively. **G-79** c; *Continue* means to go on in the same way. *Proceed* means to go on. *Expect* means to look forward to or anticipate. *Prevent* means to keep from happening. **G-80** c; *Desire* means to wish for. *Want* means to desire to have. *Have* means to own. *Try* means to attempt. **G-81** b; *Clear* means to take away obstacles. *Remove* means to take or move away. *Plant* means to set in the ground for growing. *Set* means to put into place. **G-82** c; *Care* means to provide assistance. *Tend* means to watch over. *Ignore* and *neglect* mean to pay little or no attention. **G-83** b; *Produce* means to make. *Manufacture* means to make raw material into a finished product, usually by machine. *Break* means to cause to separate into pieces. *Reduce* means to make smaller in amount or size. **G-84** c; *Survive* means to remain alive. *Recover* means to restore oneself. *Die* and *perish* both mean to stop living. **G-85** a; *Active* means to be in motion or doing something. *Busy* means to be actively engaged in something. *Quiet* and *still* mean to be inactive or not busy. **G-86** c; *Tired* means exhausted or fatigued. *Weary* means mentally or physically fatigued. *Calm* means at ease or at peace. *Rested* means renewed or having enough sleep. **G-87** b; *Curious* means strange or different. *Peculiar* means strange or different. *Familiar* means known and *similar* means alike. **G-88** b; *Personal* means of or relating to a particular person. *Private* means of or relating to the individual. *Open* means accessible. *Public* means available to people in general. **G-89** a; *Initial* means beginning. *First* means starting or initial. *Last* means final. *Middle* is between initial and final. **G-90** b; *Former* means occurring earlier in time. *Earlier* means happening before now. *Current* and *present* refer to now. **G-91** a; *Novel* means uncommon or new. *Different* means uncommon. *Familiar* means common. *Old* means not new. **G-92** a;

Earnest means <u>serious</u>. *Serious* means <u>thoughtful or subdued</u>. *Careless* and *casual* mean showing or feeling little concern. **G-93** b; *Temporary* means <u>for a limited time</u>. *Brief* means <u>for a short time</u>. *Continuous* and *permanent* mean lasting for a long time. **G-94** b; *Favorable* means <u>expressing approval</u>. *Friendly* means <u>expressing approval</u>. *Critical* and *negative* mean expressing disapproval. **G-95** c; *Clever* means <u>mentally quick</u>. *Sharp* means <u>keen and intelligent</u>. *Average* means midway between extremes. *Dull* means mentally slow. **G-96** b; *Mobile* means <u>capable of being moved</u>. *Movable* means <u>capable of being moved</u>. *Fixed* and *stationary* mean remaining in one place. **G-97** a; *Dull* means <u>uninteresting</u>. *Boring* means <u>unexciting or uninteresting</u>. *Exciting* means interesting. *Loud* means noisy or offensive in appearance or smell. **G-98** a; *Dull* means <u>not sharp</u>. *Blunt* means <u>not pointed or sharp</u>. *Even* means flat and smooth. *Sharp* means having a keen edge. **G-99** a; *Hard* means <u>not easy</u>. *Difficult* means <u>requiring great effort</u>. *Simple* means easy. *Smooth* means even or regular. **G-100** b; *Hard* means <u>solid</u>. *Firm* means <u>not giving under pressure</u>. *Easy* means requiring little effort. *Loose* means not tightly packed. **G-101** c; *Hard* means <u>practical</u>. *Realistic* means <u>practical</u>. *Fantastic* and *idealistic* mean impractical or unreal. **G-102** a; *Clear* means <u>unclouded</u>. *Bright* means <u>clear and sunny</u>. *Gloomy* and *hazy* mean cloudy or unclear. **G-103** b; *Clear* means <u>free from doubt</u>. *Certain* means <u>definite, without doubt</u>. *Blurred* and *vague* mean unclear or uncertain. **G-104** a; *Clear* means <u>free from obstruction</u>. *Bare* means <u>empty</u>. Both *clogged* and *occupied* mean filled. **G-105** b; *Fine* means <u>high-quality</u>. *Excellent* means <u>high-quality</u>. *Awful* and *poor* mean low-quality. **G-106** c; *Fine* means <u>a smooth texture</u>. *Delicate* means <u>very fine</u>. *Coarse* and *rough* are opposite of fine. **G-107** b; *Fine* means <u>narrow</u>, as in a fine line. *Thin* means <u>fine</u>. *Broad* and *wide* mean large in expanse. **G-108** a; *Fine* means <u>fair and clear</u>, as weather. *Clear* means <u>cloudless</u>. *Cloudy* and *gloomy* mean unclear. **G-109** b; *Raise* means <u>to move something to a higher position</u>. *Lift* means <u>to move something to a higher position</u>. *Lower* means to move something down. *Slide* means to move something along a surface. **G-110** a; *Raise* means <u>to make greater in amount, size, or value</u>. *Increase* means <u>to become greater in amount, size, or degree</u>. *Reduce* means to make smaller in amount, size, or value. *Use* means to put into service. **G-111** b; *Raise* means <u>to grow. Grow</u> means <u>to cultivate</u>. *Destroy* means to ruin or tear down. *Maintain* means to keep things going. **G-112** b; *Cut* means <u>to penetrate with a sharp edge</u>. *Slice* means <u>to cut</u>. *Peel* means to remove the outer covering. *Tear* means to break apart, usually with the hands. **G-113** c; *Cut* means <u>to reduce the size of</u>. *Reduce* means <u>to decrease</u>. *Hire* and *increase* mean to add on. **G-114** c; *Cut* means <u>to clip</u>. *Shave* means to <u>clip</u>. *Comb* and *dry* are other actions taken during a haircut. **G-115** b; *Cut* means <u>to thin down</u>. *Dilute* means to thin down. *Concentrate* and *thicken* are opposites of thinning. **G-116** b; *Fail* means <u>to lose strength</u>. *Decline* means <u>to fail</u>. *Cure* and *heal* mean to get better. **G-117** a; *Fail* means <u>to be less than adequate at a task</u>. *Flunk* means <u>to fail</u>. *Pass* means to complete successfully. *Win* means to succeed. **G-118** a; *Fail* means <u>to become inadequate or deficient</u>. *Dwindle* means <u>to shrink or become inadequate</u>. *Grow* means to increase. *Supply* means to give. **G-119** a; *Drop* means <u>to fall</u>. *Fall* means <u>to</u>

drop quickly. *Rise* means to go up. *Soar* means to rise or fly. **G-120** a; *Drop* means to decrease. *Decline* means to become less. *Grow* means to increase in size. *Hold* means to stay the same.

LESSON PREPARATION

OBJECTIVE AND MATERIALS

OBJECTIVE: The student will select a word with a meaning similar to a given word.

MATERIALS: Transparency of student workbook page 192 • washable transparency marker

CURRICULUM APPLICATIONS

LANGUAGE ARTS: Doing synonym exercises and vocabulary enrichment; avoiding overused words and trite expressions in compositions; paraphrasing/summarizing written or spoken sentences, paragraphs, or passages; using knowledge of word parts to determine meaning of compound words; using knowledge of prefixes and suffixes to build or comprehend new words; recognizing denotative and connotative meanings

MATHEMATICS: Recognizing key words that indicate proper function or order in word problems; reading and understanding directions for solving mathematics problems; recognizing face and place value of numbers; recognizing and using equivalent values of money, time, or measurement

SCIENCE: Following directions in performing experiments, determining meaning of unfamiliar words by using textual definitions or synonym clues

SOCIAL STUDIES: Paraphrasing or summarizing key concepts, building content vocabulary by using definition or synonym clues from text, identifying parallel or similar functions of different governmental levels

ENRICHMENT AREAS: Increasing vocabulary from pleasure reading, e.g., clues from context; recognizing foreign language vocabulary by similarity to native language words; following directions in creating a work of art or in performing a dance or musical work

TEACHING SUGGESTIONS

Encourage students to discuss why they chose an answer and explain why the other words are less correct. Class discussion is a valuable technique for having children share their acquired knowledge. Additional synonyms, other than those listed in the answer box, will result through discussion. Definitions should be tailored to the vocabulary level and needs of the students.

   Use the following cues to encourage the discussion procedure demonstrated in the lesson:
   1. Recognize/pronounce word.
   2. Define word.
   3. Select similar word (answer).
   4. Define similar word (confirm answer).
   5. Eliminate detractors (check answer).

MODEL LESSON

LESSON

Introduction

   Q: In the figural classification exercises you selected or drew figures which had similar patterns or shapes.

Explaining the Objective to Students

Q: In these exercises you will select a word with a meaning similar to a given word.

Class Activity

- Project exercise **G-73** from the transparency of student page 192.

Q: Remember that you are looking for a word that is *most like the given word*. After you have selected the word that seems to be most like the given word, check the other choices to see how they are different.

In exercise **G-73**, you are given the word *break*, followed by three words that might mean the same as *break*. *Break* means to separate into parts. *Crack* is most like *break* because *crack* means to break or split. Before you can be certain, you need to check the other words to make sure they are not more like *break*. *Mend* and *repair* both mean to put something back into good or working condition. Therefore, *crack* is most like *break* in meaning.

	SIMILARITIES—SELECT		

DIRECTIONS: Each line contains four verbs. Read the first verb and think about what it means. One of the next three verbs means almost the same thing. Underline the one that is most like the first verb in meaning.

G-73	break	a. crack	b. mend	c. repair
G-74	lead	a. attempt	b. direct	c. follow
G-75	seem	a. appear	b. have	c. need
G-76	begin	a. make	b. start	c. try
G-77	jog	a. hike	b. pace	c. run
G-78	manage	a. control	b. start	c. stop
G-79	continue	a. expect	b. prevent	c. proceed
G-80	desire	a. have	b. try	c. want
G-81	clear	a. plant	b. remove	c. set
G-82	care	a. ignore	b. neglect	c. tend
G-83	produce	a. break	b. manufacture	c. reduce
G-84	survive	a. die	b. perish	c. recover

- Underline "crack" on the transparency.

GUIDED PRACTICE

EXERCISES: **G-73** through **G-75**

- Give students sufficient time to complete these exercises. Then, using the demonstration methodology above, have them discuss and explain their choices.

INDEPENDENT PRACTICE

- Assign exercises **G-76** through **G-120**.

THINKING ABOUT THINKING

Q: What did you pay attention to in order to select a word with a similar meaning?

1. I thought about what the given word meant.

2. I found another word that meant almost the same thing.

3. I substituted the second word for the given one to check whether the words had almost the same meaning.

4. I read the other words to see why they were less similar.

PERSONAL APPLICATION

Q: When do you find it necessary or useful to recognize a word that means the same as another word?

A: Examples include following directions, understanding what others are saying, crossword puzzles or word games, taking tests.

EXERCISES G-121 to G-156

SIMILARITIES—SUPPLY

ANSWERS G-121 through G-156 — Student book pages 196–8

Guided Practice: G-121 hold, grab, catch; **G-122** pick, choose, decide; **G-123** destroy, wreck, demolish, bankrupt

Independent Practice: G-124 demand, want, crave, compel, request; **G-125** finish, fill out; **G-126** examine, wonder, regard, contemplate; **G-127** (1) hold, include, enclose; (2) control, repress; **G-128** close, seal, block; **G-129** make, invent, develop, build; **G-130** march, move, journey, pass, travel, advance, progress; **G-131** nurse, cherish, cultivate, nurture, foster; **G-132** clout, hit, sock, swat, slam, slap, beat, poke; **G-133** all, complete, total, entire; **G-134** greatest, largest; **G-135** more, additional, spare; **G-136** one, only, sole, unmarried; **G-137** yearly; **G-138** (1) beaming, luminous, radiant; (2) brainy, clever, knowing, knowledgeable, sharp, smart; **G-139** careful, discreet, considerate, vigilant, watchful, guarded; **G-140** synthetic, man-made, false, imitation, mock, fake, unreal, simulated; **G-141** civil, courteous, mannerly, well-mannered, attentive, considerate, thoughtful; **G-142** little, insignificant, petty, trivial, unimportant, trifling, small, medium, average; **G-143** (1) material, physical, gross (2) big, weighty, considerable, consequential (3) prosperous, comfortable, well-off, well-to-do; **G-144** (1) convenient, adjacent, close-by, close-at-hand, nearby (2) practical, functional, serviceable, useful; **G-145** teacher, tutor, educator, coach; **G-146** chance, opening, occasion; **G-147** description, answer, reason; **G-148** (1) skill, capacity; (2) might, force, vigor; (3) electricity, energy; **G-149** joy, pleasure, happiness, amusement; **G-150** feat, deed, exploit, accomplishment, attainment; **G-151** edge, perimeter, bounds, limits, confines, environs; **G-152** profession, calling, trade, art, craft, vocation; **G-153** part, division, member, parcel, piece, portion, segment, district, locality, subdivision, vicinity, area, zone, region, tract, territory; **G-154** declaration, advertisement, broadcast, proclamation, publication, statement; **G-155** appliance, implement, instrument, tool, utensil, apparatus, machine, mechanism, invention; **G-156** addition, complement, additive, appendix, addendum

---

LESSON PREPARATION

OBJECTIVE AND MATERIALS

OBJECTIVE: Students will supply a word with a meaning similar to a given word.

MATERIALS: Chalkboard

CURRICULUM APPLICATIONS

LANGUAGE ARTS: Doing synonym exercises and vocabulary enrichment; avoiding overused words and trite expressions in compositions; paraphrasing/summarizing written or spoken sentences, paragraphs, or passages; using knowledge of word parts to determine meaning of compound words; using knowledge of prefixes and suffixes to build or comprehend new words; recognizing denotative and connotative meanings

MATHEMATICS: Recognizing key words that indicate proper function or order in word problems; reading and understanding directions for solving mathematics problems; recognizing face and place value of numbers; recognizing and using equivalent values of money, time, or measurement

SCIENCE: Following directions in performing experiments, determining meaning of unfamiliar words by using textual definitions or synonym clues

SOCIAL STUDIES: Paraphrasing or summarizing key concepts, building content vocabulary using definition or synonym clues from text, identifying parallel or similar functions of different governmental levels

ENRICHMENT AREAS: Increasing vocabulary from pleasure reading, e.g., clues from context; recognizing foreign language vocabulary by similarity to native language words; developing directions for creating a work of art or performing a dance

TEACHING SUGGESTIONS

Encourage students to discuss and define their synonyms. Class discussion is a valuable technique for having students share their acquired knowledge. Definitions and synonyms should be tailored to the vocabulary level and needs of the students. Similar words are not intended to be finite lists; additional answers will result through discussion. These are excellent exercises for dictionary and thesaurus use. Use the following cues to encourage the discussion procedure demonstrated

1. Recognize/pronounce word.
2. Define word.
3. Supply similar word. (answer)
4. Define similar word. (confirm answer)
5. Recognize/use other synonyms.

MODEL LESSON

LESSON

Introduction

Q: In the previous exercise you selected a word with a meaning similar to a given word.

Explaining the Objective to Students

Q: In these exercises you will supply a word with a similar meaning to a given word.

Class Activity

• Write "forever" on the chalkboard.
  Q: Think of a word that means about the same as *forever*. Before you give an answer, think of the definition of *forever*.
    A: Possible answers: for all time, going on without end

  Q: Now think of other words that mean for all time.
    A: Possible answers: always, ever, eternal, constantly

• Write all answers on the chalkboard. Students may confirm answers by giving examples of each synonym or by using them in a sentence.

GUIDED PRACTICE

EXERCISES: **G-121** through **G-123**

• Give students sufficient time to complete these exercises. Using the demonstration methodology above, have them discuss and explain their choices.

INDEPENDENT PRACTICE
• Assign exercises **G-124** through **G-156**.

THINKING ABOUT THINKING
Q: What did you pay attention to in order to supply a word similar to the given word?

1. I thought about what the word meant.

2. I thought of another word that meant almost the same thing.

3. I substituted the second word for the first one to check whether the words had almost the same meaning.

PERSONAL APPLICATION
Q: When might it be necessary to provide a word that means the same as a given word?

A: Examples include giving clear written or oral directions, understanding what others are saying, crossword puzzles or word games, taking tests.

EXERCISES G-157 to G-180

HOW ALIKE?—SELECT

> **ANSWERS G-157 through G-180 — Student book pages 199–202**
> **Guided Practice: G-157** a and b (Sentence c is not true because some stamps do not have a value marked on them.) **G-158** b and c (Sentence a is not true because a king usually inherits the title from his parents rather than being elected.) **G-159** b and c (Sentence a is not true because a service such as cleaning is not an object.)
> **Independent Practice: G-160** c; **G-161** a and b; **G-162** a and b; **G-163** b and c; **G-164** a; **G-165** c; **G-166** b and c; **G-167** a and c; **G-168** a and b; **G-169** a and b; **G-170** a and c; **G-171** a and c; **G-172** a; **G-173** b and c; **G-174** b and c; **G-175** a and b; **G-176** a and b; **G-177** a and c; **G-178** a and b; **G-179** b and c; **G-180** a

LESSON PREPARATION

OBJECTIVE AND MATERIALS
OBJECTIVE: Students will select sentences that are true for both given words.
MATERIALS: Transparency of student workbook page 199 • washable transparency marker

CURRICULUM APPLICATIONS
LANGUAGE ARTS: Organizing and writing compare and contrast statements, paragraphs, or papers; recognizing denotative and connotative words or phrases
MATHEMATICS: Evaluating geometric shapes for type and congruence; interpreting word problems; interpreting different forms of statistical presentations, e.g., charts, graphs, pictures, schedules relating to the same statistics
SCIENCE: Evaluating classes of plants or animals by similar characteristics
SOCIAL STUDIES: Evaluating similarities and differences between historical events, eras, people, or artifacts

ENRICHMENT AREAS: Evaluating, contrasting, and/or comparing different works of art, music, or dance; distinguishing between two similar works of art, music, or dance

TEACHING SUGGESTIONS
Encourage students to discuss their choices. The explanations should be tailored to the vocabulary level and needs of the students.

MODEL LESSON

LESSON

Introduction
Q: In the previous exercise you supplied a word with a meaning similar to a given word.

Explaining the Objective to Students
Q: In these exercises you will select sentences that are true for two given words.

Class Activity
- Project exercise **G-157** from the transparency of student page 199, covering the right side so students cannot see the sentences they are to evaluate.

  Q: You are given the words *postage stamps* and *coins*. You need to determine how postage stamps and coins are alike.

- Uncover responses *a* through *c*.

  Q: Is sentence *a* true of both a postage stamp and a coin?
    A: Yes, both can be collected as a hobby.

  Q: Is sentence *b* true of both a postage stamp and a coin?
    A: Yes, both are produced by the government.

  Q: Is sentence *c* true of both a postage stamp and a coin?
    A: No, some stamps do not have a value printed on them. Underline sentences *a* and *b*.

HOW ALIKE?—SELECT

DIRECTIONS: Each line contains two words related to social studies. Think about the ways the two words are alike. Underline the sentence(s) that is true of both words.

G-157 postage stamps coins	a. Both can be collected as a hobby. b. Both are produced by the government. c. Both have a monetary value printed on them.
G-158 king president	a. Both are elected. b. Both are national leaders. c. Both participate in national ceremonies.
G-159 goods services	a. Both are objects. b. Both can be purchased. c. Both require workers.
G-160 globe map	a. Both are drawings of all or part of the earth. b. Both are flat. c. Both can be used to estimate distances between places.
G-161 lake ocean	a. Both are bodies of water. b. Both can be located on maps. c. Both contain drinkable water.
G-162 checks money	a. Both can be obtained at a bank. b. Both can be used to buy things. c. Both need to be endorsed.

GUIDED PRACTICE
EXERCISES: **G-157** through **G-159**
- Give students sufficient time to complete these exercises. Then, using the demonstration methodology above, have them discuss and explain their choices.

INDEPENDENT PRACTICE
- Assign exercises **G-160** through **G-180**.

THINKING ABOUT THINKING
Q: What did you pay attention to when you decided whether or not the same statement was true of two different things?

1. I thought about the meaning of each word.

2. I read each given statement to see if it was true of each word.

PERSONAL APPLICATION

Q: When might you need to decide whether a statement is true of two different things?

A: Examples include making value judgements given different situations, e.g., right/wrong, good/bad; playing word games; taking tests, especially true-false or multiple-choice objective tests; giving or following directions; developing critical reading skills.

HOW ALIKE AND HOW DIFFERENT?

EXERCISES G-181 to G-195

ANSWERS G-181 through G-195 — Student book pages 203–5
Guided Practice: G-181 ALIKE: Both are geographic divisions. DIFFERENT: A neighborhood is a small area of homes, churches, stores, and schools. A community is a collection of neighborhoods. **G-182** ALIKE: Both are elected officials. DIFFERENT: A mayor is the chief executive of a city. A governor is the chief executive of a state. **G-183** ALIKE: Both are geographic regions. DIFFERENT: A continent is one of seven very large bodies of land making up the surface of the earth. Continents are composed of smaller regions known as countries. Australia is an exception—the country occupies the whole continent.
Independent Practice: G-184 ALIKE: Both refer to weather conditions. DIFFERENT: Weather is a daily occurrence. Climate describes the long-term average weather of a region. **G-185** ALIKE: Both are forms of government. DIFFERENT: The leader of a dictatorship is appointed by a group who seizes the power of the government. The leader of a democracy is chosen by open elections. **G-186** ALIKE: Both are produced by sources and can be transmitted. DIFFERENT: Light has a variety of colors; sounds have a variety of tones. Light is detected by the eye; sound is detected by the ear. **G-187** ALIKE: Both are vertebrates that lay eggs. DIFFERENT: Amphibians have moist skin and live near the water. Reptiles have dry skin and live in dry regions. **G-188** ALIKE: Both are parts of a plant. Many fruits and seeds are edible. DIFFERENT: Fruit is the fleshy part that surrounds the seeds and is intended to nourish the seeds. **G-189** ALIKE: Both are related to getting things done. DIFFERENT: A machine is a device to make work easier. Work is the act of exerting energy. **G-190** ALIKE: Both are seen in the sky. DIFFERENT: A star is a large hot object that gives off light. A planet is often smaller than a star. Planets are cooler than stars and shine by reflecting sunlight. **G-191** ALIKE: Both have four sides (quadrilaterals) and four right angles. Both are rectangles. DIFFERENT: A square has four equal sides. **G-192** ALIKE: Both have opposite sides parallel. Both are parallelograms. DIFFERENT: A rectangle is a parallelogram that has right angles. **G-193** ALIKE: Both are parallelograms (opposite sides parallel) DIFFERENT: A rhombus is a parallelogram with four equal sides. **G-194** ALIKE: Both have a pair of parallel sides. DIFFERENT: A parallelogram

> has two pairs of parallel sides while the trapezoid has only one pair of parallel sides. **G-195** ALIKE: Both are parallelograms. DIFFERENT: A square has right angles. A rhombus has oblique angles.

LESSON PREPARATION

OBJECTIVE AND MATERIALS

OBJECTIVE: Students will write sentences comparing and contrasting two words.

MATERIALS: Transparency of student workbook page 203 • washable transparency marker

CURRICULUM APPLICATIONS

LANGUAGE ARTS: Organizing and writing compare and contrast statements, paragraphs, or papers; recognizing denotative and connotative words and phrases

MATHEMATICS: Evaluating geometric shapes for type and congruence; interpreting word problems; interpreting different forms of statistical presentations, e.g., charts, graphs, pictures, and schedules relating to the same data

SCIENCE: Evaluating classes of plants or animals by similar characteristics

SOCIAL STUDIES: Evaluating similarities and differences between historical events, eras, people, or artifacts

ENRICHMENT AREAS: Evaluating, contrasting, and/or comparing different works of art, music, or dance; distinguishing between two similar works of art, music, or dance

TEACHING SUGGESTIONS

Encourage students to discuss their answers. Class discussion is a valuable technique to encourage children to share their acquired knowledge. The explanations should be tailored to the vocabulary level and needs of the students.

MODEL LESSON

LESSON

Introduction

Q: In the previous exercise, you selected sentences that were true of two given words.

Explaining the Objective to Students

Q: In these exercises, you will write sentences to explain how the two given words are alike and how they are different.

Class Activity

• Project the transparency of exercise **G-181** from student page 203.

Q: You are given the words *neighborhood* and *community*. How are a neighborhood and a community alike?

    A: (Possible answer) Both are geographic divisions.

Q: How are a neighborhood and a community different?

HOW ALIKE AND HOW DIFFERENT?

DIRECTIONS: Each line contains two words related to social studies. Describe how the words are alike and how they are different.

G-181 neighborhood community	HOW ALIKE?
	HOW DIFFERENT?
G-182 mayor governor	HOW ALIKE?
	HOW DIFFERENT?
G-183 country continent	HOW ALIKE?
	HOW DIFFERENT?
G-184 weather climate	HOW ALIKE?
	HOW DIFFERENT?
G-185 dictatorship democracy	HOW ALIKE?
	HOW DIFFERENT?

A: (Possible answers) A neighborhood is a small area of homes, churches, stores, and schools. A community is a collection of neighborhoods.

- Write all answers on the transparency.

GUIDED PRACTICE
EXERCISES: **G-181** through **G-183**
- Give students sufficient time to complete these exercises. Ask students to discuss and explain their choices.

INDEPENDENT PRACTICE
- Assign exercises **G-184** through **G-195**.

THINKING ABOUT THINKING
Q: What did you think about when you decided how two words were alike and how they were different?
1. I thought about the meaning of each word.
2. I listed the things that were true of each word.
3. I listed the things that were different about each word.

PERSONAL APPLICATION
Q: When might you need to decide how two things are alike and how they are different?
A: Examples include making value judgements given different situations, e.g., right/wrong, good/bad; playing word games; taking tests, especially essay or objective tests; developing critical writing skills.

EXERCISES G-196 to G-201

WORD WEB—SELECT AND SUPPLY

ANSWERS G-196 through G-201 — Student book pages 206–11
Guided Practice: G-196 to G-197 See below. Examples vary.
Independent Practice: G-198 to G-201 See next page. Examples vary.

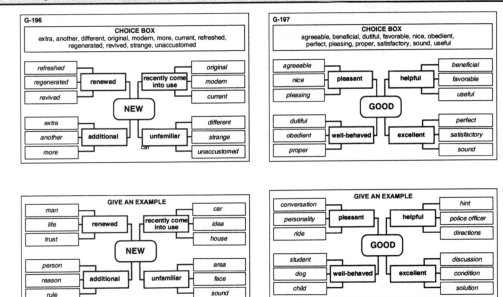

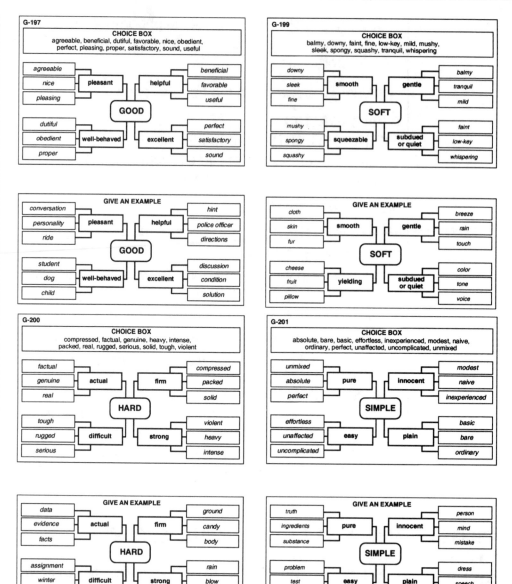

LESSON PREPARATION

OBJECTIVE AND MATERIALS

OBJECTIVE: Students will identify synonyms for different meanings of the same word.

MATERIALS: Transparency of student workbook page 206 • washable transparency marker • TM 33 (optional)

CURRICULUM APPLICATIONS

LANGUAGE ARTS: Organizing and writing compare and contrast statements, paragraphs, or papers; recognizing denotative and connotative words and phrases

MATHEMATICS: Evaluating geometric shapes for type and congruence, interpreting word problems, explaining problem solutions

SCIENCE: Describing classes of plants or animals by similar characteristics

SOCIAL STUDIES: Describing historical events, eras, people, or artifacts

ENRICHMENT AREAS: Describing works of art, music, or dance; distinguishing between two similar works of art, music, or dance

TEACHING SUGGESTIONS

The purpose of this lesson is to suggest to students more precise, descriptive, and expressive words for overused or potentially ambiguous terms. Words from the choice box may prompt students to recall common uses of the synonyms. Words in the "Give an Example" activity should convey the same meaning as the word in the center of the web, not another connotation of the synonym. For example, in the box near *additional* is the example *person*. The words in these boxes must fit with the appropriate meaning of new, as in a new or additional person. Suggest other synonyms in standard or colloquial usage that convey the meaning of each term in the four branches of the diagram; prompt students to use the words in sentences.

Your students will undoubtedly suggest examples other than those given. Encourage students to explain their examples. Create a list of common words (like *bad*) that can have many meanings, some of which may be contradictory or ambiguous.

MODEL LESSON

LESSON

Introduction

Q: In the previous exercise you made up sentences to explain how two given words were alike and how they were different.

Explaining the Objective to Students

Q: In these exercises you will identify synonyms that show different meanings for the same commonly used word.

Class Activity

- Project exercise **G-196** from the transparency of student page 206.

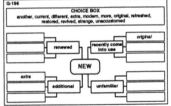

Q: *New* has so many varied meanings that describing something as new may sometimes be confusing or ambiguous. You are given four words that show different meanings for *new*. Select three words from the choice box that have the same meaning as the word on each branch. Look at the four branches. What do we mean if we say we feel like a new person?

    A: Renewed

Q: Look at the choice box and find words that are similar in meaning to *renewed*.
    A: Regenerated, refreshed, revived

Q: What do we mean by a new territory?
    A: Unfamiliar

Q: Look at the choice box and find words that are similar in meaning to *unfamiliar.*
    A: Different, strange, unaccustomed

Q: What branch word describes a new brother?
    A: Additional, as an additional child in the family

Q: Look at the choice box and find words that are similar in meaning to *additional.*
   A: Added, another, more

Q: How would you describe a new invention?
   A: Recently come into use

Q: Look at the choice box and find words that are similar in meaning to the phrase *recently come into use.*
   A: Original, modern, current

GUIDED PRACTICE
EXERCISES: **G-196** to **G-197**
• Give students sufficient time to complete these exercises. Ask students to discuss and explain their choices.

INDEPENDENT PRACTICE
• Assign exercises **G-198** through **G-201.**

THINKING ABOUT THINKING
Q: What did you pay attention to in order to select a word with a similar meaning?
   1. I thought about what the given word meant.
   2. I found another word that meant almost the same thing.
   3. I substituted the second word for the given one to check whether the words had almost the same meaning.

EXTENSION ACTIVITY (Optional)
• Photocopy TM 33. In this exercise, ask students to provide their own words. You may wish to take this opportunity to introduce the use of a thesaurus.

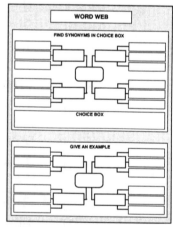

PERSONAL APPLICATION
Q: When might you need to know other words for what you want to say?
   A: Examples include when giving directions or explaining an idea to someone whose use of English is limited or who is from an area in which common English words have a different meaning; playing word games; test taking, especially essay or objective tests; descriptive, expository, or persuasive writing skills.

EXERCISES G-202 to G-204

COMPARE AND CONTRAST—GRAPHIC ORGANIZERS

> **Answers G-202 through G-204—Student book pages 212–5**
> **Guided Practice: G-202** See next page.
> **Independent Practice: G-203** and **G-204** See next page.

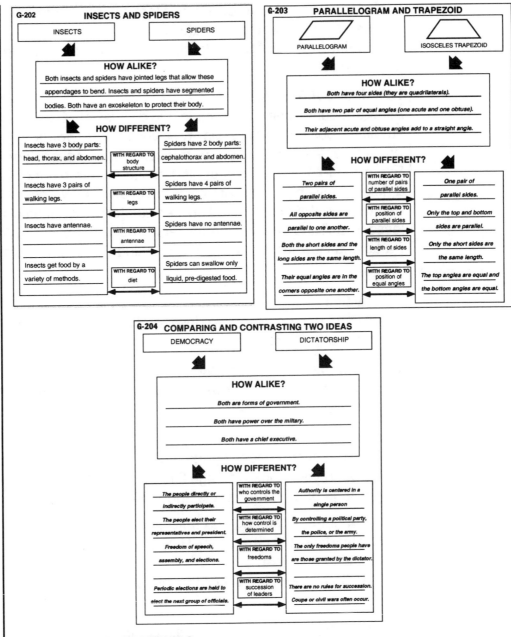

LESSON PREPARATION

OBJECTIVE AND MATERIALS

OBJECTIVE: Students will use a graphic organizer to compare and contrast ideas.

MATERIALS: Transparency of student workbook page 213

CURRICULUM APPLICATIONS

LANGUAGE ARTS: Using mind-mapping techniques for reading comprehension, organizing compare and contrast statements or paragraphs, differentiating between parts of speech or types of stories

MATHEMATICS: Identifying geometric shapes for type and congruence, interpreting word problems, writing and interpreting different forms of statistical presentations (e.g., charts, graphs, pictures, and schedules relating to the same statistics)

SCIENCE: Identifying and organizing classes of plants or animals by similar characteristics

SOCIAL STUDIES: Expressing similarities and differences between histori-cal events, eras, people, or artifacts

ENRICHMENT AREAS: Contrasting and/or comparing different works of art, music, or dance

TEACHING SUGGESTIONS

Allow adequate time for reflection and discussion. Exercise **G-203** tests your students' observational skills. Key vocabulary words in this exercise are *angle, parallel, parallelogram, trapezoid,* and *square corner* (right angle). Exercise **G-204** requires your students to research the differences between a democracy and a dictatorship. Key vocabulary words for this exercise are *democracy, dictatorship,* and *succession* (of the chief official). For additional lessons utilizing graphic organizers, see *Organizing Thinking II,* Sandra Parks and Howard Black, Critical Thinking Books and Software.

MODEL LESSON

LESSON

Introduction

Q: In an earlier lesson we described how two things were alike and how they were different.

Explaining the Objective to Students

Q: In this lesson you will use a diagram to help you explain how two things are alike and how they are different.

Class Activity

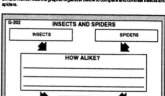
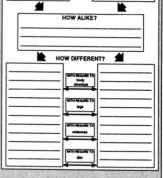

- Project transparency of page 213.

  Q: Open your books to page 212 and read the passage describing insects and spiders.

- Allow time for reading and reflection.

  Q: Read the first paragraph. How are an insect and a spider alike?

    A: Both have jointed legs that enable them to bend.

- Write the response on the first line of the transparency.

  Q: How else are a star and a planet alike?

    A: The first paragraph also tells us that they both have segmented bodies.

- Write the response on the next line of the transparency.

  Q: How else are stars and planets alike?

    A: The first paragraph tells us that they both have exoskeletons.

- Write the response on the next line of the transparency.

  Q: How are an insect and a spider different with regard to their body structure?

    A: Insects have 3 body parts: head, thorax, and abdomen. Spiders have 2 body parts: cephalothorax and abdomen.

- Write these responses on the lines.
  Q: Finish the diagram

GUIDED PRACTICE
EXERCISES: Finish the **G-202** graphic organizer "Stars and Planets."

INDEPENDENT PRACTICE
- Assign exercises **G-203** and **G-204**. Note: These exercises do not have passages to read. They will require student research and/or teacher direction.

THINKING ABOUT THINKING
Q: What did you pay attention to when you compared words or concepts?

1. I carefully read the passage.

2. I looked for the ways the two concepts were alike.

3. I recorded the similarities.

4. I looked for the ways the two concepts were different.

5. I recorded the differences.

PERSONAL APPLICATION
Q: When in your everyday life might you need to describe how two words or ideas are alike and different?

A: Examples include making value judgements (good/bad, right/wrong) in different situations, playing word games, taking tests (either essay or objective tests).

Chapter 8

VERBAL SEQUENCES
(Student book pages 218–85)

FOLLOWING DIRECTIONS—SELECT

ANSWERS H-1 through H-5 — Student book pages 218–9
Guided Practice: H-1 *C (A* has the rectangle inside the diamond; the inside shape in *B* is not a diamond)
Independent Practice: H-2 *A (B* has the circle drawn inside the triangle; *C* does not use the top of the square as the base of the triangle) **H-3** *C (A* uses the base rather than the height of the triangle as the long side of the rectangle; *b* has no rectangle and the circle is inside the square, not inside the triangle); **H-4** *C (A* reverses the directions for the designs inside the squares; *B* has the two squares side by side) **H-5** *C (A* uses the top of the square as the bottom of the rectangle; *B* has the diagonal line going from the upper right to the lower left of the square)

**LESSON
PREPARATION**

OBJECTIVE AND MATERIALS
OBJECTIVE: Students will select a figure that represents a set of directions.
MATERIALS: Transparency of student workbook page 218 • washable transparency marker

CURRICULUM APPLICATIONS
LANGUAGE ARTS: Reading and following directions in any situation involving order, number, or position, e.g., tests, worksheets, text instructions
MATHEMATICS: Following correct sequence in solving word problems, geometry proofs, and constructions
SCIENCE: Following sequence of instructions in laboratory experiments or demonstrations
SOCIAL STUDIES: Answering questions regarding charts, maps, graphs, or schedules; reading and constructing time lines
ENRICHMENT AREAS: Doing art, music, or physical education activities involving order, number, or position; following dance, drill, or sports instructions; following industrial or vocational education procedures; recognizing when directions have been followed correctly

TEACHING SUGGESTIONS
Encourage students to discuss their answers and be specific in their descriptions. Class discussion is a valuable technique for sharing acquired knowledge.

MODEL LESSON

LESSON

Introduction
Q: Every day you follow directions of some kind. When you ask someone how to get somewhere, they will usually give you directions. Sometimes you have to read directions, like when you take a test, fill out a form, or put together a model.

Explaining the Objective to Students

Q: In these exercises you will select the figure that represents the given directions.

Class Activity

*   Project the example from the transparency of page 218.

    Q: The first sentence in the directions states, "Draw a triangle with two long, equal sides." Of these three figures…

*   Indicate figures *A*, *B*, and *C*

    Q: …which have triangles with two long, equal sides?

    A: *B*, possibly *C*

    Q: The next sentence states, "Use the shortest side of the triangle as one side of a square." Which figure fits those directions?

    A: *B*

    Q: Why don't figures *A* and *C* accurately follow the directions?

    A: In figure *A*, the long sides of the triangle are not equal. In figure *C*, the base of the triangle is longer than the sides. Therefore, the square is not next to the short side of the triangle.

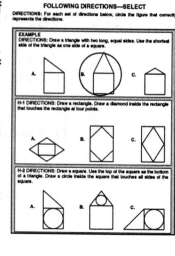

GUIDED PRACTICE

EXERCISE: **H-1**

*   Give students sufficient time to complete this exercise. Ask students to discuss and explain their choice.

INDEPENDENT PRACTICE

*   Assign exercises **H-2** through **H-5**.

THINKING ABOUT THINKING

Q: What did you pay attention to in order to select the correct figure?

1. I checked that words to describe position fit the drawing.

2. I checked that words to describe the length, width, or height fit the drawing.

3. I reread the whole description to be sure about position and size.

4. I checked why the other figures didn't fit the directions.

PERSONAL APPLICATION

Q: When might you need to select an object that correctly represents a set of written directions?

A: Examples include assembling models, games, toys, or bikes; following directions for crafts, sewing, cooking, or cleaning; doing crafts or sports activities involving order, number, or position; taking tests; using computer-tabulated questionnaires or answer sheets.

**EXERCISES
H-6 to H-13**

FOLLOWING DIRECTIONS—SUPPLY

> **ANSWERS H-6 through H-13 — Student book pages 212–4**
> **Guided Practice: H-6** See next page.
> **Independent Practice: H-7 to H-13** See next page.

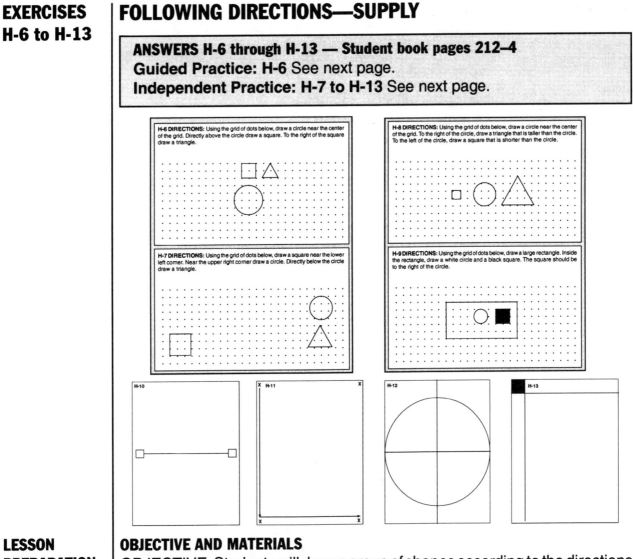

H-6 DIRECTIONS: Using the grid of dots below, draw a circle near the center of the grid. Directly above the circle draw a square. To the right of the square draw a triangle.

H-7 DIRECTIONS: Using the grid of dots below, draw a square near the lower left corner. Near the upper right corner draw a circle. Directly below the circle draw a triangle.

H-8 DIRECTIONS: Using the grid of dots below, draw a circle near the center of the grid. To the right of the circle, draw a triangle that is taller than the circle. To the left of the circle, draw a square that is shorter than the circle.

H-9 DIRECTIONS: Using the grid of dots below, draw a large rectangle. Inside the rectangle, draw a white circle and a black square. The square should be to the right of the circle.

**LESSON
PREPARATION**

OBJECTIVE AND MATERIALS

OBJECTIVE: Students will draw a group of shapes according to the directions given.
MATERIALS: TM 34 • washable transparency marker

CURRICULUM APPLICATIONS

LANGUAGE ARTS: Reading and following directions involving order, number, or position, e.g., text questions, worksheets, or tests
MATHEMATICS: Following multistep operations in solving problems
SCIENCE: Following a series of instructions in laboratory experiments or demonstrations
SOCIAL STUDIES: Reading or creating maps, charts, graphs, time lines, or schedules
ENRICHMENT AREAS: Following classroom procedures; doing art, music, or physical education activities involving order, number, or position; following dance, drill, or sports instructions

TEACHING SUGGESTIONS

Encourage students to discuss their answers. Students should recognize that all drawings need not be the same. Individual drawings, although different, may still accurately follow the directions.

MODEL LESSON

LESSON

Introduction

Q: In previous exercises you identified a figure or shape that correctly represented a set of given directions.

Explaining the Objective to Students

Q: In these exercises you will draw a group of shapes to represent the given directions.

Class Activity

• Project TM 34.

Q: You are given the following written directions for drawing a group of figures on a dot grid: "Draw a small square at the center of the grid. Draw a circle to the left of the square. Directly below the square, draw a triangle." What should be done first?

> A: Draw a small square at the center of the grid.

TRANSPARENCY MASTER 34

FOLLOWING DIRECTIONS

Draw a small square at the center of the grid. Draw a circle to the left of the square. Directly below the square, draw a triangle.

• Have a student draw the shape on the transparency.

Q: What is the next step?

> A: Draw a circle to the left of the square.

• Have student continue the drawing.

Q: What is the last step?

> A: Directly below the square, draw a triangle.

• Have student complete the drawing.

Q: Does this group of shapes accurately represent the stated directions?

• Ask students to confirm the answer by checking each statement against the drawing.

GUIDED PRACTICE

EXERCISE: **H-6**

• Give students sufficient time to complete this exercise. Ask students to discuss and explain their drawings.

INDEPENDENT PRACTICE

• Assign exercises **H-7** through **H-13**.

THINKING ABOUT THINKING

Q: What did you think about to complete each drawing?

1. I read all of the directions first.

2. I planned where I should draw each figure.

3. I drew each figure on the grid.

PERSONAL APPLICATION

Q: When might you need to follow a series of steps, rules, or directions?

A: Examples include following directions for errands or chores; following multistep directions for assembling models and toys; following written directions for crafts, sewing, cooking, cleaning, or household repairs; following rules in games or sports

**EXERCISES
H-14 to H-17**

WRITING DIRECTIONS

ANSWERS H-14 through H-17 — Student book pages 223–4
Guided Practice: (Possible Answers) **H-14** Draw a small square. Draw a large square to the left of the small square, using the left side of the smaller square as the bottom half of the right side of the large square. The bases of both squares should be aligned. **H-15** Draw a horizontal rectangle. Use the top of the rectangle as the bottom of a right triangle. The right side of the triangle is in line with the right side of the rectangle. Two sides of the triangle should be equal.
Independent Practice: (Possible Answers) **H-16** Draw a square. Divide the square in half by drawing a line from the lower left corner to the upper right corner. To the right of and touching the square, draw a rectangle as tall as the square. The rectangle should be half as wide as the square. **H-17** Draw a rectangle using a short side as the base. From the bottom left corner of the rectangle, draw a horizontal line to the left the same length as the height of the rectangle. Construct a right triangle by drawing a line connecting the top left corner of the rectangle to the end point of the horizontal line. Use the base of the triangle as the top of a second rectangle. The two rectangles should be the same size.

**LESSON
PREPARATION**

OBJECTIVE AND MATERIALS
OBJECTIVE: Students will write directions explaining how to draw a given figure.
MATERIALS: Transparency of student workbook page 223 • washable transparency marker

CURRICULUM APPLICATIONS
LANGUAGE ARTS: Setting an established style for proofing or editing manuscripts; developing formats for business letters, outlines, or essays; creating layout design for text; organizing and presenting a demonstration speech
MATHEMATICS: Solving geometry constructions and proofs, demonstrating and explaining a solution to a mathematics problem
SCIENCE: Preparing directions for scientific demonstrations
SOCIAL STUDIES: Reading maps, graphs, or charts
ENRICHMENT AREAS: Following art, industrial arts, or vocational education procedures

TEACHING SUGGESTIONS
To extend this lesson as a listening-skill exercise, instruct students to create a design with two or three geometric shapes and write directions for drawing each design. Ask each student to read his/her directions aloud and instruct the

class to draw the figure as directed. Compare drawings to confirm correct answers and to make suggestions regarding clarification of the directions. Encourage students to discuss their answers.

MODEL LESSON

LESSON

Introduction

Q: In the previous exercise you drew and positioned shapes according to given directions.

Explaining the Objective to Students

Q: In these exercises you will write directions for drawing a given figure.

Class Activity

- Project exercise **H-14** from the transparency of page 223.

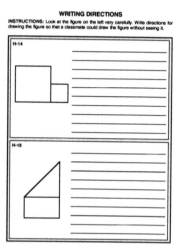

Q: What shapes do you see in this figure?
  A: A large square and a small square

Q: Where is the large square?
  A: To the left of the small square

Q: Where is the small square?
  A: To the right of the large square

Q: Is anything special about the alignment of the squares?
  A: They are touching.

Q: Is anything else special?
  A: The bases (bottoms) of the squares are in line.

Q: You have described the figure, now you need to write directions for drawing it. Remember that the directions you write should result in a figure that is the same as the given figure. How should the directions begin?
  A: Possible answer: Draw a small square. As you write the directions on the transparency, have a student draw the figure on the chalkboard.

Q: What should come next?
  A: Possible answer: Draw a large square to the left of the small square, using the left side of the smaller square as the bottom half of the right side of the larger square. The bases of the two squares should be in line with each other.

GUIDED PRACTICE
EXERCISE: **H-15**

- Give students sufficient time to complete this exercise. Ask students to discuss and explain their choices. Have students read and discuss each other's directions.

INDEPENDENT PRACTICE

- Assign exercises **H-16** and **H-17**.

THINKING ABOUT THINKING

Q: What did you pay attention to in order to write the description?

1. I identified the figures in the drawing.

2. I recalled words that describe size (height, width, length, etc.).

3. I recalled words that describe specific parts of the the figures (base, vertex, diagonal, etc.) in order to identify details about each figure.

4. I looked at the figures and thought about what I would need to say to tell the relative position of each.

5. I recalled words that describe position (right, left, above, next to, etc.).

6. I checked to see that I have used these words clearly enough that someone else could draw the figures.

PERSONAL APPLICATION

Q: When might you need to provide directions?

A: Examples include giving directions for model building or assembling toys and bikes; giving directions for crafts, sewing, cooking, cleaning, or household repairs; giving street directions; telling someone where something is located

EXERCISES H-18 to H-24

RECOGNIZING DIRECTION—A

ANSWERS H-18 through H-24 — Student book pages 225–6
Guided Practice: H-18 behind; **H-19** rectangle; **H-20** right
Independent Practice: H-21 behind; **H-22** triangle; **H-23** ahead; **H-24** square

LESSON PREPARATION

OBJECTIVE AND MATERIALS

OBJECTIVE: Students will describe the locations of four shapes.
MATERIALS: Transparency of student workbook page 225 • washable transparency marker

CURRICULUM APPLICATIONS

LANGUAGE ARTS: Providing directions to specific locations
MATHEMATICS: Doing spatial orientation exercises, locating and charting points on a graph
SCIENCE: Using a map to locate stars or planets, using a road map
SOCIAL STUDIES: Constructing and interpreting maps
ENRICHMENT AREAS: Understanding, visualizing, or following stage directions; marking or following instructions for drill team or marching band positions

TEACHING SUGGESTIONS

Encourage students to discuss their answers. Class discussion is a valuable technique for sharing acquired knowledge.

MODEL LESSON

LESSON

Introduction

Q: In previous exercises you drew and explained shapes to understand their relationships to one another.

Explaining the Objective to Students

Q: In these exercises you will describe the locations of four shapes.

Class Activity

- Project the top section of the transparency of page 225. Write the words *ahead, behind, right,* and *left* on the chalkboard or transparency.

  Q: You will use these words to describe the direction of the shapes.

- Indicate the choices.

  Q: Which shape does the arrow point to?
    A: The square

  Q: If you were standing on the circle facing in the direction of the arrow, what shape would be ahead of you?
    A: The square

  Q: What shape would be behind you?
    A: The hexagon

  Q: What shape would be to your right?
    A: The triangle

  Q: What shape would be to your left?
    A: The rectangle.

- Project the remainder of the transparency.

  Q: The example shows that ahead of the circle is a square. According to the diagram, where is the hexagon?
    A: Behind the circle

  Q: What should be written in the blank for exercise **H-18**?
    A: Behind

- Write "behind" in the blank on the transparency.

GUIDED PRACTICE
EXERCISES: **H-18 to H-20**

- Give students sufficient time to complete these exercises. Ask students to discuss and explain their choices.

INDEPENDENT PRACTICE

- Assign exercises **H-21** through **H-24**.

THINKING ABOUT THINKING

Q: What did you think about to envision what you would see if you faced various directions?

1. I imagined standing in the middle of the compass and turning to face the direction that is given.

2. I envisioned looking straight ahead from that position and imagined a line pointing to the correct shape.

3. I checked which shape is placed one position to the right.

PERSONAL APPLICATION
    Q: When might you need to recognize direction?
        A: Examples include following or making maps, giving oral directions, using a compass or sextant to determine relative location on a map.

RECOGNIZING DIRECTION—B

ANSWERS H-25 through H-34 — Student book pages 227–9
Guided Practice: H-25 square; **H-26** triangle; **H-27** triangle
Independent Practice: H-28 N; **H-29** S, hexagon; **H-30** E, triangle; **H-31** S; **H-32** E, rectangle; **H-33** N, square; **H-34** W, triangle

**LESSON
PREPARATION**

OBJECTIVE AND MATERIALS

OBJECTIVE: Using the information given, students will identify the relative direction of shapes as they change positions and determine the direction they are facing.
MATERIALS: Transparency of student workbook page 227 • washable transparency marker

CURRICULUM APPLICATIONS

LANGUAGE ARTS: Providing directions to specific locations
MATHEMATICS: Doing spatial orientation exercises, locating and charting points on a graph
SCIENCE: Using a map to locate stars or planets, orienting a road map to follow directions
SOCIAL STUDIES: Constructing and interpreting maps
ENRICHMENT AREAS: Understanding, visualizing, or following stage directions, marking or following instructions for drill team or marching band positions

TEACHING SUGGESTIONS

Encourage students to discuss their answers. Class discussion is a valuable technique for sharing acquired knowledge.

MODEL LESSON

LESSON

Introduction
    Q: In the previous exercise you identified the relative direction of shapes from a given position.

Explaining the Objective to Students
    Q: In these exercises you will use given information to identify the relative direction of shapes as you change positions and determine the direction you are facing.

Class Activity
• Project the top section from the transparency 227.

RECOGNIZING DIRECTION
DIRECTIONS: Imagine that you are standing in the circle, facing a direction given by a letter. Draw the shape you are facing and the shape on your right. For example, if you are facing north (N), as shown in the example, then the rectangle is straight ahead and the triangle is on your right. Draw a triangle in the blank in the first row. Next, imagine that you are facing west (W); draw the missing shape in the blank in the second row.

Q: You will imagine that you are facing first in one direction and then in another. Look at the arrows and the letters in the diagram. The arrow pointing upward has an N on it. What does this stand for?
  A: North

Q: The arrow pointing downward has an S on it. What does this stand for?
  A: South

Q: The arrow pointing to the left has a W on it. What does this stand for?
  A: West

Q: The arrow pointing to the right has an E on it. What does this stand for?
  A: East

- Project the example.
  Q: The example tells you that you are facing north. What shape are you facing?
    A: The rectangle

- Indicate the rectangle under the facing shape column.
  Q: What shape is to your right?
    A: The triangle.

- Draw the triangle on the indicated lines.

- Project exercise **H-25**.
  Q: What direction are you facing now?
    A: West

  Q: If the rectangle is to your right, what shape are you facing?
    A: The square.

- Draw the square in the blank.

GUIDED PRACTICE
EXERCISES: **H-26** to **H-27**
- Give students sufficient time to complete these exercises. Ask students to explain their choices.

INDEPENDENT PRACTICE
- Assign exercises **H-28** through **H-34**. Students will deduce the direction they must face to have certain shapes on the left and right.

THINKING ABOUT THINKING
Q: What did you think about to envision what you would see if you faced various directions?

1. I imagined standing in the middle of the compass and turning to face the direction that is given.

2. I envisioned looking straight ahead from that position and imagined a line pointing to the correct shape.

3. I checked which shape is placed one position to the right.

PERSONAL APPLICATION

Q: When might you need to recognize direction?

A: Examples include following or making maps, giving oral directions, using a compass or sextant to determine location in relation to a map.

EXERCISES H-35 to H-42

DESCRIBING LOCATIONS

ANSWERS H-35 through H-42 — Student book pages 230–1
Guided Practice: H-35 to **H-36** See below.
Independent Practice: H-37 See below; **H-38** R; **H-39** R; **H-40** Fourth Avenue; **H-41** Where B Street meets Second Avenue, A Street, Two blocks; **H-42** Where B Street meets First Avenue, A Street, Three blocks

H-35–37

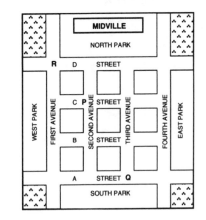

LESSON PREPARATION

OBJECTIVE AND MATERIALS

OBJECTIVE: Students will describe locations on a map.
MATERIALS: Transparency of student book page 222 • TM 33 (optional) • washable transparency marker

CURRICULUM APPLICATIONS

LANGUAGE ARTS: Writing instructional papers or giving demonstration speeches
MATHEMATICS: Identifying particular points on a graph, describing an arrangement of geometric shapes, spatial orientation exercises
SCIENCE: Stating or writing directions for construction of motors or gears, detailing the position of a star or planet
SOCIAL STUDIES: Reading maps, graphs, or charts; describing geographic locations
ENRICHMENT AREAS: Creating or following pattern plays in team sports, describing performance of a dance step or directions for creating an art project, writing or giving stage directions for a play

TEACHING SUGGESTIONS

Encourage students to discuss their answers. Class discussion is a valuable technique for sharing acquired knowledge and developing clear verbal expression.

MODEL LESSON | **LESSON**

Introduction

Q: In the previous exercise you practiced recognizing directions by using the locations of two or more given shapes.

Explaining the Objective to Students

Q: In these exercises you will describe locations on a map.

Class Activity

• Project transparency of student page 230.
Q: This is a map of Midville. What is located on the left side of the map?

• Point as students respond.
A: West Park

Q: What is located on the right side of the map?
A: East Park

Q: What is located at the top of the map?
A: North Park

Q: What is located at the bottom of the map?
A: South Park

Q: What are the names of the avenues?
A: First, Second, Third, and Fourth Avenues

Q: What are the names of the streets?
A: A, B, C, and D Streets

Q: In what direction do the streets run in Midville?
A: East and west

Q: In what direction do the avenues run?
A: North and south

Q: Now that you are familiar with the map, you will locate some crossings. Mark an "L" where Second Avenue and A Street cross.

• Have a student mark the letters on the transparency at each intersection, asking other students for verification each time. Have students mark answers in their workbooks.
Q: Mark an "M" where Third Avenue and B Street cross.

• Pause for students' response.
Q: Mark an "N" where Fourth Avenue and D Street cross.

• Pause for students' response.
Q: Mark an "O" where First Avenue and C Street cross.

• Pause for students' response.

GUIDED PRACTICE

EXERCISES: **H-35** to **H-36**

• Give students sufficient time to complete these exercises. Ask students to discuss and explain their choices.

DESCRIBING LOCATIONS
DIRECTIONS: Locate the parts of Midville described in the exercises. Read the instructions for each exercise and mark the map accordingly.

H-35 Print a "P" where Second Avenue and C Street cross.
H-36 Print a "Q" where Third Avenue and A Street cross.
H-37 Print an "R" where First Avenue and D Street cross.
H-38 Which letter (P, Q, or R) is closest to West Park?   Answer: _____
H-39 Which letter is in the northern part of Midville?   Answer: _____
H-40 Which Street or Avenue is closest to East Park?   Answer: _____

INDEPENDENT PRACTICE
• Assign exercises **H-37** through **H-42**.

THINKING ABOUT THINKING
Q: What did you pay attention to when you described specific locations on maps?
   1. I located my starting position.
   2. I carefully read the question.
   3. I checked the street and avenue names.
   4. I visualized the move from the original location to the new one.
   5. I located my new position and wrote the location.

PERSONAL APPLICATION
Q: When might you need to describe specific locations?
   A: Examples include following maps, following or giving street directions, telling someone where something is located.

**EXERCISES
H-43 to H-50**

DESCRIBING DIRECTIONS

ANSWERS H-43 through H-50 — Student book pages 232–5
Guided Practice: H-43 C Street meets First; **H-44** 2 blocks east
Independent Practice: H-45 3 blocks north and 1 block east; **H-46** 1 block east and 3 blocks north; 4 blocks; **H-47** 3 blocks south and 1 block east; **H-48** 1 block east and 3 blocks south; 4 blocks; **H-49** 1 block east, two blocks south, and 1 block east; **H-50** 1 block south, two blocks east, one block south (See map for **H-49** and **H-50** next page.)

H-49–50

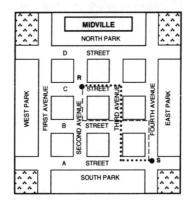

**LESSON
PREPARATION**

OBJECTIVE AND MATERIALS
OBJECTIVE: In these exercises students will locate intersections by creating or describing a given path.
MATERIALS: TM 35 • washable transparency marker • transparency of student page 230 (optional)

CURRICULUM APPLICATIONS
LANGUAGE ARTS: Using reference and cross-references in research materials

MATHEMATICS: Locating or charting consecutive points on a graph, doing spatial orientation exercises

SCIENCE: Using a map to locate stars or planets, using a sextant, constructing gears

SOCIAL STUDIES: Reading maps, graphs, or charts

ENRICHMENT AREAS: Creating or following pattern plays in team sports, putting a series of dance steps into a sequence, writing or giving stage directions for a play

TEACHING SUGGESTIONS

Encourage students to discuss their answers and be specific in their descriptions.

MODEL LESSON

LESSON

Introduction

Q: In the previous exercise you described locations or positions on a map.

Explaining the Objective to Students

Q: In these exercises you will locate intersections by creating or describing a given path.

Class Activity

Note: If it has been a few days since the Describing Locations lesson, use the lesson on page 230 for review.

- Project TM 35.

  Q: This map shows a path in Midville. Look at the part of the path from point *P* to point *Q*.

- Point as students respond.

  Q: Which park is closest to point *P*?

  A: East Park

  Q: Which park is closest to point *Q*?

  A: West Park

  Q: When describing a path, it is useful to indicate that it goes from one direction to another. How can you describe the direction of the path from point *P* near East Park to point *Q* near West Park?

  A: It goes from east to west.

Q: Now look at the path from point *Q* to point *R*. Which park does the arrow indicate?

  A: North Park

Q: Which park is behind point *Q*?

  A: South Park

Q: Describe the direction of the path from point *Q* to point *R*.

  A: It goes from south to north.

Q: Now look at the lengths of the paths. How many blocks is it from point *P* to point *Q*?

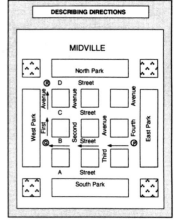

TRANSPARENCY MASTER 35

DESCRIBING DIRECTIONS

MIDVILLE

© 1998 CRITICAL THINKING BOOKS & SOFTWARE • WWW.CRITICALTHINKING.COM • 800-458-4849

A: Three blocks

Q: How many blocks is it from point *Q* to point *R*?
   A: Two blocks

Q: How could you direct a person who wants to take this path from point *P* to point *R*?
   A: Go three blocks west, then turn right and go two blocks north.

GUIDED PRACTICE
EXERCISES: **H-45** to **H-46**
• Give students sufficient time to complete these exercises. Then, using the demonstration methodology above, have them discuss and explain their choices.

INDEPENDENT PRACTICE
• Assign exercises **H-47** through **H-50**.

THINKING ABOUT THINKING
Q: What did you pay attention to when you described specific locations or directions on maps?
   1. I located my starting position.
   2. I carefully read the question.
   3. I checked the street and avenue names.
   4. I visualized the move from the original location to the new one.
   5. I located my new position and wrote the location.

PERSONAL APPLICATION
Q: When do you want or need to find a location?
   A: Examples include following or giving street directions, reading a road map to find out how to get from one place to another (sometimes by more than one route), writing or following clues in a treasure hunt game.

EXERCISES H-51 to H-73

TIME SEQUENCE—SELECT, RANK, SUPPLY

ANSWERS H-51 through H-73 — Student book pages 236–8
Guided Practice: H-51 arrive; **H-52** spend; **H-58** eat; (or cook, eat, clean); **H-59** dial, talk, hang up; **H-65** die
Independent Practice: H-53 occupy; **H-54** result; **H-55** late; **H-56** cut; **H-57** rise; **H-60** shop, buy, use; **H-61** attack, battle, defeat; **H-62** lesson, practice, performance; **H-63** start, continue, finish; **H-64** wash, rinse, dry; **H-66** harvest; **H-67** end, finish, complete; **H-68** future; **H-69** noon, afternoon, day, evening; **H-70** heal; **H-71** exhale, breathe out; **H-72** buy, purchase; **H-73** graduate, finish, complete

LESSON PREPARATION

OBJECTIVE AND MATERIALS
OBJECTIVE: Students will arrange words in their order of occurrence.

MATERIALS: Transparencies of student workbook pages 236 and 237 • washable transparency marker

CURRICULUM APPLICATIONS

LANGUAGE ARTS: Relating correct chronological order, e.g., writing narratives or letters; relating story plots; selecting adverbs and verbs to express order or time

MATHEMATICS: Solving word problems involving transitivity

SCIENCE: Recognizing and predicting frequency variance, following sequential directions and writing organized reports of science demonstrations, classifying physical phenomena chronologically

SOCIAL STUDIES: Recognizing and using chronological order to place historical events

ENRICHMENT AREAS: Understanding and using correct time-sequence procedures, recognizing and describing degrees of expertise

TEACHING SUGGESTIONS

Give students sufficient time to complete these exercises. Then using the methodology below, have them discuss and explain their choices. In exercises **H-65** through **H-73** students must supply a word to continue the sequence.

The following cues will encourage discussion for exercises **H-51** through **H-57**:

1. What do all the words concern? (Topic)

2. Which of the word choices continues the sequence? (Answer)

3. Why don't the other choices fit the time sequence? (Elimination of detractors)

The following cues will encourage discussion for exercises **H-58** through **H-64**:

1. What do all the words concern?

2. Which action would happen first?

3. Which action would happen last?

4. In what time sequence would the actions normally occur? (Answer)

MODEL LESSON | ## LESSON

Introduction

Q: In previous exercises you located and described directions or paths that started at one point and went to another. Many of the things you do follow a sequence, much like giving directions or following a path.

Explaining the Objective to Students

Q: In these exercises you will arrange words in their order of occurrence.

Class Activity

Q: Sometimes you do things in a particular order out of habit and sometimes out of necessity. For example, most of you probably follow the same pattern every school morning. This is a time sequence of habit. When you prepare a meal, you usually follow a time sequence of necessity.

• Project exercise **H-51** on the transparency of student page 236.

Q: In this exercise you are given the words *leave* and *travel* and asked to select a word from the column on the right to continue the sequence. What do the words *leave* and *travel* concern?

  A: Taking a trip

Q: Look at the answer choices. Which word continues the trip sequence *leave, travel?*

  A: Arrive

Q: How does *arrive* continue the sequence?

  A: First you leave, then you travel, and last you arrive.

Q: Why is *depart* not the answer?

  A: *Depart* means the same as leave; it is the first thing that happens in a trip sequence.

Q: Why is *drive* not the answer?

  A: *Drive* means the same as travel; it is the second thing that happens when taking a trip.

• Project the transparency of page 237.

Q: These exercises are similar to the one you just did, but here you must determine the correct order of the given words. In exercise **H-58** you are given the words *clean, cook, and eat.* What do these words concern?

  A: Preparing food for a meal

Q: You need to arrange these words so the first word represents the first thing done and the last word represents the last thing done. Which action takes place first?

  A: Clean the food (or cook the meal)

Q: Which action happens last?

  A: Eat the food (or clean the table and dishes)

Q: In what order do these three actions normally occur?

  A: Clean, cook, eat (Note: If students consider clean as "to clean up after a meal," the answer would be cook, eat, clean.)

Q: What do the words in exercise **H-59**—*dial, hang up, and talk*—have in common?

  A: They all concern making a telephone call.

Q: Which action usually takes place first?

  A: Dial

Q: Which do you do last?

  A: Hang up

Q: In what time sequence do these three actions normally occur?
  A: Dial, talk, hang up

GUIDED PRACTICE
EXERCISES: **H-51, H-58** to **H-59, H-65**

INDEPENDENT PRACTICE
• Assign exercises **H-52** through **H-57**; **H-60** through **H-64**; **H-66** through **H-73**.

THINKING ABOUT THINKING
Q: What did you pay attention to when you decided which word came next?

1. I looked for the relationship between the words.

2. I determined whether the sequence was increasing or decreasing.

3. I decided which word would come next in the sequence.

4. I checked that the other words didn't fit the pattern.

PERSONAL APPLICATION
Q: When might you need to determine, arrange, or supply what comes next in time?
  A: Examples include following sequential directions for errands or chores; following directions for crafts, sewing, cooking, cleaning, or household repairs; games involving chronological order, e.g. military board games; telling and understanding jokes, puns, or stories; word puzzles and games; understanding and describing test or game results.

EXERCISES H-74 to H-119

DEGREE OF MEANING—SELECT, RANK, SUPPLY

ANSWERS H-74 through H-119 — Student book pages 239–44
Guided Practice: H-74 freezing; **H-75** behind; **H-88** pleased, delighted, thrilled; **H-89** safety, threat, danger; **H-102** mayor, governor, president; **H-103** front, side, back
Independent Practice: H-76 demand; **H-77** hopeless; **H-78** plenty; **H-79** excellent; **H-80** downpour; **H-81** harsh; **H-82** different; **H-83** excited; **H-84** average; **H-85** terrified; **H-86** exhausted; **H-87** disgusted; **H-90** doze, nap, sleep; **H-91** bright, dim, dark (or dark, dim, bright); **H-92** desert, prairie, jungle; **H-93** pond, lake, ocean; **H-94** state, country, continent; **H-95** pupil, class, school; **H-96** tender, sore, painful; **H-97** swell, full, burst; **H-98** empty, full, overflowing; **H-99** starving, hungry, full; **H-100** pint, quart, gallon; **H-101** inch, foot, yard; The following are possible answers: **H-104** few, many, most; **H-105** far, farther, farthest; **H-106** more, some, none; **H-107** word, sentence, paragraph; **H-108** same, similar, different; **H-109** good, better, best; **H-110** cool, warm, hot; **H-111** short, average, tall; **H-112** dark, dawn, daylight; **H-113** day, week, month; **H-114** caterpillar, cocoon, butterfly; **H-115** scene, act, play; **H-116** home,

neighborhood, community; **H-117** foal, colt, horse; **H-118** duet, trio, quartet; **H-119** tenor, baritone, bass

LESSON PREPARATION

OBJECTIVE AND MATERIALS
OBJECTIVE: Students will arrange words according to degree of meaning.
MATERIALS: Transparency of student workbook pages 239 and 241 • washable transparency marker

CURRICULUM APPLICATIONS
LANGUAGE ARTS: Using comparative and superlative rank of adjectives or adverbs; doing exercises involving chronological order, e.g., writing narratives or letters, relating story, plots; selecting nouns and verbs to express degree, rank, or order
MATHEMATICS: Solving word problems involving transitivity or inequality, describing geometric proportions in angle or size
SCIENCE: Recognizing and predicting variance of size or frequency, writing organized reports of science demonstrations
SOCIAL STUDIES: Recognizing degrees of meaning in economics, history, or geography texts; recognizing divisions and subdivisions of governmental or political structures; recognizing rank in social, military, or governmental institutions
ENRICHMENT AREAS: Describing gradations of color or size in art; describing gradations of pitch, rhythm, or volume in music; recognizing and describing degrees of expertise

TEACHING SUGGESTIONS
Encourage students to discuss their answers. Class discussion is a valuable technique for having students share their acquired knowledge. Often a student's words will communicate in a more meaningful way than words a teacher may use.

Give students sufficient time to complete these exercises. Then, using the demonstration methodology in the lesson, have them discuss and explain their choices. In exercises **H-102** through **H-119**, students must supply a word to continue the sequence. You may want to break these exercises into two or three separate lessons.

MODEL LESSON

LESSON

Introduction
Q: In previous exercises you arranged words in order of occurrence.

Explaining the Objective to Students
Q: In these exercises you will arrange words according to degree of meaning.

Class Activity
• Project exercise **H-74** from student page 239.
Q: You are given the words *chilly* and *frosty* and asked to select a word from the column on the

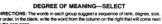

DEGREE OF MEANING—SELECT
DIRECTIONS: The words in each group suggest a sequence of rank, degree, size, or order. In the blank, write the word from the column on the right that will come next in the sequence.

H-74 chilly, frosty, _____	brisk / cool / freezing
H-75 ahead, beside, _____	behind / beneath / between
H-76 hint, ask, _____	demand / request / suggest
H-77 sad, depressed, _____	hopeless / sorry / unhappy
H-78 scarce, adequate, _____	enough / few / plenty
H-79 satisfactory, admirable, _____	average / ordinary / excellent
H-80 mist, light rain, _____	downpour / drizzle / fog

right to continue the sequence. *Chilly* and *frosty* refer to degrees of what?
  A: Degrees of coldness or temperature

Q: Look at the answer choices. Which word continues the degree-of-coldness sequence?
  A: *Freezing*

Q: How does *freezing* continue the sequence?
  A: *Frosty* is colder than *chilly*, and *freezing* is colder than *frosty*.

Q: Why is *brisk* not the answer?
  A: *Brisk* means about the same as *chilly*, possibly slightly warmer than *chilly*.

- Project exercise **H-88** from student page 241.
  Q: You are given the words *delighted, pleased,* and *thrilled*. The directions say that you are to arrange the words in increasing (ascending) order, from least or smallest to greatest or largest. These words name degrees of what?
  A: Degrees of happiness

  Q: Which word names the least degree of happiness?
  A: *Pleased*

  Q: Which is the greatest degree of happiness?
  A: *Thrilled*

  Q: Rank these words in order of increasing degrees of happiness.
  A: *Pleased, delighted, thrilled*

DEGREE OF MEANING—RANK

DIRECTIONS: On the lines below, rewrite each group of words in order from lowest or smallest to highest or largest in degree, rank, size, or order.

H-88 delighted, pleased, thrilled
_____ _____ _____

H-89 danger, safety, threat
_____ _____ _____

H-90 doze, nap, sleep
_____ _____ _____

H-91 bright, dark, dim
_____ _____ _____

H-92 desert, jungle, prairie
_____ _____ _____

H-93 lake, ocean, pond
_____ _____ _____

H-94 continent, country, state
_____ _____ _____

GUIDED PRACTICE
EXERCISES: **H-74** to **H-75**; **H-88** to **H-89**; **H-102** to **H-103**
- In exercises **H-102** through **H-119** students must supply a word to continue the sequence.

INDEPENDENT PRACTICE
- Assign exercises **H-76** through **H-87**; **H-90** through **H-101**; **H-104** through **H-119**.

THINKING ABOUT THINKING
Q: What did you pay attention to when you decided which word came next?

1. I looked for the relationship between the words.

2. I determined whether the sequence was increasing or decreasing.

3. I decided which word would come next in the sequence.

4. I checked that the other words didn't fit the pattern.

PERSONAL APPLICATION
Q: When do you want or need to know what comes next in a given order or ranking?

A: Examples include understanding and describing test or game results; telling and understanding jokes, puns, or stories; distinguishing the size or worth of objects; playing word puzzles and games; understanding consumer product terms describing size or volume.

TRANSITIVITY—COMPARISON/COMMON SEQUENCES

ANSWERS H-120 through H-132 — Student book pages 245–51
Guided Practice: H-120 Airedale, fox terrier, Westie; **H-121** monorail, subway, bus, bicycle; **H-125** George Washington, John Adams, Thomas Jefferson, John Quincy Adams; **H-126** Augustine, Jamestown, Plymouth
Independent Practice: H-122 Mary, Michelle, Elizabeth, Gloria; **H-123** Victorian, colonial, modern; **H-124** John, Taryn, Eric, Christine, Jesse; **H-127** a. 4, b. 1, c. 2, d. 3; **H-128** a. 2, b. 1, c. 4, d. 3; **H-129** Purchase film, load film, focus camera, click shutter, process film; **H-130** 1. Lift receiver, 2. dial one, 3. dial area code, 4. dial seven-digit number, 5. talk, hang up; **H-131** 1. Decide on type, 2. find recipe, 3. buy materials, 4. cook candy, 5. package candy, 6. sell candy; **H-132** 1. Ask family, 2. talk about kind, 3. go to shelter, 4. pick out dog, 5. pay license and fee, 6. take dog home

OBJECTIVE AND MATERIALS
OBJECTIVE: Students will compare objects according to common characteristics and compare events in order of their occurrence.
MATERIALS: Transparencies of student workbook pages 245 and 247 • washable transparency marker

CURRICULUM APPLICATIONS
LANGUAGE ARTS: Expressing comparative and superlative rank of adjectives or adverbs; writing narratives or letters, relating story plots, or doing other exercises involving chronological order; selecting nouns and verbs to express degree, rank, or order
MATHEMATICS: Solving word problems involving transitivity or inequality, describing geometric proportions in angle or size
SCIENCE: Recognizing and predicting variance, size, or frequency; writing organized reports of science demonstrations; describing size comparisons in plants and animals
SOCIAL STUDIES: Recognizing chronological order and using it to place historical events, eras, artifacts, cultures, and people into proper time relationships; recognizing divisions and subdivisions of governmental or political structures
ENRICHMENT AREAS: Describing gradations of color or size in art; describing gradations of pitch, rhythm, or volume in music; recognizing and describing degrees of expertise

TEACHING SUGGESTIONS
Encourage students to discuss their answers and check their completed charts against the information in the paragraph.

MODEL LESSON | LESSON

Introduction

Q: In previous exercises you arranged words according to order in time or degree of meaning.

Explaining the Objective to Students

Q: In these exercises you will arrange information from sentences. Sometimes you will compare objects according to some characteristic they have in common, and sometimes you will organize events according to their order of occurrence.

Class Activity

- Project the transparency of exercise **H-120** on student page 245.

  Q: You are given a paragraph that describes three different kinds of terriers.

- Read the paragraph aloud.

  Q: What are you being asked to compare?

    A: The size of the dogs

  Q: What information tells you which is the largest or smallest terrier?

    A: The last sentence says that the Airedale is the largest dog in the terrier breed.

  Q: Where does this information go?

    A: In the top (Largest) blank

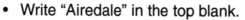

- Write "Airedale" in the top blank.

  Q: The first sentence compares the fox terrier to the Westie. Which dog is smaller?

    A: The Westie

  Q: How do you know?

    A: The first sentence tells you that the fox terrier is taller than the Westie.

- Write "Westie" in the last (Smallest) blank.

  Q: What should be written in he second blank?

    A: Fox terrier

  Q: You have now arranged the names according to the decreasing size of the dogs—Airedale, fox terrier, Westie. Check the arrangement against the information given in the paragraph. The first sentence states that the fox terrier is taller than the Westie. Does the chart agree with that information?

- Indicate the last two lines.

    A: Yes

  Q: The second sentence says that the Airedale is the largest dog in the terrier breed. Does the chart agree with that information?

- Indicate the top line.
  A: Yes

- Project exercise **H-125** from student page 247.
  Q: You are given a paragraph concerning the time three men served as president of the United States. You are to arrange their names in order from earliest to latest.

- Read the paragraph aloud.
  Q: What facts are you given about John Quincy Adams?

- Point to the first sentence.
  A: He was the sixth president of the United States and was the son of John Adams, the second president.

  Q: Which would come later in time, the sixth president or the second president?
  A: The sixth president

- At the side of the transparency, write "J.A." Then under it write "J.Q.A."
  Q: When did John Adams become president?

- Point to the second sentence.
  A: After two terms as vice president under George Washington

  Q: Which of these two men, John Adams or George Washington, was president first?
  A: George Washington

- Write "G.W." above J.A. at the side of the transparency.
  Q: Check this order against the information given in the paragraph. The first sentence says that John Adams was the second president and John Quincy Adams was the sixth president. Does the chart show this order?
  A: Yes

  Q: The last sentence says that John Adams was president after George Washington. Does the chart show this order?
  A: Yes

  Q: List the presidents in order from earliest to latest.
  A: George Washington, John Adams, Thomas Jefferson, John Quincy Adams

GUIDED PRACTICE
EXERCISES: **H-120** to **H-121**, **H-125** to **H-126**
- Give students sufficient time to complete these exercises. Then, using the demonstration methodology above, have them discuss and explain their choices.

INDEPENDENT PRACTICE

- Assign exercises **H-122** through **H-124** and **H-127** through **H-132**.

THINKING ABOUT THINKING

Q: What did you pay attention to when you decided which word came next?

1. I looked for the relationship between the words.

2. I determined whether the sequence was increasing or decreasing.

3. I decided which word would come next in the sequence.

PERSONAL APPLICATION

Q: When might you need to determine order or rank from given information?

A: Examples include recreational reading; understanding and describing test or game results; understanding and telling jokes, puns, or stories; distinguishing among size or worth of objects; solving word puzzles and games; understanding consumer product terms describing size, volume, or value.

EXERCISES H-133 to H-136

TRANSITIVITY—FAMILY TREE

ANSWERS H-133 through H-136 — Student book pages 252–6
Guided Practice: H-133 See below.
Independent Practice: H-134 1. Helen, 2. Bill, 3. Helen, 4. Jim; See diagram below. **H-135** 1. Brown, 2. John and Ruth Cooper; See next page. **H-136** Information will vary.

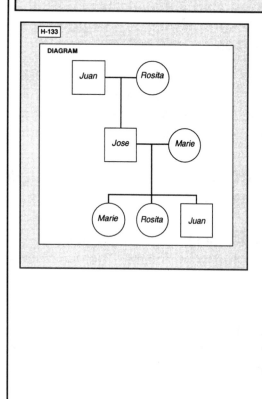

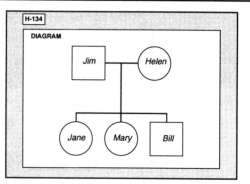

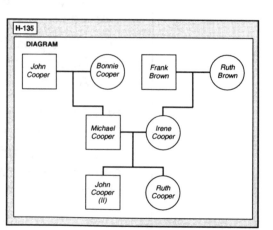

LESSON PREPARATION

OBJECTIVE AND MATERIALS

OBJECTIVE: Students will use clues to complete a diagram of a family tree.

MATERIALS: Transparencies of student workbook pages 252 and 253 • washable transparency marker

CURRICULUM APPLICATIONS

LANGUAGE ARTS: Doing reading comprehension activities regarding family relationships

MATHEMATICS: Tracking and recording generations

SCIENCE: Doing genetics research

SOCIAL STUDIES: Tracing family histories, tracing technological or industrial developments

ENRICHMENT AREAS: Tracing development of vocations

TEACHING SUGGESTIONS

Encourage students to discuss their answers and to check their completed diagrams against the clues. They should state which clue gave them the indicated information.

In exercise **H-136**, students will complete a family tree diagram based on their own family. You may want to assign this exercise for homework.

LESSON

Introduction

Q: In previous exercises you arranged information in order. Sometimes objects were compared, and sometimes events were arranged in order of time.

Explaining the Objective to Students

Q: In these exercises you will use clues to complete a diagram of a family tree.

Class Activity

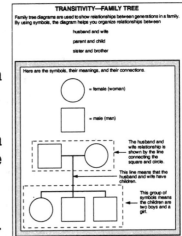

TRANSITIVITY—FAMILY TREE

Family tree diagrams are used to show relationships between generations in a family. By using symbols, the diagram helps you organize relationships between

husband and wife

parent and child

sister and brother

Here are the symbols, their meanings, and their connections.

= female (woman)

= male (man)

The husband and wife relationship is shown by the line connecting the square and circle.

This line means that the husband and wife have children.

This group of symbols means the children are two boys and a girl.

- Project the transparency of page 252.
  Q: In these diagrams, circles...

- Point to the circle.
  Q: ...mean that the person represented is a female, and squares...

- Point to the square.
  Q: ...mean that the person represented is a male. A horizontal line connecting a square and a circle...

- Point to the line.
  Q: ...means the man and woman are married. A vertical line...

- Point.
  Q: ...means the husband and wife have children.

- Project the transparency of page 253. Point to the rows of the diagram.

Q: This family tree diagram has three rows. What does the bottom row represent?
    A: The children in the family.

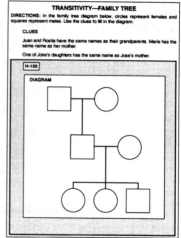

- Write "children" beside the bottom row.
  Q: What does the middle row represent?
      A: The parents of the children.

- Write "parents" beside the middle row.
  Q: What does the top row represent?
      A: The grandparents of the children (father's parents).

- Write "grandparents" beside the top row.
  Q: You are to use clues from the paragraph to correctly complete the diagram of the family tree. The first sentence states that Juan and Rosita have the same names as their grandparents. What do you know from this clue?
      A: The names of the two children and the names of the grandparents are Juan and Rosita.

  Q: Can you fill in any of the diagram using this information?
      A: Yes; put the grandparents' names in the top row and put in two of the children's names.

  Q: Where should you write the children's names?
      A: On the bottom line. Put "Juan" in the square and "Rosita" in one of the circles.

- Write the grandparents' names in the top row and the children's names in the square and a circle.
  Q: The next sentence states that Marie has the same name as her mother. What can you determine from this clue?
      A: The remaining child's circle and the circle in the parents' row should be filled in with the name Marie.

- Write "Marie" in both circles.
  Q: How do you know the name that belongs in the last empty square?
      A: The last clue states that one of Jose's daughters has the same name as Jose's mother.

- Write "Jose" in the empty square.
  Q: You can check that Jose's name belongs in the square. Look at the diagram. What is the name of Jose's mother?
      A: Rosita.

- Point to the circle in the top row.
  Q: What is the name of one of Jose's daughters?
      A: Rosita.

- Point to the circles in the bottom row.
  Q: The diagram agrees with the clue.

178

GUIDED PRACTICE
EXERCISES: **H-133** to **H-134**

INDEPENDENT PRACTICE
• Assign exercises **H-135** through **H-136**.

THINKING ABOUT THINKING
Q: What did you think about as you completed the family tree?

1. I read the clues carefully.

2. I used information from the clues to determine family relationships.

3. I filled in the diagram according to the information.

4. I checked the diagram from top to bottom to be sure it agreed with the clues.

PERSONAL APPLICATION
Q: When might you need to identify relationships or arrange a family by generations?

A: Examples include recording or explaining family histories or completing medical records.

EXERCISES H-137 to H-147

DEADUCTIVE REASONING

DEDUCTIVE REASONING

ANSWERS H-137 through H-147 — student book pages 257–64

Guided Practice: H-137 Abraham, Salem; James, Dartmouth; Nathaniel, Bourne; **H-138** Onju, 5th; Pedro, 4th; Richard, 3rd

Independent Practice: H-139 Cicero, mouse; Ego, rabbit; Fred, tiger; **H-140** David, swimming; Hector, football; Maria, baseball; **H-141** Anita, cook; Beth, typist; Juan, nurse; **H-142** Mr. Allen, art; Mr. Franklin, first; Ms. Smith, second; Mrs. Townsend, third; **H-143** George, math teacher; Nancy, programmer; Shannon, astronaut; **H-144** Graham, coupe; Mario, hatchback; Pancho, Spyder; First: Graham, coupe; Second: Pancho, Spyder; Third: Mario, hatchback; **H-145** Bob, blue; Chris, white; Nancy, green; Pat, red; **H-146** Bill, axe; Jane, pliers; Kim, hammer; Tom, saw; **H-147** Small, plankton; Medium, plants; Large, meat and plants; Very Large, meat

DETAILED SOLUTIONS

H-137 Clue *b* tells you that Abraham's parents settled in Salem just before he was born; therefore, he was probably born in Salem. Place a *Y* (for Yes) in the Salem cell under Abraham. If Abraham were born in Salem, he could not have been born anywhere else, so mark the Dartmouth and Bourne cells

	Abraham	James	Nathaniel
Bourne	NO	NO	YES
Dartmouth	NO	YES	NO
Salem	YES	NO	NO

under Abraham *N* (for No). You also know that if Abraham were born in Salem, none of the other ancestors were born there. Mark the James and the Nathaniel cells next to Salem *N* also. Clue *c* tells you that the youngest

Bradford was born in Dartmouth. From clue *a* you know that Nathaniel is not the youngest, i.e., he is older than James. You then know that Nathaniel was not born in Dartmouth and can mark cell Dartmouth *N*. The chart now gives you the information that neither Nathaniel nor Abraham was born in Dartmouth. Thus, only James could have been born there. Place a *Y* in the Dartmouth cell under James and an *N* in the Bourne cell. This leaves only one cell blank, so Nathaniel must have been born in Bourne. Place a *Y* in the Bourne cell.

H-138 Clue *a* tells you that neither Pedro nor Onju is in the third grade. Mark this information by placing an *N* in the Onju and Pedro cells under 3rd. Only one cell is blank in the 3rd-grade column, so mark the Richard cell *Y*. Since Richard is in third grade, he cannot be in any other grade. Mark the Richard cells under 4th and 5th with an *N*. Clue *b* tells you that Onju is in a higher grade

	3rd	4th	5th
Onju	NO	NO	YES
Pedro	NO	YES	NO
Richard	YES	NO	NO

than Pedro. The only two students not yet identified are in the fourth and fifth grades. If Onju is in a higher grade, then he must be in the fifth grade. Mark the cell next to Onju under 5th with a *Y* and the cell under 4th with an *N*. That means Pedro is in the 4th grade. Mark the appropriate cells *Y* and *N*.

H-139 Clue *a* tells you that Ego is larger than a mouse; therefore, he is not the mouse. Mark an *N* in the Ego/Mouse cell. In Clue *b*, Cicero is older than the rabbit but younger than the tiger, so Cicero is neither the rabbit nor the tiger. Mark an *N* in the Cicero/Rabbit and the Cicero/Tiger cells. You now know that Cicero must be the mouse, so mark the mouse cell *Y*. Then

	Mouse	Rabbit	Tiger
Cicero	YES	NO	NO
Ego	NO	YES	NO
Fred	NO	NO	YES

Fred cannot be the mouse, so place an *N* in the Mouse cell. Clue *c* tells you that Fred is older than Cicero, but clue b says that Cicero is older than the rabbit. Thus, Fred cannot be the rabbit. Place an *N* in the Fred/Rabbit cell. This means Fred is the tiger. Place a *Y* in the Fred/Tiger cell. Then Ego is not the tiger, he is the rabbit. Mark the appropriate cells *Y* and *N*.

H-140 Clue *a* tells you that Maria is probably not on the swimming team. Mark cell Maria/Swimming *N*. Clue *c* tells you that Hector is a quarterback. Since only football has a quarterback, Hector must play football. Mark the cell H/Football *Y* and the other two cells in the H row *N*. By examining the chart, you can see that Maria must be

	Baseball	Football	Swimming
D	NO	NO	YES
H	NO	YES	NO
M	YES	NO	NO

a member of the baseball team. This leaves only one sport for David—swimming—and clue *b* reinforces that information.

H-141 From clue *a* you know that Juan cannot type; therefore, he is not the typist. Mark cell J-Typist *N*. Clue *b* tells you that Anita is neither the nurse nor the typist. Mark cells A-Nurse and A-Typist *N*. The only profession remaining for Anita is cook. Mark cell A-Cook *Y* and all other cells in column C *N*, for if Anita is the cook then no one else is. Then Juan must be the nurse. Mark cell J-Nurse *Y* and cell B-Nurse *N*. (If Juan is the nurse, then Beth cannot be the nurse.) This leaves Beth as the typist.

	Cook	Nurse	Typist
A	YES	NO	YES
B	NO	NO	NO
J	NO	YES	NO

H-142 Since one expects that first-, second-, and third-grade teachers would teach either reading or arithmetic and clue *a* tells you that Mr. Allen teaches neither, put an *N* in the 1st, 2nd, and 3rd column cells of row A. This means Mr. Allen must teach art, so mark column A-ART *Y*. If Mr. Allen teaches art, then none of the other teachers do, so put an *N* in all other cells under column ART. Clue *b* tells you that Ms. Smith teaches a "middle" grade—lower than Mrs. Townsend and higher than Mr. Franklin. This would be 2nd grade. Mark a *Y* in cell S-2nd, and fill in an *N* in each remaining cell of the 2nd column and the S row. Clue *b* also tells you that Mr. Franklin teaches 1st grade (lower than Ms. Smith) and Mrs. Townsend teaches 3rd grade (higher than Ms. Smith).

	1st	2nd	3rd	Art
A	NO	NO	NO	YES
F	YES	NO	NO	NO
S	NO	YES	NO	NO
T	NO	NO	YES	NO

H-143 You are told that George is neither the astronaut nor the computer programmer (*a*), and that Nancy is not the astronaut (*b*). If the astronaut is neither George nor Nancy, it must be Shannon. Mark cell A/Shannon *Y*, and all other cells in the Shannon column *N*. This leaves only Nancy to be the computer programmer. Place a *Y* in cell CP/Nancy and an *N* in cell MT/Nancy. Then George is the math teacher.

	George	Nancy	Shannon
A	NO	NO	YES
CP	NO	YES	NO
MT	YES	NO	NO

H-144 Clue *a* tells you that Mario was not driving the coupe, since the coupe beat Mario's car. Put an *N* in the Mario/Coupe cell. Clue *b* tells you that Mario was not driving the Spyder either, so an *N* goes in the Mario/Spyder cell. So Mario must have been driving the hatchback. Place a *Y* in the Mario/Hatchback cell and mark the other cells under the column with an *N*. Clue *d* tells you that Graham's car won first place, so Graham should be written on the second chart in the 1st-DRIVER cell. Clue *e* tells you the Spyder

	Coupe	Hatch-back	Spyder
Graham	YES	NO	NO
Mario	NO	YES	NO
Pancho	NO	NO	YES

came in second. Write Spyder in the 2nd-CAR cell. The first chart now gives you the information that Graham must have been driving the coupe, since he was driving neither the hatchback nor the Spyder. Place a *Y* in the coupe column next to Graham and an *N* next to Pancho. This leaves only one car for Pancho—the Spyder. Mark a *Y* in the cell Pancho/Spyder.

Place	Car	Driver
First	Coupe	Graham
Second	Spyder	Pancho
Third	Hatchback	Mario

Now use the first chart to complete the second chart. From chart 2, you know that Graham came in first, and from chart 1 you know that Graham drove the coupe. Write coupe in the 1st-CAR cell. Chart 2 also tells you the Spyder came in second. From chart 1 you know that Pancho drove the Spyder. Write Pancho in cell 2nd-DRIVER. This leaves Mario, driving the hatchback, for third place.

H-145 From clue *f* you learn that the red bike is a one-speed. Since Bob and Chris have ten-speeds (a), neither owns the red bike. Mark an *N* in the Red row under Bob and Chris. From clue *c* we know that Nancy has a three-speed, so she cannot own the red bike. That means that Pat does. Mark *N* under Nancy and a *Y* under Pat in the red row, and mark *N* in the other cells in the Pat column. From clue *c* you learn that Nancy does not own the white bike (her friend does), and from clue *d* you learn that Nancy does not own the blue bike (her

	Bob	Chris	Nancy	Pat
Red	NO	NO	NO	YES
Blue	YES	NO	NO	NO
Green	NO	NO	YES	NO
White	NO	YES	NO	NO

brother does). That means Nancy owns the green bike. In the Nancy column, mark the cells for White and Blue with an *N;* in the Green row, mark the cells under Bob and Chris with *N*. Clue *d*, when combined with clue *a*, tells you that either Bob or Chris must own the blue bike, i.e., they have the ten-speeds (a), and one of the ten-speeds is blue (d). Chris does not own the blue bike (b), so Bob must own it. In the Blue row, mark the cell under Bob with *Y* and the cell under Chris with *N*. Then Chris owns the white bike. Mark the appropriate cells.

H-146 Kim brought her mom's hammer (c), and Bill brought an axe (d)—although it didn't do much good! In Kim's row, mark all cells with an *N* except for the cell under hammer, which you will mark *Y*. In Bill's row, you can mark all cells N except for the cell under axe., which you mark with a Y. You can also mark the other cells in the hammer and axe columns *N*, since no

	Axe	Hammer	Pliers	Saw
Bill	YES	NO	NO	NO
Jane	NO	NO	YES	NO
Kim	NO	YES	NO	NO
Tom	NO	NO	NO	YES

one else brought either the axe or the hammer. Since a girl had the pliers *(a)*, you can match Jane with the pliers (*Y* in cell Jane/Pliers) and Tom with the saw (*Y* in cell Tom/Saw).

H-147 Clue *a* tells you that the large animal eats neither meat nor plankton; put an *N* in the Large/Meat and the Large/Plankton cells. NOTE: You cannot, however, assume that the large animal does not eat both meat and plants. Clue *b* tells you that the medium-sized animal is larger than the plankton eater. Since there is

	Meat	Plant	Meat & Plant	Plankton
Small	NO	NO	NO	YES
Medium	NO	YES	NO	NO
Large	NO	NO	YES	NO
Very Large	YES	NO	NO	NO

only one animal smaller than the medium-sized animal, the small animal must eat plankton. Put a *Y* in the Small/Plankton cell. If the small animal eats plankton, then none of the other animals eat plankton, so all other cells under plankton should be marked *N*. Likewise, if the small animal eats plankton, it does not eat any of the other foods; mark all remaining cells in the Small row *N*. From clue *c*, you gain the information that the meat eater is larger than the plant eater. You can deduce from this that the medium animal is not the meat eater, since the only animal that it is larger than eats plankton. Mark cell Medium/Meat *N*. Finally, clue *d* tells you that the plant eater is not large, so cell Large/Plant can also be marked *N*.

By examining the chart, you can see that only one cell is blank in the Large row. This means that the large animal eats meat and plants. Mark cell Large/Meat & Plant *Y* and place an *N* in the remaining cells in the meat and plant column since no other animal can now fit into that category. This leaves the medium animal to eat plants and the very large animal to eat meat.

LESSON PREPARATION

OBJECTIVE AND MATERIALS
OBJECTIVE: Students will complete a matrix by matching items with their characteristics.
MATERIALS: Transparencies of student workbook pages 257 and 258 • washable transparency marker

CURRICULUM APPLICATIONS
LANGUAGE ARTS: Doing comprehension exercises involving transitive order or process of elimination, determining chronological events in stories or dramatizations
MATHEMATICS: Doing transitivity or inequality exercises, solving word problems
SCIENCE: Evaluating experiment results
SOCIAL STUDIES: Comprehending chronological order, comparing statistics
ENRICHMENT AREAS: Interpreting chronological events in dramatic productions

TEACHING SUGGESTIONS
Encourage students to discuss their answers and explain how each choice was eliminated. Answers may not always be arrived at by following the same order of clues. Listen to answers carefully, following the student's own line of reasoning.

MODEL LESSON | LESSON

Introduction

Q: In previous exercises you used clues to arrange generations of families.

Explaining the Objective to Students

Q: In these exercises you will use clues to answer several related questions.

Class Activity

• Project the transparency of page 257 first.
Q: You will identify the owners of three pets by using a chart to mark information given in the clues.

• Follow the Example from the two transparencies step-by-step, indicating the charted information as you read.

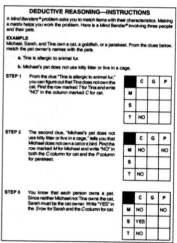

DEDUCTIVE REASONING—INSTRUCTIONS

GUIDED PRACTICE

EXERCISES: **H-137** to **H-138**

• Give students sufficient time to complete these exercises. Then, using the demonstration methodology above, have them discuss and explain their choices

INDEPENDENT PRACTICE

• Assign exercises **H-139** through **H-147**. These exercises may be divided into two lessons, **H-138** through **H-142** and **H-143** through **H-147**.

THINKING ABOUT THINKING

Q: How did you use the clues to solve the problem?
1. I looked for clues that were specific to one item.

2. I looked for clues that eliminated a characteristic for an item.

3. I matched each item with its characteristics.

PERSONAL APPLICATION

Q: When might you need to deduce information from clues?
A: Examples include games or puzzles requiring deductive reasoning, e.g., card games, mystery games, logic puzzles; recreational reading, especially detective novels or mysteries; comparison shopping; correct interpretation of chronological events in news articles, television shows, movies, or plays.

EXERCISES H-148 to H-150 | FOLLOWING YES–NO RULES—A

ANSWERS H-148 through H-150 — Student book pages 265–6
Guided Practice: H-148 See next page.
Independent Practice: H-149 to **H-150** See next page.

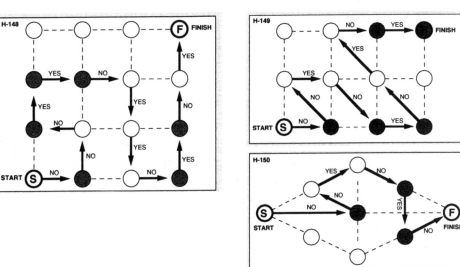

LESSON PREPARATION

OBJECTIVE AND MATERIALS

OBJECTIVE: Students will complete a path having a sequence of eight or more color changes by following the given rule.

MATERIALS: Transparency of TM 36 • washable transparency marker

CURRICULUM APPLICATIONS

LANGUAGE ARTS: Arranging topics into a two- or three-step outline; recognizing the effect of *no* or *not* on meaning; interpreting double negatives; following rules of capitalization or punctuation

MATHEMATICS: Recognizing proper multistep operations in mathematics problems; recognizing or analyzing similarity and congruence in geometry

SCIENCE: Recognizing the change of a single variable in science demonstrations or experiments; tracing the path of an electrical circuit

SOCIAL STUDIES: Preparing for deductive reasoning involving truth value; following or creating a chart or mapping a route

ENRICHMENT AREAS: Creating computer programs; learning or duplicating dance steps; duplicating plays in organized sports or games; following instructions for art, needlework, or craft projects

TEACHING SUGGESTIONS

Encourage students to discuss their answers. Class discussion is a valuable technique for having students share their acquired knowledge. Often a student's words will communicate in a more meaningful way than words a teacher may use.

MODEL LESSON

LESSON

Introduction

Q: In previous exercises you solved deductive reasoning problems using clues in the form of yes-no statements.

Explaining the Objective to Students

Q: In these exercises you will follow color-change rules to complete a path having a sequence of eight or more changes.

Class Activity

- Project TM 36.

  Q: You are to darken the correct circles. According to the Rule Box…

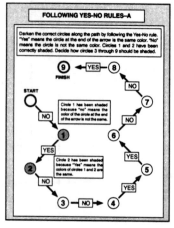

TRANSPARENCY MASTER 36

- Point.

  Q: …if YES is written on the arrow, the next circle should be the same color as the preceding circle. If NO is written on the arrow, the next circle should be the opposite color. The first arrow from the Start position has a NO on it.

- Point.

  Q: Should circle 1 be the same color?
    A: No

  Q: What should be done to the circle?
    A: It should be shaded so it will not be the same as the first circle, which is white.

- Point to the second arrow.

  Q: The second arrow is marked YES.

- Point to circles 2 and 3.

  Q: Should these circles be the same color?
    A: Yes

  Q: What should be done to circle 2 on this path?
    A: It should be shaded so it will be the same as circle 1.

- Point to the third arrow. Continue this line of questioning until the path is complete.

GUIDED PRACTICE

EXERCISES: **H-148**

- Give students sufficient time to complete this exercise. Then, using the demonstration methodology above, have them discuss and explain their choices.

INDEPENDENT PRACTICE

- Assign exercises **H-149** to **H-150**.

EXTENSION ACTIVITY

What's My Logic?, computer software

THINKING ABOUT THINKING

Q: What did you pay attention to when you determined the rule?
1. I looked carefully at the circles each arrow connects.
2. I decided whether or not to darken a circle or write "yes" or "no."

PERSONAL APPLICATION

Q: When might you need or be asked to follow a series of steps or rules?
A: Examples include strategy games, e.g., chess, cards, checkers;

following multistep directions in assembling games or models; using on-off switches.

**EXERCISES
H-151 to
H-158**

FOLLOWING YES–NO RULES—B/WRITING YES–NO RULES

ANSWERS H-151 through H-158 — Student book pages 267–70
Guided Practice: H-151 No, Yes, Yes, No, Yes, No, No
Independent Practice: H-152 No, Yes, No, Yes, No, Yes, No, Yes;
H-153 No, No, Yes, No, No, Yes, No, Yes; **H-154** No, No, Yes, Yes, No, No, No, Yes; **H-155** The solid path alternates between Yes and No; Each part of the dashed line path follows the No rule; **H-156** Each part of the dotted path follows the No rule; Each part of the solid path follows the Yes rule; The dashed line path alternates Yes and No

**LESSON
PREPARATION**

OBJECTIVE AND MATERIALS
OBJECTIVE: Students will write rules to describe the changes in a completed path.
MATERIALS: Transparency of TM 37 • washable transparency marker • student handouts of TM 37 (optional)

CURRICULUM APPLICATIONS
LANGUAGE ARTS: Determining whether usage, spelling, grammar, or paragraph construction examples follow a given set of rules
MATHEMATICS: Recognizing correctly completed multistep operations, recognizing similarity and congruence in geometric shapes
SCIENCE: Explaining basic experimental reactions and their causes, recognizing the change of a single variable in science demonstrations
SOCIAL STUDIES: Placing artifacts according to usage, era, or culture; determining specifics from a map, e.g., type of road, size of city, elevations, points of interest; deductive reasoning involving truth value
ENRICHMENT AREAS: Deciding the time signature for a piece of music from written samples of the music, learning the rules of a game by playing rather than by reading instructions, playing hidden-rule games on a computer or video

TEACHING SUGGESTIONS
Encourage students to discuss their answers. Class discussion is a valuable technique for having students share their acquired knowledge. Often a student's words will communicate in a more meaningful way than words a teacher may use.

MODEL LESSON

LESSON

Introduction
    Q: In the previous exercise you followed yes-no rules regarding color changes in circles.

Explaining the Objective to Students
    Q: In these exercises you will write the rules to describe the color changes.

Class Activity
• Project the transparency of TM 37.

Q: In this exercise you are to write YES or NO on the arrows between the circles. If the circles are the same color, write YES on the arrow. If the circles are not the same color, write NO on the arrow.

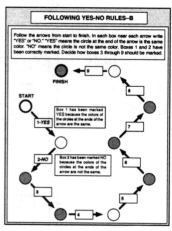

- Point to arrow 3, the first unmarked arrow.
  Q: Are the circles connected by this arrow the same color?
    A: Yes

  Q: What should be written on the arrow?
    A: Yes

- Write "Yes" on the arrow then point to arrow 4.
  Q: How should this arrow be marked?
    A: No

  Q: Why?
    A: The circles are not the same color.

- Write "No" on arrow 4 then point to the next arrow.
  Q: Are the circles connected by the next arrow the same color?
    A: Yes

  Q: What should be written on this arrow?
    A: Yes

- Write "Yes" on arrow 5. Continue this line of questioning until the transparency has been filled in, or duplicate the transparency master as a handout and ask students to finish the example as a guided practice exercise.

GUIDED PRACTICE
EXERCISE: **H-151**
- Give students sufficient time to complete this exercise. Ask students to discuss and explain their choices.

INDEPENDENT PRACTICE
- Assign exercises **H-152** through **H-158**. In Exercises **H-155** and **H-156**, students write the yes or no rule for each path. Exercises **H-157** and **H-158** are student-generated problems utilizing the blank graphics provided on page 270 of the student book.

EXTENSION ACTIVITY
What's My Logic?, computer software

THINKING ABOUT THINKING
Q: What did you pay attention to when you determined the rule?
1. I looked carefully at the circles each arrow connected.
2. I decided what to write above the arrow. (*Yes* if the circles were the same color and *No* if they were not.)

PERSONAL APPLICATION

Q: When might you need to use a number of examples to determine a rule?

A: Examples include strategy games, e.g., chess, cards, checkers; assembling games or models involving multistep directions; using on-off switches; watching a game or sport with which you are unfamiliar.

EXERCISES H-159 to H-161

COMPLETING TRUE—FALSE TABLES

ANSWERS H-159 through H-161 — Student book pages 271–2

Guided Practice: H-159 IT IS BLACK: True, False, False, True, False, False; IT IS STRIPED: False, True, False, False, True, False; IT IS CHECKED: False, False, True, False, False, True; IT IS SQUARE: True, True, True, False, False, False

Independent Practice: H-160 IT IS BLACK: False, False, True; IT IS STRIPED: False, True, False; IT IS NOT BLACK: True, True, False; **H-161** IT IS BLACK: False, False, False, True, True, False; IT IS STRIPED: False, True, True, False, False, False; IT IS NOT BLACK: True, True, True, False, False, True; IT IS NOT STRIPED: True, False, False, True, True, True

LESSON PREPARATION

OBJECTIVE AND MATERIALS

OBJECTIVE: Students will complete a matrix by deciding whether statements are true or false.

MATERIALS: Transparencies of TM 29 and 38 • washable transparency marker

CURRICULUM APPLICATIONS

LANGUAGE ARTS: Proofreading papers for errors in spelling, grammar, or punctuation; answering true/false questions over an aspect of a story or selection; judging when formatting instructions have been followed

MATHEMATICS: Checking computations to determine if correct procedures were followed, choosing correct answer sets to a problem, checking computations by estimation

SCIENCE: Verifying animal or plant characteristics in laboratory demonstrations, reading or completing genetic probability charts

SOCIAL STUDIES: Finding facts to support or negate statements, determining correct time in different time zones, deductive reasoning involving truth value

ENRICHMENT AREAS: Determining whether instructions and/or rules have been followed in sports or recreation activities

TEACHING SUGGESTIONS

Some students may experience difficulty in determining the truth value of negative statements. Encourage students to discuss and explain their answers.

MODEL LESSON

LESSON

Introduction

Q: In previous exercises you identified or followed yes-no rules in completing a path.

Explaining the Objective to Students

Q: In these exercises you will complete a matrix by deciding whether statements are true or false.

Class Activity

- Project TM 29.

    Q: Do you remember this exercise from Figural Classifications? This is a matrix. A matrix has rows and columns.

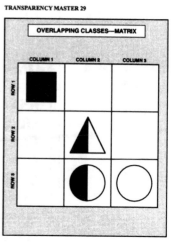

- Indicate rows and columns. Project TM 38.

    Q: This is another kind of matrix called a True-False table. What is the heading for Column 1?
    A: It Is Square

    Q: What is the heading for Column 2?
    A: It Is Black

    Q: What is the heading for Column 3?
    A: It Is White

    Q: What is the shape at the beginning of Row 1?
    A: A black square

    Q: As you move across the black square row, write True if the statement at the head of that column is true for a black square and False if the statement is not true for a black square. Look at the heading of Column 1, It Is Square. Is this statement true for a black square?
    A: Yes

    Q: What should be written in the Row 1, Column 1 cell?

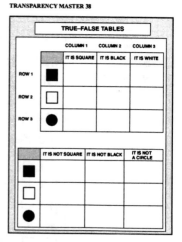

- Indicate the top left cell.
    A: True, because the statement is true for a black square.

- Write "True" in the cell.

    Q: Now move to the next column in Row 1. What is the heading?
    A: It Is Black.

    Q: Is the statement "It Is Black" true for a black square?
    A: No

    Q: What should be written in the Row 1, Column 2 cell?
    A: False, because the statement is not true for a black square.

- Write "False" in the cell.

    Q: Now move to Column 3 in Row 1. What is the heading?
    A: It Is White

    Q: Is the statement "It Is White" true for a black square?
    A: Yes

Q: What should be written in the Row 1, Column 3 cell?
 A: True, because the statement is true for a black square.

- Write "True" in the cell.
 Q: What is the shape at the beginning of Row 2?
  A: A white square

 Q: Look at the heading of Column 1 and ask yourself, "Is the statement It Is Square true for the white square?"
  A: Yes

 Q: What should be written in this cell?
  A: True

- Write "True" in the Row 2, Column 1 cell. Repeat a similar line of questioning until all the cells in the True-False Table have been filled. Continue with the second table on the transparency.

GUIDED PRACTICE
EXERCISE: **H-159**
- Give students sufficient time to complete this exercise. Encourage students to discuss and explain their choices.

INDEPENDENT PRACTICE
- Assign exercises **H-160** to **H-161**.

THINKING ABOUT THINKING
Q: What did you pay attention to when you decided whether a statement was true or false?

1. I looked at the shape being tested.

2. I read the heading of the column.

3. If the shape matched the heading, I wrote true in the box.

4. If the shape did not match the heading, I wrote false in the box.

PERSONAL APPLICATION
Q: When might you need to decide whether a statement is true or false or whether a rule is being followed correctly?
 A: Examples include observing whether operating instructions or directions have been correctly followed, recognizing whether recipes or directions for taking medicine are being correctly followed, answering true/false questions on a test, recognizing that negative statements can be either true or false.

EXERCISES H-162 to H-171

FOLLOWING IF–THEN RULES—A

ANSWERS H-162 through H-171 — Student book pages 273–6
Guided Practice: H-162 Gray circle
Independent Practice: H-163 to **H-171** See next page.

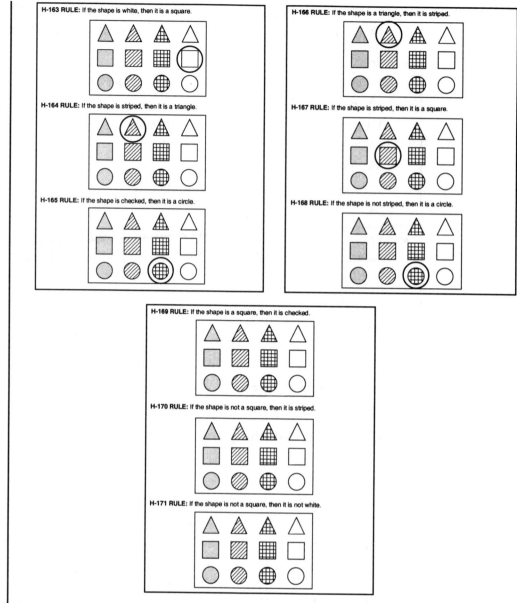

LESSON PREPARATION

OBJECTIVE AND MATERIALS

OBJECTIVE: Students will apply the If-Then rule to a given matrix of figures.
MATERIALS: Transparency of TM 39 • washable transparency marker

CURRICULUM APPLICATIONS

LANGUAGE ARTS: Understanding conditional and exclusive statements; recognizing and stating causal relationships; knowing and following rules of grammar, spelling, usage, and punctuation
MATHEMATICS: Recognizing and understanding geometric proofs
SCIENCE: Stating causal relationships in laboratory reports
SOCIAL STUDIES: Developing deductive reasoning involving conditional statements, recognizing and applying laws
ENRICHMENT AREAS: Understanding stated consequences for actions, matching tools or materials to correct usages

TEACHING SUGGESTIONS

Encourage students to discuss and explain their answers verbally. Students may have difficulty with the concept that only the shapes mentioned in the if-statement are to be considered. The following example may help clarify this concept.

> Q: Can you think of an example of a rule that applies to one grade here at school that does not apply to your grade?
>> A: Possible answers: Lunchtime is different for different grades. Special activities are usually scheduled at different times for different grades.

> Q: Now restate that rule as an if-then rule.
>> A: Lunch schedule: If you are in the fourth grade, then your lunch period is 11:30 to 12:00. Special activities: If you are in the first grade, then your assembly is at 10:00.

> Q: Does this rule apply to all grades?
>> A: Lunch schedule: No, only to fourth graders. So the students in other grades are not required to follow the rule. Special activities: No, only to first graders. So the students in the other grades are not required to follow the rule.

> Q: Describe someone who does not follow this rule: "If you are in the fourth grade, then your lunch period is from 11:30 to 12:00."
>> A: A fourth grader who goes to lunch from 12:00 to 12:30 (or any time other than 11:30 to 12:00).

MODEL LESSON

LESSON

Introduction

> Q: In the previous exercise you completed a matrix in which the columns represented statements that were either true or false.

Explaining the Objective to Students

> Q: In these exercises you are given a matrix of figures and asked to follow a new rule called the *If-Then* rule.

Class Activity

• Project a transparency of TM 39. Indicate the rows.

> Q: In this matrix the rows represent shapes. Row 1 represents triangles, Row 2 represents squares, Row 3 represents circles. What characteristics do the columns represent?
>> A: Color, shading, or pattern

> Q: Column 1 is for gray shapes, Column 2 is for striped shapes, Column 3 is for checked shapes, Column 4 is for white shapes. You will use this matrix of shapes to follow If-Then rules. If-Then rules have two parts. The first part begins with the word *If,* and the second part begins with the word *Then.* For example, "IF the shape is a square, THEN it is white." The If part of the statement directs your attention to a particular part of the given group of shapes. It means, "Pay attention to only this part of the group."

TRANSPARENCY MASTER 39

IF–THEN RULES

RULE: If the shape is a square, then it is white.

In the Example, the if-statement, "IF the shape is a square,…" directs your attention to the row of squares. It tells you that in this statement triangles and squares are not to be considered. You can emphasize the if-statement by drawing an oval around the four squares.

- Draw an oval around the row of squares on the transparency.
  Q: Now look at the Then part of the statement , "…THEN it is white." You can emphasize the "then-statement" by drawing an oval around the three white shapes.

- Draw an oval around the column of three white shapes.
  Q: Notice that there is only one shape contained in both ovals, the white square. This means that only white squares follow the given If-Then rule.

- Clean the transparency so it can be used with exercise **H-162**.
  Q: Look at exercise **H-162** on page 265 in your workbook. The rule says, "If the shape is a circle, then it is gray." What is the if-statement?
    A: "If the shape is a circle,…"

  Q: Which row of shapes should be boxed to indicate that only these shapes are being considered?
    A: Row 3 (the circles)

- Draw an oval around the circles.
  Q: What should be done to the triangles and squares?
    A: Nothing, they are not being considered; only circles can follow the rule.

  Q: How can you tell which of the circles follow the rule?
    A: Look at the then-statement.

  Q: What does the then-statement tell you?
    A: That it is gray.

- Draw an oval around the gray shapes.
  Q: Which circle is enclosed by both ovals?
    A: The gray circle

  Q: Which circle follows the "if-then rule"?
    A: The gray circle

GUIDED PRACTICE
EXERCISE: **H-162**
- Give students sufficient time to complete this exercise. Ask students to discuss and explain their choices.

INDEPENDENT PRACTICE
- Assign exercises **H-163** through **H-171**.

THINKING ABOUT THINKING
Q: What did you pay attention to as you decided which figures fit the rule?
1. I read the first part of the rule.

2. I circled the shapes indicate.

3. I read the second part of the rule and circled the second group of shapes indicated.

4. I looked to see which figure was included in both circles.

PERSONAL APPLICATION

Q: When might you need to determine which members of a group are affected by a rule and which ones are following the rule?

A: Examples include following parliamentary procedure in meetings; following rules for sports; refereeing sports matches; knowing if and how laws apply to you.

EXTENDING ACTIVITIES
What's My Logic?, Computer Software

EXERCISES H-172 to H-181

FOLLOWING IF-THEN RULES—B

ANSWERS H-172 through H-181 — Student book pages 277–80

Guided Practice: H-172 Shapes in all 4 groups fit the rule. REASONS: The only checked shapes in Groups 1, 2, and 4 are square. Group 3 also fits the rule because it contains no checked shapes.

Independent Practice: H-173 Shapes in groups 2 and 3 fit the rule. REASONS: Group 1 contains two circles that are not striped. Group 4 contains a large gray circle which does not fit the rule. **H-176** a. Yes, striped circles are allowed, as are any other marked circles. b Yes, checked squares are allowed, as well as all other marked squares. **H-177** a. No, only the triangles are striped. b. Yes, the non-triangles can have any non-striped pattern. NOTE: According to the rule, squares may be any pattern, including checked. No other shape, however, may have a checked pattern. **H-180** a. Yes. b. No, all squares must be checked. **H-181** a. No. b. Yes, striped squares are not prohibited by the if-statement. Only checked non-squares are prohibited. (**H-174, H-175, H-178,** and **H-179** See below.)

H-174 **RULE:** If the shape is a triangle, then it is striped.

H-178 **RULE:** If the shape is a square, then it is checked.

H-175 **RULE:** If the shape is striped, then it is a triangle.

H-179 **RULE:** If the shape is checked, then it is a square.

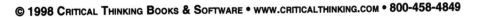

LESSON PREPARATION	**OBJECTIVE AND MATERIALS**

OBJECTIVE AND MATERIALS

OBJECTIVE: Students will determine which groups of shapes fit a given rule and state their reasons.

MATERIALS: Transparency of student workbook page 277 • washable transparency marker

CURRICULUM APPLICATIONS

LANGUAGE ARTS: Understanding conditional and exclusive statements; recognizing and stating causal relationships; knowing and following rules of grammar, spelling, usage, and punctuation

MATHEMATICS: Recognizing and understanding geometric proofs

SCIENCE: Stating causal relationships in laboratory reports

SOCIAL STUDIES: Developing deductive reasoning involving conditional statements, recognizing and applying laws

ENRICHMENT AREAS: Understanding stated consequences for actions, matching tools or materials to correct usages

TEACHING SUGGESTIONS

Encourage students to discuss and explain their answers verbally. Students may have difficulty with the concept that only the shapes mentioned in the if-statement are to be considered. Reviewing the example in the previous exercise may help clarify this concept.

MODEL LESSON

LESSON

Introduction

Q: In previous exercises you followed the If-Then rule with the same group of shapes.

Explaining the Objective to Students

Q: In these exercises you will follow the same If-Then rule for several different groups of shapes.

Class Activity

• Project the transparency of page 277.
  Q: In this exercise you are given the rule, "IF the shape is checked, THEN it is square." Use these groups of shapes…

FOLLOWING IF–THEN RULES—B
DIRECTIONS: Decide which groups of shapes (1, 2, 3, 4) fit the rule.

• Indicate the shapes in the boxes.
  Q: …to find the group or groups in which all of the shapes follow the stated If-Then rule. Remember that the IF part of the statement directs your attention to a particular part of the given groups. It says, "Pay attention to only this part of the whole group." In this exercise the if-statement, "IF the shape is checked,…" directs your attention only to the checked shapes. The gray, white, or striped shapes are not to be considered and are not affected by the rule. Only checked shapes are to be tested. You can emphasize the if-statement by drawing boxes around the checked shapes.

- Draw boxes around the three checked shapes on the transparency.
  Q: Now look at the then-statement, "…THEN it is square." This means that of the checked figures, only the squares follow the If-Then rule. Checked shapes that are not square do not follow the rule. Are there any checked shapes that are not square?
     A: No, all the checked shapes are square.

  Q: In which groups of figures do all the shapes fit the rule?
     A: Students will probably reply that squares in groups 1, 2, and 4 fit the rule. If so, direct their attention to group 3.

  Q: Are there any checked shapes in group 3?
     A: No

  Q: Since there are no checked shapes in group 3, none of these shapes are covered by the rule. They are exempt from the rule, so they fit the rule also.

GUIDED PRACTICE
EXERCISE: **H-172**
- Give students sufficient time to complete this exercise. Encourage students to discuss and explain their choices. Students should cross out any selected shapes that do not fit the rule.

INDEPENDENT PRACTICE
- Assign exercise **H-173** through **H-181**. In exercises **H-174** through **H-181**, students will mark a group of shapes according to a given rule.

THINKING ABOUT THINKING
Q: How did you determine which groups of shapes fit the rule?
1. I read the first part of the rule and found the shapes that fit.
2. I read the second part of the rule and found the shapes that fit.
3. I then found the shapes that fit both parts of the rule.

PERSONAL APPLICATION
Q: When might you need to determine which members of a group are affected by a rule and which are following the rule?
   A: Examples include following parliamentary procedure in meetings; following rules for sports games; refereeing sports matches; knowing if and how laws apply to you.

EXTENDING ACTIVITIES
What's My Logic?, Computer Software

EXERCISES H-182 to H-184

GRAPHIC ORGANIZERS—CYCLES

ANSWERS H-182 through H-184 — Student book pages 281–3
Guided Practice: H-182 See next page.
Independent Practice: H-183 and **H-184** See next page.

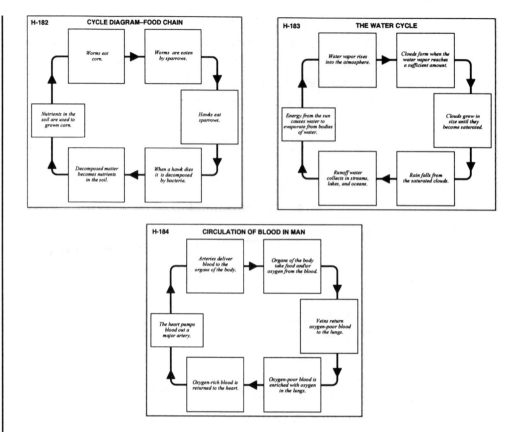

LESSON PREPARATION

OBJECTIVE AND MATERIALS
OBJECTIVE: Students will use graphic organizers to depict cycles.
MATERIALS: Transparency of page 281 in student book

CURRICULUM APPLICATIONS
LANGUAGE ARTS: Outlining, organizing the steps in writing a report, sequencing events in a story
MATHEMATICS: Outlining the steps in converting measurements, fractions, etc.; solving word problems involving a series of steps
SCIENCE: Illustrating changes within the plant or animal kingdoms, sequencing the developmental stages of organisms, illustrating changes between elements in a compound or mixture
SOCIAL STUDIES: Analyzing historical events and periods chronologically and in order of significance; depicting steps in legislative processes, election processes, and judicial processes; recognizing divisions and subdivisions of governmental or political structures
ENRICHMENT AREAS: Prioritizing the steps in decision making, writing instructions, organizing study skills, charting a musical progression

TEACHING SUGGESTIONS
If possible, coordinate one or more of these cycle lessons with your science program.

MODEL LESSON

LESSON

Introduction
Q: You have used graphic organizers to compare and contrast ideas.

Explaining the Objective to Students

Q: In this lesson you will use cycle diagrams to show natural events that repeat.

Class Activity

• Project transparency of page 281.

Q: This is a transparency of exercise **H-182** on page 281.

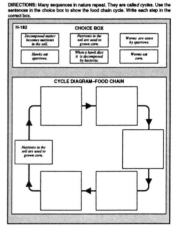

• Read the statement written on the left side of the cycle.

A: Nutrients in soil are used to grow corn.

Q: What key word do you think belongs in the next step in the cycle?

A: Probably *corn*

Q: Which statement contains the word *corn?*

A: Worms eat corn.

Q: Write that phrase on your diagram and I will do the same on the transparency.

Q: What key word do you think belongs in the next step in the cycle?

A: Probably *worm*

Q: Which statement contains the word *worm?*

A: Worms are eaten by sparrows.

Q: Write that phrase on your diagram and I will do the same on the transparency.

Q: You can now proceed with the cycle.

GUIDED PRACTICE

EXERCISE **H-182**

• Allow time for completing the lesson then proceed with a similar line of questioning to complete the diagram.

INDEPENDENT PRACTICE

• Assign exercises **H-183** and **H-184**.

THINKING ABOUT THINKING

Q: What did you pay attention to when you completed a cycle?

1. I read the first step carefully and looked for key words that would need to be in the next step of the cycle.

2. I looked for these key words in the remaining responses.

3. I found the correct response and wrote it in the next box.

4. I repeated steps 1–3 until the cycle was complete.

PERSONAL APPLICATION

Q: When do you want or need to show the steps in doing a task?

A: Examples include writing a check, completing an assignment, scheduling your time, operating a bank machine, planning after school activities.

**EXERCISES
H-185 to
H-186**

GRAPHIC ORGANIZERS—TIME LINES

ANSWERS H-185 through H-186 — Student book pages 284–5
Guided Practice: H-185 See below.
Independent Practice: H-186 See below.

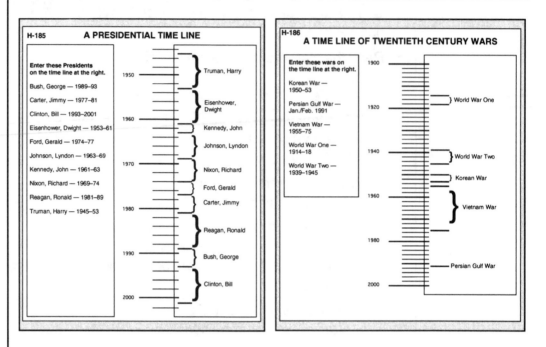

**LESSON
PREPARATION**

OBJECTIVE AND MATERIALS

OBJECTIVE: Students will use graphic organizers to depict historical time lines.
MATERIALS: Transparency of student workbook page 284

CURRICULUM APPLICATIONS

LANGUAGE ARTS: Outlining, organizing the steps in writing a report, sequencing events in a story
MATHEMATICS: Outlining the steps in converting measurements, fractions, etc.; solving word problems involving a series of steps
SCIENCE: Illustrating changes within the plant or animal kingdoms, sequencing the developmental stages of organisms, illustrating changes between elements in a compound or mixture
SOCIAL STUDIES: Analyzing historical events and periods chronologically and in order of significance; depicting steps in legislative processes, election processes, and judicial processes; recognizing divisions and subdivisions of governmental or political structures
ENRICHMENT AREAS: Prioritizing the steps in decision making, writing instructions, organizing study skills, charting a musical progression

TEACHING SUGGESTIONS

If possible, coordinate these time line lessons with your social studies program.

MODEL LESSON | **LESSON**

Introduction

Q: You have used graphic organizers to show the sequence of steps in a cycle.

Explaining the Objective to Students

Q: In this lesson you will use time lines to show a continuous historical event and a random series of historical events.

Class Activity

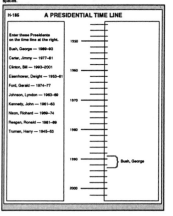

- Project transparency of student page 284.

  Q: This is a transparency of exercise **H-185** on page 284. Count the number of spaces between the ten-year period 1950 and 1960. (Students sometimes have difficulty counting spaces, they tend to count lines.)

  A: There are five spaces.

  Q: How much time does each space represent?

  A: Two year

  Q: How did you determine that one space equals two years?

  A: If five spaces equal ten years, then ten divided by five equals two years for each space.

  Q: Notice where President Bush appears on the time line. Why does his bracket not fall on a line?

  A: His term was from 1989 until 1993. The line for 1989 is halfway between the 1988 and 1990 lines. The 1993 mark is halfway between the 1992 and 1994 lines.

  Q: The next president on the alphabetical list is President Jimmy Carter—1977–81. Find these years on the time line.

- Ask a student to mark them on the transparency. Then write the president's name.

  Q: Now finish the rest of the time line on your own and we will go over it after you are done.

GUIDED PRACTICE
EXERCISE H-185

- Allow time for completing the diagram then proceed with a similar line of questioning to complete the lesson.

INDEPENDENT PRACTICE

- Assign exercise **H-186**.

THINKING ABOUT THINKING

Q: What did you pay attention to when you completed a time line?

1. I marked the dates on the time line, remembering that if the date was

an odd number I made a mark halfway between the even number dates.

2. I repeated step 1 until the time line was complete.

PERSONAL APPLICATION

Q: When do you want or need to show a sequence of historical events?

A: Examples include keeping a log of important events in your life, making a family history, and social studies lessons.

Chapter 9

VERBAL CLASSIFICATIONS
(Student book pages 288–336)

PARTS OF A WHOLE—SELECT

ANSWERS I-1 through I-19—Student book pages 288–90
Guided Practice: I-1 WHOLE: book PARTS: chapter, index, table of contents; **I-2** WHOLE: newspaper PARTS: comics, editorial, sports
Independent Practice: I-3 WHOLE: library PARTS: books, shelves, card file; **I-4** WHOLE: debate PARTS: argument, rebuttal, statement of proposition; **I-5** WHOLE: magazine PARTS: advertisements, articles, photographs; **I-6** WHOLE: block PARTS: alleys, streets, buildings; **I-7** WHOLE: neighborhood PARTS: churches, homes, schools; **I-8** WHOLE: city PARTS: downtown, neighborhood, suburb; **I-9** WHOLE: county PARTS: cities, rural areas, towns; **I-10** WHOLE: state PARTS: cities, counties, townships; **I-11** WHOLE: nation PARTS: forests, mountains, rivers; **I-12** WHOLE: Earth PARTS: continents, atmosphere, oceans; **I-13** WHOLE: plant PARTS: leaves, root, stem; **I-14** WHOLE: mammal PARTS: backbone, brain, heart; **I-15** WHOLE: tulip PARTS: bulb, stem, blossom; **I-16** WHOLE: fruit PARTS: pulp, seeds, skin; **I-17** WHOLE: insect PARTS: antennae, jointed legs, segmented abdomen; **I-18** WHOLE: fish PARTS: backbone, gills, scales; **I-19** WHOLE: bird PARTS: beak, feathers, wings

---

OBJECTIVE AND MATERIALS
OBJECTIVE: In these exercises you will determine which word names the class to which all the other words belong.
MATERIALS: Transparency of student workbook page 288 • washable transparency marker

CURRICULUM APPLICATIONS
LANGUAGE ARTS: Identifying parts of speech, parts of a book, parts of a letter; identifying the topic sentence and its supporting statements from a paragraph; utilizing heads and subheads in outlines; constructing elements of a poem or screenplay; writing specific definitions
MATHEMATICS: Identifying components in arithmetic, e.g., addends and sums in an addition problem
SCIENCE: Identifying significant parts of living organisms; observing components of constellations, stars, planets, or the solar system
SOCIAL STUDIES: Examining dwellings, artifacts, costumes, communities, and governments to identify component parts; using keys or legends to identify map components
ENRICHMENT AREAS: Recognizing component parts of written music, e.g., the concepts of measure, phrase, notes; art projects utilizing positive and negative space, focal point, and elements of composition; sewing; crafts

TEACHING SUGGESTIONS

Encourage students to discuss their answers. It is sometimes difficult for younger children to distinguish between parts of a whole and members of a class, for in each of these relationships a smaller item is being compared to a larger item or group. To reinforce parts of a whole and class/subclass concepts, identify these two important relationships in content lessons. Use bulletin board displays and discuss their application to classroom objects.

MODEL LESSON

LESSON

Introduction

Q: In previous figural exercises you grouped figures according to shared characteristics.

Explaining the Objectives to Students

Q: In these exercises you will decide which word names the class or whole to which the other words belong or are part of.

Class Activity

- Project the example from the transparency of page 288.

Q: The first step in this kind of classifying is to identify which of the given words name the whole and which name parts of that whole. You are given the words *closing, greeting, letter,* and *signature.* Is a closing part of a greeting?

  A: No, a closing is at the end and a greeting is at the beginning.

Q: Is a closing part of a letter?

  A: Yes, a closing would be at the end of a letter.

Q: Is a closing part of a signature?

  A: No, a signature comes after the closing.

Q: By comparing the first word to the other words, you have found that a closing is part of a letter. Are the greeting and signature also parts of a letter?

  A: Yes

Q: Then what is the whole?

  A: The letter

Q: What are the parts?

  A: The closing, greeting, and signature

- Project the solution to confirm answers.

GUIDED PRACTICE

EXERCISES: **I-1** to **I-2**

- Give students sufficient time to complete these exercises. Then, using the demonstration methodology above, have them discuss and explain their choices.

THINKING ABOUT THINKING

Q: What did you pay attention to when you decided which was the whole and which were the parts?

1. I looked carefully at each word.

2. I decided which word represented a whole thing.

3. I checked to see whether the other words represented parts of the whole.

4. I wrote the words on the appropriate lines.

INDEPENDENT PRACTICE

• Assign exercises **I-3** through **I-19**.

PERSONAL APPLICATION

Q: When might you need to distinguish between a whole and its parts?

A: Examples include assembling or disassembling models, appliances, or construction toys; examining household objects, recipes, clothing construction, or food preparation instruments.

EXERCISES I-20 to I-40

CLASS AND MEMBERS—SELECT

ANSWERS I-20 through I-40—Student book pages 291–3

Guided Practice: I-20 CLASS: fiction MEMBERS: drama, novel, short story; **I-21** CLASS: personal histories MEMBERS: autobiographies, diaries, journals

Independent Practice: I-22 CLASS: articles MEMBERS: a, an, the; **I-23** CLASS: sentences MEMBERS: exclamations, questions, statements; **I-24** CLASS: figures of speech MEMBERS: metaphors, personification, similes; **I-25** CLASS: parts of speech MEMBERS: adjectives, adverbs, nouns; **I-26** CLASS: reference book MEMBERS: almanac, atlas, dictionary; **I-27** CLASS: goods MEMBERS: appliances, clothing, food; **I-28** CLASS: leaders MEMBERS: kings, presidents, prime ministers; **I-29** CLASS: government MEMBERS: city, federal, state; **I-30** CLASS: social sciences MEMBERS: economics, geography, history; **I-31** CLASS: school MEMBERS: elementary, high, middle; **I-32** CLASS: service MEMBERS: cleaning, repairing, protecting; **I-33** CLASS: government MEMBERS: democracy, monarchy, republic; **I-34** CLASS: grain MEMBERS: corn, oats, wheat; **I-35** CLASS: mammal MEMBERS: ape, man, whale; **I-36** CLASS: flower MEMBERS: daisy, rose, tulip; **I-37** CLASS: fruit MEMBERS: apple, banana, pear; **I-38** CLASS: insect MEMBERS: beetle, fly, grasshopper; **I-39** CLASS: fish MEMBERS: guppy, perch, trout; **I-40** CLASS: bird MEMBERS: heron, penguin, sandpiper

LESSON PREPARATION

OBJECTIVE AND MATERIALS

OBJECTIVE: Given a group of words, students will identify which word names a class and which words are members of that class.

MATERIALS: Transparency of student workbook page 291 • washable transparency marker

CURRICULUM APPLICATIONS

LANGUAGE ARTS: Using proper form when defining nouns, i.e., stating the general class and the characteristics that distinguish it within that class; using reference books to locate information on a topic, e.g., *Reader's Guide*, encyclopedias, atlases

MATHEMATICS: Using cue words to determine functions for solving word problems, using set theory

SCIENCE: Describing phyla; identifying natural objects in the same manner as nouns, e.g., name, general class, distinguishing characteristics

SOCIAL STUDIES: Defining terms; identifying people, events, artifacts, groups, or eras

ENRICHMENT AREAS: Classifying music according to type, e.g., classical, jazz, operatic; classifying paintings by given characteristics, e.g., artist's techniques, type of medium used; classifying dances according to style, e.g., folk, modern, tap, jazz, ballroom, ballet

TEACHING SUGGESTIONS

Encourage students to discuss their answers. Although the specific language may seem tedious, a basic objective of this lesson is to teach students to use precise words in describing common terms. Precision of language fosters clarity of thinking and is a necessary tool for vocabulary development and clear expression. To reinforce this concept, use the process of naming characteristics and special qualities whenever you or your students need to define terms. Identify classroom objects by general classes, e.g., tools, texts, furniture, paper products, objects which can be magnetized, building materials, and by members. When writing definitions of nouns, students should identify the category (general class) and the characteristics that distinguish this particular member from others in that class. Use this format:

A _____ is a _____ that _____ .
　　(noun)　　　　　　　(general class)　　　(specific characteristics)

For example: A mallard is a wild duck that is characterized by the male's green head and black neck band. Use the questioning technique demonstrated in this lesson to define words in other academic areas.

MODEL LESSON

LESSON

Introduction

Q: In the previous exercise you identified words that named a whole and those that named parts of that whole.

Explaining the Objective to Students

Q: In these exercises you will decide the class to which a group of things belong.

Class Activity

• Project item **I-20** from the transparency of student page 291.

Q: You are to identify the class and the

CLASS AND MEMBERS—SELECT

DIRECTIONS: On each line are four words from language arts lessons. Read the words and decide which word represents the class to which the other words belong. On the lines below each group, write the word that represents the class then list the words that are members of that class.

I-20 drama, fiction, novel, short story

CLASS _____ MEMBERS _____ , _____ , _____

I-21 autobiographies, diaries, journals, personal histories

CLASS _____ MEMBERS _____ , _____ , _____

I-22 a, an, articles, the

CLASS _____ MEMBERS _____ , _____ , _____

I-23 exclamations, questions, sentences, statements

CLASS _____ MEMBERS _____ , _____ , _____

I-24 figures of speech, metaphors, personification, similes

CLASS _____ MEMBERS _____ , _____ , _____

I-25 adjectives, adverbs, nouns, parts of speech

CLASS _____ MEMBERS _____ , _____ , _____

I-26 almanac, atlas, dictionary, reference book

CLASS _____ MEMBERS _____ , _____ , _____

members of that class from the given words *drama, fiction, novel, short story*. Can a drama be fiction?

   A: Yes

Q: When the answer is yes, you should see if the other given words are also correct answers to the same question. For example, can a novel be fiction?

   A: Yes

Q: Can a short story be fiction?

   A: Yes

Q: Now that you have three "yes" answers, you have determined that the class is *fiction* and the members are *drama, novel,* and *short story.*

- NOTE: This is an appropriate place to help students distinguish between parts of a whole and class/subclass. Project exercise **I-21** from the transparency. Point to each corresponding word as you ask the determining questions.

  Q: Are autobiographies kinds of diaries? Are autobiographies kinds of journals? Are autobiographies kinds of personal histories? Think about these questions, and raise your hand when you have determined which word names the class and which names members of that class.

     A: The class is *personal histories.* The members are *autobiographies, diaries,* and *journals.*

- Write the words on the transparency then use the technique modeled to confirm the answer.

GUIDED PRACTICE
EXERCISES: **I-20** to **I-21**
- Give students sufficient time to complete these exercises. Encourage students to discuss and explain their choices.

INDEPENDENT PRACTICE
- Assign exercises **I-22** through **I-40**.

THINKING ABOUT THINKING
Q: What did you pay attention to when you determined the class to which the members belonged?

1. I thought about the characteristics of each item.

2. I asked myself two questions about each word: (1) Did this word represent a group of many different kinds of things? (2) Did this word represent something that was described by another word among the choices?

3. I checked to see that the rest of the words were members of the class I chose.

PERSONAL APPLICATION
Q: When might you need to find or name things by the class to which they belong?

**EXERCISES
I-41 to I-51**

A: Examples include finding items in a supermarket, hardware store, mall directory, telephone book yellow pages, or classified ads; answering identification questions on essay tests; using the Dewey Decimal System to locate sources in a library.

SENTENCES CONTAINING CLASSES AND SUBCLASSES

ANSWERS I-41 through I-51—Student book pages 294–7
Guided Practice: I-41 (1) vegetable (2) bean (3) lima; **I-42** (1) pastry (2) pie (3) cherry pie
Independent Practice: I-43 (1) books (2) fiction (3) mysteries; **I-44** (1) vehicle (2) recreational vehicle (3) camper van; **I-45** (1) lumber (2) boards (3) pine boards; **I-46** (1) insect (2) beetle (3) ladybug; **I-47** (1) plants (2) weed (3) dandelion; **I-48** (1) arachnid (2) spider (3) black widow spider; **I-49** (1) insect (2) honeybee (3) worker honeybee; **I-50** (1) reptile (2) tortoise (3) Galapagos tortoise; **I-51** (1) bird (2) wading bird (3) heron

**LESSON
PREPARATION**

OBJECTIVE AND MATERIALS

OBJECTIVE: Students will classify and arrange words in order from the most general to the most specific within a class.
MATERIALS: Transparency of TM 40 • washable transparency marker

CURRICULUM APPLICATIONS

LANGUAGE ARTS: Using proper form when defining nouns, i.e., stating the general class and the characteristics that distinguish it within that class; organizing and writing descriptive paragraphs; organizing topic or passage outlines
MATHEMATICS: Using cue words to determine functions for solving word problems, using set theory
SCIENCE: Describing phyla; identifying natural objects in the same manner as nouns, e.g., name, general class, distinguishing characteristics
SOCIAL STUDIES: Defining social studies terms or identifying people, events, artifacts, groups, or eras; recognizing specific examples of general social science categories, e.g., geography includes the study of maps, physical features, climates, and natural resources
ENRICHMENT AREAS: Classifying music according to type, e.g., classical, jazz, operatic; classifying paintings by given characteristics, e.g., artist's techniques, type of medium used; classifying dances according to style, e.g., folk, modern, tap, jazz, ballet, ballroom

TEACHING SUGGESTIONS

Encourage students to discuss their answers. When writing proper definitions of nouns, students should identify the category (general class) and the characteristics that distinguish it from others in that class. Use this format:

A _____ is a _____ that _____ .
       (noun)   (general class)   (specific characteristics)

To identify terms from the most general to the most specific, students should continue to follow the procedure of identifying the class and specific characteristics. This allows clear conceptualization of terms used in academic areas. Develop the habit of using this technique in defining words and in accepting student responses. For example, a duck is a water bird that has webbed feet and a flattened beak. A male mallard is a duck that is characterized by his green head and black neck band. The concept *mallard* has been developed from the general concept *bird* with sufficient distinction that the learner can follow the differentiation: bird—duck—mallard. The student realizes that the mallard is a kind of duck and not a separate species of bird.

MODEL LESSON

LESSON

Introduction

Q: In the previous exercise you selected the class to which a group of things belonged.

Explaining the Objective to Students

Q: In these exercises, you will classify and arrange words from the most general to the most specific within a class.

Class Activity

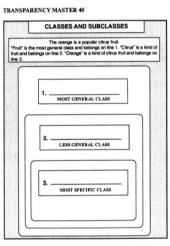

- Project the transparency of TM 40. Students may look at the example in their workbooks, page 294.

  Q: This example from your workbook on page 294 contains three words that name members of a class. You are to identify the members of the class then arrange them from the most general to the most specific class. In this sentence, which three words name the classes?

  A: Orange, citrus, and fruit

- Help students identify citrus as a kind of fruit.

  Q: Which is the most general class?

  A: Fruit

- Write "fruit" on the most general class line (1) of the transparency .

  Q: Which word, *orange* or *citrus*, is the most specific? That is, which is an example of the other?

  A: Orange. An orange is an example of a citrus fruit.

- Write "orange" on the most specific class line (3).

  Q: The most general word, *fruit*, has been written on line one and the most specific word, *orange*, has been written on line three. The remaining word, *citrus*, will be written on line two.

- Write "citrus" on the less general class line (2).

  Q: To check that the answer is correct, ask yourself if answer three (3) is a member of class two (2) and if answer two (2) is a member of class one (1).

  A: Yes, an orange is a kind of citrus fruit, and citrus is a kind of fruit.

> Q: Look at exercise **I-41** in your workbook. Which three words in this sentence identify the classes?
> A: Vegetable, lima, and beans

- Write the words on the transparency.
> Q: Which word names the most general class, that is, the class to which the other members belong?
> A: Vegetable

> Q: Which word is the most specific?
> A: Lima. Lima is a kind of bean.

> Q: Which word names a class between vegetable and lima?
> A: Beans

> Q: If you arrange the words in order from most general class to most specific class, what should go on each line?
> A: (1) vegetable, (2) beans, (3) lima

- Write the answers on the transparency.
> Q: How can you check your answer?
> A: A lima (3) is a kind of bean (2), and a bean (2) is a kind of vegetable (1).

GUIDED PRACTICE
EXERCISES: **I-41** to **I-42**
- Give students sufficient time to complete these exercises. Encourage students to discuss and explain their choices.

INDEPENDENT PRACTICE
- Assign exercises **I-43** through **I-51**.

THINKING ABOUT THINKING
> Q: What did you think about as you identified the class members and ranked them from most general to most specific class?
> 1. I looked for most general word.
> 2. I looked for the most specific word.
> 3. I decided which word names a class between the most general and the most specific.
> 4. I stated the pattern from general to specific to check the order.

PERSONAL APPLICATION
> Q: When might you need to find information, then arrange it from most general to most specific?
> A: Examples include finding items in a supermarket, hardware store, mall directory, telephone book yellow pages, or classified ads; answering identification or definition questions on essay tests; using the Dewey Decimal System to locate sources in a library; locating related topics in books, reference sources, or card catalogs; differentiating among tools or utensils for specific jobs

**EXERCISES
I-52 to
I-100**

HOW ARE THESE WORDS ALIKE?—SELECT

ANSWERS I-52 through I-100—Student book pages 298–302
Guided Practice: I-52 c (warning); **I-53** a (blemish); **I-54** b (strange)
Independent Practice: I-55 b (money); **I-56** c (plan); **I-57** b (hold); **I-58** c (warning); **I-59** b (edge); **I-60** c (smooth); **I-61** b (fiction); **I-62** b (measuring devices); **I-63**; b (kitchen tools); **I-64** c (woodworking tools); **I-65** a (drawing tools); NOTE: Answers **I-66** through **I-77** are either high, line, or show. **I-66** line; **I-67** show; **I-68** high; **I-69** show; **I-70** line; **I-71** show; **I-72** high; **I-73** show; **I-74** line; **I-75** high; **I-76** show; **I-77** show NOTE: Answers **I-78** through **I-89** are either band, change, fair, or spring. **I-78** fair; **I-79** spring; **I-80** change; **I-81** fair; **I-82** band; **I-83** spring; **I-84** band; **I-85** change; **I-86** fair; **I-87** band; **I-88** change; **I-89** fair; NOTE: Answers **I-90** through **I-100** are either flow, kind, party, or pass. **I-90** flow, pass; **I-91** party; **I-92** flow; **I-93** pass; **I-94** kind; **I-95** flow, pass; **I-96** pass; **I-97** party; **I-98** pass; **I-99** flow; **I-100** kind

**LESSON
PREPARATION**

OBJECTIVE AND MATERIALS

OBJECTIVE: Students will select the word that best describes the class to which a group of given words belong.
MATERIALS: Transparency of student workbook page 298 • washable transparency marker

CURRICULUM APPLICATIONS

LANGUAGE ARTS: Diagramming sentences according to functions of words, choosing proper reference books when researching reports, recognizing parts of speech or types of literature, using an index or table of contents to locate information in books
MATHEMATICS: Distinguishing among types of arithmetic problems, recognizing numerical or geometrical properties, grouping numbers according to place or face values
SCIENCE: Naming and recognizing attributes of different phyla of plants or animals, naming and recognizing properties of various elements or compounds
SOCIAL STUDIES: Classifying types of architectural structures, governmental divisions, or community institutions according to their functions or other attributes
ENRICHMENT AREAS: Naming the attributes of types of dance, art, or music; naming functions and attributes of different tools in art, shop, or home economics

TEACHING SUGGESTIONS

Encourage students to discuss their answers. Class discussion is a valuable technique for having students share their acquired knowledge.

MODEL LESSON

LESSON

Introduction

Q: In the previous exercise you selected and arranged groups of words according to their class and subclass.

Explaining the Objective to Students

Q: In these exercises you will look at similarities among words and choose the word that best describes the class to which three given words belong.

Class Activity

- Project exercise **I-52** from the transparency of page 298.

Q: You are given the words *alarm, horn,* and *siren.* From the column on the right, you are to choose the word which best describes the class to which all three words belong. Are alarms, horns, and sirens kinds of bells?

    A: No, a bell is a similar noisemaking device.

Q: Are alarms, horns, and sirens kinds of safety?
    A: No, they are used to warn of danger.

Q: Are alarms, horns, and sirens kinds of warning?
    A: Yes, they all warn of danger.

HOW ARE THESE WORDS ALIKE?–SELECT

DIRECTIONS: Circle the letter in front of the answer that **best** describes the class of words.

I-52	alarm, horn, siren b. safety c. warning	a. bell
I-53	blotch, smear, stain b. rip c. tear	a. blemish
I-54	different, odd, peculiar b. strange c. weak	a. little
I-55	dollar, peso, pound b. money c. penny	a. coin
I-56	aim, design, intend b. finish c. plan	a. draw
I-57	grab, grasp, grip b. hold c. try	a. hit
I-58	caution, slow, yield b. stop light c. warning	a. intersection

- Circle the letter *c* on the transparency.

GUIDED PRACTICE
EXERCISES: **I-52** to **I-54**

- Give students sufficient time to complete these exercises. Ask students to discuss and explain their choices.

INDEPENDENT PRACTICE

- Assign exercises **I-55** through **I-100**. You may wish to divide this into two lessons.

THINKING ABOUT THINKING

Q: What did you think about when you chose the class for several things?
1. I thought about the characteristics of each item.

2. I asked myself, "What characteristics do these items have in common?"

3. I selected the class that best described each group of words.

PERSONAL APPLICATION

Q: When might you need or want to find a class name for several individual items?
    A: Examples include finding items in a supermarket, hardware store, mall directory, telephone book yellow pages, or classified ads; locating related topics in text books, reference books, or card catalogs; developing a filing system; grouping files on a computer disk.

EXERCISES I-101 to I-127

HOW ARE THESE WORDS ALIKE?—EXPLAIN

ANSWERS I-101 through I-127—Student book pages 303–306
Guided Practice: I-101 They are all hard and sharp parts of animals.

I-102 They are all sports arenas. I-103 They are all light beams. **Independent Practice: I-104** treatment of disorders; **I-105** low level of sound; **I-106** decorations; **I-107** ways to question something; **I-108** things airborne objects do; **I-109** ways to change water to steam or water vapor; **I-110** types of running; **I-111** soft talking; **I-112** relating to expectation; **I-113** loud noises; **I-114** courage; **I-115** treatment, care, or pleasant ways to be; **I-116** heavy; **I-117** thin; **I-118** dependability or stability; **I-119** strength; **I-120** not moving or inactive; NOTE: **I-121** through **I-127** are all weather terms. **I-121** light rain; **I-122** below average temperature; **I-123** high degree of visibility; **I-124** high winds; **I-125** low degree of visibility; **I-126** high humidity; **I-127** heavy rain

LESSON PREPARATION

OBJECTIVE AND MATERIALS

OBJECTIVE: Students will explain how the given words are alike.

MATERIALS: Transparency of student workbook page 303 • washable transparency marker

CURRICULUM APPLICATIONS

LANGUAGE ARTS: Diagraming sentences according to functions of words, choosing proper reference books when researching reports, recognizing parts of speech or types of literature, writing descriptive paragraphs, understanding figures of speech

MATHEMATICS: Distinguishing among types of arithmetic problems, recognizing geometric or numerical properties, grouping numbers according to place or face values

SCIENCE: Naming and recognizing attributes of different phyla of plants or animals

SOCIAL STUDIES: Classifying types of architectural structures, governmental divisions, or community institutions according to their functions or other attributes

ENRICHMENT AREAS: Naming attributes of types of dance, art, or music; naming functions and attributes of different tools in art, shop, or home economics

TEACHING SUGGESTIONS

Encourage students to discuss their answers and be specific in their definitions. Class discussion is a valuable technique for having students share their acquired knowledge.

MODEL LESSON

LESSON

Introduction

Q: In the previous exercise you chose the word or phrase which best described the class to which three given words belonged.

Explaining the Objective to Students

Q: In these exercises you will also look for similarities among words, but now you will need to explain how the given words are alike.

Class Activity

* Project the example words from the transparency of page 303.

  Q: You are given the words *chalk, plaster,* and *sugar.* Before you can tell how things are alike, you must describe each of them. What is chalk and how is it used?

  A: Chalk is a soft, white material used to write on hard surfaces.

  Q: What is plaster and how is it used?

  A: Plaster is a white material made from a powder and used to cover walls.

  Q: What is sugar and how is it used?

  A: Sugar is a white substance used to sweeten foods and drinks.

  Q: What do all three things have in common?

  A: They are all white powders.

* Project the solution to confirm answers.

HOW ARE THESE NOUNS ALIKE?—EXPLAIN
DIRECTIONS: Each group of three nouns has a similar meaning. Explain how the nouns in each group are alike.
EXAMPLE: chalk, plaster, sugar
These materials are all white powders.
I-101 claws, horns, tusks
I-102 court, diamond, rink
I-103 glare, gleam, ray
I-104 cure, medication, remedy
I-105 hush, quiet, still
I-106 adornment, ornament, ribbon

GUIDED PRACTICE

EXERCISES: **I-101** through **I-103**

* Give students sufficient time to complete these exercises. Encourage students to discuss and explain their choices.

INDEPENDENT PRACTICE

* Assign exercises **I-104** through **I-127**.

THINKING ABOUT THINKING

Q: What did you pay attention to when you named the class for a group of items?

1. I defined each item.

2. I looked for a common class that each definition fit.

3. I described the common class.

PERSONAL APPLICATION

Q: When might you need or want to explain how several items are alike?

A: Examples include finding items in a supermarket, hardware store, mall directory, telephone book yellow pages, or classified ads.

EXERCISES I-128 to I-141

EXPLAIN THE EXCEPTION

> **ANSWERS I-128 through I-141—Student book pages 307–9**
> **Guided Practice: I-128** Umbrella is the exception to the class "weather terms." **I-129** Corn is the exception to the class "leafy vegetables."
> **Independent Practice: I-130** Work is the exception to the class "quiet actions." **I-131** Hear is the exception to the class "visual words." **I-132**

Water is the exception to the class "solids." **I-133** Minnows is the exception to the class "shellfish." **I-134** Eggs are the exception to the class "meat." **I-135** Basket is the exception to the class "containers with lids." **I-136** Pocket is the exception to the class "fasteners." **I-137** Newscast is the exception to the class "fictional television programs." **I-138** Clock is the exception to the class "distance-measuring devices." **I-139** Violin is the exception to the class "wind instruments." **I-140** Bicycle is the exception to the class "engine-powered vehicles." **I-141** Strainer is the exception to the class "containers for liquids."

LESSON PREPARATION

OBJECTIVE AND MATERIALS

OBJECTIVE: Students will compare four words to determine which word is different and then explain the exception.

MATERIALS: Transparency of student workbook page 307 • washable transparency marker

CURRICULUM APPLICATIONS

LANGUAGE ARTS: Diagramming sentences according to functions of words, eliminating certain reference books when researching reports, recognizing sentences that do not support a topic, making an outline as a prewriting exercise by choosing only those subheads or points which support the main idea

MATHEMATICS: Distinguishing among types of arithmetic problems, recognizing numerical or geometrical properties, grouping numbers according to place or face values

SCIENCE: Naming and recognizing plants or animals that do not belong in a particular phyla, naming and recognizing differing properties of elements or compounds, classifying foods into basic food groups or determining nutritional values

SOCIAL STUDIES: Eliminating architectural structures, governmental divisions, or community institutions that do not fit a given class of functions or other attributes

ENRICHMENT AREAS: Recognizing types of dance, art, or music that do not fit stated criteria; naming functions and attributes of different tools in art, shop, or home economics

TEACHING SUGGESTIONS

Encourage students to discuss their answers and to state the similarities and differences as specifically as possible. Class discussion is valuable for sharing acquired knowledge.

MODEL LESSON

LESSON

Introduction

Q: In the previous exercise you explained how three given words could fit into the same class by stating how they were alike.

Explaining the Objective to Students

Q: In these exercises you will look at the similarities and differences among four words then explain how three of the words are alike and how the fourth word is different.

Class Activity

- Project the example from the transparency of page 307.

  Q: You are given the words *candle, eye, lamp,* and *star.* Before you can tell how these words are alike or different you must define them. What is a candle?

  A: A candle is an object that produces light by burning.

  Q: Define *eye.*

  A: An eye is the part of the body that collects light and allows one to see.

  Q: Define *lamp.*

  A: A lamp is an object that converts electricity or fuel into light.

  Q: Define *star.*

  A: A star is a source of light in the sky.

  Q: All of these words concern light, yet three are more closely related than the fourth. Which word is the exception?

  A: *Eye*

  Q: Why is *eye* the exception?

  A: An eye is not a source of light, it receives light; the other words all name light sources.

EXPLAIN THE EXCEPTION

DIRECTIONS: Each group of four words contains one member that is an exception to the class. Explain how the similar words are alike and how the exception is different.

EXAMPLE: candle, eye, lamp, star

Candle, lamp, and star are similar because they give off light. Eye is the exception to the class "things that give off light." The eye receives light but does not give off light.

I-128   cloud, rain, snow, umbrella

I-129   cabbage, corn, lettuce, spinach

I-130   relax, rest, sleep, work

I-131   hear, look, read, see

GUIDED PRACTICE
EXERCISES: **I-128** to **I-129**

- Give students sufficient time to complete these exercises. Ask students to discuss and explain their choices.

INDEPENDENT PRACTICE

- Assign exercises **I-130** through **I-141**.

THINKING ABOUT THINKING

Q: What did you pay attention to when you identified something that did not fit into the same category or class as other things?

1. I thought about the meaning of each word.

2. I looked for three things that had something in common.

3. I named the class of three things.

4. I explained how the fourth word did not fit into this class.

PERSONAL APPLICATION

Q: When might it be important to identify something that does not fit into a specific category or class?

A: Examples include putting away items at home or in school; replacing items in a supermarket, warehouse, workshop, or library; finding items in a supermarket, hardware store, mall directory, telephone book yellow pages, or classified ads.

**EXERCISES
I-142 to
I-145**

SORTING INTO CLASSES

ANSWERS I-142 through I-145—Student book pages 310–3
Guided Practice: I-142 HAPPY: content, delighted, fortunate, joyous, lucky, satisfied, successful; SAD: discouraged, dismal, displeased , dreary , groaning, miserable, sorrowful, cheerless
Independent Practice: I-143 PEOPLE: actor, captain, doctor, friend , nurse, pilot, teacher, crew; PLACES: airport, beach, factory, garden, house, office, school, station, zoo; THINGS: bicycle, book, computer, stove, vegetable, television, newspaper; **I-144** WHO: all, anybody, anyone, everybody, everyone, nobody, no one, some, somebody, someone; WHEN: always, never, early, later, long ago, now, sometimes, sooner, today, tomorrow, yesterday; WHERE: downstairs, downtown, far away, inside, in town, nearby, next door, outside, upstairs, uptown; (NOTE: In **I-145** optionally classified words are enclosed in parentheses.) **I-145** BIRDS: crow, eagle, heron, loon, ostrich, owl, pelican, penguin; FOREST ANIMALS: beaver, chipmunk, cougar, (crow), (eagle), elk, (frog), moose, (owl), raccoon, sloth, weasel; WATER ANIMAL: (beaver), dolphin, eel, frog, (heron), (loon), (pelican), (penguin), porpoise, shark, whale

**LESSON
PREPARATION**

OBJECTIVE AND MATERIALS

OBJECTIVE: Students will sort a group of words into two classes.
MATERIALS: Transparency of student workbook page 310 • washable transparency marker

CURRICULUM APPLICATIONS

LANGUAGE ARTS: Differentiating among literary genres and types of works within genre; classifying examples of figures of speech, parts of speech, or paragraph types
MATHEMATICS: Differentiating among number properties and problem types
SCIENCE: Differentiating among phyla of plants and animals, classifying elements or compounds according to properties
SOCIAL STUDIES: Classifying types of dwellings, weapons, household articles, or tools belonging to various eras or cultures
ENRICHMENT AREAS: Recognizing music, art, architecture, or dance by era, culture, or type

TEACHING SUGGESTIONS

Some words can be listed in more than a single classification. Encourage students to use each word only once, then discuss and explain why each fits into the chosen category.

MODEL LESSON

LESSON

Introduction

Q: You often take a group of items and sort or classify them into two different categories or classifications. Suppose it's time to buy some new clothes and you want to give the clothes you have outgrown to your younger sister or brother. To do this, you go to your closet and divide your clothing into two groups: clothes that fit and clothes that are too small.

Explaining the Objective to Students
Q: In these exercises you will sort a group of words into two given classes.

Class Activity
* Project the transparency of page 310.

  Q: Fifteen words are listed in the choice box at the top of this chart. You are to sort them into two groups: words that suggest happiness and words that suggest sadness. Does the first word, *cheerless*, suggest happiness or sadness?

    A: Sadness

* Write "cheerless" in the Sad column on the transparency.

  Q: The second word is *content*. Does *content* suggest happiness or sadness?

    A: Happiness. Write "content" in the Happy column on the transparency.

  Q: Does the third word, *delighted*, suggest happiness or sadness?

    A: Happiness. Write "delighted" in the Happy column on the transparency.

GUIDED PRACTICE
EXERCISE: Remainder of **I-142**
* Give students sufficient time to complete this exercise. Ask students to discuss and explain their choices.

INDEPENDENT PRACTICE
* Assign exercises **I-143** through **I-145**.

THINKING ABOUT THINKING
Q: What did you pay attention to when you chose the class for each word?
1. I thought about the characteristics of each word.
2. I asked myself, "Which class matches these characteristics?"
3. I selected the class that had a similar characteristic.

PERSONAL APPLICATION
Q: When might you need or want to sort a list of items into specific classes?

  A: Examples include sorting tools, utensils, toys, clothes, coupons, records, or books for storage and easy retrieval; making an organized shopping list; making lists for special projects or occasions, e.g., Hanukkah, Christmas, planning a party or school project; filing records or letters in an office; finding items in a supermarket, hardware store, mall directory, telephone book yellow pages, or classified ads.

**EXERCISES
I-146 to
I-147**

BRANCHING DIAGRAMS

ANSWERS I-146 through I-147 — Student book pages 314–6
Guided Practice: I-146 TEAM SPORTS: baseball, football, hockey, soccer; INDIVIDUAL SPORTS: golf, gymnastics, skating, skiing; TABLE GAMES: checkers, chess; MOVEMENT GAMES: hopscotch, jump rope, tag
Independent Practice: I-147 INSECTS: ant, bee, butterfly; BIRDS: chicken, ostrich, robin; FISH: minnow, shark, tuna; MAMMALS: cat, elephant, horse; TREES: maple, oak, pine; FLOWERS: rose, tulip, violet; VEGETABLES: bean, carrot, potato

**LESSON
PREPARATION**

OBJECTIVE AND MATERIALS

OBJECTIVE: Students will sort a group of given words into two large classes and then into subclasses.
MATERIALS: Transparency of student workbook page 314 • washable transparency marker

CURRICULUM APPLICATIONS

LANGUAGE ARTS: Differentiating among literary genres and types of works within genre; classifying examples of figures of speech, parts of speech, or paragraph types
MATHEMATICS: Differentiating among number properties and problem types
SCIENCE: Differentiating among phyla classes and orders of plants and animals, classifying elements or compounds according to properties and subproperties
SOCIAL STUDIES: Classifying types of dwellings, weapons, household articles, or tools belonging to various eras or cultures
ENRICHMENT AREAS: Classifying music, art, architecture, or dance by era, culture, and type

TEACHING SUGGESTIONS

Encourage students to discuss their answers. Class discussion is a valuable technique for having children share their acquired knowledge. Often a student's words will communicate in a more meaningful way than the words a teacher may use.

MODEL LESSON

LESSON

Introduction

Q: In the previous exercise you sorted words into particular groups or classes.

Explaining the Objective to Students

Q: In these exercises you will sort given words into two large classes, then sort those classes into subclasses.

Class Activity

• Project the transparency of page 314.

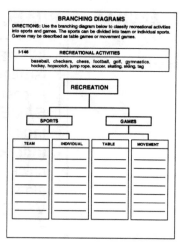

Q: You are given thirteen words that name recreational activities. First you are to classify them into two major groups: Sports and Games. You are then asked to divide the Sports group into Team sports and Individual sports and the Games group into Table games and Movement games. First classify the activities into Sports and Games. Does the first word, *baseball*, name a sport or a game?
   A: A sport

• Write an *S* above the word *baseball* or write "baseball" on the left side of the transparency.
   Q: Does the next word, *checkers*, refer to a sport or a game?
   A: A game

• Write a *G* above the word *checkers* or write "checkers" on the right side of the transparency.

• Continue this line of questioning until all the words have been classified as either a sport or a game.
   A: The sports are baseball, football, golf, gymnastics, hockey, soccer, skating, and skiing. The games are checkers, chess, hopscotch, jump rope, and tag.

Q: Now look at the sports group and decide which of the sports is a team sport and which is an individual sport. A team sport is one in which you cannot participate alone. An individual sport is one in which you can compete alone, even though that sport may also have organized teams, such as swimming. Is baseball a team sport or an individual sport?
   A: A team sport

• Write "baseball" in the Team box.
   Q: Which of these words names an individual sport that you can play even if you are not on a team?
   A: Golf, gymnastics, skating, skiing (etc.).

• Write the selected answer in the Individual box.
   Q: Now look at the Games list. Which of the words in this class names a table game?
   A: Checkers, chess (etc.).

• Write the selected answer in the Table box.
   Q: Which one is an example of a movement game?
   A: Hopscotch, jump rope, tag (etc.).

• Write the selected answer in the Movement box.

GUIDED PRACTICE
EXERCISE: Remainder of **I-146**
• Give students sufficient time to complete this exercise. Ask students to discuss and explain their choices.

INDEPENDENT PRACTICE
• Assign exercise I-147.

THINKING ABOUT THINKING
Q: What did you think about as you sorted things into classes and subclasses?

1. I thought about the characteristics of each word.

2. I asked myself, "Which class matches these characteristics?"

3. I selected the class that had a similar characteristic.

4. I then further divided the words into more specific subclasses.

PERSONAL APPLICATION
Q: When might you need or want to sort items into given classes and subclasses?

A: Examples include sorting tools, utensils, toys, clothes, coupons, records, or books for storage and easy retrieval; making a shopping list; making lists for special projects or occasions, e.g., Hanukkah, Christmas, planning a party or school project; filing records or letters in an office or computer file.

EXERCISES I-148 to I-159

DIAGRAMMING CLASSES—SELECT

ANSWERS I-148 through I-159 — Student book pages 317–21
Guided Practice: I-148 A. Coins for collecting are separate from coins for spending. **I-149** B. All dimes are coins and all coins are money
Independent Practice: I-150 A. Coins and dollar bills are both kinds of money, but no coin is a dollar bill. **I-151** C. Both fruit and food that grows on vines are kinds of food. Since some fruit grows on vines, fruit that grows on vines is shown in the intersection of the circles. **I-152** A. Food contains the class fruit which contains the subclass oranges. **I-153** B. No fruit is a vegetable. **I-154** B. No chicken is a duck. **I-155** C. Ducks and wild birds would be in separate circles. However, some ducks are wild, so these would be included in the intersection. **I-156** A. All hens are chickens and all chickens are birds. **I-157** B. Mothers and fathers are parents, but no mother is a father. **I-158** C. The intersection represents female teachers who are also mothers. **I-159** A. All mothers are women and all women are people.

LESSON PREPARATION

OBJECTIVE AND MATERIALS
OBJECTIVE: Students will select a circle diagram that shows how a given group of words can be classified.
MATERIALS: Transparency of student workbook page 317 • washable transparency marker

CURRICULUM APPLICATIONS
LANGUAGE ARTS: Doing reading comprehension activities involving *all, none, some, not, and , or;* selecting diagrams for illustrating an article, report, or presentation

MATHEMATICS: Creating or interpreting mathematical diagrams
SCIENCE: Using diagrams to understand relationships within phyla of plants and animals
SOCIAL STUDIES: Using diagrams to show relationships between or among ideas, groups, or organizations
ENRICHMENT AREAS: Using diagrams to illustrate relationships between various works of an author, composer, or artist who share at least one common characteristic

TEACHING SUGGESTIONS

This exercise provides students with experience using diagrams to depict class relationships. Whenever the opportunity arises, ask students to identify similar relationships in curricular areas and use the diagrams for clear conceptualization of class relationships. Encourage students to discuss their answers.

MODEL LESSON

LESSON

Introduction

Q: In previous exercises you sorted words into groups, classes, and subclasses using charts and branching diagrams.

Explaining the Objective to Students

Q: In these exercises you will use circle diagrams to sort groups of words into classes and subclasses and to illustrate their relationship to each other.

Class Activity

• Project the transparency of student page 317. Indicate the individual diagrams as you speak.

DIAGRAMMING CLASSES—THREE EXAMPLES

EXAMPLE 1: bicycles, trucks, vehicles
The first diagram pictures two distinctly different classes within a common class. The large circle represents vehicles. The smaller circles represent bicycles and trucks.

A bicycle is a kind of vehicle, and a truck is a kind of vehicle. However, no truck is a bicycle.

B = bicycles
T = trucks

EXAMPLE 2: truck, van, vehicles
The second diagram pictures a class-subclass relationship. All of the items in one class are members of a larger class.

A truck is a kind of vehicle, and a van is a kind of truck. The smaller circle representing trucks is inside the large circle representing vehicles. The smallest circle representing vans is inside the circle representing trucks because all vans are trucks.

EXAMPLE 3: bicycles, mopeds, motorcycles, vehicles
Is there a form of bicycle that is also a form of motorcycle?

A moped can be operated by peddling like a bicycle. A moped can also be powered by an engine like a motorcycle. This relationship can be shown by an overlapping diagram like this one.

B = bicycles
C = motorcycles
M = mopeds

Q: These diagrams are like the ones you will be using. Diagram number 1 is used to represent a class with two subclasses that are distinctly different. Diagram number 2 is used to represent a class-subclass relationship. This means that all of the items in one class are members of the larger class. Diagram number 3 is used to represent an overlapping relationship. This means that the two subclasses share some items, but not all. As an example, consider the words *bicycles, trucks,* and *vehicles* for the first diagram.

• Write "bicycles," "trucks," and "vehicles" at the top of the transparency.
Q: Which of these words names the most general class or the class to which the other words belong?
   A: Vehicles

Q: To check that vehicles is the most general class, test the other words. Are all bicycles and all trucks vehicles?
   A: Yes, all bicycles and all trucks are vehicles.

Q: Which circle in this first diagram would represent vehicles?
   A: The largest circle

- Write "V" in the largest circle.
    Q: Which words belong in the small circles?
    A: Bicycles and trucks

    Q: Why are the small circles inside the large circle?
    A: Because all bicycles and all trucks are vehicles

    Q: The small circles do not touch or overlap each other. Since this kind of diagram is only used to represent subclasses that are distinctly different from each other, you must determine that the subclasses are different by testing two statements: "No truck is a bicycle," and "No bicycle is a truck." Is each of these statements true?
    A: Yes.

- Write "B" and "T" in the smaller circles.

- Write "trucks," "vans," and "vehicles" above the second diagram.
    Q: Classifying the words *trucks, vans,* and *vehicles* will show you when to use the second kind of diagram. Which names the most general class and where should it go on the diagram?

A: *Vehicles* is the most general class so it should go in the largest circle.

- Write "V" in the largest circle.
    Q: What question do you ask to verify the general class?
    A: Are all trucks and vans vehicles?

    Q: For this diagram, use the definition that a van is a kind of truck. Of the subclasses trucks and vans, which is the more general?
    A: Trucks

    Q: Which circle should represent trucks?
    A: The middle circle

- Write "T" in the middle circle.
    Q: If a van is a kind of truck, then vans are a subclass of trucks. Which circle represents vans?
    A: The small inner circle

- Write "V" in the small inner circle.
    Q: An overlapping diagram like this…

- Point to the last diagram.
    Q: …is used when some members of the group can belong to more than one of the given classes. Consider the words *bicycles, mopeds, motorcycles,* and *vehicles.*

- Write the words above the diagram.
    Q: Which names the most general class?
    A: Vehicles

    - Write "V" in the largest circle.

    Q: Why is vehicle the most general class?
    A: Because all bicycles, mopeds, and motorcycles are kinds of vehicles

Q: Define bicycle.
  A: A bicycle is a two-wheeled vehicle that you pedal.

Q: Define motorcycle.
  A: A motorcycle is a two- or three-wheeled vehicle that is powered by an engine.

Q: What is a moped?
  A: It is a two-wheeled vehicle that can be propelled either by pedaling or by an engine

Q: How is a moped like a bicycle?
  A: They both can be pedaled.

Q: How is a moped like a motorcycle?
  A: They both can be run by an engine.

Q: Look at the overlapping circles diagram. If you mark a "B" for bicycle in one circle and a "C" for motorcycle in the other circle…

• Mark the two circles on the transparency.
  Q: …the space where the two circles overlap represents vehicles that are like both bicycles and motorcycles. Mopeds would fit into this class.

• Write "M" on the overlapping section.

GUIDED PRACTICE
EXERCISES: **I-148** to **I-149**
• Give students sufficient time to complete these exercises. Ask students to discuss and explain their choices.

INDEPENDENT PRACTICE
• Assign exercises **I-150** through **I-159**.

THINKING ABOUT THINKING
Q: What did you think about as you identified the class members and ranked them from most general to most specific class?
  1. I looked for the relationship between the words.

  2. I determined the sequence from general to specific.

  3. I decided which word would come next in the sequence.

  4. I checked that the other words didn't fit the pattern.

PERSONAL APPLICATION
Q: When might you use a diagram for illustrating class relationships?
  A: Examples include interpreting or drawing diagrams in advertising, magazines, and newspapers; explaining or clarifying class relationships in any area.

**EXERCISES
I-160 to
I-174**

DIAGRAMMING CLASSES—SELECT AND EXPLAIN

**ANSWERS I-160 through I-174 — Student book pages 322–6
Guided practice: I-160 to I-162 See next page.
Independent practice: I-163 through I-174 See next page.**

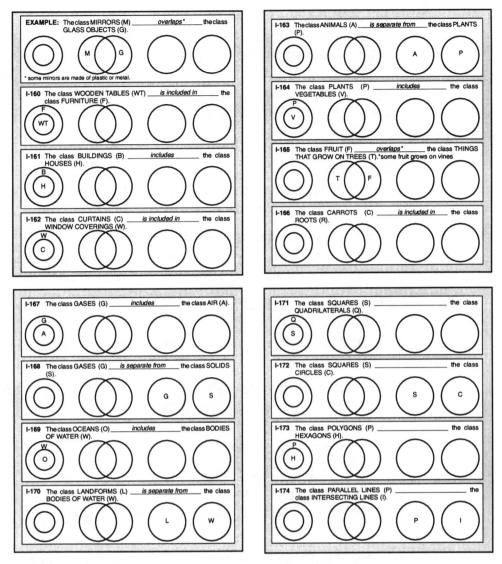

LESSON PREPARATION

OBJECTIVE AND MATERIALS

OBJECTIVE: Students will sort words using circle diagrams and then explain the relationship illustrated.

MATERIALS: Transparency of TM 41 • transparencies of student workbook pages 322 and 323 • washable transparency marker

CURRICULUM APPLICATIONS

LANGUAGE ARTS: Doing reading comprehension activities involving *all, none, some, not, and, or*; selecting diagrams for illustrating an article, report, or a presentation

MATHEMATICS: Creating or interpreting mathematical diagrams

SCIENCE: Using diagrams to understand relationships within phyla of plants and animals

SOCIAL STUDIES: Using diagrams to show relationships between or among ideas, groups, or organizations

ENRICHMENT AREAS: Using diagrams to illustrate relationships between various works of an author, composer, or artist; illustrating relationships between or among artists, authors, or composers who share at least one common characteristic

TEACHING SUGGESTIONS

This exercise provides students with experience using diagrams to depict class relationships. Identify similar relationships in other academic areas and use the diagrams for clear conceptualization of class relationships. Encourage students to discuss and explain their answers. Use a transparency of TM 39 to summarize this lesson.

MODEL LESSON

LESSON

Introduction

   Q: In the previous exercises, you used circle diagrams to help sort groups of words into classes and subclasses.

Explaining the Objective to Students

   Q: In this exercise you will continue to use circle diagrams to sort words into classes, but you will also explain what each diagram means.

Class Activity (optional)

- Project TM 41.
  Q: You will be using the same diagrams as before.

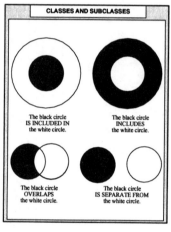

- Point to the first diagram.
  Q: This diagram represents the idea that one class is included in the other. The black circle is included in the white circle.

- Point to the second diagram.
  Q: This diagram shows how one class includes the other. The black circle includes the white circle.

- Point to the third diagram.
  Q: This diagram represents the idea that one class overlaps the other. The black circle overlaps the white circle.

- Point to the fourth diagram.
  Q: This diagram represents the idea that one class is separate from the other. The black circle is separate from the white circle.

Class Activity

- Project a transparency of student page 322. Students can follow along in their workbooks.
  Q: You will be using the same diagrams as before.

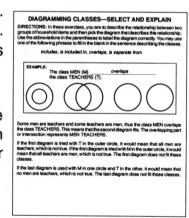

- Point to the first diagram.
  Q: This diagram represents the idea that one class is included in the other. All the things in the small circle are also members of the larger circle.

- Point to the second diagram.

Q: This diagram represents the idea that one class overlaps the other. Some, but not all, members of the first group are also members of the second.

- Point to the third diagram.
  Q: This diagram represents the idea that one class is separate from the other. No member of the first group is a member of the second one.

- Write this sentence on the chalkboard: "The class Teachers (T) blank the class Men (M)."
  Q: Complete the sentence by stating the correct relationship between the two classes then choose and mark the diagram which illustrates that relationship. First you need to determine the relationship between the two classes.

- Indicate the first diagram on page 322.
  Q: Does one of the words name the class to which all members of the other class belong? Can you say that the class Teacher includes the class Men?
    A: No. If the class Teacher included the class Men, it would mean that all men are teachers. That cannot be true, for many men have other occupations.

  Q: Can you say that the class Teacher is included in the class Men?
    A: No. All teachers are not men; some teachers are women. Therefore, the class Teacher is not included in the class Men.

  Q: All teachers are not men, nor are all men teachers. Two of the relationship word choices have been eliminated: *includes* and *is included in.* Two of the diagram choices have also been eliminated. Which ones?
    A: The first one and the second one

- Cross out the eliminated diagrams and their corresponding sentences on the transparency. Point to the fourth diagram.
  Q: Is no member of one class a member of the other class? Can you say that the class Teacher is separate from the class Men? Are no teachers men and no men teachers?
    A: No, some teachers are men.

  Q: Which diagram and relationship word does this statement eliminate?
    A: The separated circles diagram and the relationship "is separate from."

- Cross out the eliminated responses on the transparency.
  Q: You are left with one diagram and its matching statement.

- Write the statement on the transparency as you say it.
  Q: The class Teacher (overlaps) the class Men. Now you need to mark the diagram. Which section of the diagram represents men?
    A: Either of the circles

- Mark an "M" on one circle.
  Q: Which section of the diagram represents teachers?
    A: The other circle

- Mark a "T" on the other circle.
  Q: Which section of the diagram represents teachers who are men?
    A: The overlapping section

- Mark "MT" in the overlapping section. Project a transparency of page 323 exposing the Example.

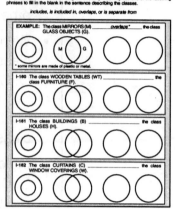

  Q: In the Example on page 323 you are given the partial statement: "The class Mirrors (M) blank the class Glass objects (G)." Which relationship description best completes the statement? Does the class Mirrors include all glass objects?

    A: No, some glass objects are not mirrors.

  Q: Is the class Mirrors included in the class Glass objects?
    A: No, not all mirrors are glass objects; some mirrors are made of metal or plastic.

  Q: Are some mirrors made of glass?
    A: Yes

  Q: Which diagram represents this "some" statement?
    A: The second diagram that represents one class overlapping another class.

  Q: Which circle in this diagram represents mirrors (M)?
    A: Either

- Write "M" in the left circle.
  Q: Which circle represents glass objects (G)?
    A: The other circle. Write "G" in the right circle.

  Q: Which phrase completes the statement?
    A: Overlaps: The class Mirrors (M) *overlaps* the class Glass objects (G).

- Write "overlaps" in the blank.
  Q: Look at exercise I-163. "The class Animals (A) blank the class Plants (P)." Does the class Animals include plants? Are all plants animals?
    A: No, no plants are animals.

  Q: Is the class Animals included in the class Plants? Are all animals plants?
    A: No, no animals are plants.
  Q: Which diagram has been eliminated?
    A: The first one

  Q: Does the class Animals overlap the class Plants? Are some animals also plants?
    A: No, these classes are either plants or animals.

  Q: Which diagram has been eliminated?
    A: The overlapping circles diagram

Q: Is the class animals separate from the class plants? Is any animal also a plant?
   A: No animal is a plant; the classes are separate.

Q: Which phrase completes the statement?
   A: Is separate from: The class Animals (A) *is separate from* the class Plants (P).

* Write "is separate from" in the blank.
   Q: Which diagram represents this statement?
     A: The separated-circles diagram

   Q: How should the diagram be marked?
     A: Mark one circle with an "A" and one with a "P."
   GUIDED PRACTICE

EXERCISES: **I-160** through **I-162**

* Give students sufficient time to complete these exercises. Encourage students to discuss and explain their choices.

INDEPENDENT PRACTICE

* Assign exercises **I-163** through **I-174**.

THINKING ABOUT THINKING

Q: What did you think about as you identified the class members and ranked them from most general to most specific class?

1. I looked for the relationship between the words.

2. I determined the sequence from general to specific.

3. I decided which word would come next in the sequence.

4. I checked that the other words didn't fit the pattern.

PERSONAL APPLICATION

Q: When might using a diagram help you understand or explain the relationship between classes or items?
   A: Examples include diagrams used in advertising, magazines, and newspapers.

EXERCISES I-175 to I-177

OVERLAPPING CLASSES—MATRIX

ANSWERS I-175 through I-177 Student book pages 327–9
Guided Practice: I-175 Boys Band: Bruce, Carl; Boys Chorus: Harold, Ivan; Girls Band: Donna, Jane, Kathy; Girls Chorus: Anne, Mary, Ruth
Independent Practice: I-176 PLASTIC Fasteners: button, (bolt), clothespin, paper clip; Cleaners: brush, (mop), paint scraper; Containers: ice cream carton, jar, styrofoam sandwich carton, tank, toothpaste tube, trash bag; METAL Fasteners: nail, button, bolt, paper clip, safety pin, staple, wire; Cleaners: paint scraper, steel wool, wire brush, Containers: can, aluminum foil, frying pan, kettle, tank; OTHER Fasteners: (button), cotton string, glue, masking tape, rubber band; Cleaners: brush, eraser,

> mop, rag; Containers: ice cream carton, jar, paper cup, pocket, tank, trash bag; **I-177** GENERALLY FAVORABLE Taste: ripe, delicious, soothing; Touch: cool, furry, soft, soothing; Sound: beautiful, musical, soft, sweet, soothing; Appearance: ripe, beautiful, cool, fine, sharp, handsome; GENERALLY UNFAVORABLE Taste: bitter, sharp, spoiled; Touch: rough, scalding; Sound: deafening, dull, sour, noisy; Appearance: blinding, dull, loud, rough, spoiled, ugly; SOMETIMES FAVORABLE & SOMETIMES UNFAVORABLE: Taste: salty, sweet, sour; Touch: icy, sharp, warm, wet; Sound: loud, sharp; Appearance: bright, plain, soft, wet

LESSON PREPARATION

OBJECTIVE AND MATERIALS
OBJECTIVE: Students will use a matrix to classify words or items with two common characteristics.
MATERIALS: Transparency of student workbook page 327 • washable transparency marker

CURRICULUM APPLICATIONS
LANGUAGE ARTS: Comparing or contrasting several elements from different works of literature; using a matrix to organize points or paragraphs in a composition, e.g., main character, point of view, meter of poetry
MATHEMATICS: Constructing or reading probability or arithmetic charts
SCIENCE: Reading or constructing probability charts for experiments or genetics, presenting experiment results using a matrix, classifying objects using more than one characteristic, reading a periodic chart
SOCIAL STUDIES: Using a matrix to present survey results; interpreting information presented on a matrix; using a matrix to organize information, e.g., branches of government, types of juries, duties of officers
ENRICHMENT AREAS: Using a matrix to compare or contrast characteristics of multiple works of art, artists, music, or dance; using a matrix to compare teams or types of sports

TEACHING SUGGESTIONS
Students may approach matrices in various ways. Some will begin with the first word on the word list, classify it, write it on the matrix, then go to the next word, repeating the process until all words are placed. Other students may proceed cell by cell, noting the characteristics of each cell, then choosing words from the list that fit those characteristics. Encourage students to discuss and explain their answers.

MODEL LESSON

LESSON

Introduction
Q: In the previous exercise you used circle diagrams to explain the relationship between two or more given classes.

Explaining the Objective to Students
Q: In these exercises you will use matrix diagrams to classify words or items that have two characteristics in common.

Class Activity

- Project the transparency of page 327.
  Q: What do the rows represent?
    A: Boys or girls

  Q: What do the columns represent?
    A: Music activities, either band or chorus

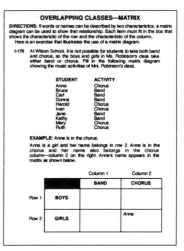

- Point to the top left cell.
  Q: What names would go in this cell of the matrix?
    A: Boys who are in the band

- Point to the top right cell.
  Q: What names would go in this cell of the matrix?
    A: Boys who are in the chorus

- Point to the lower left cell.
  Q: What would go in this cell of the matrix?
    A: Girls who are in the band

- Point to the lower right cell.
  Q: What would go in this cell of the matrix?
    A: Girls who are in the chorus

  Q: At the top of the page is a list of students' names and their activities. First, decide whether each student is a boy or a girl, then find the correct row and place the name in the correct activity box. The first name on this list, Anne, is a girl's name. Anne is in the chorus. Notice that her name has been entered in the Row 2 (girls), Column 2 (chorus) cell. The next name on the list, Bruce, is in the band. In which row does his name belong?
    A: Row 1 (boys)

  Q: In which column of Row 1 should you write Bruce's name?
    A: Column 1, since Bruce is in the band

- Write "Bruce" in the Row 1, Column 1 cell.
  Q: Find a name that belongs in the Row 1, Column 2 cell. What two characteristics should this person have?
    A: Row 1 means it should be a boy; Column 2 means he should be in the chorus. The name of the first boy who is in the chorus is Harold.

- Write "Harold" in the Row 1, Column 2 cell.
  Q: Find a name that belongs in the Row 2, Column 1 cell. What two characteristics should this person have?
    A: Row 2 means it should be a girl; Column 1 means she should be in the band. The name of the first girl who is in the band is Donna.

- Write "Donna" in the Row 2, Column 1 cell.

GUIDED PRACTICE

EXERCISE: remainder of **I-175**

• Give students sufficient time to complete this exercise. Encourage students to discuss and explain their choices.

INDEPENDENT PRACTICE

• Assign exercises **I-176** and **I-177**.

THINKING ABOUT THINKING

Q: What did you think about as you identified the class members and ranked them from most general to most specific class?

1. I looked for the relationship between the words.

2. I determined the sequence from general to specific.

3. I decided which word would come next in the sequence.

4. I checked that the other words didn't fit the pattern.

PERSONAL APPLICATION

Q: When might you use a matrix to understand or sort information?

A: Examples include reading matrix tables, e.g., bus, train, or airplane schedules; making or reading class schedules; interpreting sports data from scoreboard columns; organizing study or work schedules; reading product comparison charts.

EXERCISES I-178 to I-189

RELATIONSHIPS—EXPLAIN

ANSWERS I-178 through I-189 — Student book pages 330–2
Guided Practice: I-178 Each member of group B is *a kind of* its corresponding member in group A. **I-179** Each member of group B is *a part of* its corresponding member of group A. **I-180** Each member of group A is *a measure of* its corresponding member of group B, i.e., rhythm is measured in beats, temperature is measured in degrees, etc. **I-181** Each member of group B is *the top part of* its corresponding member of group A
Independent Practice: I-182 Each member of group B is *the opposite of* its corresponding member of group A. **I-183** Each member of group B is *an extreme form of* its corresponding group A member. **I-184** Each member of group B is *the bottom part of* its corresponding member of group A. **I-185** Each member of group B describes *the action of* its corresponding A member. **I-186** Each member of group B is *the opposite of* its corresponding member of group A. **I-187** Each member of group A is *a measure of* its corresponding member of group B, i.e., an acre is a measure of area, etc. **I-188** Each member of group B is *an extreme form of* its corresponding A member. **I-189** Each member of group B is *a kind of* its corresponding member of group A.

LESSON PREPARATION

OBJECTIVE AND MATERIALS

OBJECTIVE: Students will explain the relationship between two group of words.

MODEL LESSON

MATERIALS: Transparency of student workbook page 330 • washable transparency marker

CURRICULUM APPLICATIONS

LANGUAGE ARTS: Diagramming sentences according to functions of words, choosing proper reference books when researching reports, recognizing parts of speech or types of literature, using an index or table of contents to locate information in books

MATHEMATICS: Distinguishing among types of arithmetic problems, recognizing numerical or geometrical properties, grouping numbers according to place or face values

SCIENCE: Naming and recognizing attributes of different phyla of plants or animals, naming and recognizing properties of various elements or compounds

SOCIAL STUDIES: Classifying types of architectural structures, governmental divisions, or community institutions according to their functions or other attributes

ENRICHMENT AREAS: Naming the attributes of types of dance, art, or music; naming functions and attributes of different tools in art, shop, or home economics

TEACHING SUGGESTIONS
Encourage students to discuss their answers.

LESSON

Introduction

Q: In the previous exercises you classified words according to one or two characteristics.

Explaining the Objective to Students

Q: In these exercises you will explain the relationship between two groups of words.

Class Activity

• Project the transparency of page 330.

Q: The words on the first line are *bird* and *robin*. The words on the second line are *book* and *novel*. Can you think of a common relationship that these word pairs share?

   A: A robin is a type of bird and a novel is a kind of book.

Q: Test this relationship on the remaining three pairs. Is a setter a kind of dog?

   A: Yes

Q: Is a lemon a kind of fruit?

   A: Yes

Q: Is a lizard a kind of reptile?

   A: Yes

RELATIONSHIPS—EXPLAIN

DIRECTIONS: Each word in box A is related in the same way to the word on the same line in box B. Describe how the words in box A are related to the words in box B.

GUIDED PRACTICE

EXERCISES: **I-178** through **I-181**

Give students sufficient time to complete these exercises. Then, using the demonstration methodology above, have them discuss and explain their choices.

INDEPENDENT PRACTICE

- Assign exercises **I-182** through **I-188**.

THINKING ABOUT THINKING

Q: How did you explain the relationship between the two groups of words?

1. I looked at each word pair and decided how they were related.

2. I thought of a common relationship that both pairs shared.

3. I tested this relationship on the remaining word pairs.

PERSONAL APPLICATION

Q: When might you need to determine the relationship between two groups of words?

A: Examples include finding items in a supermarket, hardware store, mall directory, telephone book yellow pages, or classified ads; locating related topics in text books, reference books, or card catalogs; developing a filing system; grouping files on a computer disk.

EXERCISES I-190 to I-193

CLASSIFYING SHAPES—GRAPHIC ORGANIZERS

ANSWERS I-190 through I-193 — Student book pages 333–6
Guided Practice: I-190 Most General: Quadrilateral; Less General: Parallelogram; More Specific: Rectangle; Most Specific: Square
Independent Practice: I-191 through **I-193** See diagrams below and on next page.

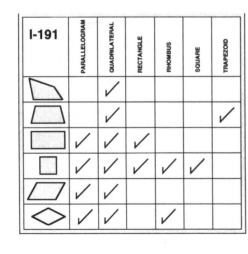

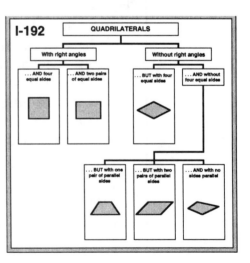

LESSON PREPARATION

MODEL LESSON

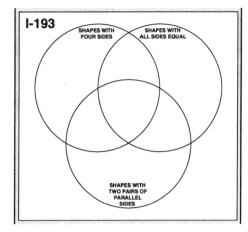

I-193

SHAPES WITH FOUR SIDES

SHAPES WITH ALL SIDES EQUAL

SHAPES WITH TWO PAIRS OF PARALLEL SIDES

OBJECTIVE AND MATERIALS

OBJECTIVE: Students will use four types of graphic organizers to classify quadrilaterals.

MATERIALS: Transparency of student book page 333.

CURRICULUM APPLICATIONS

LANGUAGE ARTS: Doing multiple-meaning exercises in reading or spelling; choosing exact words to express meaning in both descriptive and persuasive writing and speaking; using connotation and denotation exercises; understanding, using, and interpreting figures of speech

MATHEMATICS: Recognizing and using cue words to determine processes for solving word problems

SCIENCE: Following directions in conducting experiments, writing laboratory reports

SOCIAL STUDIES: Classifying historical documents by type (speeches, letter, records, etc.)

TEACHING SUGGESTIONS

Collect jokes, comic strips, or puns with double-meaning "punch lines" to share with students. Students will find that the same word can have more than one meaning and be used in more than one way, often with humorous results.

LESSON

Introduction

Q: You have used each of these organizers in previous exercises to classify different kinds of information.

Explaining the Objective to Students

Q: In this activity you will classify the same information using four different types of graphic organizers.

Class Activity

• Project the transparency of page 333.

Q: Read the definitions beside each of the pictures to find the most general shape.

CLASSIFYING SHAPES WITH A BULL'S EYE DIAGRAM

DIRECTIONS: Read the definitions of these shapes, complete the diagram below, and draw a conclusion. Hint: Use *all* in your conclusion, as in "*all* fathers are men and *all* men are males."

I-190

SHAPES / DEFINITIONS

This is a parallelogram. It is a special quadrilateral with two pairs of parallel sides.

This is a quadrilateral. It is a general four-sided figure with no special properties.

This is a rectangle. It is a special parallelogram with four square corners.

This is a square. It is a special rectangle with four sides that are the same length.

CLASSIFYING SHAPES WITH A BULL'S EYE DIAGRAM

MOST GENERAL CLASS

LESS GENERAL CLASS

MORE SPECIFIC CLASS

MOST SPECIFIC CLASS

CONCLUSION

- Allow time for reflection.

  Q: What is the most general shape?

    A: The quadrilateral is the most general shape.

  Q: What clue did you use?

    A: The definition "It is a general four-sided figure with no special properties."

  Q: What class of shapes belongs in the less general class?

    A: The parallelogram is less general than the quadrilateral.

  Q: What clue did you use?

    A: The parallelogram is defined as a special quadrilateral.

  Q: What statement, using "all", can you make about parallelograms and quadrilaterals?

    A: All parallelograms are quadrilaterals.

  Q: Finish the exercise.

- Ask the students to explain how they arrived at their answers. Write the answers on the transparency as the discussion proceeds.

GUIDED PRACTICE
EXERCISE: **I-190**

- Finish the diagram.

INDEPENDENT PRACTICE

- Assign **I-191** through **I-193**.

THINKING ABOUT THINKING

Q: What did you pay attention to when you figured out the class to which the members belonged?

1. I thought about the characteristics of each shape.

2. I asked myself two questions about each shape: (1) Which is the largest group of many kinds of shapes? and (2) Which shapes belong in a larger category?

3. I checked to see that the rest of the shapes were members of the class I chose.

PERSONAL APPLICATION

Q: When is it helpful to find or name things by identifying the class to which they belong?

  A: Examples include finding items in the supermarket, hardware store, mall directory, telephone book yellow pages, or classified ads in newspapers; answering identification-type questions on essay tests; locating information in a library.

Chapter 10

VERBAL ANALOGIES
(Student book pages 338–67)

ANALOGIES—SELECT

ANSWERS — Student book pages 338–47
Guided Practice: J-1 hear (synonym); **J-2** purchase (synonym); **J-3** found (antonym); **J-4** instruct (synonym); **J-5** false (antonym);
Independent Practice: J-6 lock (used to open); **J-7** shell (enclosed in); **J-8** bottle (kept in); **J-9** spring (part of); **J-10** books (kept in); **J-11** hair (similar parts); **J-12** boat (holds in place); **J-13** cloth; **J-14** gas; **J-15** look; **J-16** fuel; **J-17** jewel; **J-18** picture; **J-19** fish; **J-20** forest; **J-21** candle; **J-22** music; **J-23** class; **J-24** zoo; **J-25** year; **J-26** store; **J-27** compute; **J-28** record; **J-29** attack; **J-30** turn; **J-31** dry; **J-32** pumps; **J-33** tells; **J-34** prays; **J-35** expands; **J-36** informs; **J-37** plays; **J-38** one (synonym); **J-39** few (synonym); **J-40** much (synonym); **J-41** many (synonym); **J-42** one (synonym); **J-43** much (antonym); **J-44** one (antonym); **J-45** many (antonym); **J-46** one (synonym); **J-47** weight; **J-48** area; **J-49** area; **J-50** volume; **J-51** area; **J-52** volume; **J-53** volume; **J-54** volume; **J-55** area

LESSON PREPARATION

OBJECTIVE AND MATERIALS
OBJECTIVE: Students will learn to recognize different types of analogous relationships.
MATERIALS: Transparencies of student workbook pages 338 (optional), 339, and 340 • washable transparency marker

CURRICULUM APPLICATIONS
LANGUAGE ARTS: Recognizing and using word analogies; using context clues to infer meaning of unfamiliar words; using paraphrasing skills; identifying and stating the relationship shown by pairs or groups of words, sentences, passages, or selections
MATHEMATICS: Changing numerical information to graphic or verbal information and vice versa; recognizing and using part-to-whole analogies in measurements of time, weight, size, or volume; identifying the relationship between fractional parts and fractions
SCIENCE: Comparing phyla of plants or animals, conducting laboratory experiments and writing reports on them
SOCIAL STUDIES: Recognizing historic, geographic, or cultural parallels
ENRICHMENT AREAS: Recognizing and using comparative note values in music; comparing styles in music, art, dance, or drama; comparing sports statistics or teams

TEACHING SUGGESTIONS
Encourage students to discuss their answers. They should state the relationship shown in the two pairs of words, as well as why the other choices are incorrect. If students are not familiar with analogies, you may wish to use a

transparency of student workbook page 328 to introduce the concept. These exercises may be divided into two lessons: **J-6** through **J-37** and **J-38** through **J-55**. Exercises **J-48** through **J-55** on page 337 may require preteaching of length, area, volume, and weight concepts.

MODEL LESSON

LESSON

Introduction

Q: In previous exercises you examined how words were alike and how they were different. You put words into sequential order and separated words into classes.

Explaining the Objective to Students

Q: In these exercises you will recognize how two pairs of words are related. This relationship is called an analogy.

Class Activity

- Project the transparency of page 339. NOTE: If students are not familiar with analogies, you may wish to use a transparency of student workbook page 338 to introduce the concept.

  Q: You will look at the relationship between two pairs of words. Both pairs of words must be related in the same way. The first analogy reads, "wrist is to arm as ankle is to blank." How are *wrist* and *arm* related?

  A: The wrist is the joint at the lower end of the arm.

  Q: Think about which answer is related to ankle in the same way arm is related to wrist. Remember, the wrist is the joint at the lower end of the arm. Look for a word that completes the statement, "The ankle is the joint at the lower end of the blank." Try each choice, starting with foot. Is the ankle the joint at the lower end of the foot?

  A: No, the ankle is the joint at the upper end of the foot.

  Q: Now try *joint*. Is the ankle the joint at the lower end of the joint?

  A: No, joint describes the relationship, but does not fit the analogy sentence.

  Q: Now try *leg*. Is the ankle the joint at the lower end of the leg?

  A: Yes

- Write "leg" in the blank of the example.

- Project the example from the transparency of page 340.

  Q: In this example how are *fair* and *just* related?

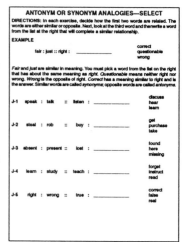

A: They have similar meanings (synonyms).

Q: Can you find a word in the column on the right that is similar to *right?*
A: *Correct*

* Write "correct" in the blank of the example.
Q: Why does *questionable* not fit the analogy?
A: *Questionable* means not decided yet; it could be either right or wrong.

Q: Why does *wrong* not fit the analogy?
A: *Wrong* means the opposite of right.

GUIDED PRACTICE
EXERCISES: **J-1** through **J-5**
* Give students sufficient time to complete these exercises. Ask students to discuss and explain their choices.

INDEPENDENT PRACTICE
* Assign exercises **J-6** through **J-55**.

THINKING ABOUT THINKING
Q: What did you think about as you selected a word to complete each analogy?
1. I decided how the first pair of words was related.
2. I read the third word and looked for another word in the list that would complete a similar relationship.
3. I tried the other word choices to be sure they did not fit the analogy.

PERSONAL APPLICATION
Q: When might you need or want to recognize and duplicate the relationship between two items?
A: Examples include explaining family relationships; teaching someone to use a tool or construct a model; recognizing different items that can be used for similar purposes or functions

EXERCISES J-56 to J-94

ANALOGIES—SELECT A PAIR/TWO

ANSWERS — Student book pages 348–51

Guided Practice: J-56 have : possess (synonyms); **J-57** send : receive (antonyms of cycle of goods); **J-58** all : none (antonyms of amount); **J-65** mayor : <u>city</u> :: governor :: <u>state</u> (elected leader of); **J-66** city : <u>county</u> :: county : <u>state</u> (part of); **J-67** road : <u>country or county</u> :: avenue : <u>city</u> (belongs in)

Independent Practice: J-59 have : possess (synonyms); **J-60** all : none (antonyms of amount); **J-61** send : receive (antonyms of cycle, communication); **J-62** all : none (antonyms of amount); **J-63** have : possess (synonyms); **J-64** send : receive (antonyms of cycle, gifts); **J-68** governor : <u>state</u> :: president : <u>nation</u> (elected leader of); **J-69** county : <u>state</u> :: state : <u>nation</u> (part of); **J-70** police chief : <u>city</u> :: sheriff : <u>county</u> (peace officer of);

J-71 acre : <u>country</u> :: block : <u>city</u> (measurement of area); **J-72** garden : <u>city</u> :: farm : <u>country</u> (scale of growing things); **J-73** books : <u>read</u> :: audio tapes : <u>hear</u> (used to); **J-74** discuss : <u>talk</u> :: listen : <u>hear</u> (synonyms); **J-75** examine : <u>see</u> :: study : <u>read</u> (synonyms); **J-76** inspect : <u>see</u> :: converse : <u>talk</u> (synonyms); **J-77** television : <u>see</u> :: stereo : <u>hear</u> (used to); **J-78** blind : <u>see</u> :: deaf : <u>hear</u> (association, inability to); **J-79** actors : <u>talk</u> :: editors : <u>read</u> (association, occupation); **J-80** sounds : <u>hear</u> :: sights : <u>see</u> (association, can be); **J-81** observe : <u>see</u> :: chatter : <u>talk</u> (synonyms); **J-82** telescope : <u>see</u> :: telephone : <u>hear/talk</u> (used to [distance]); **J-83** microphone : <u>talk</u> :: microscope : <u>see</u> (used to intensify); **J-84** fur : <u>bear</u> :: scales : <u>fish/tuna</u> (part of); **J-85** eagle : feather :: <u>bear : fur</u>, or <u>tuna/fish : scales</u> (part of, body covering); **J-86** bear : mammal :: <u>robin : bird</u>, or <u>tuna : fish</u> (kind of); **J-87** tuna : fish :: <u>robin</u> : bird (kind of); or <u>scales</u> : fish :: <u>feathers</u> : bird (part of); **I-88** <u>robin</u> : flies :: <u>tuna</u> : swims ; or <u>bird</u> : flies :: <u>fish</u> : swims (action); **J-89** lungs : <u>bear, bird, or robin</u> :: gills : <u>fish/tuna</u> (part of); **J-90** <u>bear</u> : growls :: <u>robin/bird</u> : sings (action); **J-91** wing : <u>bird/robin</u> :: fin : <u>fish/tuna</u> (part of); **J-92** hair : <u>bear</u> :: feather : <u>bird/robin</u> (part of); **J-93** scales : <u>fish/tuna</u> :: feathers : <u>bird/robin</u> (part of); **J-94** tuna : <u>fish</u> :: robin : <u>bird</u> (kind of)

LESSON PREPARATION

OBJECTIVE AND MATERIALS
OBJECTIVE: Students will select two words to complete an analogy.
MATERIALS: Transparencies of student workbook pages 348 and 349 • washable transparency marker

CURRICULUM APPLICATIONS
LANGUAGE ARTS: Recognizing and using word analogies; organizing and writing compare/contrast paragraphs or essays; using context clues to infer meaning of unfamiliar words; using paraphrasing skills; identifying and stating relationships shown by pairs or groups of words, sentences, passages, or selections
MATHEMATICS: Changing numerical information to graphic or verbal information and vice versa; recognizing and using part-to-whole analogies in measurements of time, weight, size, or volume; identifying the relationship between fractional parts and fractions
SCIENCE: Contrasting or comparing phyla of plants or animals, conducting laboratory experiments, reporting experiment results
SOCIAL STUDIES: Recognizing and explaining historic, geographic, or cultural parallels
ENRICHMENT AREAS: Recognizing and using comparative note values in music; choosing complementary colors or styles in decorating or art projects; comparing styles in music, art, dance, or drama; comparing sports teams or statistics

TEACHING SUGGESTIONS
Encourage class discussion of each analogy, including identification of the type of analogy or the association of the words.

MODEL LESSON | **LESSON**

Introduction

Q: In previous exercises you selected one word to complete an analogy.

Explaining the Objective to Students

Q: In these exercises you will select two words to complete an analogy.

Class Activity

- Project the transparency of page 348.

  Q: As before, you will be looking at the relationship between two pairs of words. Both pairs of words must be related in the same way. The first analogy reads, "need is to require as blank is to blank." *Need* and *require*, the first word pair, are synonyms. Find a pair of words in the choice box that are synonyms. Look at all three choices and determine the relationship in each pair. How are *all* and *none* related?

  A: They are opposites (antonyms) describing amounts.

  ANTONYM OR SYNONYM ANALOGIES—SELECT A PAIR

  DIRECTIONS: In each exercise, read the pair of words and decide how they are related. Next, select a pair of words from the choice box that will complete the analogy. The pairs in the choice box may be used more than once.

CHOICE BOX		
all : none	have : possess	send : receive

J-56	need : require	::	_____ : _____
J-57	sell : buy	::	_____ : _____
J-58	everything : nothing	::	_____ : _____
J-59	make : create	::	_____ : _____
J-60	full : empty	::	_____ : _____
J-61	talk : listen	::	_____ : _____
J-62	everyone : no one	::	_____ : _____
J-63	hold : own	::	_____ : _____
J-64	give : get	::	_____ : _____

  Q: How are *have* and *possess* related?

  A: They have the same meaning (synonyms).

  Q: How are *send* and *receive* related?

  A: They are opposites (antonyms) describing parts of a cycle or the flow of something.

  Q: Which pair of words has the same relationship as *need* and *require?*

  A: Have and possess. Write "have" and "possess" in the blanks.

  Q: In exercise **J-57** how are *sell* and *buy* related?

  A: They are opposites having to do with the purchase of something (economic cycle).

  Q: Which pair is most related to *sell* and *buy?*

  A: Send and receive

  Q: Why is "send is to receive" the better choice of the two antonym pairs?

  A: They are opposites having to do with parts of a cycle. What one person sells, another person buys, and what one person sends, another person receives.

  Q: Why is "all is to none" not a better antonym choice?

  A: They are opposites having to do with amount. *Sell* and *buy* are not related to amount, as one may buy or sell any amount.

  Q: Why is "have is to possess" not the correct pair?

  A: They are synonyms, not antonyms.

- Project the transparency of page 349.

  Q: In these exercises you must also select two words, but they are to be put into different positions in the analogy. In the example "garage is to blank as barn is to blank," the two words from the choice box that complete this analogy are *city* and *country.* Barns are located in the country, not in the city. The analogy will read, "garage is to city as barn is to country."

> A: Look at exercise **J-65**, "mayor is to blank as governor is to blank." What do a mayor and a governor have in common?

> A: They are both officials elected to head their sections of government.

Q: Look at the words in the choice box. Which word names the government headed by a mayor?

> A: A city is headed by a mayor.

- Write "city" in the first blank.
  Q: Which word names the government headed by a governor?
  > A: A state is headed by a governor.

- Write "state" in the last blank.
  Q: The complete analogy reads, "mayor is to city as governor is to state." Confirm your analogy by filling in the relationship. A mayor is the official elected to head a city, and a governor is the official elected to head a state.

GUIDED PRACTICE
EXERCISES: **J-56** through **J-58** and **J-65** through **J-67**.
- Give students sufficient time to complete these exercises. Encourage students to discuss and explain their choices.

INDEPENDENT PRACTICE
- Assign exercises **J-59** through **J-64** and **J-68** through **J-94**.

THINKING ABOUT THINKING
Q: How did you select the two words to complete the analogy?
1. I looked at the given word in each analogy pair.
2. I determined the type of relationship shown in the analogy.
3. I selected two words from the choice box that would complete each pair of words.
4. I checked to be sure that each pair of words showed the same kind of relationship.

PERSONAL APPLICATION
Q: When might you want or need to recognize, explain, or duplicate the relationship between two items?
> A: Examples include explaining family relationships, teaching someone to use a tool or construct a model, explaining or recognizing relationships between items in a test question, recognizing different items which can be used for similar purposes or functions.

ASSOCIATION ANALOGIES—SELECT TWO
DIRECTIONS: In this exercise, two members of an association analogy are supplied. Select two words from the choice box that will complete the analogy. Words in the choice box may be used more than once.

EXAMPLE: garage : _____ :: barn : _____
A garage is associated with the city, while a barn is associated with the country.

CHOICE BOX
city, country, county, nation, state

J-65	mayor :	_____ ::	governor :	_____
J-66	city :	_____ ::	county :	_____
J-67	road :	_____ ::	avenue :	_____
J-68	governor :	_____ ::	president :	_____
J-69	county :	_____ ::	state :	_____
J-70	police chief :	_____ ::	sheriff :	_____
J-71	acre :	_____ ::	block :	_____
J-72	garden :	_____ ::	farm :	_____

EXERCISES
I-95 to I-113

ANALOGIES—EXPLAIN

ANSWERS — Student book pages 352–5
Guided Practice: J-95 ANTONYMS; Bored and excited are opposite physical feelings, and rested and weary are opposite physical feelings. **J-96** KIND OF; A hamburger is a kind of cooked beef just as french fries are a kind of cooked potato. **J-97** SYNONYM; The words of each pair have similar meanings dealing with judgement. **J-98** USED TO; A hammer is used to hit a nail just as a bat is used to hit a ball.
Independent Practice: J-99 KIND OF; A beetle is a kind of insect just as a snake is a kind of reptile. **J-100** ASSOCIATION; A teacher is associated with instruction and a musician is associated with entertainment. **J-101** SYNONYM; The words of each pair have similar meanings dealing with intensity of examination. **J-102** ANTONYM; The words of each pair have opposite meanings dealing with wind strength. **J-103** USED TO; Pliers are used to grip and a hammer is used to pound. **J-104** PART OF; A wick is part of a candle just as a bulb is part of a light. **J-105** ASSOCIATION; A budget is a plan for money, and a schedule is a plan for time. **J-106** SYNONYMS; The words of each pair have similar meanings dealing with texture. **J-107** USED TO; A hook is used to hang things, and an anchor is used to hold things. **J-108** ANTONYMS; The words of each pair have opposite meanings dealing with direction. **J-109** PART OF; A dial is part of a radio, and a switch is part of a lamp. **J-110** USED TO; A cloth is used to wash just as a towel is used to dry. **J-111** ASSOCIATION; Fly is associated with sky, and float is associated with water. **J-112** USED TO; A ballot is used to vote, and a check is used to pay. **J-113** KIND OF; A yam is a kind of potato, and a lima is a kind of bean.

LESSON PREPARATION

OBJECTIVE AND MATERIALS

OBJECTIVE: Students will classify each analogy and then explain the relationship between the word pairs.

MATERIALS: Transparency of student workbook page 352 • washable transparency marker

CURRICULUM APPLICATIONS

LANGUAGE ARTS: Recognizing and using word analogies; using context clues to infer meaning of unfamiliar words; paraphrasing skills; identifying and stating the relationship shown by pairs or groups of words, sentences, passages, or selections

MATHEMATICS: Changing numerical information to graphic or verbal information and vice versa; recognizing and explaining part-to-whole analogies in measurements of time, weight, size, or volume; identifying and explaining the relationship between fractional parts and fractions

SCIENCE: Distinguishing among phyla of plants or animals, explaining and/or writing reports on laboratory experiments

SOCIAL STUDIES: Recognizing and explaining historic, geographic, or cultural parallels

ENRICHMENT AREAS: Recognizing and explaining comparative note values in music; explaining the choice of complementary colors or styles in decorating or art projects; explaining the relationship between the life and work of an author, musician, or artist

TEACHING SUGGESTIONS

Encourage students to discuss their answers. Class discussion is a valuable technique for sharing acquired knowledge.

MODEL LESSON

LESSON

Introduction

Q: In previous exercises you completed many different kinds of analogies by choosing the correct word or words to determine a relationship.

Explaining the Objective to Students

Q: In these exercises you will classify analogies and explain your reasoning.

Class Activity

• Project the example from the transparency of page 352.

Q: You will look at the relationship between two pairs of words, then use the given list to classify that relationship. Both pairs of words must be related in the same way. In this analogy, "banana is to fruit as carrot is to vegetable," the relationship shown is that of "kind of." A banana is a kind of fruit just as a carrot is a kind of vegetable. In exercise **J-95** you are given the analogy "bored is to excited as rested is to weary." What relationship is illustrated by this analogy?

A: Antonyms; *bored* and *excited* are opposite mental feelings, and *rested* and *weary* are opposite physical feelings.

• Write "antonymns" and the explanation on the transparency.

GUIDED PRACTICE

EXERCISES: **J-95** through **J-98**

• Give students sufficient time to complete these exercises. Encourage students to discuss and explain their choices.

INDEPENDENT PRACTICE

• Assign exercises **J-99** through **J-113**.

THINKING ABOUT THINKING

Q: What did you pay attention to when you classified the analogy?

1. I looked at each pair of words and decided how they were related.

2. I used the list of kinds of analogy to classify the relationship between each pair of words

3. I then explained the relationship.

PERSONAL APPLICATION

Q: When might you need to identify and explain the relationship between two words or a group of words?

A: Examples include explaining family relationships, teaching someone to use a tool or construct a model, explaining or recognizing relationships between items in a test question, recognizing and explaining the use of different items for similar purposes or functions.

EXERCISES J-114 to J-217

ANALOGIES—SUPPLY

ANSWERS — Student book pages 356–63

Guided Practice: (Possible answers) J-114 visitor (synonym); **J-115** top (antonym); **J-116** fall (synonym); **J-117** soon (synonym); **J-118** find (synonym); **J-119** hole (synonym)

Independent Practice: J-120 far (antonym of distance); **J-121** kid (synonym); **J-122** noisy (antonym); **J-123** open or unlock (synonym); **J-124** dull (antonym); **J-125** walk or hike (synonym); **J-126** meal (synonym); **J-127** prince (male adult-child relationship); **J-128** rock or stone (synonym, increasing size); **J-129** floor (covers); **J-130** mountain (increasing size); **J-131** black (increasing intensity); **J-132** cub (adult-child); **J-133** cry or sob (cause/effect); **J-134** student (provider-consumer); **J-135** plan or blueprint (producer/product); **J-136** music or score (uses); **J-137** uncle (male-female); **J-138** patient (provider-consumer); **J-139** snow (extreme form) **J-140** truck; **J-141** furniture; **J-142** shoes; **J-143** nut; **J-144** liquid; **J-145** drink; **J-146** fruit; **J-147** metal or ore; **J-148** insect; **J-149** candy; **J-150** chair; **J-151** car, automobile; **J-152** song, poem; **J-153** elephant, walrus; **J-154** house, building, wall; **J-155** blouse, coat, shirt; **J-156** book; **J-157** car, truck; **J-158** arm; **J-159** school; **J-160** grass; **J-161** building; **J-162** television; **J-163** furnace, air conditioner; **J-164** car, other vehicle with brakes; **J-165** clock; **J-166** eat; **J-167** color, draw; **J-168** see; **J-169** cut; **J-170** sweep; **J-171** measure; **J-172** tie; **J-173** taste; **J-174** walk; **J-175** drink; **J-176** roof (cover); **J-177** hold; **J-178** angle (measure); **J-179** learns or studies; **J-180** catches; **J-181** drives; **J-182** turns or opens; **J-183** builds, saws, or nails; **J-184** burns; **J-185** writes; **J-186** plays; **J-187** buys; **J-188** melts; **J-189** produces or makes; **J-190** flashes; **J-191** floats; **J-192** busy (antonym); **J-193** giggle (synonym); **J-194** swims (action); **J-195** rooster (association: female-male); **J-196** death (antonym); **J-197** arm (part of); **J-198** shirt (association); **J-199** drop (made of); **J-200** clothing (kind of); **J-201** word (part of); **J-202** push (synonym); **J-203** egg (comes from); **J-204** hear (association); **J-205** chew or bite (used for); **J-206** feel (synonym); **J-207** catch (antonym); **J-208** strong (antonym); **J-209** lose (synonym); **J-210** write (used to); **J-211** liquid (kind of); **J-212** cattle (group of); **J-213** real (synonym); **J-214** drop (antonym); **J-215** buy (synonym); **J-216** cheap (antonym); **J-217** doctor (synonym)

LESSON PREPARATION

OBJECTIVE AND MATERIALS

OBJECTIVE: Students will supply a word to complete an analogy.

MATERIALS: Transparency of student workbook page 356 • washable transparency marker

CURRICULUM APPLICATIONS

LANGUAGE ARTS: Recognizing and using word analogies; using context clues to infer meaning of unfamiliar words; paraphrasing skills; identifying and stating the relationship shown by pairs or groups of words, sentences, passages, or selections; choosing words with desired connotation or denotation

MATHEMATICS: Changing numerical information to graphic or verbal information and vice versa; recognizing and using part-to-whole analogies in measurements of time, weight, size, or volume; identifying the relationship between fractional parts and fractions

SCIENCE: Distinguishing among phyla of plants or animals, conducting laboratory experiments, writing laboratory reports

SOCIAL STUDIES: Recognizing and explaining historic, geographic, or cultural parallels

ENRICHMENT AREAS: Recognizing and using comparative note values in music, choosing complementary colors or styles in decorating or art projects

TEACHING SUGGESTIONS

Encourage students to discuss their answers. Class discussion is a valuable technique for sharing acquired knowledge. NOTE: These exercises may be divided into three lessons: **J-120** through **J-152**; **J-153** through **J-178**; and **J-179** through **J-217**.

MODEL LESSON

LESSON

Introduction

Q: In previous exercises you selected words to complete an analogy and identified and explained the relationship expressed by an analogy.

Explaining the Objective to Students

Q: In these exercises you will supply a word to complete an analogy.

Class Activity

• Project the transparency of page 356.

Q: Look at the relationship between the two pairs of words and remember that both pairs of words must be related in the same way. In the first analogy, "passenger is to traveler as guest is to blank," the relationship is that *passenger* and *traveler* are synonyms. A passenger is one who travels, or a traveler. To complete the analogy, you need a word that has the same relationship to *guest*, "A guest is one who blanks, or a blank."

A: A guest is one who visits, or a visitor.

ANTONYM OR SYNONYM ANALOGIES—SUPPLY

DIRECTIONS: Look at the first two words. Think about how they are related. The words are either similar or opposite. Next, look at the third word and produce a word from your memory that has a similar relationship as the first two words.

J-114 passenger : traveler :: guest : _____

J-115 valley : peak :: bottom : _____

J-116 twilight : dusk :: autumn : _____

J-117 frequently : often :: shortly : _____

J-118 hunt : search :: locate : _____

J-119 stick : pole :: pit : _____

J-120 close : distant :: near : _____

J-121 insect : bug :: child : _____

J-122 quiet : loud :: silent : _____

J-123 shut : close :: unfasten : _____

J-124 bright : dim :: shiny : _____

J-125 dash : race :: stroll : _____

J-126 sprinkle : rain :: snack : _____

- Write "visitor" in the blank.
  Q: In exercise **J-115**, how are *valley* and *peak* related?
    A: They are antonyms (opposite locations).

  Q: Can you think of a word that names a location opposite to bottom?
    A: Top.

- Write "top" in the blank.

GUIDED PRACTICE
EXERCISES: **J-114** through **J-119**
- Give students sufficient time to complete these exercises. Then, using the demonstration methodology above, have them discuss and explain their choices.

INDEPENDENT PRACTICE
- Assign exercises **J-120** through **J-217**.

THINKING ABOUT THINKING
Q: What did you think about supplying a word to complete each analogy?
1. I decided how the first pair of words was related.

2. I read the third word and thought of another word that would complete a similar relationship.

PERSONAL APPLICATION
Q: When might you need or want to know a word that shows a particular relationship to another word?
  A: Examples include explaining family relationships, teaching someone to use a tool or construct a model, explaining or recognizing relationships between items in a test question, recognizing different items which can be used for similar purposes or functions.

EXERCISES J-218 to J-236

ANALOGIES—EXPLAIN AND SUPPLY A PAIR /
ANALOGIES—PRODUCE

ANSWERS — Student book pages 364–7
Guided Practice: (Possible Answers) **J-218** sailor : navy; pilot : air force; student : class; worker : business; secretary : office (PART OF: A soldier is a member or employee of an army.); **J-219** grimy : washed; soiled : spotless; illegal : legal (ANTONYM: Dirty is the opposite of clean.); **J-220** apple, pear, strawberry, peach, or orange : fruit; lettuce, peas, beans, carrots, or potatoes : vegetable; beef, mutton, or pork : meat (KIND OF: Oats is a kind of grain.)
Independent Practice: J-221 car, truck, bus, or van : highway; boat, ship : ocean, sea, or river (ASSOCIATION: A train runs on a track.); **J-222** author : writes; musician : composes; actor : performs; (ACTION: creative pursuits); **J-223** president : country; governor : state; mayor : city (ASSOCIATION: The chief is the head of the tribe.); **J-224** still : noisy; dull

: bright; soft : hard; smooth : rough; ripe : rotten (ANTONYM: Quiet is the opposite of loud and deals with the sense of hearing; any antonym pair is correct, but a pair associated with the senses is best.); **J-225** intelligent : smart; bright : alert (SYNONYM: Silly is the same as foolish.) **J-226** sugar, candy, cake : sweet (ASSOCIATION: A lemon tastes sour.) **J-227** stripes : tiger or zebra; trunk : elephant; mane : lion (ASSOCIATION or CHARACTERISTIC OF: Spots are a characteristic of a leopard.) **J-228** beverage : drink (USED TO: Food is used to eat.) **J-229** through **J-236** NOTE: Any of the following analogies may be used: fins : fish :: wings : birds; wings : birds :: legs : horse; fly : wings :: walk : legs; fly (insect) : wings :: horse : legs; fins : swim :: legs : walk; legs : walk :: wings : fly; fly : sky :: swim : sea; sea : swim :: land : walk; bird : fly :: fish : swim; fish : swim :: horse : walk; bird : sky :: fish : sea; fish : sea :: horse : land; fins : sea :: wings : sky; wings : sky :: legs : land

LESSON PREPARATION

OBJECTIVE AND MATERIALS

OBJECTIVE: Students will explain the relationship between two given words and then supply another pair of words with the same relationship to complete the analogy.

MATERIALS: Blank transparency or access to a chalkboard • washable transparency marker or chalk

CURRICULUM APPLICATIONS

LANGUAGE ARTS: Recognizing and using word analogies; using context clues to infer meaning of unfamiliar words; paraphrasing skills; identifying and stating the relationship shown by pairs or groups of words, sentences, passages, or selections

MATHEMATICS: Changing numerical information to graphic or verbal information and vice versa; recognizing and using analogies in measurements of time, weight, size, or volume; identifying the relationship between fractional parts and fractions

SCIENCE: Distinguishing among phyla of plants or animals; conducting, explaining, and writing reports of laboratory experiments

SOCIAL STUDIES: Drawing and explaining historic, geographic, or cultural parallels

ENRICHMENT AREAS: Recognizing and using comparative note values in music; choosing and explaining complementary colors or styles in decorating or art projects; comparing artists, musicians, music, art forms, dramas, or dances

TEACHING SUGGESTIONS

Encourage students to refer to the analogy types on student workbook pages 340 through 345 to identify the kind of analogy they are using. Have students state the relationship between the given word pair as specifically as possible and evaluate their supplied pair of words to see how closely it matches the relationship shown by the first pair.

MODEL LESSON | **LESSON**

Introduction

Q: In previous exercises you determined relationships between pairs of words, selected or supplied words to show the same relationship to a third word, and explained types of analogies.

Explaining the Objective to Students

Q: In these exercises you will explain the relationship between two given words, then supply another pair of words that show the same relationship.

Class Activity

- Write "gallon : volume :: _____ : _____" at the top of the blank transparency or on the chalkboard.

  Q: Here you have a given pair of words, *gallon* and *volume,* and the beginning of an analogy, "gallon is to volume as blank is to blank." You are to determine the relationship, then complete the analogy. What is the relationship between *gallon* and *volume?*

  A: A gallon is a measure of volume.

  Q: What two words might be used to show the same relationship?

  A: Possible answers: inch, foot, yard, meter, mile, or kilometer to distance, perimeter, or size; square inch, square foot, square yard, square centimeter, or square mile to area; pound, ton, ounce, gram, or kilogram to weight.

- Write all answers on the chalkboard without discussion, then use the pairs of words given by students to fill in each of the blanks in the following sentence. If a pair is rejected as not being analogous, ask students to explain why the pair does not fit, then erase it from the list.

  Q: If you say that a gallon is a measure of volume, can you also say that a (_____) is a measure of (_____)?

- Continue this manner of questioning until all word pairs have been tried.

  Q: Any of the word pairs here can be used to correctly complete the analogy because they all have the same relationship as *gallon* to *volume.* They all express the relationship that a unit of measurement has to the quantity being measured.

GUIDED PRACTICE

EXERCISES: **J-218** through **J-220**.

- Give students sufficient time to complete these exercises. Ask students to discuss and explain their choices.

INDEPENDENT PRACTICE

- Assign exercises **J-221** through **J-236**. NOTE: For exercises **J-229** through **J-236**, students are asked to produce complete analogies from a given group of words.

THINKING ABOUT THINKING

Q: What did you think about in order to complete the analogy?

1. I determined the relationship between the first pair of words.

2. I thought of two more words that might be used to show the same relationship.

3. I then tried each word pair to see if it fit.

PERSONAL APPLICATION

Q: When might you need to identify the relationship shown by a pair of words, then think of another pair that is related in the same way?

A: Examples include explaining family relationships, teaching someone to use a tool or construct a model, explaining or recognizing relationships between items in a test question, recognizing different items which can be used for similar purposes or functions.

TRANSPARENCY MASTER 1

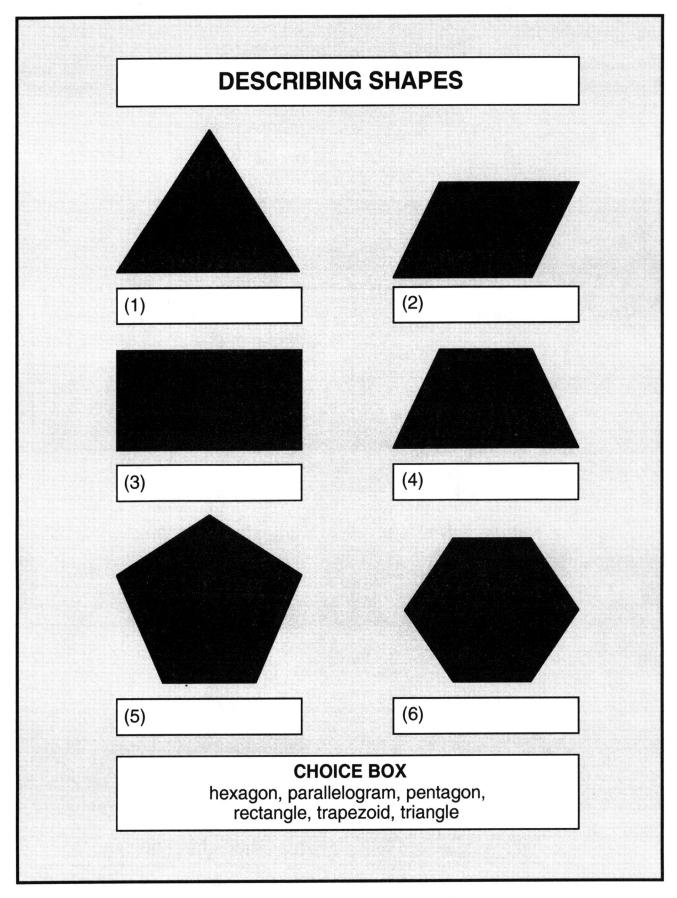

TRANSPARENCY MASTER 2

COMPARING SHAPES

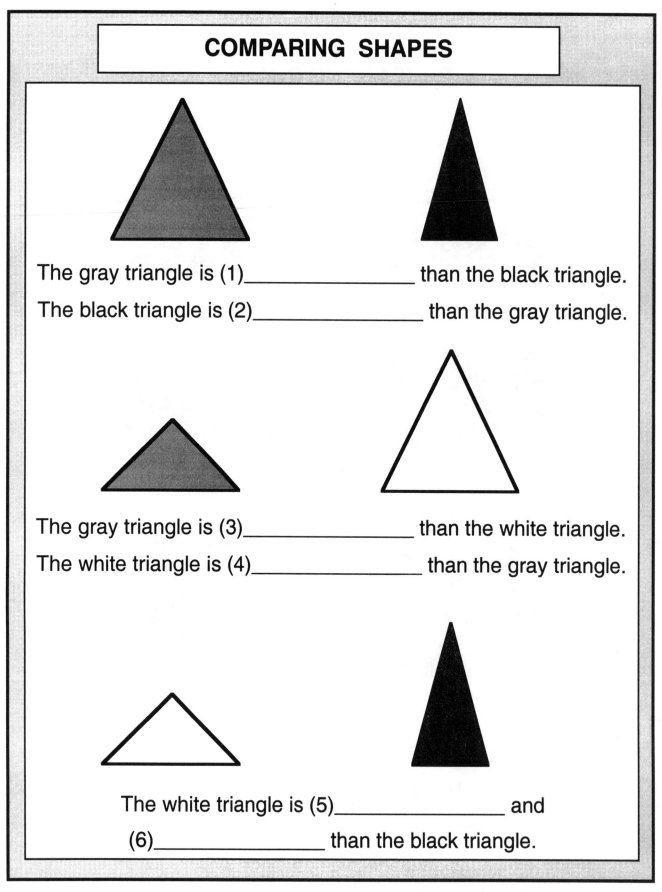

The gray triangle is (1)_____ than the black triangle.

The black triangle is (2)_____ than the gray triangle.

The gray triangle is (3)_____ than the white triangle.

The white triangle is (4)_____ than the gray triangle.

The white triangle is (5)_____ and

(6)_____ than the black triangle.

TRANSPARENCY MASTER 3

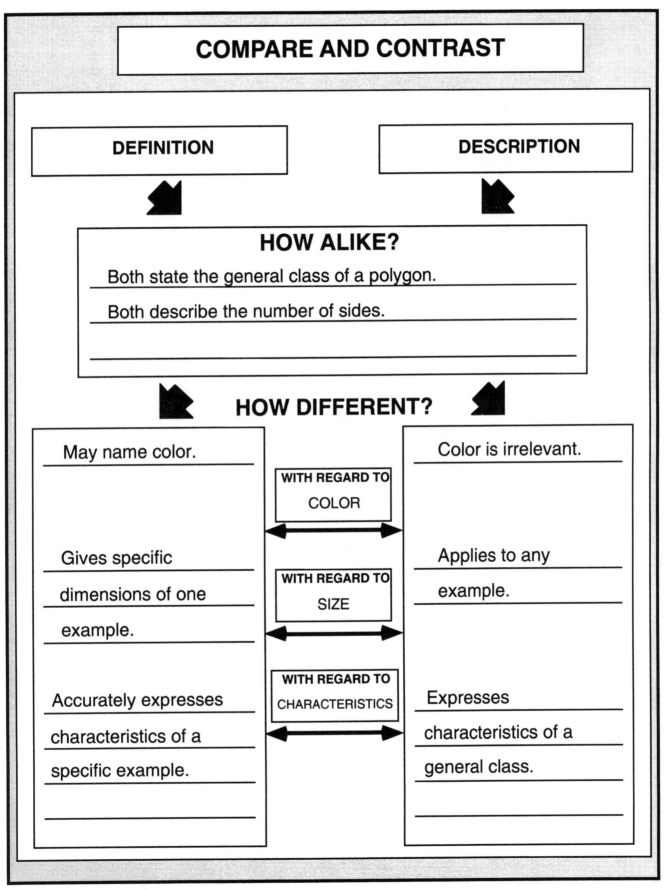

COMPARE AND CONTRAST

DEFINITION

DESCRIPTION

HOW ALIKE?

Both state the general class of a polygon.

Both describe the number of sides.

HOW DIFFERENT?

	WITH REGARD TO COLOR	
May name color.		Color is irrelevant.
Gives specific dimensions of one example.	WITH REGARD TO SIZE	Applies to any example.
Accurately expresses characteristics of a specific example.	WITH REGARD TO CHARACTERISTICS	Expresses characteristics of a general class.

TRANSPARENCY MASTER 4

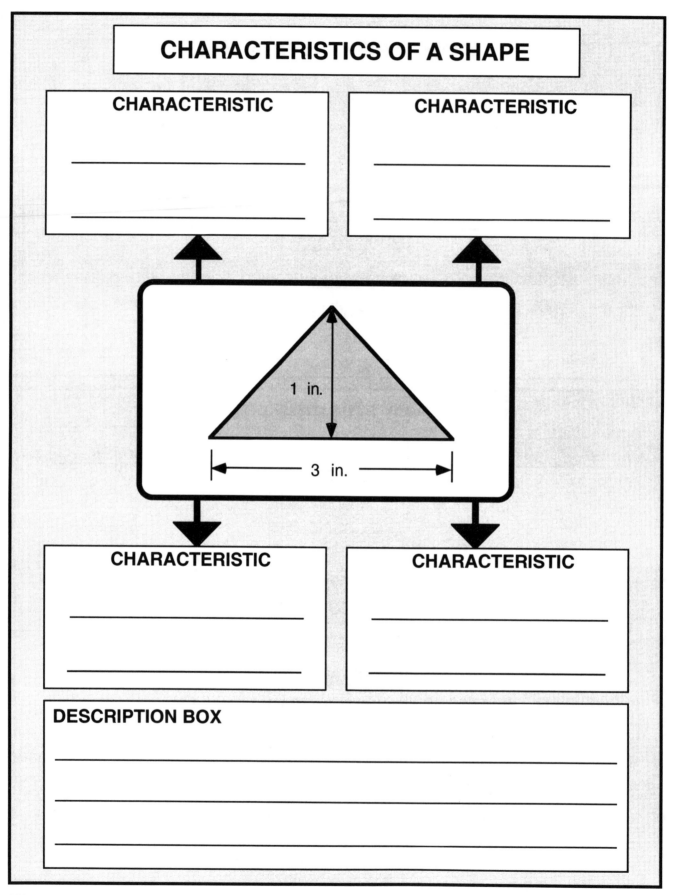

CHARACTERISTICS OF A SHAPE

CHARACTERISTIC

CHARACTERISTIC

1 in.

3 in.

CHARACTERISTIC

CHARACTERISTIC

DESCRIPTION BOX

TRANSPARENCY MASTER 5

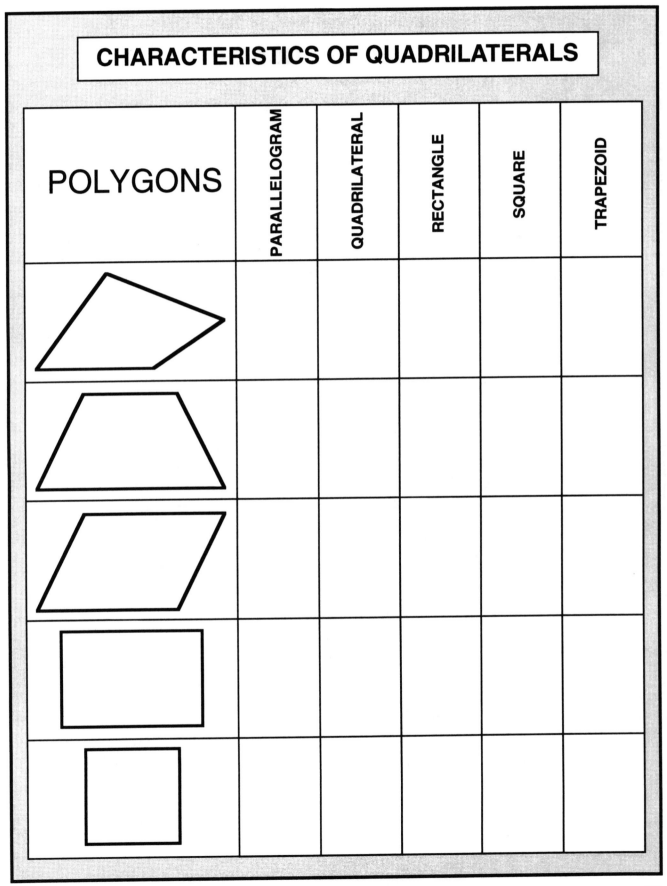

CHARACTERISTICS OF QUADRILATERALS					
POLYGONS	PARALLELOGRAM	QUADRILATERAL	RECTANGLE	SQUARE	TRAPEZOID

TRANSPARENCY MASTER 6

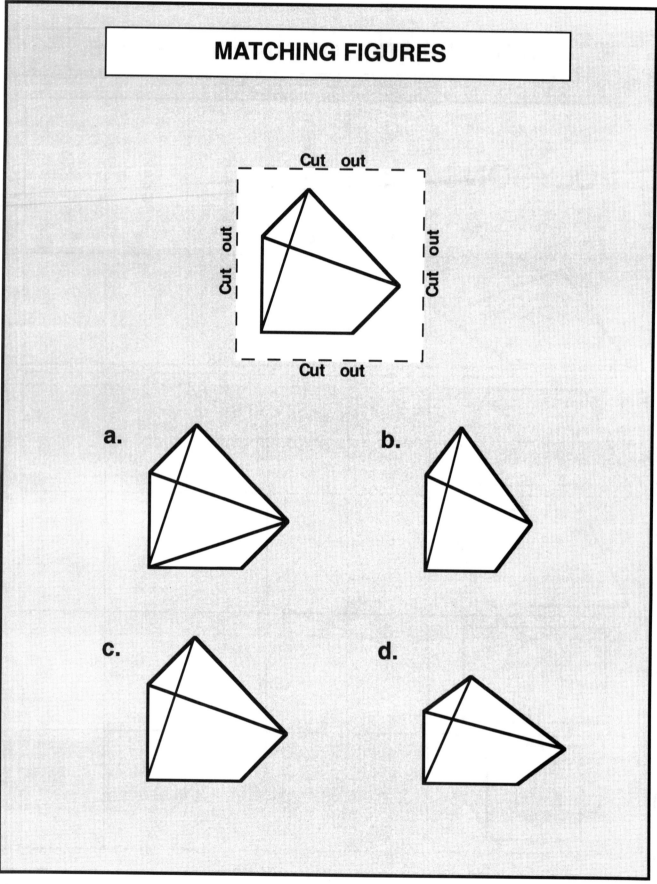

MATCHING FIGURES

a.

b.

c.

d.

TRANSPARENCY MASTER 7

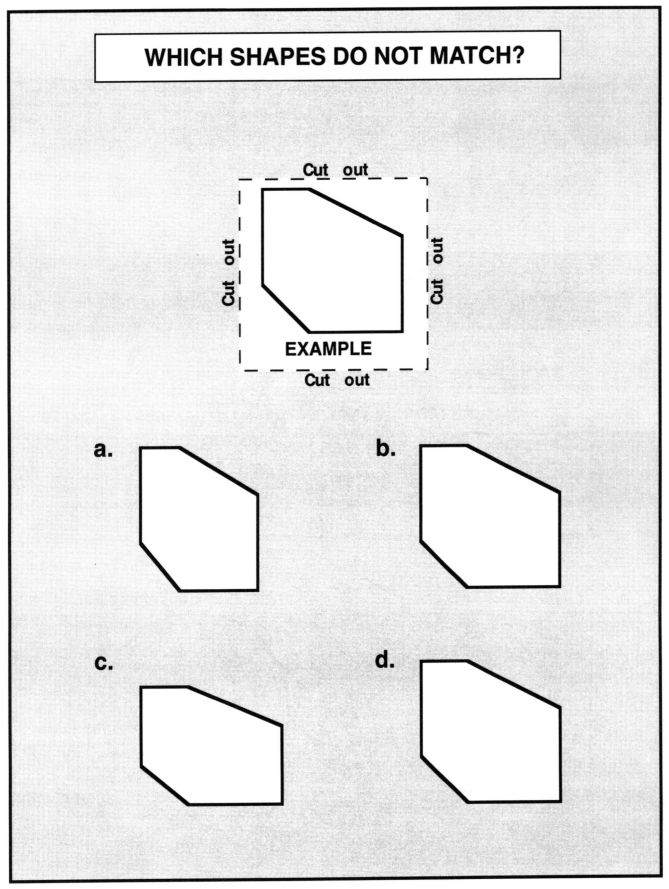

TRANSPARENCY MASTER 8

FINDING SHAPES

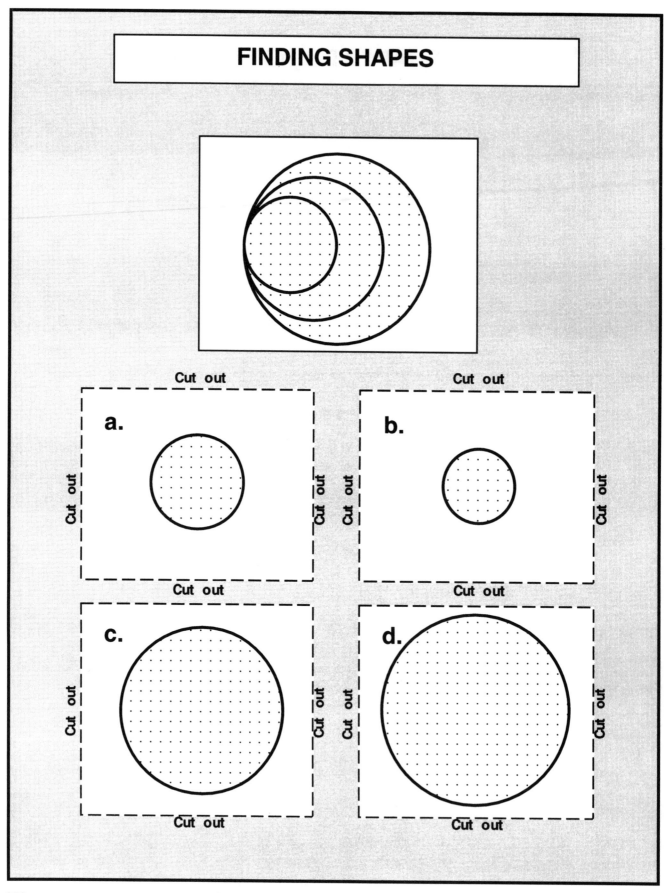

Cut out

a.

Cut out

Cut out

Cut out

Cut out

b.

Cut out

Cut out

Cut out

Cut out

c.

Cut out

Cut out

Cut out

Cut out

d.

Cut out

Cut out

TRANSPARENCY MASTER 9

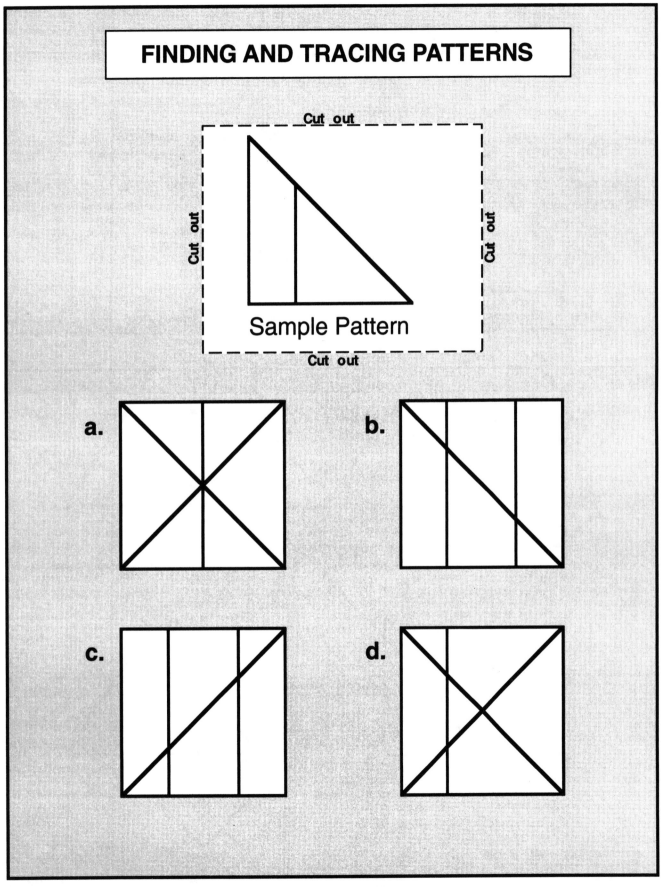

FINDING AND TRACING PATTERNS

Cut out

Cut out

Cut out

Cut out

Sample Pattern

a.

b.

c.

d.

TRANSPARENCY MASTER 10

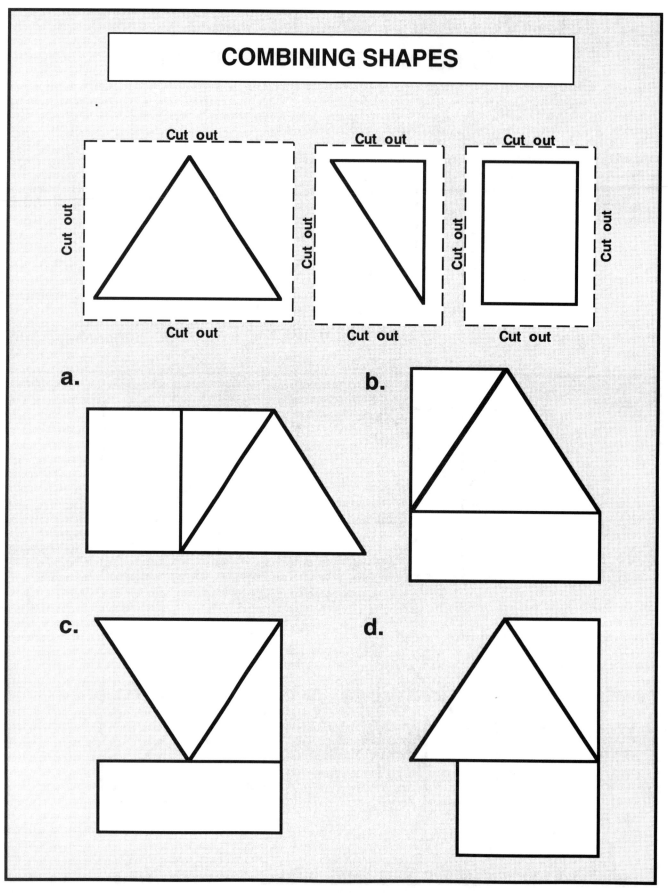

COMBINING SHAPES

Cut out
Cut out
Cut out
Cut out
Cut out
Cut out
Cut out
Cut out
Cut out
Cut out
Cut out
Cut out

a.

b.

c.

d.

TRANSPARENCY MASTER 11

DIVIDING SHAPES INTO EQUAL PARTS

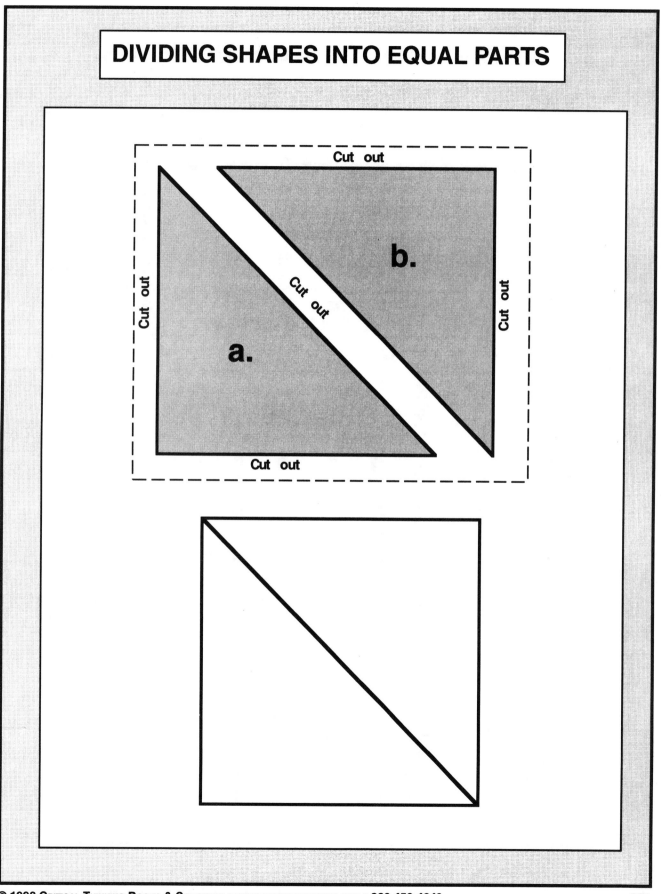

TRANSPARENCY MASTER 12

DIVIDING SHAPES INTO EQUAL PARTS

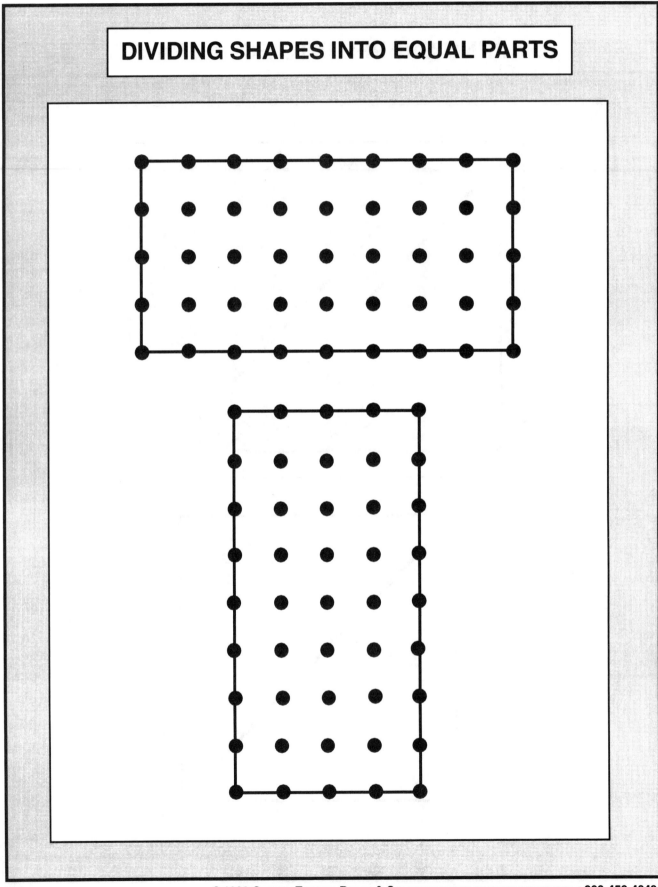

TRANSPARENCY MASTER 13

PAPER FOLDING

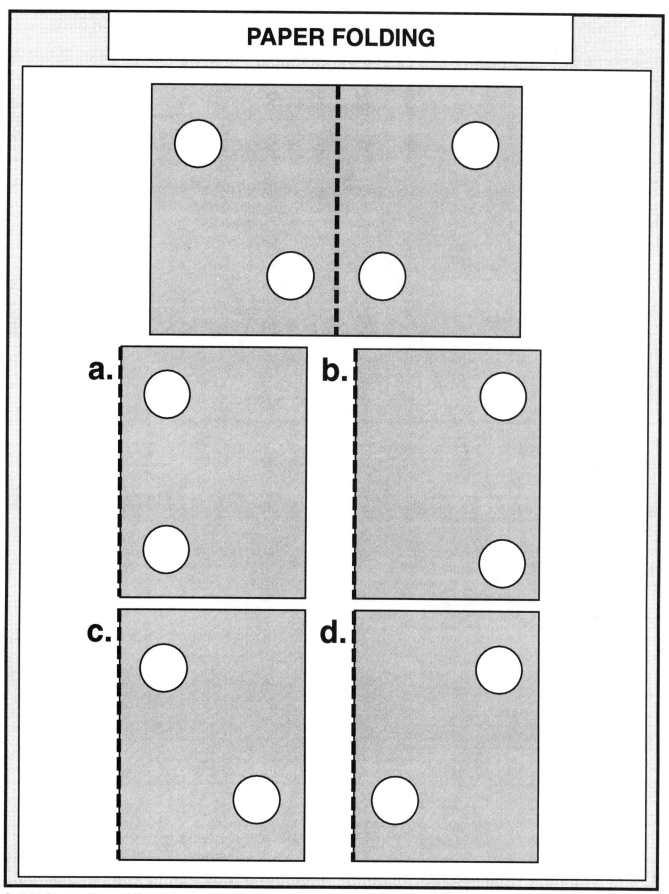

TRANSPARENCY MASTER 14

AXIS OF SYMMETRY

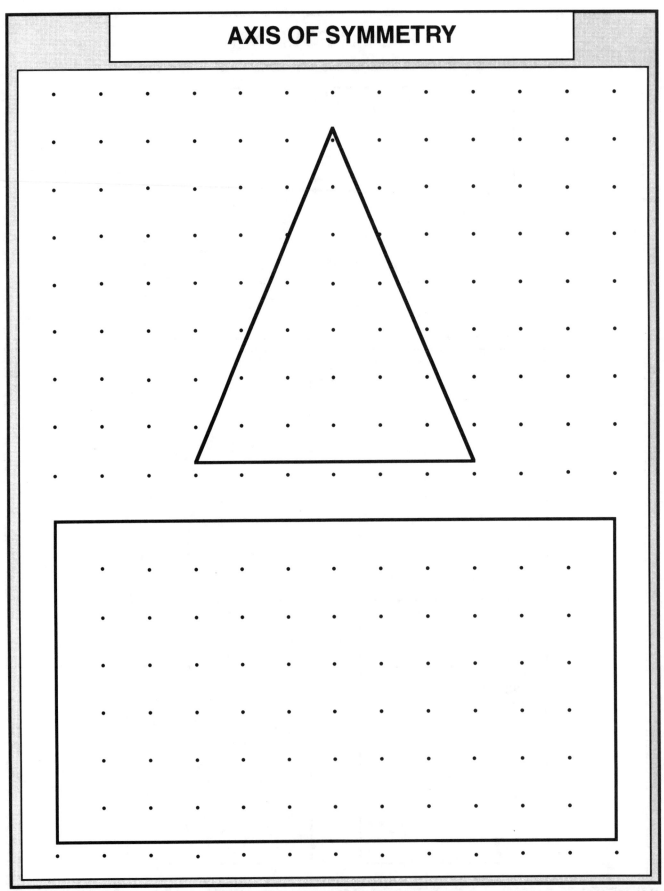

TRANSPARENCY MASTER 15

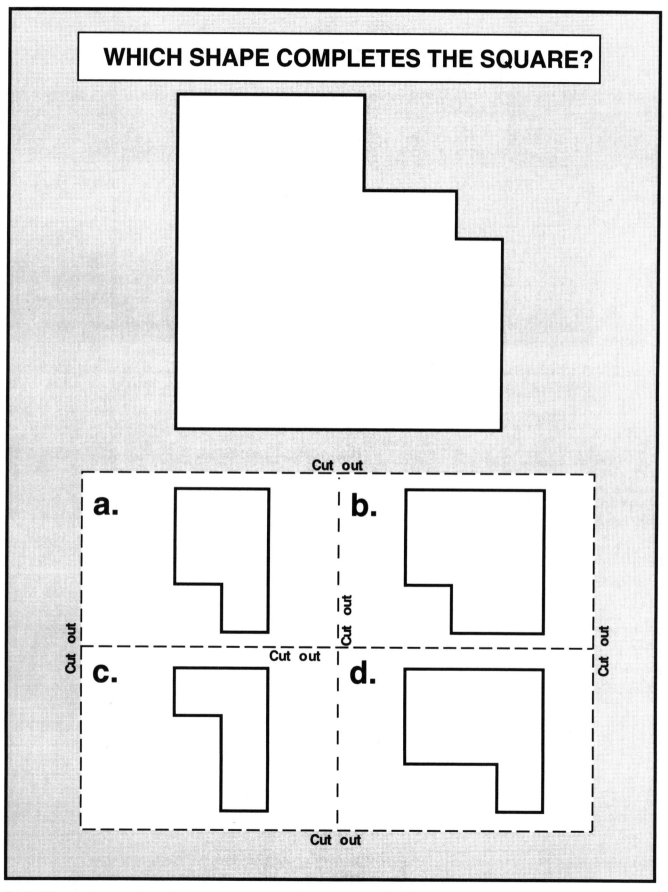

WHICH SHAPE COMPLETES THE SQUARE?

Cut out

a.

b.

Cut out

Cut out

Cut out

c.

d.

Cut out

Cut out

TRANSPARENCY MASTER 16

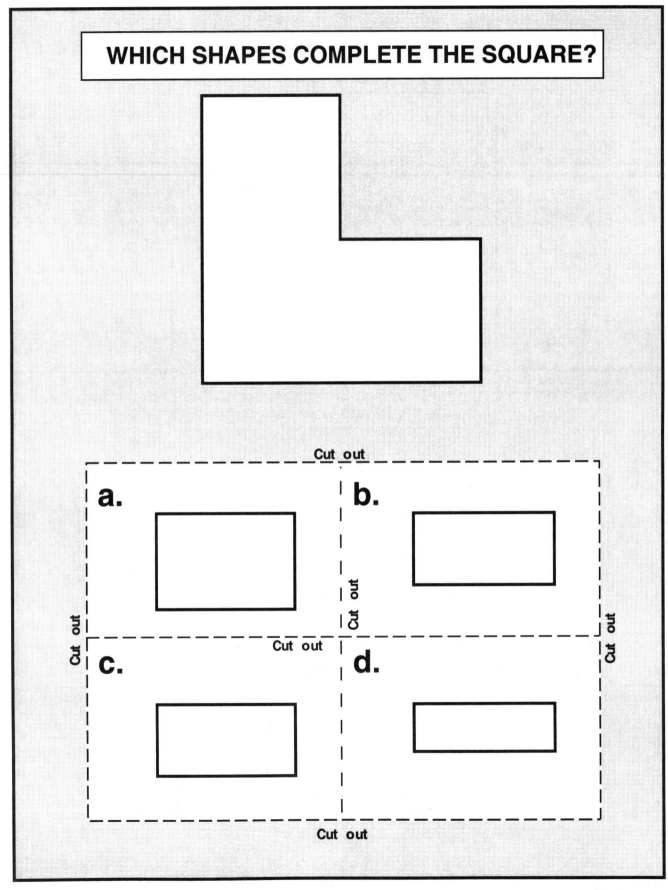

WHICH SHAPES COMPLETE THE SQUARE?

Cut out

a.

b.

Cut out

Cut out

Cut out

Cut out

c.

d.

Cut out

TRANSPARENCY MASTER 17

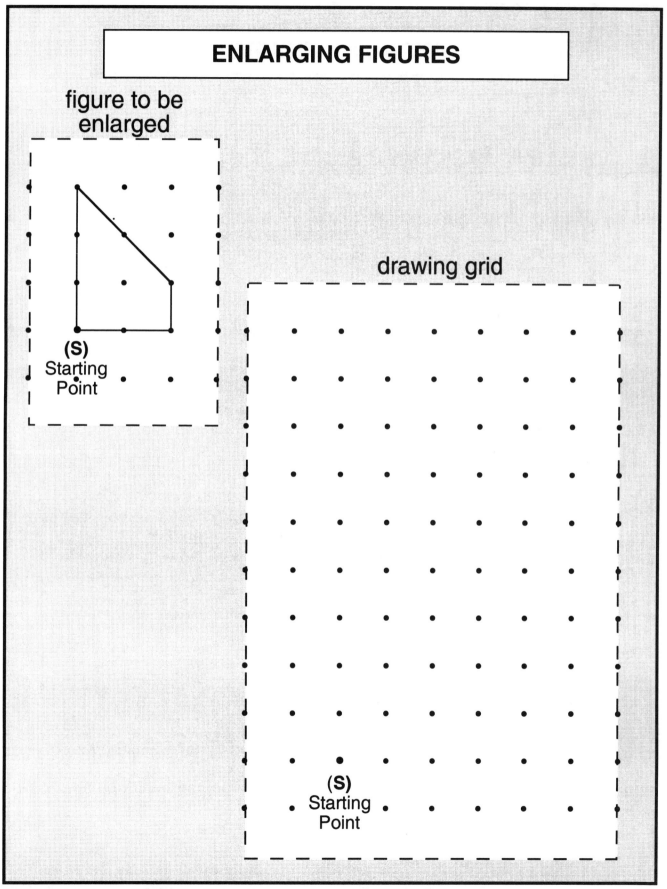

ENLARGING FIGURES

figure to be enlarged

(S)
Starting
Point

drawing grid

(S)
Starting
Point

TRANSPARENCY MASTER 18

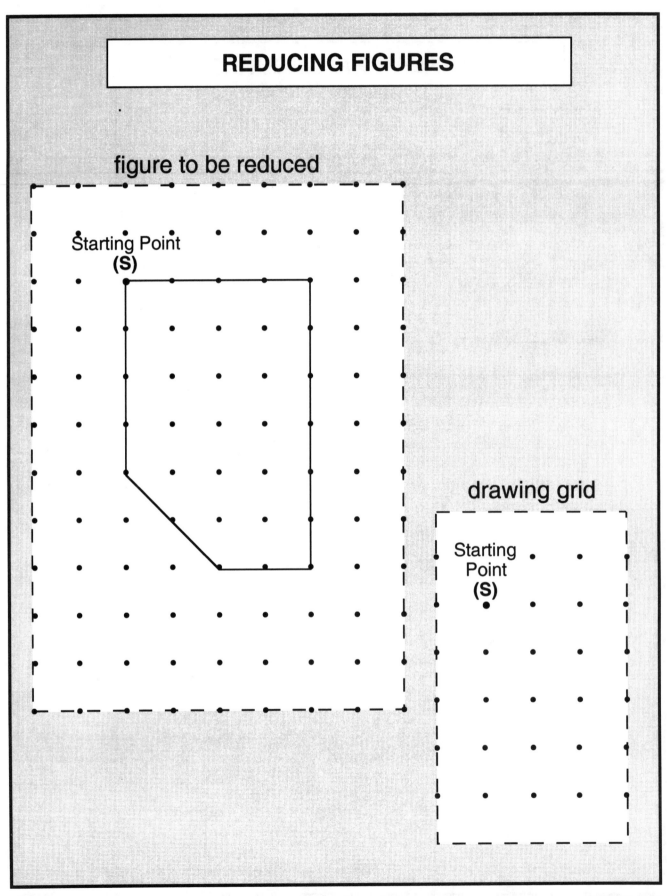

REDUCING FIGURES

figure to be reduced

Starting Point
(S)

drawing grid

Starting
Point
(S)

TRANSPARENCY MASTER 19

COMPARING SHAPES

Shape 1 _____

Shape 2 _____

HOW ALIKE?

_____

_____

HOW DIFFERENT?

WITH REGARD TO

Shape 1 _____

_____

_____

_____

Shape 2 _____

_____

_____

_____

TRANSPARENCY MASTER 20

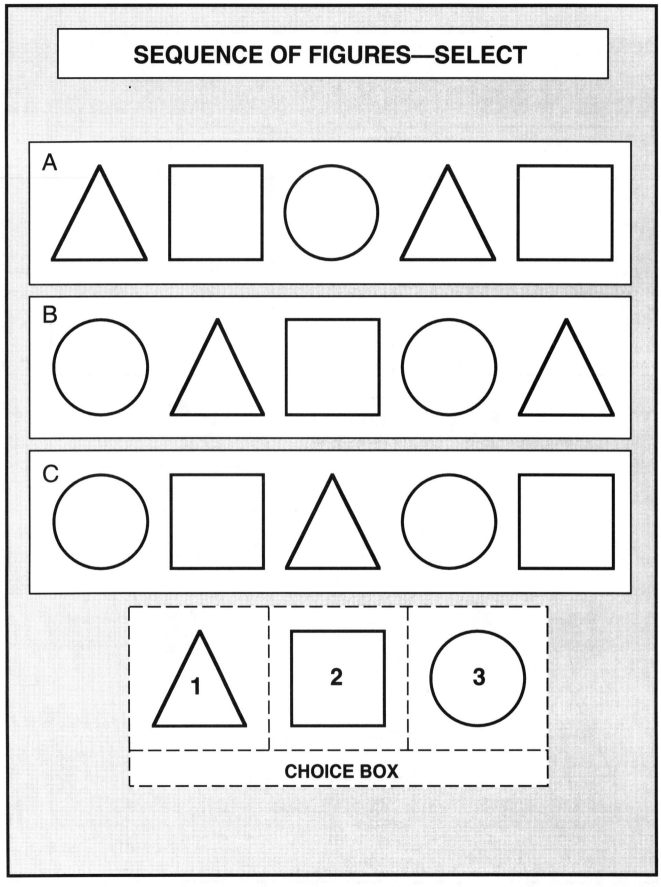

SEQUENCE OF FIGURES—SELECT

TRANSPARENCY MASTER 21

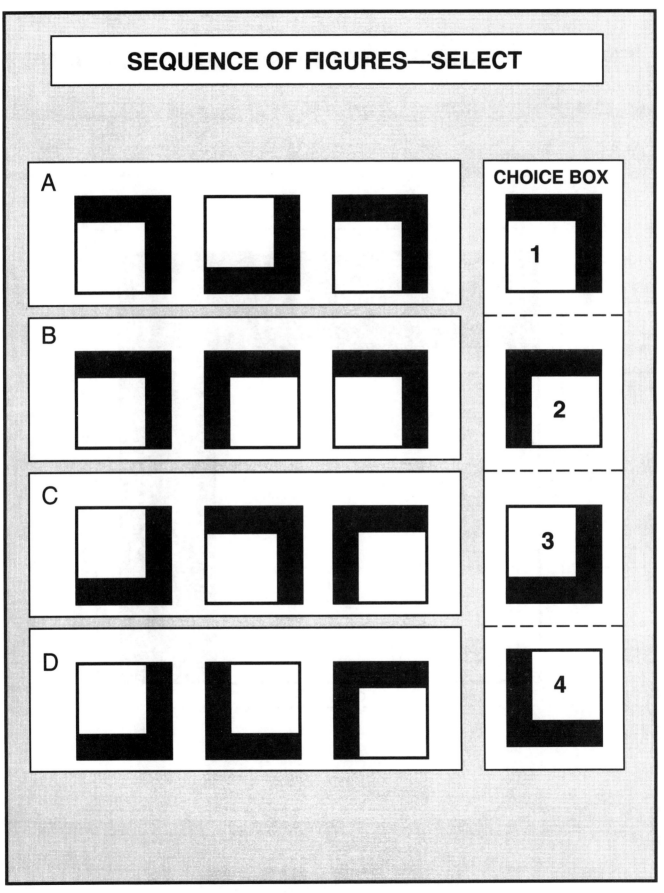

SEQUENCE OF FIGURES—SELECT

TRANSPARENCY MASTER 22

ENLARGED FIGURE—ROTATIONS AND REFLECTIONS

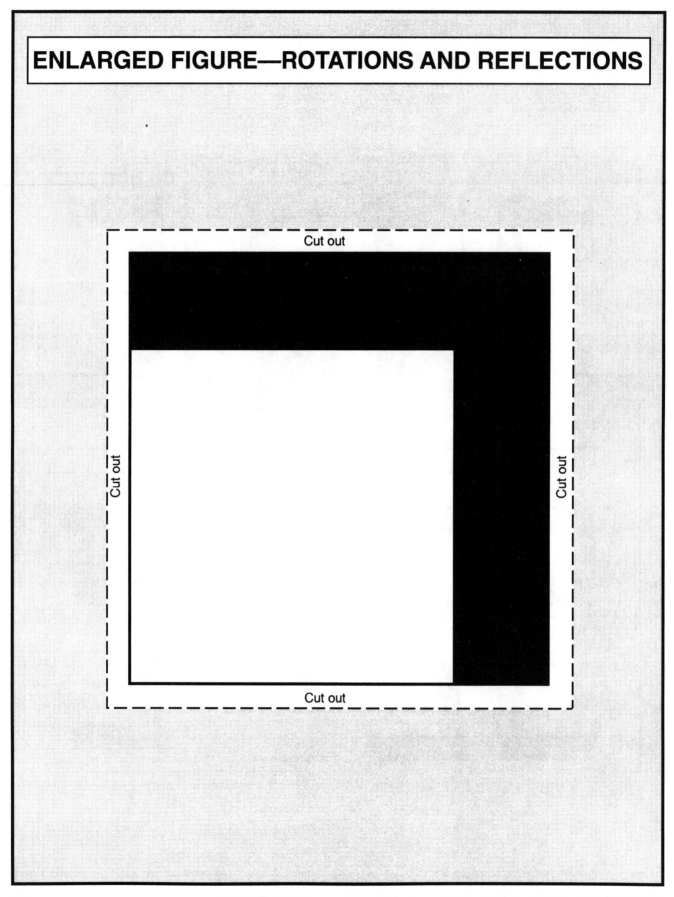

Cut out

Cut out

Cut out

Cut out

TRANSPARENCY MASTER 23

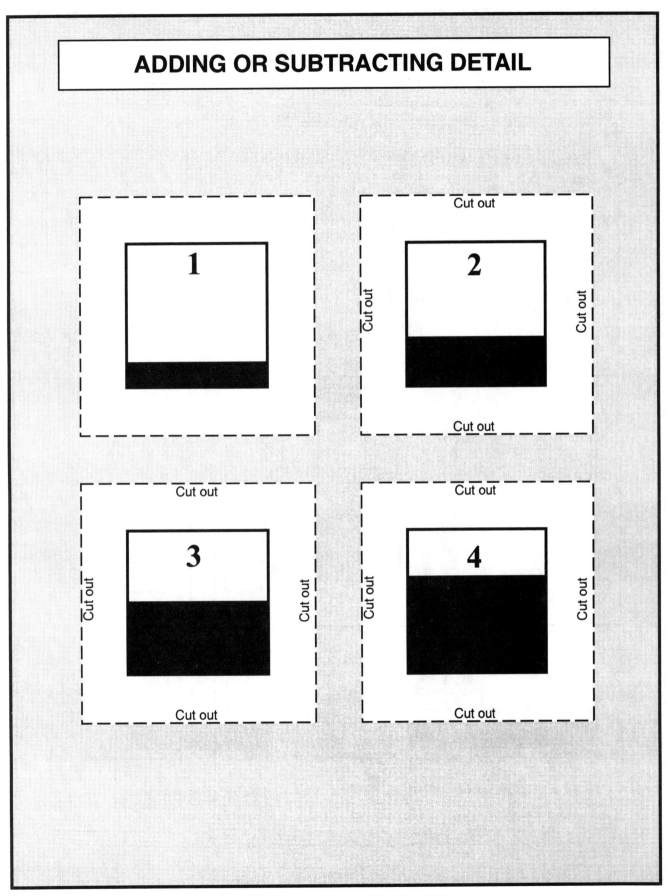

ADDING OR SUBTRACTING DETAIL

TRANSPARENCY MASTER 24

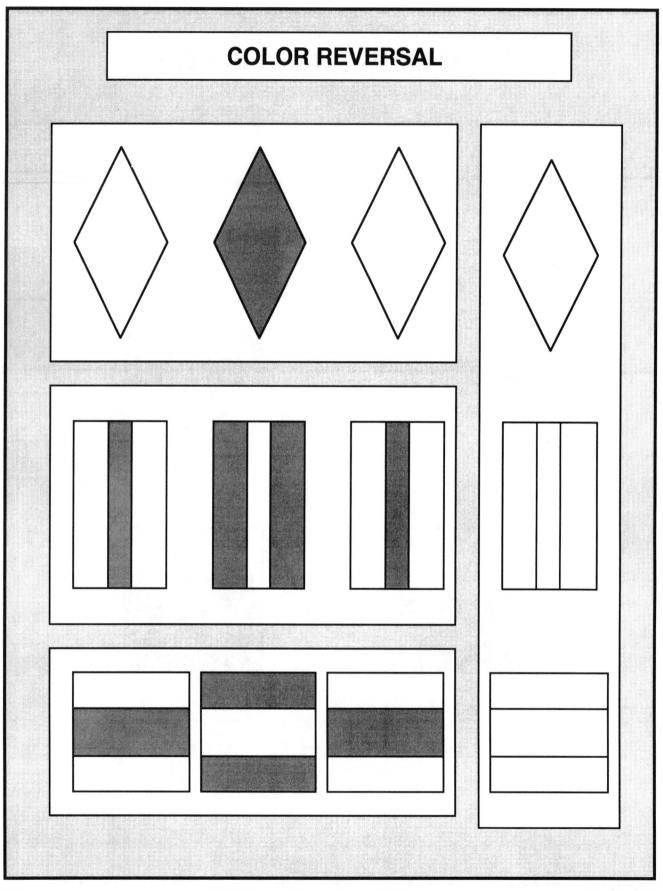

COLOR REVERSAL

ROTATING FIGURES

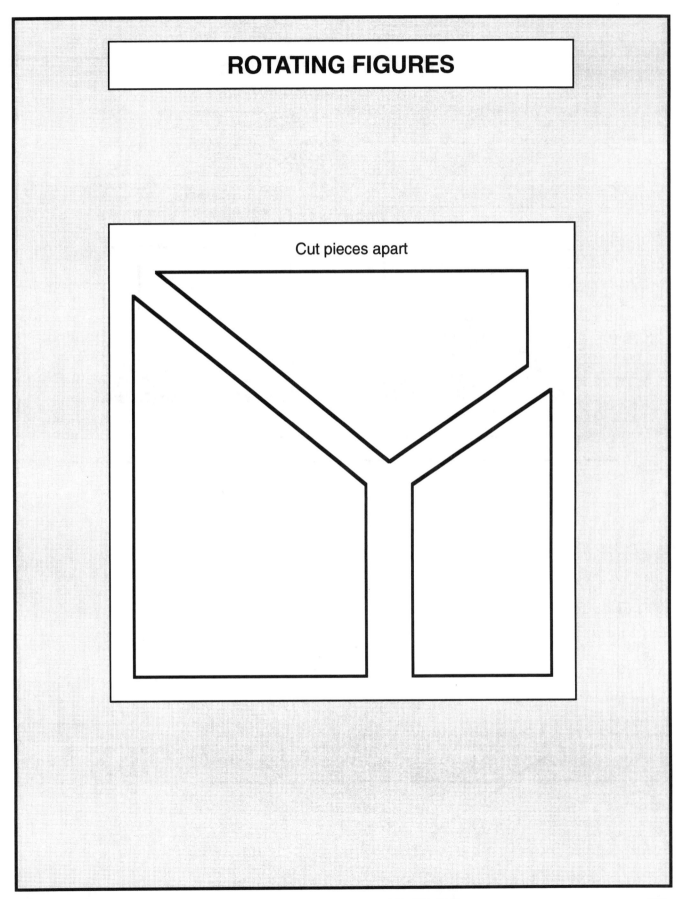

Cut pieces apart

TRANSPARENCY MASTER 26

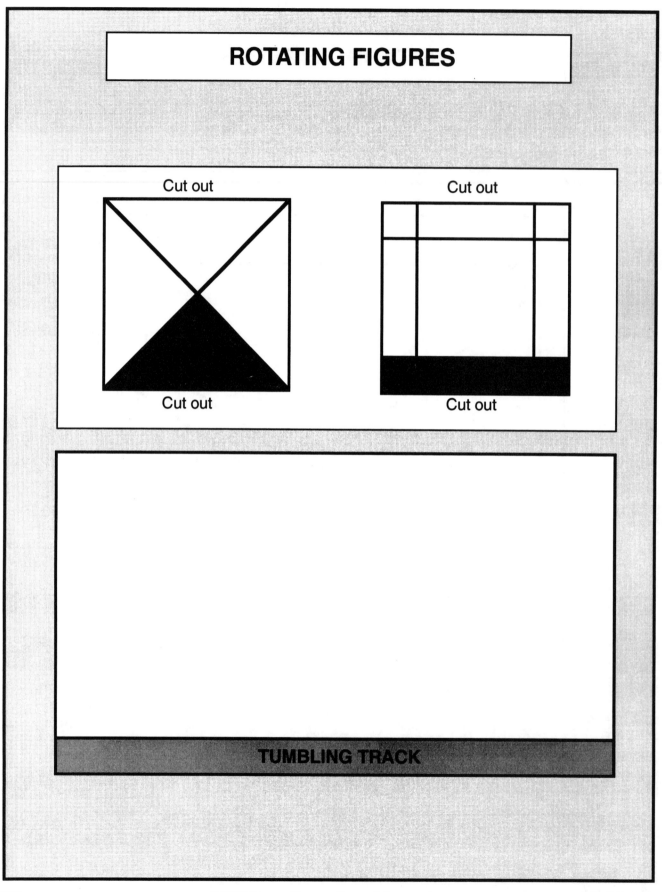

ROTATING FIGURES

Cut out

Cut out

Cut out

Cut out

TUMBLING TRACK

TRANSPARENCY MASTER 27

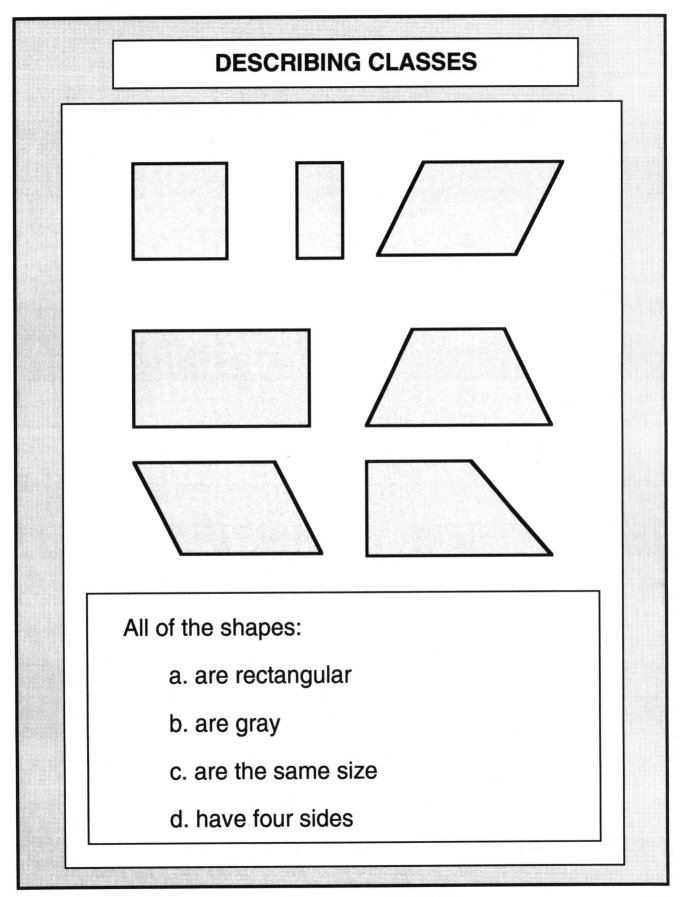

DESCRIBING CLASSES

All of the shapes:

   a. are rectangular

   b. are gray

   c. are the same size

   d. have four sides

TRANSPARENCY MASTER 28

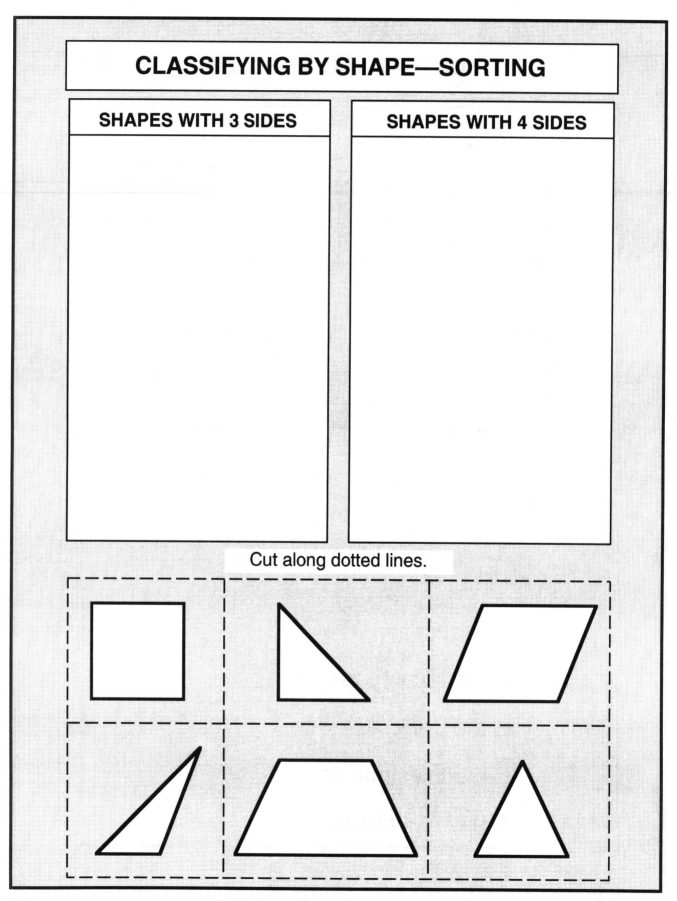

CLASSIFYING BY SHAPE—SORTING

SHAPES WITH 3 SIDES	SHAPES WITH 4 SIDES

Cut along dotted lines.

TRANSPARENCY MASTER 29

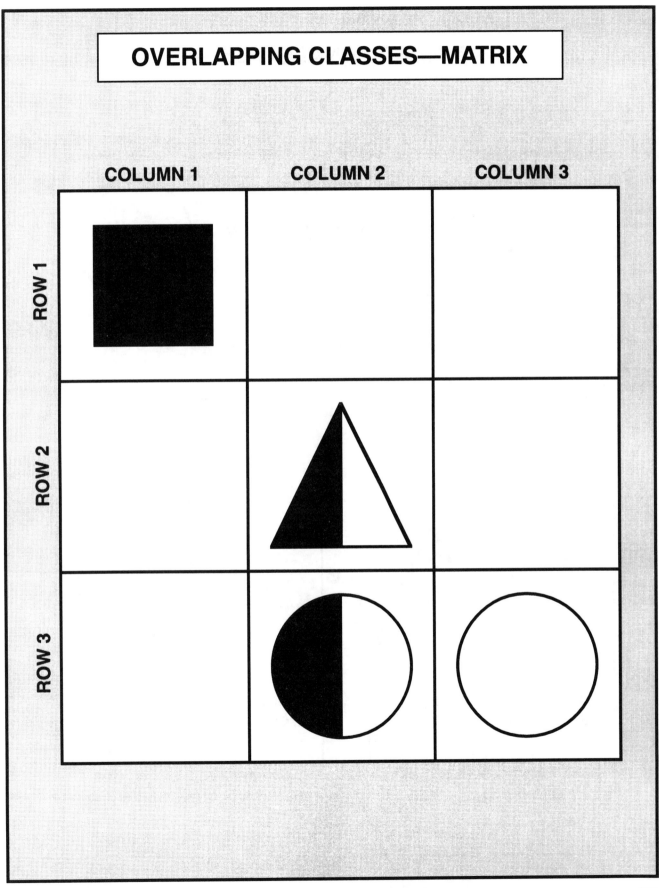

TRANSPARENCY MASTER 30

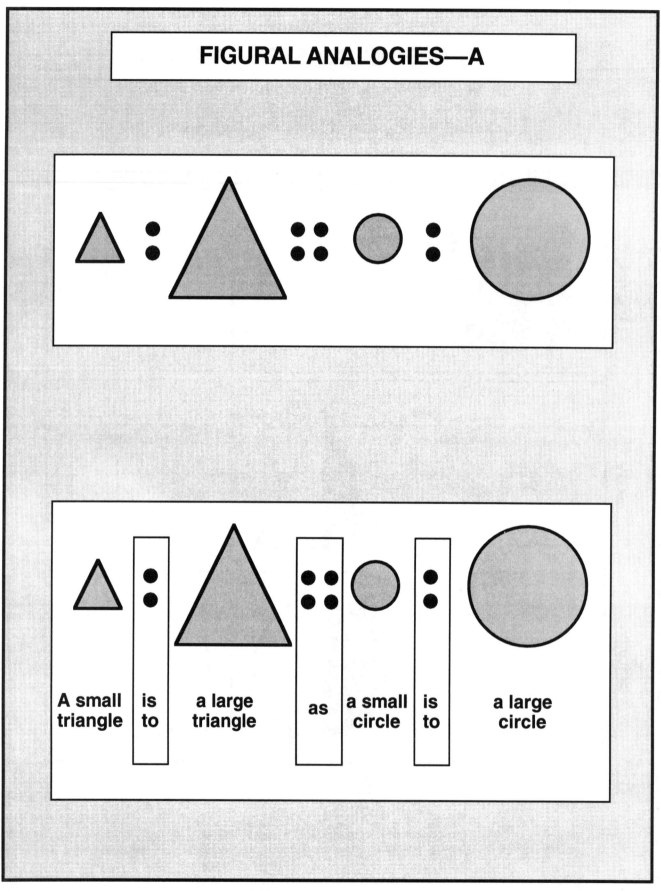

FIGURAL ANALOGIES—A

A small triangle | is to | a large triangle | as | a small circle | is to | a large circle

TRANSPARENCY MASTER 31

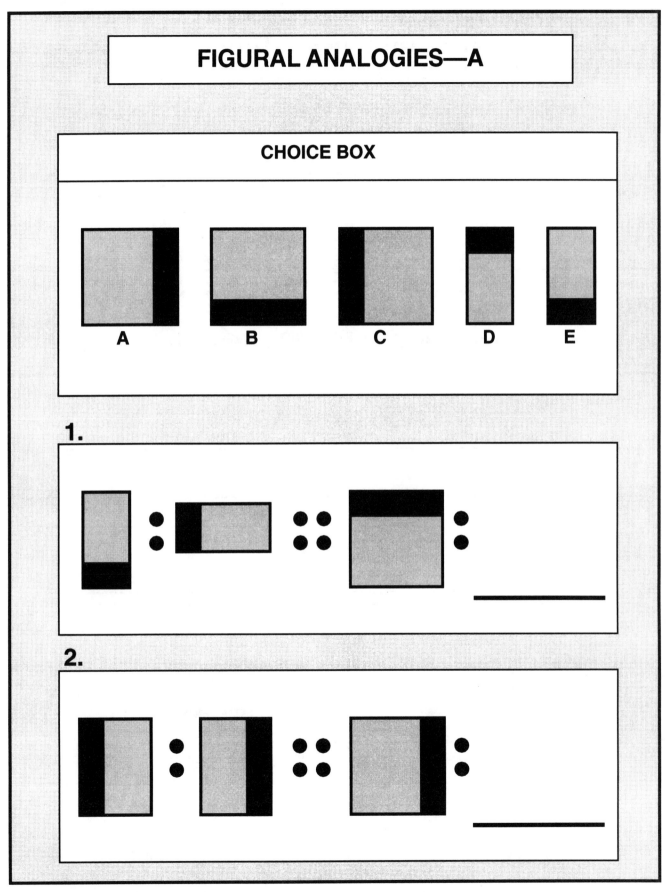

FIGURAL ANALOGIES—A

CHOICE BOX

A   B   C   D   E

1.

2.

TRANSPARENCY MASTER 32

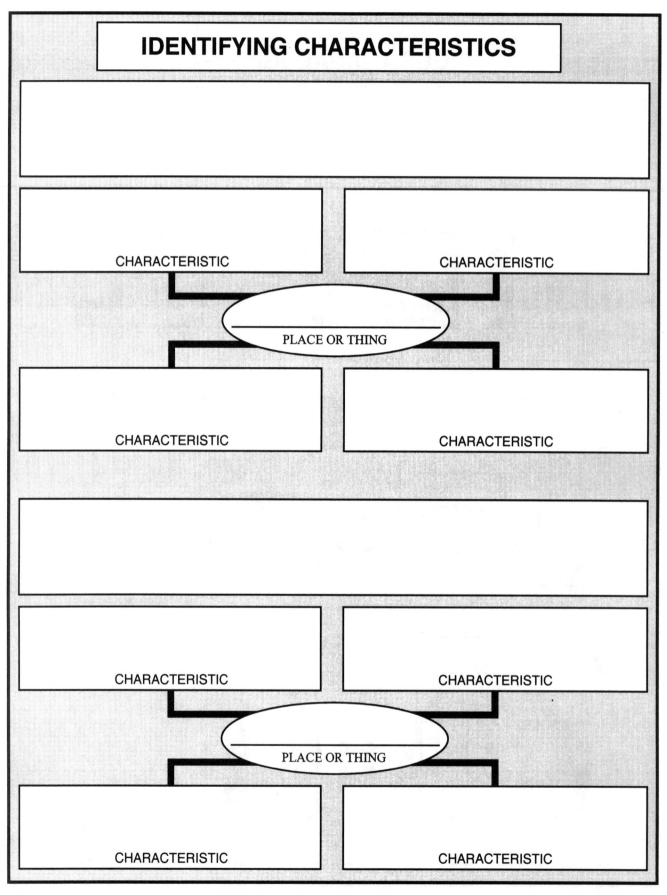

IDENTIFYING CHARACTERISTICS

CHARACTERISTIC

CHARACTERISTIC

PLACE OR THING

CHARACTERISTIC

CHARACTERISTIC

CHARACTERISTIC

CHARACTERISTIC

PLACE OR THING

CHARACTERISTIC

CHARACTERISTIC

TRANSPARENCY MASTER 33

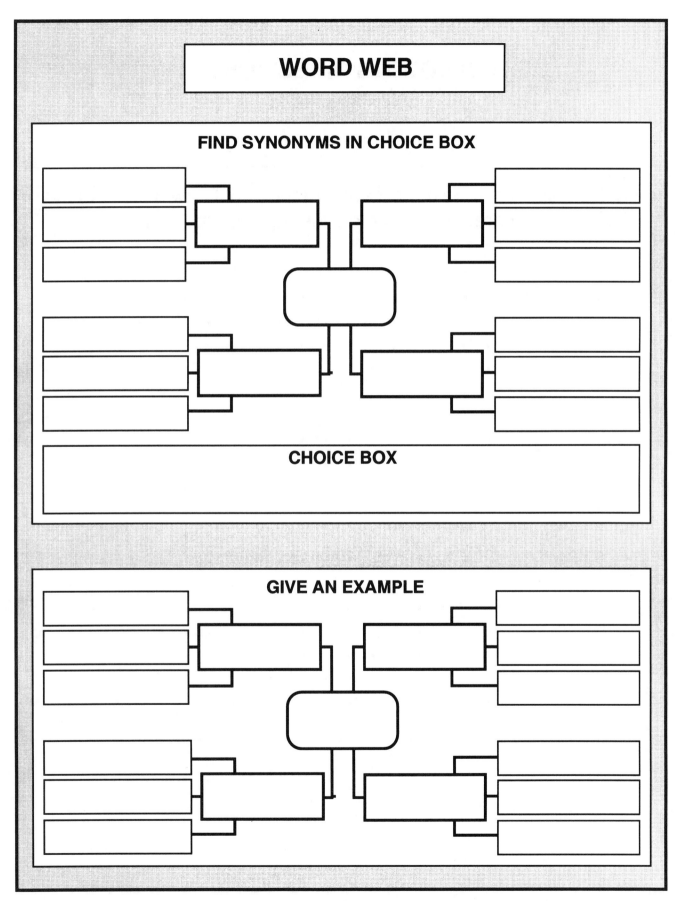

TRANSPARENCY MASTER 34

FOLLOWING DIRECTIONS

Draw a small square at the center of the grid. Draw a circle to the left of the square. Directly below the square, draw a triangle.

TRANSPARENCY MASTER 35

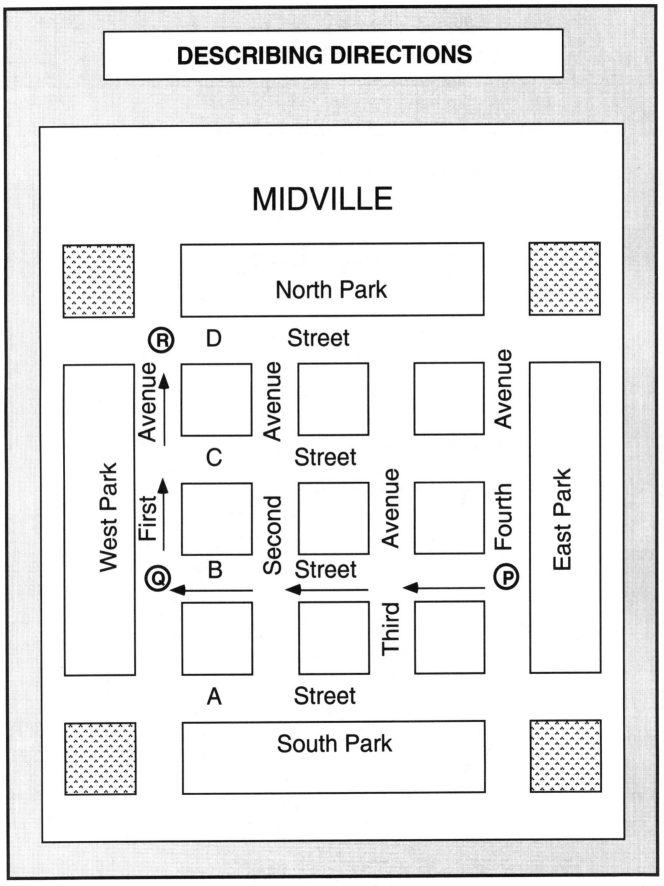

DESCRIBING DIRECTIONS

MIDVILLE

North Park

D Street

West Park

North Park

First Avenue

Second Avenue

Third Avenue

Fourth Avenue

East Park

C Street

B Street

A Street

South Park

TRANSPARENCY MASTER 36

FOLLOWING YES-NO RULES–A

Darken the correct circles along the path by following the Yes-No rule. "Yes" means the circle at the end of the arrow is the same color. "No" means the circle is not the same color. Circles 1 and 2 have been correctly shaded. Decide how circles 3 through 9 should be shaded.

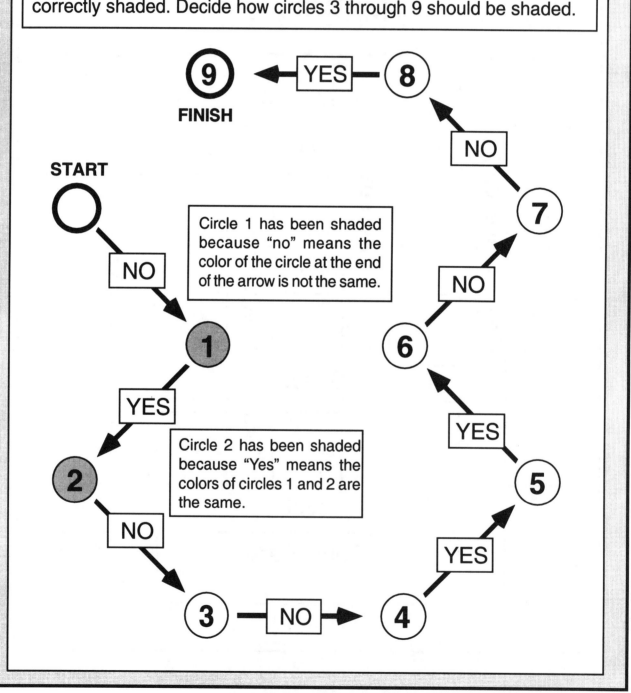

TRANSPARENCY MASTER 37

FOLLOWING YES-NO RULES–B

Follow the arrows from start to finish. In each box near each arrow write "YES" or "NO." "YES" means the circle at the end of the arrow is the same color. "NO" means the circle is not the same color. Boxes 1 and 2 have been correctly marked. Decide how boxes 3 through 9 should be marked.

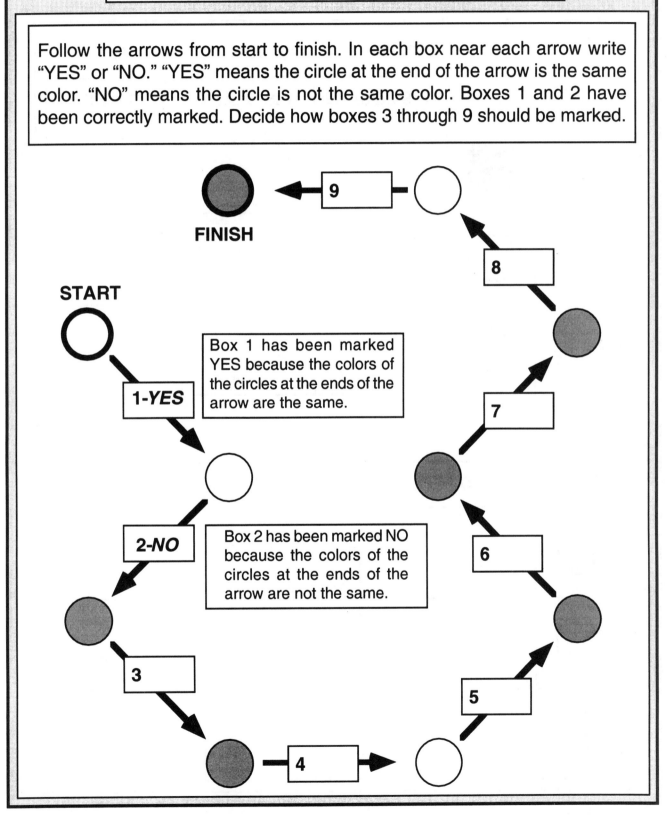

FINISH

START

1-YES

Box 1 has been marked YES because the colors of the circles at the ends of the arrow are the same.

2-NO

Box 2 has been marked NO because the colors of the circles at the ends of the arrow are not the same.

3

4

5

6

7

8

9

TRANSPARENCY MASTER 38

TRUE–FALSE TABLES

	COLUMN 1 IT IS SQUARE	COLUMN 2 IT IS BLACK	COLUMN 3 IT IS WHITE
ROW 1 ■			
ROW 2 □			
ROW 3 ●			

	IT IS NOT SQUARE	IT IS NOT BLACK	IT IS NOT A CIRCLE
■			
□			
●			

TRANSPARENCY MASTER 39

IF–THEN RULES

RULE: If the shape is a square, then it is white.

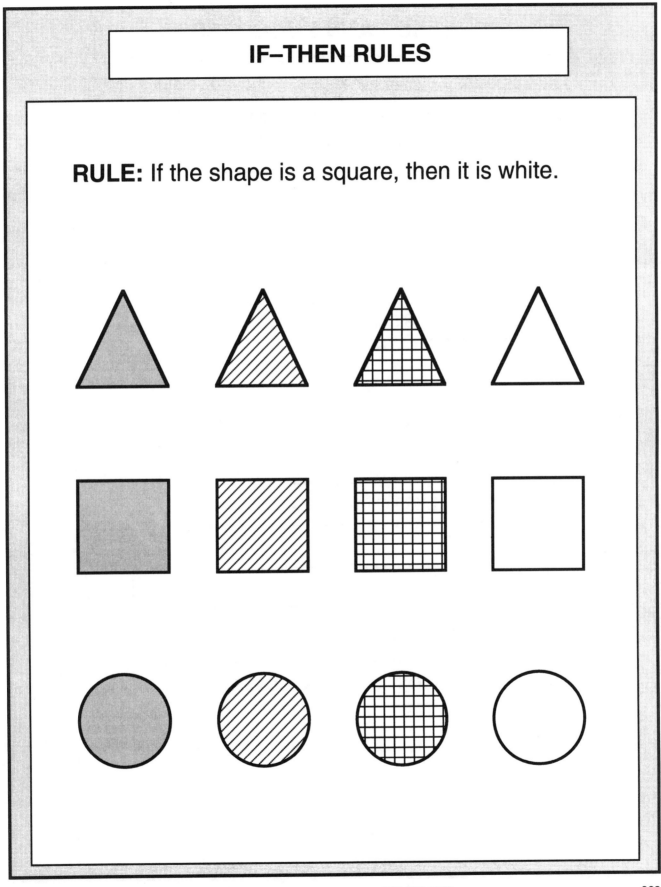

TRANSPARENCY MASTER 40

CLASSES AND SUBCLASSES

The orange is a popular citrus fruit.
"Fruit" is the most general class and belongs on line 1. "Citrus" is a kind of fruit and belongs on line 2. "Orange" is a kind of citrus fruit and belongs on line 3.

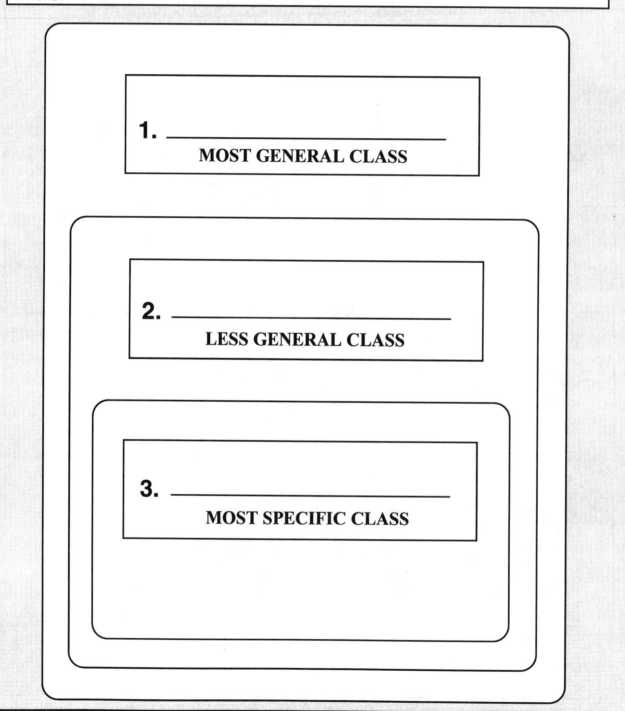

1. _____
    MOST GENERAL CLASS

2. _____
    LESS GENERAL CLASS

3. _____
    MOST SPECIFIC CLASS

TRANSPARENCY MASTER 41

CLASSES AND SUBCLASSES

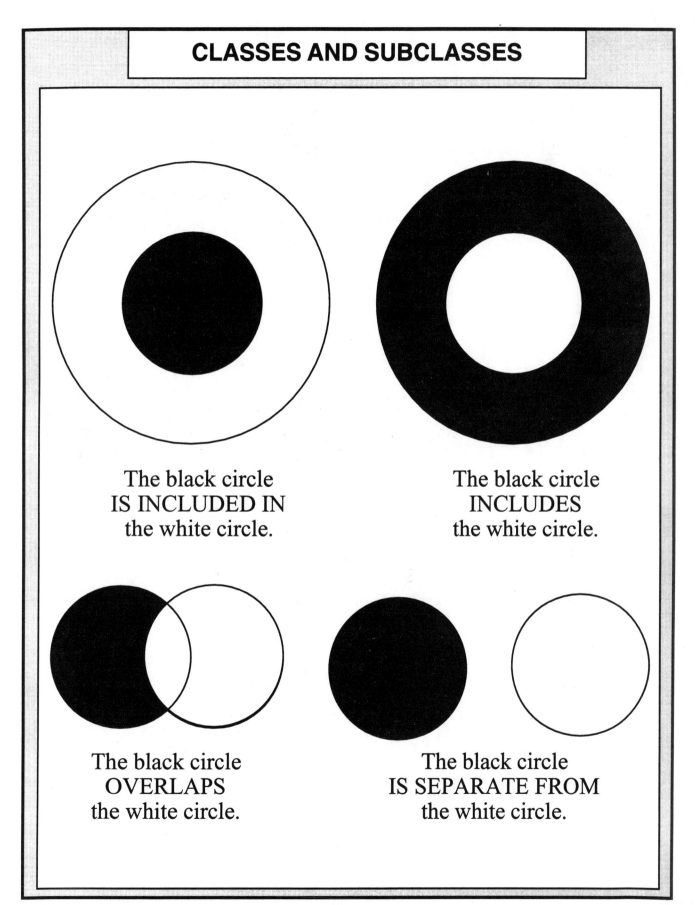

The black circle
IS INCLUDED IN
the white circle.

The black circle
INCLUDES
the white circle.

The black circle
OVERLAPS
the white circle.

The black circle
IS SEPARATE FROM
the white circle.